THE
WRITERS'
AMERICA

National Association of Book Publishers poster, by N. C. Wyeth

The AMERICAN HERITAGE *History of*

THE
WRITERS'
AMERICA

By Marshall B. Davidson

and

THE EDITORS OF AMERICAN HERITAGE

PUBLISHED BY
AMERICAN HERITAGE PUBLISHING COMPANY, INC., New York

BOOK TRADE DISTRIBUTION BY
McGRAW-HILL BOOK COMPANY

Staff for this Book

EDITOR
Marshall B. Davidson

ART DIRECTOR
Murray Belsky

MANAGING EDITOR
Kaari Ward

ASSOCIATE EDITOR
Angela H. Weldon

PICTURE EDITOR
Maureen Dwyer

EDITORIAL ASSISTANT
Deborah Agrest

CONSULTANT LIBRARIAN
Laura A. Lane

GENERAL CONSULTANT
Richard C. Robey

AMERICAN HERITAGE PUBLISHING CO., INC.

PRESIDENT AND PUBLISHER
Paul Gottlieb

EDITOR-IN-CHIEF
Joseph J. Thorndike

SENIOR EDITOR, BOOK DIVISION
Alvin M. Josephy, Jr.

EDITORIAL ART DIRECTOR
Murray Belsky

GENERAL MANAGER, BOOK DIVISION
Kenneth W. Leish

Library of Congress Cataloging in Publication Data
Davidson, Marshall B.
 The American heritage history of the writers' America.

 Half title: The writers' America.
 1. American literature—History and criticism.
I. American heritage. II. Title. III. Title: The writers' America.
PS88.D28   810'.9   73-10280
ISBN 0-07-015435-X
ISBN 0-07-015436-8 (de luxe)

ISBN 07-079482-0 de luxe boxed set with The American heritage history of the artists' America

CONTENTS

INTRODUCTION

In one of his best essays Oscar Wilde observed that nature is always imitating art, always creating men and women, landscapes, shapes, and just things in art's image. The truth conveyed by that paradox has become increasingly self-evident in the years since Wilde wrote. Art can indeed lead us to look at nature in new ways, to find new forms and values in what we observe of the world about us. For example, no one who has enjoyed Monet's renderings of the cathedral at Rouen can gaze at the actual structure without first seeing it as the artist did in his shimmering images of its façade. Coming closer to home, if George Washington were to return to earth he would have to resemble Gilbert Stuart's portraits of him or go unrecognized.

Literature has the same transforming quality as painting. To a very large extent every nation is the invention of its poets, novelists, and other authors who have written about the land and its people, about the dreams and aspirations of their countrymen as well as about the observed realities of their daily lives. America is no exception; America is a state of mind and spirit created in good part by the books that have emerged from American experience —as truly, certainly, as it is a political entity shaped by historical circumstance. We are all, so to speak, the spiritual heirs of Poor Richard, Father Knickerbocker, Natty Bumppo, Hiawatha, Huckleberry Finn, and a long succession of other cherished figures from our literary past. They have fashioned our national image, not only in our own eyes but in the eyes of the world at large.

As told on the pages immediately following, the New World was, in fact, "invented" long before the land had ever been seen by a white man. From ancient times both pagan prophecies and Christian legends had postulated a world beyond the western Sea of Darkness, a world large and free enough to accommodate the timeless dreams of man. That credulous expectancy did not by any means vanish with the first eyewitness reports of the western hemisphere by Christopher Columbus, Amerigo Vespucci, and other early explorers. More than three and a half centuries after Columbus' landfall, Henry Thoreau wrote from his rude sanctuary at Walden Pond, near Concord, Massachusetts, that every sunset he witnessed inspired him "to go to a West as distant and as fair as that into which the sun goes down. . . . We dream all night of those mountain-ridges in the horizon though they may be of vapor only, which were last gilded by his rays. The island of Atlantis, and the islands and gardens of the Hesperides, a sort of terrestrial paradise, appear to have been the Great West of the ancients, enveloped in mystery and poetry. Who has not seen in imagination, when looking into the sunset sky, the gardens of the Hesperides, and the foundation of all those fables?"

However, there was fact as well as fable to be faced for those who came to America to settle and to spread out over the continent; dreams had to be accommodated to realities that were for the most part unprecedented in the lives of those colonists and immigrants who chose America as a new homeland. That need to reconcile the *idea* of America with the actualities of American experience is a recurrent theme throughout the entire course of this country's literature.

The writers' America—one might as well say the American mind—had its true birth in the literature of discovery, exploration, and settlement, penned by those who first faced the actualities of life in the New World. It is a literature deeply rooted in the rich tradition of Elizabethan and Miltonian England, and it reflects the intellectual excitement of those vital times. Colonists to new lands instinctively try to re-create those aspects of the world they leave behind them, those, at least, that they best remember and most highly value. The Englishmen who settled along the Atlantic seaboard of America in the seventeenth century were no exception. However different may have been some of their beliefs and opinions from those that prevailed in England, they hoped in good time to reproduce in the New World the familiar and cherished amenities of life they had known at home. Thus the houses they raised and their furnishings were, as closely as could be contrived, replicas of Old World models. Thus, too, in their writing they chose as models contemporary English prose and poetry. It was to their supreme advantage that they had as their most revered model the majestic utterances of the King James Bible, published first in 1611.

There was little enough time or occasion in colonial America for writing polite literature, and nothing produced here in those early days can compare with the stylish creations of such contemporary English authors as Milton, Dryden, and Pope. For reading matter of that nature the colonists could and did depend on a plentiful supply of books imported from the Old World. It was in the nature of circumstances that much early American writing was functional—writing in which the matter under discussion was deemed of more importance than the fashion in which it was presented. Thus, until after the Revolution the most representative literary output of the country took the form of histories, travel accounts, personal journals, and political tracts—works intended to report, explain, elucidate, and argue. Among the colonists there were indefatigable penmen who wrote in a plain and readable manner of the new world about them and the physical and spiritual adventures they encountered there. They often told of such things as were barely dreamed of in the sedate parlors and studies of distant England. The colorful reports from Virginia by that doughty braggart, Captain John Smith, and the grim and pious history of Governor William Bradford of Plymouth Plantation were worlds apart from common English experience. Such works may lack high literary quality, but as historical documents they are both fascinating and invaluable. In later years the polemical writing produced during the political crises of the Revolutionary and Civil Wars sometimes achieved a rare brilliance. Neither Thomas Jefferson nor Abraham Lincoln thought of himself particularly as a man of letters, but the Declaration of Independence and the Gettysburg Address display such a superb command of the language that they can rightly be considered among the classics of world literature.

For long years American writers clung faithfully to their English heritage in matters of style, whatever the content of their messages. As a youthful reporter, that most American of Americans, Benjamin Franklin, assiduously studied and paraphrased the polished essays in Addison and Steele's London *Spectator* to perfect his own style. Franklin did in fact become a master of the King's English, but in his maturity he wrote with a wit, clarity, brevity, and homely wisdom, briefly and clearly expressed, that in sum breathed a fresh and rare American spirit. His unfinished *Autobiography* remains a classic of Western literature and of American prose.

With American independence came a demand, notably from the famed lexicographer Noah Webster, for an independent American language. That could not be accomplished by decree, of course, but a more or less distinctive American language was already taking shape in the normal course of events. From England such developments were viewed as unpardonable violations of the mother tongue. In 1787 Jefferson was taken severely to task in a British review for using American idioms in his writing; but he clearly understood that such "aberrations" were both natural and desirable. As in the case of painting and the other arts, American writing would find new and appropriate ways of expression that would bear the unmistakable imprint of the native environment and culture and that would change with the times and circumstances.

However, the influence of English style was strong, long, and persistent. Washington Irving, the first American man of letters to win an international reputation, was hailed abroad because he wrote the way an Englishman should write, regardless of his subject matter and in spite of the fact that he wrote from "the wilds of America." (He was also spoken of as the most fashionable fellow in London during a residence there.) On the other hand, comparisons of English and American writers could be odious. James Fenimore Cooper was highly irritated by the intended compliment that dubbed him the American Walter Scott. Not only did that assign him a secondary status; it also suggested a dependence on English rather than his own, American standards of style and taste.

In the case of such later writers as Walt Whitman and Mark Twain comparisons of that nature were, of course, impossible. Their books represented to the world a distinctive, indigenous American literature that was clearly recognizable as such. Since their day, a wide variety of talented authors have contributed to a further development of a native tradition of letters. In our own time American literature is widely regarded as one of the most vital expressions of thought and imagination in the world. The current of influence has been reversed, and what is written in the New World has become an energizing factor in the writing of other lands.

The following pages offer a panoramic view of the American scene and the American people—of American experience, in short, as it has appeared to American writers, from the first days of settlement until modern times. To cover such a large topic between the covers of a single book demands a degree of selectivity. Inevitably, for reasons of space, some deserving authors have been omitted in favor of other deserving authors. However, those whose works are here discussed seem representative of the best and most interesting writing that has been produced in this country throughout its history. Even as these words are written, new writers of exceptional merit are offering fresh insights into the nature of American experience in this rapidly changing world. Fashions in reading and writing constantly fluctuate, as do literary reputations. We must look to the future for a fair judgment of their contributions.

ERRANDS INTO THE WILDERNESS

The trail, photographed opposite, leads to the site of Meronocomoco, King Powhatan's village, where Capt. John Smith claimed to have been rescued by Pocahontas, the ruler's daughter. In The Generall Historie of Virginia (1624) Smith relates that he had been exploring the wilderness of the Jamestown area and had "proceeded so farre that with much labour by cutting of trees insunder he made his passage." The captain was then "beset with 200. Salvages," who carried him off to Powhatan's capital. The Pocahontas episode has become a favorite American folk legend.

In its final passage the Nuremberg Chronicle, published in July, 1493, explained that the historical accounts that were therein compiled included all "the events most worthy of notice from the beginning of the world to the calamity of our time." With deep foreboding a few blank pages were added for recording such events as might occur before the Day of Judgment forever ended the story of mortal man. Divided by discordant forces within and threatened by Mongol hordes at its borders, disillusioned by the recent past and discontented with the present, Christian Europe was obviously in a sorry state of mind.

At almost precisely the same time, however, another publication appeared, in Barcelona, that would cast a new light on things. In printed copies of a letter written by Christopher Columbus the epochal discovery of that explorer was first publicly announced to the Western world. This small pamphlet, which was quickly translated into several languages, was a very modest publication for one of the most significant revelations in the history of the world. Since the time of Plato there had been rumors of a strange and wonderful land beyond the western limits of the known world; it was occasionally imagined as an earthly paradise, a sanctuary for departed spirits that was recalled as late as World War I when the dying soldier "went west," as Homer's heroes had done millenniums earlier.

That the earth was round was no secret to informed persons over earlier centuries; three hundred years before Christ, Eratosthenes had even estimated the circumference of the globe with fair accuracy. And during the decades before Columbus' first journey across the Atlantic, along the wharves and in the taverns and warehouses frequented by sailors, there was undoubtedly more current gossip and information about landfalls across the western sea than reached most mapmakers and geographers of that time. Reports of the actual existence of such "fantastic islands" were, quite possibly, among the inciting causes of Columbus' "Enterprise of the Indies."

However, Columbus' letter was the first printed eyewitness report of the New World. To his dying day he thought he had skirted the fringes of the fabulous Orient, whose great and glorious cities held the most profitable markets on earth. Had he known that he had instead stumbled on a barbarous

9

"The Letter to Santangel," in which Columbus announced his discovery of America, was translated into several languages and issued as a pamphlet with small woodcut illustrations. Above, we see the native Americans fleeing from Columbus, from a 1493 Paris edition of the letter. In 1555 Guillaume le Testu, the noted French chartmaker, drew the world map, opposite. The dark areas are the continents—the North American continent is indicated at the upper left—and the light areas represent the world's oceans tossed by the blowing winds.

wilderness half a world distant from his true goal, Columbus would have been a bitterly frustrated man. Nevertheless, his letter gave a glowing report of what he had actually encountered. "This is a land to be desired," he wrote, "and once seen, never to be relinquished"; and that estimate held up in the years to come.

Columbus' letter was not known in English until the *Edinburgh Review* published a translation in 1816. However, before the first British colonies were planted (they were, in fact, referred to as "plantations"), a wealth of literature in a variety of languages, including English, was available to those who cared to know what America was like, what was happening there and along the sea lanes that led there. Accounts of the voyages and adventures of Elizabethan seamen along those ocean lanes and along the coasts of the American continents fired the imagination of the English people. Such tales of heroic valor and enterprise gave the nation a new sense of pride and of imperial destiny. As recounted in the books of Richard Hakluyt in the late sixteenth century, they made a rich contribution to English literature, and so far as they concern the founding of the colonies on these shores, they provide in the majestic cadences of Elizabethan prose a broad background for the history of American literature—for the writers' America.

One notable result of those exploits was, in fact, the growth of active interest in the English colonization of the New World. England was almost the last of the great European colonizing powers to undertake permanent settlements. Before this could be done, the oceans of the world had to be swept clean of Spanish interference, and with martial spirit this the Elizabethan sea dogs and gentlemen adventurers proceeded to do. "Singeing the King of Spain's beard" was from the outset profitable enterprise on the open sea. In the *Golden Hind* Francis Drake spread terror over both coasts of Spain's American lands. After plundering the great treasure ship *Nuestra Señora de la Concepción*, "the chiefest glory of the whole South Sea," Drake entertained the astonished and defeated Spanish admiral with "all possible kinds of delicacies" served on a silver plate to the accompaniment of violin music, and then returned to England to be knighted. Spanish carracks, gorged "with rubies, carbuncles, and sapphires," fell prey to other British marauders. After one conquering voyage in the Pacific, Thomas Cavendish sailed up the Thames, his ships rigged with sails of damask and his sailors in silk suits and bedecked with chains of pure gold. By such remarkable deeds Elizabethan England opened a right of way to an American empire. As Drake wrote Lord Burleigh, there was now "a very great gap" opened through the diminishing lines of the Spanish maritime forces. English ships could sail the seas unchallenged, and through that widening gap they carried the growing swarms of colonists who would people the American wilderness.

Hakluyt himself had pointed out the material benefits that he believed would quickly and easily be realized from such ventures—"as great a profit to the Realme of England," he predicted, "as the Indies to the King of Spain." Here could be found everything from gold, silver, pearls, and emeralds to copper and lead, from spices, drugs, and silk worms "fairer than ours of Europe" to cotton, wine grapes, and olives for oil, and from tall trees for masts and hemp for cordage to "all kinde of precious furres" from the northern climes. One might "well and truly conclude," he wrote, "that all the com-

modities of our olde decayed and daungerous trades in all Europe, Africa, and Asia haunted by us, may in short space and for little or nothinge, in a manner be had in that part of America which lieth betweene 30 and 60 degrees of northerly latitude." Sir Walter Raleigh, poet and statesman and "the very perfect knight errant of his age," had enduring faith that he would live to see this land an English nation.

Bitter experiences in the century to come demolished most of those sanguine expectations. Riches there were in abundance, but for the most part they had to be patiently earned by toil and sweat. (William Penn prudently advised prospective emigrants in 1685: "Be moderate in Expectation, count on Labour before a Crop, and Cost before Gain.") Before that rude awakening there were others who also heralded this land of incredible wealth. In 1606, just before an expedition set out for Virginia, the poet Michael Drayton hymned an ode in praise of the land he had never seen. Hakluyt, "Whose reading shall inflame Man to seake fame," had inspired his verses. Drayton wrote:

> And cheerefully at sea,
> Successe you still intice,
>   To get the pearle and gold,
>   And ours to hold,
> Virginia,
> Earthe's onely paradise.

It was a "delicious land" of "lushious smell," as Drayton described it, where cedars reached to kiss the sky and where the harvests were all greater than might be wished for.

Such prospects were held forth in a spate of promotional literature, much of it prompted by speculators with mercenary interests in exploiting the resources of America. (That genre of literature, most of it with nothing like Drayton's lyricism, continued through much of the nineteenth century when steamship companies, railroad combines, and land speculators advertised in the same spirit to entice hopeful emigrants from Europe with colorful legends of this land of promise.) Even while the pitiful survivors of the first Jamestown settlement were devouring their horses, the snakes of the forests, their leather

Two engravings, above, from John Smith's Generall Historie *depict Smith being captured by Indians (left) and being rescued by Pocahontas (center). In* A True Relation *(1608) Smith represented Powhatan as a friendly individual, and wrote nothing about having been saved by an Indian maiden. A braggart, he probably invented the romantic rescue story after Pocahontas married John Rolfe, an English gentleman. The princess, shown in the 1793 engraving (right) after a portrait of 1616, took the Christian name Rebecca.*

boots, and ultimately the carcasses of their dead comrades in a desperate effort to survive, the Virginia Company of London was blithely describing the advantages of life in their colony. During that "starving time" the author of *Nova Britannia* hailed the delights and resources of every description that awaited prospective planters in Virginia. As an additional lure he advised that native Indians were "generally very loving and gentle."

In 1622, shortly after those "friendly" but inconstant savages had all but annihilated the colonists at Jamestown, John Donne, poet and dean of St. Paul's, preached a sermon boosting the colony in the name of God and king. His words were published and distributed, and for this blurb he was given some stock in the company. In that same year, on the other hand, prospective settlers were more realistically advised to bring with them firearms, powder and shot, swords, and among other equipment, complete suits of armor. Such tracts, specious, overdrawn, or true enough as they sometimes were, also take their place in the background of the history of American letters.

The early trials of the Jamestown colony will forever be associated with the almost legendary figure of Captain John Smith. As he recalled and wrote about his career, in his youth Smith had fought for the Holy Roman Empire against the Turks, who captured him and took him as a slave to Constantinople; there the pasha's wife fell in love with him and managed his freedom. And so on goes his story, which has tested the credulousness of historians and laymen alike over the centuries. He arrived at Jamestown by way of the Canaries and the West Indies in 1607. Whether he was, in fact, there rescued from death by the fair Indian princess Pocahontas, as he said, is far from certain. "Two great stones were brought before *Powatan*, then as many as could laid hands on him," wrote Smith in the third person, "and dragged him to them, and thereupon laid his head, and being ready with their clubs, to beat out his brains, Pocahontas, the King's daughter, when no entreaty could prevaile, got his head in her arms, and laid her owne upon his to save him from death: whereat the emperor was contented he should live to make him hatchets, and her bells, beads, and copper. . . ."

Pocahontas, at least, was no figment of Smith's imagination. The heart of

14

John Rolfe (the Virginia settler who introduced the regular cultivation of tobacco into the colony) was "so intangled and enthralled in so intricate a laborinth" by that unbelieving creature that he took her to wife—one of the few Englishmen to marry a native. He also took her to London, where she was received at court and, according to Ben Jonson, where she was occasionally spied slipping through tavern doors. But in that chill and alien land the ill-fated lady died before she could return to her native shores, and was buried at Gravesend. (Back in Virginia, Rolfe met his end, in all probability at the hands of murderous Indians.)

Smith's account of the princess was written in 1624, some years after the alleged episode of his deliverance from the Indians. Earlier, in 1608, he had published an account of the beginning of our first permanent settlement, and that date might be chosen as the birth date of American literature. He wrote with gusto and in a rich and racy style that allied him with the robust pamphleteers and narrators of the Elizabethan Age. However many tall tales may be interlarded in his accounts of adventure, it is fair to conclude that without his practical efforts Jamestown might have quickly perished. Upon his arrival he realized that a supply of food was of first importance, even before picking up precious stones. Very few among the first settlers were accustomed to the hard labor required for those pioneering beginnings. The colonists who came, Smith complained, were "ten times more fit to spoil a common-wealth than either begin one, or but help to maintain one." Under such cir-cumstances, he wrote, "a plaine soldier that can use a pickaxe and a spade is better than five knights." The true "first families of Virginia" were hard-working yeomen, not cavaliers.

Quite aside from the inducements of promoters and rhapsodists, the lure of free land to be had overseas was incentive enough for the many English-men who were being forced from their land at home with the enclosure of the open fields and commons at a time when unemployment was rising and the city streets of England were swarming with "rogues and sturdy beggars." As John Winthrop observed before he himself sailed westward to become the first governor of Massachusetts Bay Colony, "this land grows weary of her inhabitants." And, he asked himself, "Why then should we stand striving here for places of habitation . . . & in the meane time suffer a whole Continent as fruitfull & convenient for the use of men to lie waste without any improve-ment?" That was a good if somewhat rhetorical question that was answered by a mounting tide of emigration. A ballad, "Summons to New England," was sung in the streets of English towns and a "great giddiness" to emigrate swept the land. The poor of England had almost no means of improving their lot or of affecting any course of action determined by those who ruled the land. Even King Charles' poor laws provided little help for them. Between 1620 and 1642 almost 80,000 (2 per cent of all Englishmen) left Britain—and about 58,000 of them ventured across the Atlantic. What is known as the Great Migration was under way.

John Smith's Virginia exploits have tended to overshadow his vital role as a "founder" of New England, which he explored, mapped, named, and de-scribed. He was an accomplished and influential promoter in his own right. He later wrote that when the time came for the Pilgrims' overseas journey, to save expenses they declined the expert services he proffered, "saying my

NOVA BRITANNIA.
OFFRING MOST
Excellent fruites by Planting in
VIRGINIA.
Exciting all such as be well affected
to further the same.

LONDON
Printed for SAMVEL MACHAM, and are to be fold at
his Shop in Pauls Church-yard, at the
Signe of the Bul-head.
1609.

Nova Britannia, *a promotional tract, was printed in London in 1609, when the Jamestown colonists were suffering from starvation. The overly optimistic pamphlet, however, promised Virginia immigrants plentiful food and "mountains making a sen-sible proffer of hidden treasure."*

books and maps were much better cheape to teache them, than myselfe."
(One of his excellent maps shows "Plimouth," which he named six years
before the Pilgrims arrived there.) In much the same vein, shortly after his
arrival in Salem in 1629, the Reverend Francis Higginson wrote *New England's Plantation,* a guide for prospective pilgrims heading for the New
World. "I advise them," he wrote in this book (which quickly went through
three editions), "to buy Captaine John Smith's book of the description of
New England in folio, and reade from fol. 203 to the end; and there let the
reader expect to have full content."

Protestantism played its part in English colonial policy. To extend the reach
of empire was to spread the reformed faith that would confound the designs
of the papacy. It was, indeed, a form of patriotism—and it included saving the
souls of heathen red savages for the glory of God and the true faith. With his
practical common sense, John Smith had his doubts about this kind of moti-
vation to settlement. "I am not so simple to think," he wrote in his *Description of New England,* "that ever any other motive than wealth, will ever erect
there a Commonweale; or draw companie from their ease and humours at
home, to stay in New England."

In this, of course, he was dead wrong. Although it was of a strain repugnant
to the British establishment, religion gave the greatest impetus to the early
settlement of New England. It started with the landing of the Pilgrims at
Plymouth in 1620. That was the story, wrote one historian, "of a small and
feeble enterprise, glorified by faith and hope and charity, but necessarily and
always limited by the slender resources of the poor and humble men who
originated it." But, in spite of formidable obstacles, that settlement endured,
and it was quickly followed by the erection of several other commonwealths
in that area, which also endured. (Had the *Mayflower* kept on to its original
destination in Virginia the history of the Pilgrims' adventure might have been
altogether different; they might, in fact, have been quite forgotten.)

These were no light undertakings. To face the real perils of the ocean
crossing and the anticipated hardships—and others not to be imagined—of
securing footholds in the "hideous and desolate wilderness, full of wild
beasts and wild men," was an act of insuperable faith. Those perils and hardships, wrote William Bradford, first governor of Plymouth Plantation, were
such as "could not but move the very bowels of men to grate within them and
make them weak to quake and tremble." Even that steadfast Puritan John
Winthrop recorded in his diary more than a decade after the founding of the
Massachusetts Bay Colony that, had he foreseen the trials he suffered during
the first years of that settlement, he would never have left home. More than
a few of those who came to America found the prospects far from their expectations and returned home to advertise their complaints.

But such defectors were persons of little or no faith, as the Pilgrims and
Puritans understood the word. Not all of those who persevered were goaded
solely by religious zeal, to be sure. Many had come to further their fortunes
rather than, or at least as well as, to escape the "many popish Injunctions"
that threatened their consciences in England. Cotton Mather recalled that
when one minister enjoined a congregation somewhere Down East from
Boston to remain a firmly religious people lest they "contradict the main end
of planting this wilderness," a prominent member of that assembly cried, "Sir,

*As a boy in Suffolk, England, John
Winthrop, later the first governor
of the Massachusetts Bay Colony,
began to discipline himself to
Puritan reserve and sobriety. In
1629, when he lost his post as an
attorney in London's Court of
Wards because of his religious
views, he became interested in
emigrating to America. That year
he was chosen governor of the
newly chartered Massachusetts
Bay Company. Winthrop's* Journal, *begun when the* Arbella *was
preparing to set sail for New England, is a valuable record of life
and morality in the Bay Colony.*

you are mistaken, you think you are preaching to the people at the Bay; our main end was to catch fish." However, the stated purpose and the solid intent of the leaders of those early New England commonwealths was to found the perfect society and the kingdom of God's select. To this end, preached William Stoughton, later a judge in the Salem witch trials, "God sifted a whole nation that He might send choice grain over into this wilderness."

Those choice souls were in good part a bookish, immensely well-read lot. Archbishop William Laud helped in the selection of emigrants by hounding some of the sharpest nonconformist minds out of England, including among numerous others John Cotton, who in 1633 fled his post at St. Botolph's at Boston, in Lincolnshire, to become the "mightiest man in New England." (The town of Boston in the Bay Colony was named after that older Boston in England where Cotton had preached.) Laud's purges are reminiscent of the persecutions of Adolf Hitler that, three centuries later, brought so many European refugee savants to America. At least one hundred thirty graduates of Oxford and Cambridge came to New England before 1646, and among other emigrants there were many who had been solidly educated in the English grammar schools. Those men were the accepted leaders of the Puritan migration, for in this society of believers learning was next to godliness.

Thus it was, as an anonymous pamphlet of 1643 reported:

> After God had carried us safe to *New England,* and wee had builded our houses, provided necessaries for our liveli-hood, rear'd convenient places for Gods worship, and settled the Civill Government; One of the next things we longed for, and looked after was to advance *Learning,* and perpetuate it to Posterity, dreading to leave an illiterate Ministry to the Churches, when our present Ministers shall lie in the dust . . . it pleased God to stir up the heart of one Mr. Harvard . . . to give the one halfe of his Estate . . . towards the erecting of a College, and all his Library.

And thus it was that in 1647 the Massachusetts School Act was passed for expressly establishing a system of schooling in the colony, lest knowledge become "buried in the graves of our fore-fathers in Church and Common-wealth." As early as 1637 Boston had a "Bookebynder" to serve its reading public, and a decade later a bookshop. Wandering hawkers supplied the back country with literature. In April, 1705, the Boston *News-Letter* reported the death of one such salesman "That used to go up and down the Country selling of Books, who left a considerable Estate behind him"—an accomplishment not often matched by booksellers of our own day.

From the pens of such men issued a remarkable flow of writings, considering the circumstances. Books they had in fair supply, and more books arrived with the cargo of each incoming ship from abroad. But these authors had no libraries to turn to comparable to those in London or at Cambridge, Oxford, and elsewhere in England; nowhere in New England was there a diversified and cosmopolitan society such as in old England responded to the works of Shakespeare, Beaumont and Fletcher, Ben Jonson, and the others whose brilliant creations shed glory over the generation following the death of Queen Elizabeth. (Almost incredibly, Increase Mather, president of Harvard from 1685 to 1701, seems not to have known of Shakespeare or Jonson, although he read Hebrew, Latin, Greek, French, Spanish, and even one of the Indian

St. Botolph's Church (above), in the English town of Boston, Lincolnshire, was the parish church of John Cotton, one of the many Puritans who fled to New England after William Laud (below) became Archbishop of Canterbury.

17

tongues and wrote in most of those languages, and in his writings quoted from a variety of other sources and reference works.) Puritan New England produced no plays, no fiction, and very little poetry that got into print. However, the histories and chronicles, the voluminous private journals and diaries, the theological essays and sermons that came forth from the wilderness world in the seventeenth century constituted the first solid growth of an American literature. Whatever their literary merits—and they were often enough considerable within very restricted limits—those writings are of absorbing historical interest. The distinctive social and moral order of the Puritans as it is therein expressed had a persistent influence that spread out over the whole continental United States in years to come.

The authors of those early books and pamphlets were not professional writers; there would be none such in America for many long years to come. But they were highly articulate in the fashion of their time and place, and they could rise to an eloquence that continues to appeal to us over the intervening centuries. They tell of their first encounters with the New World and its aborigines with a mixture of awe and foreboding, of surprise, bewilderment, and delight that still enchants with its direct and often colorful descriptions. In all this there was none of the self-conscious exaltation that inspired the romantics two centuries later. Consider, for example, just one passage in William Wood's *New England's Prospect*, published in 1634, in which he describes Massachusetts Bay with a direct and spontaneous lyricism. It "is both safe, spacious, and deep," he wrote, "free from such cockling seas as run upon the coast of Ireland, and in the channels of England. . . . The mariners . . . may behold the two capes embracing their welcome ships in their arms, which thrust themselves out into the sea in form of a half-moon, the surrounding shores being high, and showing many white cliffs in a most pleasant prospect. . . . This harbor is made by a great company of islands, whose high cliffs shoulder out the boisterous seas."

The dark forests and the tawny natives posed immediate problems that had to be met face on with little experience to guide the first arrivals, except their conviction that God's work must be done—and, somewhat more practically, with the advice of friendly Indians when they could get such. William Bradford of Plymouth Plantation spoke plainly for his shipmates on the *Mayflower* as he surveyed their plight and their prospects upon arrival. "Being thus passed the vast ocean and a sea of troubles . . . they now had no friends to welcome them, nor inns to entertain or refresh their weather-beaten bodies, no houses or much less towns to repair to, to seek for succor." The "savage barbarians" who greeted them, he remarked, "were readier to fill their sides full of arrows than otherwise." As he stood there at Plymouth on that narrow strip of land between the two infinities of ocean and wilderness, he reflected that "summer being done, all things stand upon them with a weather-beaten face; and the whole country, full of woods and thickets, represented a wild and savage hue." Half his company did indeed die during the following winter. In later years he could not but wonder and greatly "admire the marvelous providence of God, that notwithstanding the many changes and hardships that these people went throwgh, and the many enemies they had and difficulties they mette with all, that so many of them should live to very olde age!" (The *Mayflower* passengers who survived that first cruel winter lived

Tee Yee Ga Row, one of five Iroquois sachems who visited England in 1709–10, is shown in John Simon's engraving after a painting by John Verelst. The Indian "kings" were a fashionable novelty in London and attracted enormous attention; they even had an audience with Queen Anne, who "ordered them presents."

an average of thirty-seven years afterward.)

In a different vein, when Francis Higginson touched ground in the Bay Colony after six weeks on the ocean, it was the full tide of summer, and he could not conceal his delight with the gladness of nature that welcomed him. Strawberries were in season, "and all manner of Berries and Fruits." The woods were full of turkeys, "farre greater then our English Turkies, and exceeding fat, sweet and fleshy . . . all the yeere long." He could even get a quart of milk for a penny, he exulted. When he added that "a sup of New England's air is better than a whole draught of Old England's ale," we can assume that he was indulging in a bit of deliberate promotion of the new colony at Salem. However, he is more objective and believable when he describes the Indians, ever a source of wonder and curiosity to white men until they actually had to cope with the hostilities and perversities of beleaguered red men. Those Higginson first met, he wrote, were "a tall and strong-limbed people. Their colors are tawny. . . . Their hair is generally black, and cut before, like our gentlewomen, and one lock longer than the rest, much like to our gentlemen, which fashion, I think, came from hence into England."

Some of the early observers were carried away by the utter novelty of what they saw, or perhaps they had that penchant for tall tales that became an enduring tradition in our frontier literature. In his *New England Rarities Discovered*, published in 1672, the English naturalist John Josselyn gravely reported that the American Indians had extemporary discussions "in perfect hexameter verse." He wrote of frogs "which chirp in the spring like sparrows, and croak like toads in autumn," and which in some cases were "as big as a child of a year old"; and of the "pilhannaw," a bird so large and formidable that when it took to the air all other feathered creatures hid themselves. (Such stories remind one of Benjamin Franklin, a century later, solemnly assuring his English readers that to see whales leaping up the falls of Niagara like so many salmon was an impressive sight to behold.) Josselyn once mistook a hornet's nest for a rare fruit "as big as the crown of a woman's hat," until he touched it and the "wasps" came swarming out. "By the time I was come into the house," he wanly related, " . . . they hardly knew me but by my garments." Occasionally, after his more extravagant statements, he paused to reproach readers who, "muttering out of their scuttle-mouths," might express disbelief in his stories. Like so many other early visitors to these shores, Josselyn was intrigued by the Indians he saw. Thus in his account he described the native squaws:

> The men are somewhat horse-faced and generally faucious, i.e., without beards; but the women, many of them, have very good features; seldom without a come-to-me, or *cos amoris,* in their countence; all of them black-eyed; having even, short teeth, and very white; their hair black, thick, and long; broad-breasted; handsome, straight bodies, and slender, considering their constant loose habit; their limbs cleanly, straight, and of a convenient stature, generally as plump as partridges; and, saving here and there, one of a modest deportment.

Josselyn's writings were noticed by the Royal Society in London as valuable contributions.

The earliest, the most authoritative, and the most moving of all the narratives concerning early New England is William Bradford's *History of*

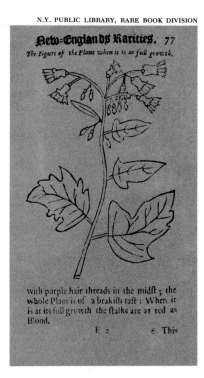

The English naturalist John Josselyn made two voyages (1638 and 1663) to America, where he studied the flora and fauna. Reproduced above is one page from his New-Englands Rarities Discovered in Birds, Beasts, Fishes, Serpents, and Plants of that Country, *a lively compendium of fact and fantasy, first published in London in 1672.*

being ready to departe, they had a day of solemne humiliation their pastor taking his text from Ezra 8.21 And ther at ye river, by Ahaua, ye proclaimed a fast, that we might humble our selves before our god, and seeke of him a right way for us, and for our children, and for all our substance. | Upon which he spente a good parte of ye day very profitably, and suitable to their presente occasion, the rest of the time was spente in powering out prairs to ye Lord, with great fervencie; mixed with abundance of tears. And ye time being come that they must departe, they were accompanied with most of their brethren out of ye citie, unto a towne sundrie miles of called Delfs-Haven wher the ship lay ready to receive them. So they lefte ye goodly & pleasante citie, which had been ther resting place nere 12 years; but they knew they were pilgrimes, & looked not much on these things; but lift up their eyes to ye heavens, their dearest cuntrie, and quieted their spirits. When they came

The band of Separatists who founded Plymouth Colony in 1620 called themselves Old Comers; they were not known as Pilgrims until the 1840's. The term comes from the phrase "they knew they were pilgrimes," in William Bradford's History of Plymouth Plantation; *a manuscript page from the work is reproduced above. The Pilgrim meetinghouse, built in Plymouth in 1683, is pictured below.*

MEETING HOUSE

PILGRIM HALL, PLYMOUTH

Plymouth Plantation. Like a latter-day Moses, Bradford felt duty-bound to chronicle the exodus of his people—his pilgrims in quest of a promised land. (He was the first to use the term "Pilgrims.") This he purported to do "in plaine stile, with a singular regard unto ye simple trueth in all things." As the brief quotations already given from this book suggest, Bradford's "plaine stile" had an almost biblical sonority. These "scribled Writings," as he referred to his manuscript, are grave and dignified, but they are enlivened by Bradford's sense of drama and his eye for color—occasionally even by sparkles of malicious wit and sarcasm.

Bradford was ideally equipped for his task. He was a student of many books and a number of languages—Dutch, French, Latin, and Greek, besides English; and in his later years he diligently studied Hebrew to familiarize himself with that ancient tongue "in which God and angels spake to the holy patriarchs of old time." Beyond that, he wrote with special insights as a principal actor in the events he recounted and as a chief of the inner councils at Plymouth where matters of moment were intimately discussed. He did not tell the whole truth at times when that might discredit the Pilgrim enterprise, but he often described the daily life of his fellow settlers with a candor that completely destroys the stereotyped conceptions of these men and women that still remain a prominent part of their legend. He showed them for what they were in flesh and blood; not as plaster saints, but as human beings with all too many frailties and vanities along with their rugged strengths and their austere convictions.

These were not meek, drab souls forever going to meetings with downcast eyes and pious tread, as they were so often pictured in the nineteenth century. They knew and appreciated the pleasures of the food and drink that were available. (The cargo of the *Mayflower* included a precious supply of "hot waters" and beer; John Alden, the cooper, was charged with maintaining the barrels these were stored in.) And they were certainly not above the conceits of finery. William Brewster, one of the more venerable Pilgrims, occasionally sported a violet-colored coat, a green waistcoat, silk stockings, a red or white cap, and—sight unseen—"1 paire of green drawers." (Both Alden and Brewster were ancestors of Henry Wadsworth Longfellow, who, two centuries later, himself had a penchant for finery.)

Bradford could be remarkably frank about the sinful behavior that broke out in the colony—"especially drunkenness and uncleanness; not only incontinency between persons unmarried . . . but some married persons also. But that which is worse, even sodomy and buggery . . . have broke forth in this land oftener than once." "Horrible it is to mention," wrote Bradford, "but the truth of the history requires it." Obviously, not all who came to Plymouth or to the Bay Colony were of the sifted wheat. However, Bradford philosophically concluded, he was "verily persuaded" to believe that such evils were no more common at Plymouth than elsewhere; they were just discovered and punished more quickly by the Pilgrims than by the authorities in other colonies.

For a time Bradford was deeply disturbed by the frivolous, bibulous, and libidinous colonists (as he viewed them) who had settled nearby on the site of what is now Quincy, Massachusetts, while Thomas Morton served as their leader. Morton was an Anglican of a conventional sort, a lawyer and an adventurer, and back in England he sometimes drank and rollicked with the immortal Ben Jonson at the Mermaid Tavern in London. He named, or renamed, the colony "Ma-re-Mount" (Mountain by the Sea), which the Pilgrims quickly termed Merry Mount and which they condemned for the "beastly practises of ye madd Bachianalians" who lived there. Morton's crew was also guilty of outwitting the Pilgrims in trading with the Indians, which Bradford considered a substantial loss to the Plymouth economy, and in the course of their negotiations of supplying the natives with firewater and firearms, which was a real menace to all white men.

But the moral issues were most condemnable. To celebrate the renaming of the colony, Morton had set up and trimmed an eighty-foot-tall pine tree to serve as a Maypole, about which his men and laughing Indian girls danced

Contrary to a widespread misconception, Puritan youngsters did not always wear somber clothes, as evidenced by this group portrait of the Mason children, painted in 1670 by an unknown Massachusetts artist. In keeping with the artistic convention of the period, the children are dressed and portrayed as miniature adults.

21

hand in hand chanting in chorus one of Morton's compositions:

Drinke and be merry, merry, merry boyes;
Let all your delight be in Hymen's joyes,
Joy to Hymen, now the day is come,
About the merry Maypole take a Roome.

Make greene garlons, bring bottles out;
And fill sweet Nectar, freely about,
Uncover thy head, and feare no harme,
For hers good liquor to keepe it warme.

✿　✿　✿　✿

Then drinke and be merry, merry, merry boyes;
Let all your delight be in Hymen's joyes,
Joy to Hymen, now the day is come,
About the merry Maypole take a Roome.

Bradford decided to put an end to such profane nonsense. Myles Standish, whom Morton contemptuously referred to as "Captain Shrimpe," was dispatched to take Morton into custody, which he did in a comic-opera sort of skirmish. The episode, along with other details concerning Indian life and the natural features of America, Morton later wrote up in his *New English Canaan*, published at Amsterdam in 1637 and one of the liveliest and wittiest books to come out of the early American experience.

Such a curious byway in colonial history has captured the imagination of other writers over the years. Two centuries after the fact, Nathaniel Hawthorne created an allegorical romance out of the history of Merry Mount. "The future complexion of New England was involved in this important quarrel," he wrote in "The May-Pole of Merry Mount," one of his *Twice-Told Tales*, making the quarrel somewhat more important than it actually was. "Should the grisly saints establish their jurisdiction over the gay sinners, then would their spirits darken all the clime, and make it a land of clouded visages, of hard toil, of sermon and psalm forever. But should the banner-staff of Merry Mount be fortunate, sunshine would break upon the hills, and flowers would beautify the forest, and late posterity do homage to the May-pole." At the end, he reflected, "As the moral gloom of the world overpowers all systematic gaiety, even so was their home of wild mirth made desolate amid the sad forest. They returned to it no more."

Most of us are much more familiar with Hawthorne's version of the story than with the contemporary records of Bradford or Morton. However, to understand the Pilgrims' role in the history of life in America, it is necessary to look to Bradford's book. He did not plan these jottings for publication, but as an immediate record of events and circumstances, lest the trials and triumphs of his people be forgotten by generations to come, and in this he showed a clear sense of destiny. Bradford's manuscript has an interesting history of its own. Early in the eighteenth century it found its way to the library of the Old South Church in Boston, whence it was probably stolen by some British soldier during the Revolutionary War. Three-quarters of a century later it was rediscovered in the library of the Bishop of London. Shortly thereafter, in 1856, it was finally published—and some years later the manuscript was returned to America.

The ever-merry Thomas Morton of Merry Mount, "a lord of misrule," was a thorn in the Pilgrims' side. He set up a Maypole, as depicted in the 19th-century woodcut reproduced above, and scandalized Plymouth with his sinful revelry. In his New English Canaan *(1637) Morton explained that "The setting up of this Maypole was a lamentable spectacle to the precise Separatists that lived at New Plymouth. They termed it an idol . . . and stood at defiance with the place . . . threatening to make it a woeful mount and not a merry mount."*

In a sense it might be said that this publication was the beginning of Pilgrim history. Over the two hundred years that Bradford's manuscript lay all but forgotten, the true story of the Pilgrims, as Bradford had feared, was largely neglected. Plymouth Rock was all but unnoticed until the eve of the Revolution, just another granite boulder among the glacial debris of the Cape until it was moved about from one spot to another (it was broken in the process), finally coming to rest at its original site beneath the Greek temple that now shelters it. The very word "Pilgrims," referring to those early forefathers, was itself virtually forgotten until nearly the middle of the last century. Much that has long passed as the saga of the Pilgrims, so basic to American tradition, was an invention of the nineteenth century, an often fanciful mixture of patriotism, ignorance, and romantic sensibility. With the belated publication of Bradford's *History* a substantial part of the true story became a matter of public record.

For the earnest Puritan, life on earth was an anxious way station in the passage either to eternal salvation or to damnation, depending upon the inscrutable will of God. Every event revealed the interposition of a special providence; every incident conveyed a "sign" that, properly construed, would provide some evidence of spiritual portent. Nothing was too trivial for God's close attention. Thus, when the diarist Samuel Sewall suffered a sore throat one evening, he ascribed this malaise to his having neglected his morning's private prayers. When Cotton Mather had one of his periodic toothaches, he wondered whether he might have sinned with his teeth by excessive eating or by some evil speech. In 1640 mice got into John Winthrop's library of more than a thousand books, but the little rodents providentially selected for destruction only the Book of Common Prayer that was bound in with the Greek Testament and the Psalms (it was later suggested in a review of the episode that, rather than a sign of divine disapprobation of the Episcopal prayer book, it might have been that the mice disliked psalmody and did not understand Greek).

To explain many of the chances of life, as one historian has observed, the Puritans held a comfortable "heads I win, tails you lose" point of view. An individual's misfortune could mean to him that the Lord chastens those whom he loves. His adversary's misfortune proved that God took vengeance on the wicked. However, in the end, only the Lord knew the true portent of things that happened in life; these he would make manifest, but only in his good time. It would be arrogant to claim sure knowledge of God's will. The doubts about one's spiritual status could drive a person quite mad, as in the case of a Boston woman who, unable any longer to endure the uncertainty, threw her baby down a well with the assurance that now at last she was surely damned. Our present world is not free from such phenomenal attitudes, although we refer to them as superstitions. But it is difficult to realize that both Increase Mather and his illustrious son Cotton, two of the most learned and enlightened —and orthodox—men in seventeenth century New England, wrote serious books relating endless examples demonstrating the persistent interference of the Deity in the minute private affairs of men and women.

The so-called Mather dynasty, which spanned three generations, through the lives of Richard, Increase, and Cotton, played a dominant role in the intellectual life of Puritan New England. As an old epitaph put it:

The Mather dynasty dominated the theological life of Puritan New England. Grandfather Richard (top) edited The Bay Psalm Book; *son Increase (center) served as president of Harvard; grandson Cotton (bottom) penned the* Magnalia Christi.

23

Indian Horrors, *printed in the 1890's and including these illustrations, offered tales of "terrible personal encounters with the red men, hairbreadth escapes, thrilling captures, and bloody massacres"—subjects that have appealed to readers from colonial times down to the present day.*

> Under this stone lies Richard Mather,
> Who had a son greater than his father,
> And eke a grandson greater than either.

All three were prolific writers and sermonizers. Richard Mather, founder of the dynasty, spent his whole, industrious life among books, reading and writing, until he no longer had the strength to crawl to his study. To his contemporaries he was a "mighty man," immensely learned, and a formidable presence in the pulpit. "His voice," his grandson recalled, "was loud and big; and uttered with deliberate vehemency, it procured unto his ministry an awful and very taking majesty."

Richard's son Increase Mather preached his first sermon from his father's pulpit at the age of eighteen, and went on to deliver sermons that hit his audience like "the fall of thunderbolts." Before he died in the ripeness of old age, Increase had published at least 130 titles on subjects ranging from crime and politics to Indians and earthquakes, from drunkenness and smallpox to dancing and ignorance. Yet his son Cotton, in his turn, outdid both his elders in the magnitude of his accomplishment. In his lifetime he produced no less than 450 works, including his *Magnalia Christi Americana*, a compendious ecclesiastical history that, when she read it many years later, made Harriet Beecher Stowe feel the very ground she walked on "to be consecrated by some special dealing of God's providence." That book was, as the author himself observed, "a bulky thing," running to some thirteen hundred pages. It was the most impressive publication written in the colonies.

Mather had had some difficulty finding a publisher. In his distress over this problem, in the dead of an April night and after singing some psalms, Cotton cast himself "prostrate into the dust, on my study-floor, before the Lord" and "confessed unto him the sins for which he might justly reject me and all my services." (Before or since, many hopeful authors have experienced such anguish.) Six months later the book was in print, and Mather thanked God for his "watchful and gracious providence over that work." For all his prolixity and the heavy burden of his learned allusions, Cotton Mather could tell a good story, and as many New England writers of the last century learned, his *Magnalia* is an indispensable source book for his period. "The Memorable Action at Wells," a part of the *Magnalia* dealing with Indian warfare in the North, remains thrilling reading to this day.

This section of his great opus tells of the ten-year battle, from 1688 to 1698, with the savages to the North, a conflict Mather claimed was no less epic in its way than the Trojan War. For, as he wrote, "the walls of Troy were, it seems, all made of poet's paper; and the siege of the town, with the tragedies of the wooden horse, were all but a piece of poetry. And if a war between us and a handful of Indians do appear no more than a *Batrachomyomachia* [*The Battle of the Frogs and Mice*, a parody of Homer's epic story] to the world abroad, yet unto us at home it hath been considerable enough to make a history." He then proceeds to describe the action in a brisk narrative with colorful and gory detail, as in his account of an episode wherein one of the colonists, "poor John Diamond," fell into the hands of the Indians:

> . . . they fell to torturing their captive, John Diamond, after a manner very diabolical. They stripped him, they scalped him alive, and after

24

a castration, they finished that article in the punishment of traitors upon him; they slit him with knives between his fingers and his toes; they made cruel gashes in the most fleshy parts of his body, and stuck the gashes with fire-brands which were afterwards found sticking in the wounds. Thus they butchered one poor Englishman with all the fury that they would have spent upon them all, and performed an exploit for five hundred furies to brag of at their coming home. Ghastly to express! What was it then to suffer?

The Puritan mission to save the souls of red men was often thwarted by the more immediate and urgent need to protect themselves from savage attacks by the natives. All the settlers were moving into land that from the Indians' vantage was not theirs, and this was a point of conscience that sometimes bothered the white men. In 1609 Robert Gray asked in his *Good Speed to Virginia*, "By what right or warrant can we enter into the land of these Savages, take away their rightful inheritance from them, and plant ourselves in their places, being unwronged or unprovoked by them." The complex relationship between the two races cannot easily be understood or explained. The Indians left little or no record of their side of the story, but the white men left an ample record of theirs. By far the most lurid account of this conflict of interest was penned by Mrs. Mary Rowlandson of Lancaster, Massachusetts, who spent eleven anguished weeks as a captive of the Indians who had sacked and burned that village and slaughtered many of its inhabitants. Mrs. Rowlandson's story of her adventures, written in a lively narrative style that makes the book a classic of its kind, was published in 1682 and went through more than thirty editions. She spared no detail of the action that destroyed her town and killed so many of her friends—and her own child:

Now is the dreadful hour come that I have often heard of (in time of war, as it was the case of others), but now mine eyes see it. Some in our house were fighting for their lives, others wallowing in their blood, the house on fire over our heads, and the bloody heathen ready to knock us on the head if we stirred out. Now might we hear mothers and children crying out for themselves and one another, 'Lord, what shall we do?' ... The bullets flying thick, one went through my side, and the same (as would seem) through the bowels and hand of my dear child in my arms. One of my elder sister's children, named William, had then his leg broken, which the Indians, perceiving they knocked him on head. Thus were we butchered by those merciless heathen, standing amazed, with the blood running down to our heels. My eldest sister being yet in the house and seeing those woeful sights, the infidels haling mothers one way and children another, and some wallowing in their blood, and her elder son telling her that her son William was dead and myself was wounded, she said, 'And, Lord, let me die with them!'—which was no sooner said, but she was struck with a bullet, and fell down dead. . . .

A good part of the literary output of the Mathers was comprised of their almost endless sermons. The sermon was, indeed, the most characteristic product of the Puritan mind and the most important form of prose literature in early New England. To a later age these hours-long discussions seem like incredible feats of endurance, too trying for modern minds to accept with anything more than impatience and boredom. Even an occasional contem-

Cotton Mather published some 450 titles, including The Wonders of the Invisible World *(1693), an account of the Salem witchcraft scare and trials. Mather, here shown with the Devil, lived in an age that believed Satan, like God, was an active presence on earth.*

Thomas Savage of Boston, captain of the Ancient and Honorable Artillery Company (an elite organization for the defense of Boston), is shown in all his finery in a 1679 portrait attributed to Thomas Smith. In his bright, almost gaudy uniform—lace-trimmed coat, fringed sash, and gold-topped cane—he belies the image of the drably clad Puritan so familiar in romantic 19th-century literature and legend.

porary was overwhelmed by the length and tedium of such performances. "Wee have a strong weaknesse in New England," wrote one whimsical satirist of the time, himself a preacher, "that when wee are speaking, we know not how to conclude: wee make many ends, before we make an end: the fault is in the climate; we cannot helpe it, though we can, which is the Arch infirmity of all morality."

For the most part, only students and historians nowadays bother to read these lengthy preachments. Yet, contemporary audiences often sat spellbound when the right minister was in the pulpit. (Also, as one parishoner gratefully recalled later, the fire-and-brimstone messages delivered during those long sessions could take the winter's chill off the coldest meetinghouse.) The sermons were primarily meant to be heard before they were read, and from the printed page we can gather only a dim notion of the message as it was orally delivered by men with passionate conviction and evangelical fervor. The audiences were in a sense captives of a theocratic state, but in their measure they shared the preachers' interest in religion and looked to their spiritual leaders' reasoning for the practical guidance they needed in their daily lives—men and women who took notes with their inkhorn and paper and were ready with comments. They were largely plain folk of modest attainments—men who plowed the earth or kept their shops, who plied their crafts or fished the ocean waters, and women who went about the infinite variety of their daily household chores and who raised large families. And to them the truths of Holy Writ were explained in a plain and homely style through analogies with their familiar workaday lives. "Sweep your hearts," preached the Reverend Thomas Hooker, "and clense those roomes, clense every sinke, brush downe every cobweb, and make roome for Christ. . . . And when thou hast swept every corner of thy house, doe not leave the dust behind the doore, for that is a sluts tricke: doe not remove sin out of thy tongue, and out of thy eye, and out of thy hand, and leave it in thy heart." Or again, "Meditation is not a flourishing of a mans wit, but hath a set bout at the search of the truth, beats his brain as wee use to say, hammers out a buisiness, as the Gouldsmith with his mettal, he heats it and beats it, turnes it on this side and then on that, fashions it on both that he might frame it to his mind." Such an analogy was not lost on those who had watched the goldsmiths John Hull and Robert Sanderson work over their anvils in Boston.

For style as well as for content, the sermonists and writers of Puritan New England relied upon the Bible. It was their ultimate source book, with images and illustrations to suit every occasion and with a model language that could scarcely be challenged. Biblical style was "penned by the Holy Ghost" and could only be perfect. Those who followed its "simplicitie" and "plainnesse" in their writings and their preachings communicated directly with their congregations in a familiar pattern.

In the nineteenth century the Puritan legend, like that of the Pilgrims, was distorted by romantics searching for a picturesque American past. From surviving sermons and other formal literature it was all too easy to think of those remote forefathers as rather forbidding effigies everlastingly somber in thought and drab in appearance. Their morals were high, no doubt, but they were not arbitrary. From the start those earnest souls needed their rugged virtues if they were to firmly establish "Mount Sion in the Wildernesse." But they also had their share of human weaknesses. "As to truth and godliness," wrote one critical contemporary reporter, "you must not expect more of them than of others"; and, it was said, "Drinking and fighting occur there [in New England] not less than elsewhere." In 1675 Cotton Mather complained that every other house in Boston was an alehouse. The *Twice-Told Tales* and *The Scarlet Letter* of Nathaniel Hawthorne hardly prepare us for the actual portrait of Captain Thomas Savage of the Ancient and Honorable Artillery Company in his gold-fringed outfit, his sash, lace, red breeches, and other trappings. If Hester Prynne had a scarlet letter (beautifully embroidered) for her shame as an adulteress, Governor Richard Bellingham had a scarlet coat as the mantle of his respectability and authority. In spite of sumptuary laws, conformity and demureness in matters of dress are hardly apparent in the intimate historical evidence. As one other example, there is a strangely topical ring in John Endicott's protest against Harvard students "Wearing long hair in the manner of Ruffians."

In this connection, and also as a happy deviation from the "plaine stile" of writing, it is refreshing to turn to one of the most unusual and entertaining books produced in colonial America, Nathaniel Ward's *The Simple Cobler of Aggawam* [Ipswich] *in America*, published in London in 1647. Ward was another refugee from Archbishop Laud's displeasure. Before that turn of events he had some sort of association with Frederick V, Elector Palatine, and his wife, Princess Elizabeth, daughter of King James I of England. Apparently, during his sojourn on the Continent he had held in his arms that couple's child, who later, as Prince Rupert, became known as "the Mad Cavalier" and who served prominently as a Royalist officer during the English Civil War. "I wish I had him there now [that is, in his arms] . . . ," Ward later wrote, "I would pray hard to his Maker to make him a right Roundhead . . . to forgive all his sins, and at length to save his soul, notwithstanding all his God-damn-me's."

Ward became a sharp critic of society, both in New England and old England, who delivered his shafts with a gusty humor and an eccentric style that were unique in the history of Puritan literature. ("To speak to light heads with heavy words," he explained, "were to break their necks.") In *The Simple Cobler* he described himself as one "Willing to help 'mend his Native Country, lamentably tattered, both in the upper-Leather and sole, with all the honest stiches he can take." On the subject of woman's attire, particularly, he exercised merciless wit. He railed against any woman "with a ruff like a sail . . . with a feather in her cap like a flag in her top, to tell, I think, which way the wind will blow." "I am neither Nigard, nor Cinick . . . ," he wrote, "but when I heare a nugiperous Gentledame inquire what dresse the Queen is in this week: what the nudiustertian fashion of the Court; I meane the very newest. . . . I look at her as the very gizzard of a trifle, the product of a quarter of a cypher, the epitome of nothing, fitter to be kickt, if shee were a kickable substance, than either honour'd or humour'd." He had seen a number of such in Boston, and he could not abide their presence.

All those curious quirks and turns of phrase, "new-quoddled words" he called them, did not in the end disguise the fact that Ward was a sincere and impassioned reformer of independent spirit, a man whose radical thoughts fought with his conservative temperament. The very suggestion of religious

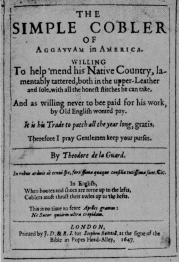

Nathaniel Ward's The Simple Cobler of Aggawam *(1647), whose first edition title page is shown above, is a vehement, witty tirade against back-sliding Puritans.*

27

toleration or free thought set him off on other tirades. He proclaimed to the world, in the name of New England, "that all Familists, Antinomians, Anabaptists, and other enthusiasts, shall have free liberty—to keep away from us; and such as will come—to be gone as fast as they can, the sooner the better." It was in that spirit of intolerance that the Quakers who insisted upon coming to the Bay Colony were persecuted, hanged, banished, or otherwise discouraged from lingering there.

Yet, in 1641, Ward, who in his younger days had studied law, drew up for the Massachusetts colony the "Body of Liberties," an enlightened and relatively humane code of laws and principles that is still considered a fundamental document in American constitutional history. Just a century ago, at the time of the nation's centennial celebration, one eminent scholar claimed that "for its liberality and comprehensiveness" that document "may vie with any similar record from the days of Magna Charta." It is difficult to judge whether it was because of his misogynistic attitudes or in spite of them that Ward wrote an article into this legislation assuring that "everie marryed woeman shall be free from bodilie correction or stripes by her husband, unlesse it be in his own defense upon her assalt." Another article stated that "No man shall exercise any Tirranny or Crueltie towards any bruite Creatures which are usuallie kept for man's use." With such provisions, cows, oxen, and married women would fare better under the law than the Quakers would.

Neither the Pilgrims nor the Puritans have always enjoyed a good press. (In his *History of England* Thomas Macaulay remarked that the Puritans hated bearbaiting, not because it gave pain to the bears, but because it gave pleasure to the spectators.) In the 1920's it was fashionable to regard them both as joyless hypocrites—as people filled with "the haunting fear that someone, somewhere, may be happy." H. L. Mencken had his little joke when he wrote that "When the Pilgrim Fathers landed, they fell upon their knees—and then upon the aborigines." He was applauded by *Vanity Fair*, in 1921, "because he has for years been almost our only bold assailant of the national Puritanism." It was the lingering strain of Puritanism that was blamed for Prohibition—and everything else that inhibited the pursuit of pleasure.

That cynical re-evaluation of the Puritans' role in American history was partly a reaction to the romantic idealization of our forefathers that had followed the centennial excitements of 1876—a sort of veneration that was enthusiastically shared by hordes of immigrants who swarmed into America during the last decades of the nineteenth century. The anthropologist Margaret Mead has remarked that in this country there has been an odd blending of the future with the past in which another man's grandfather becomes the symbol of one's grandson's future. Newcomers, often from outlandish places and fresh from the packed holds of immigrant ships, learned to associate their own destiny with the deeds of their adopted ancestors, to sing of this "land where my fathers died, land of the pilgrim's pride."

Liberal historians, Fourth of July orators, and sentimentalists of various stripes praised the Puritans for virtues that were not theirs—that they would not have considered virtues in the first place. They were acclaimed as pioneers of religious liberty, which, as already indicated, was the policy furthest from their minds. They were hailed as the prophets of American democracy, a form of government that was actually dreaded by the pious and select men

On January 21, 1621, the entire company of the Mayflower *came ashore for the first time (they stayed for only a few hours) and held their first meeting for public worship on American soil. The event is depicted in George Johann Schwartze's 19th-century painting, though the original thatched Common House bears little resemblance to this grand hall.*

who guided the early colonists on their "errand into the wilderness." "Democracy I do not conceive that God did ever ordain as a fit government for either church or commonwealth," counseled John Cotton. "If the people be governors, who shall be governed? As for monarchy and aristocracy, they are both clearly approved and directed in the Scriptures. . . . He setteth up theocracy . . . as the best form of government in the commonwealth as in the church." Democracy, added John Winthrop, "has always been accounted the meanest and worst of all forms of government."

Yet, on another occasion, Winthrop made a fervent appeal for a proper and just balance between authority and individual liberties that, paraphrased in modern idiom, would serve as an essay on civil rights in today's newspaper. In the spring of 1645, led by their minister and his three stout brothers, the people of Hingham, Massachusetts, mutinied over the question of an unpopular militia officer who had been imposed upon them by the General Court. In dealing with this sedition Winthrop was accused by his political enemies of exceeding his authority, and he was haled before the Court in what was, in effect, a trial for his impeachment. In the end he was acquitted, and his Hingham opponents were fined. When the verdict was reached, Winthrop rose and made his memorable "little speech," concluding:

> Concerning liberty, I observe a great mistake in the country about that. There is a two fold liberty, natural (I mean as our nature is now corrupt) and civil or federal. The first is common to man with beasts and other creatures. By this, man, as he stands in relation to man simply, hath liberty to do what he lists; it is a liberty to evil as well as good. This liberty is incompatible and inconsistent with authority, and cannot endure the least restraint of the most just authority. The exercise and maintaining of this liberty makes men grow more evil, and in time to be worse than brute beasts: . . . The other kind of liberty I call civil or federal. . . . This liberty is the proper end and object of authority, and cannot subsist without it; and it is a liberty to that only which is good, just and honest. This liberty you are to stand for, with the hazard (not only of your goods, but) of your lives, if need be. Whatsoever crosseth this, is not authority, but a distemper thereof. This liberty is maintained and exercised in a way of subjection to authority; it is of the same kind of liberty wherewith Christ hath made us free. . . .

In the permissive and laissez-faire atmosphere of the booming 1920's the Puritan's regulation of business, fixing of just prices, and restricting of individual profits in the larger interests of the commonwealth—all curtailments of free, competitive enterprise—seemed archaic and somewhat ridiculous. However, those economic theories and practices were deemed vital for the welfare of communities whose very survival remained for a time in question. Faced by the perils of total war in the early 1940's, the United States turned back to similar policies.

Few topics in the study of American history have been so widely debated as the nature of Puritanism and its influence, for better or for worse, in shaping American traditions. New evidence continues to emerge from records of the past, adding heat and light to the discussion. Only within the last several generations have earnest collectors and antiquarians, combing old inventories and ferreting about in barns and attics, revealed that neither Puritanism

Although they abhorred extravagance, Puritan artists and artisans had an appreciation of beauty. John Hull and Robert Sanderson, the leading Puritan silversmiths of mid-17th-century Boston, fashioned the dram cup (top) in 1651. Sanderson made the two-quart tankard (above, right) in 1668, and the silver candlestick (above, left), recalling a medieval column, was worked in 1686 by Jeremiah Drummer, once Hull's apprentice. The room at right in the Abraham Browne house, in Watertown, Mass., represents a typical colonial "hall," with a Turkey "carpitt" on the table top and an elaborately curtained bed.

nor the exacting problems of pioneering blighted the creative side of human nature. The Puritans may have eschewed extravagance, but they were not indifferent to beauty, as is clearly indicated by the handsomely designed silverware, the colorfully painted furniture, and the other tasteful furnishings of their seventeenth-century homes.

More recently and even more surprisingly, in the late 1930's, the poems of the Reverend Edward Taylor were brought to light and published after remaining virtually unknown for centuries past. For unknown reasons Taylor had instructed his heirs never to publish his poems, but when they finally appeared in print they were immediately recognized as an artistic achievement unequaled in New England for almost two hundred years. This sensational discovery gave a new perspective to the appreciation of Puritan literature. No other American of his time wrote with such rich imagery and inventive fancy, with such unorthodox use of sensuous allusion. In spite of his pious intent, Taylor might well have distracted his readers with carnal thoughts had they read the verses of his "Sacramental Meditations," such as:

> My Lovely One, I fain would love thee much,
>   But all my Love is none at all I see;
> Oh! let thy Beauty give a glorious touch
>   Upon my Heart, and melt to Love all mee.
>   Lord, melt me all up into Love for thee,
>   Whose Loveliness excells what love can bee.

Or another sampling from the same series:

> Shall I not smell thy sweet, oh! Sharons Rose?
>   Shall not mine Eye salute they Beauty? Why?
> Shall thy sweet leaves their Beautious sweets unclose?
>   As halfe ashamde my sight should on them ly?

Even Taylor's homespun images are filled with a mood of exaltation and rapture that lifts the mind beyond the level of everyday associations, as in a verse from "Huswifery":

> Make me, O Lord, thy Spin[n]ing Wheele compleat;
>   Thy Holy Worde my Distaff make for mee.
> Make mine Affections thy Swift Flyers neate,
>   And make my Soule they holy Spoole to bee.
> My Conversation make to be thy Reele,
>   And reele the yarn thereon spun of thy Wheele.

Taylor was the best but far from the only Puritan poet. Almost everyone in early New England who could read at all, read poetry, and many of those

30

turned their hand to versifying. The first book published in the colonies, *The Bay Psalm Book*, printed at Cambridge in 1640 (copies of the work command fantastic prices on today's market), was a poetic phenomenon of sorts, a makeshift metrical version of David's Psalms, to which the venerable Richard Mather contributed; it was designed to meet the need for divine songs for use in religious meetings. "If . . . the verses are not alwayes so smooth and elegant as some may desire or expect," wrote Mather in a preface, "let them consider that Gods altar needs not our pollishings."

However, only ten years later Anne Bradstreet, daughter of Governor Thomas Dudley and wife of Simon Bradstreet, who also became governor, published the earliest poems by an American Puritan of either sex. They first appeared in London under the engaging title, *The Tenth Muse Lately sprung up in America. Or Severall Poems, compiled with great variety of Wit and Learning, full of delight,* and were followed by more that were published in Boston after her death in 1672. It is hard to realize that such a lyric note could be struck by this frail, devout woman in the time she could spare from her laborious housewifely chores and from her devoted care of eight children in a frontier village of "glacial" New England.

Most of her poems were religious in character, many of them were dull and derivative, but when she explored her own private feelings as a woman, she combined piety with sexual passion, a liberated spirit, and an inspired grace in a way that was equaled only two centuries later in the intensely personal poems of Emily Dickinson. Hear Anne Bradstreet in a poem to her "dear and loving husband":

> If ever two were one, then surely we.
> If ever man were loved by wife, then thee.
> If ever wife were happy in a man,
> Compare with me, ye women, if you can.
> I prize thy love more than whole mines of gold,
> Or all the riches that the East doth hold.
> My love is such that rivers cannot quench,
> Nor ought but love from thee give recompense.
> Thy love is such I can no way repay;
> The Heavens reward thee manifold, I pray.
> Then, while we live, in love let's so persever,
> That when we live no more we may live ever.

The North Andover, Mass., home of Puritan poet Anne Bradstreet, reproduced here from a 19th-century engraving, was built in 1667 in characteristic New England salt-box style. There she had access to the library amassed by her husband, Governor Simon Bradstreet.

With all her love for and devotion to her husband, she could not quietly ignore the fact that Puritan New England was a man's world, a world in which the arbitrary authority and the superiority of men over women were firmly established by old tradition. In the "Body of Liberties" Nathaniel Ward had protected women from wife-beating, unless they brought it upon themselves by physically assaulting their mates; in one of his essays Samuel Sewall went so far as to concede that there might even be a place for women in Heaven, along with all other creatures; but Anne Bradstreet, feeling the sting of such absurdities, spoke out strongly for her "less noble gender":

> Now say, have women worth? or have they none?
> Or had they some, but with our Queen [Queen Elizabeth I] is't gone?
> Nay, Masculines, you have thus taxt us long,
> But she, though dead will vindicate our wrong.

An anonymous artist produced the above view of Boston in the early 1700's, when the city was a community of some 10,000 inhabitants. Throughout the 18th century most New Englanders looked to the sea for their fortunes, and Boston, with its ample harbor, was the "principal mart of trade in North America"; it was also considered the literary capital of America.

Let such as say our sex is void of Reason,
Know tis a Slander now, but once was Treason.

One close contemporary of the poet, "a feeble little shadow of a man" with the implausible name Michael Wigglesworth, earned extraordinary fame with his long theological poem *The Day of Doom* (subtitled *A Poetical Description of the Great and Last Judgment*). A small sampling of this mournful doggerel of doom and damnation is enough to discourage the modern reader, as when Christ appears to judge the sinner of the world:

> Before his face the heav'ns give place,
>   and skies are rent asunder,
> With mighty voice, and hideous noise,
>   more terrible than thunder.

Penny-dreadful as such jog-trot balladry sounds to our ears, however, it won Wigglesworth a popularity far surpassing Anne Bradstreet's or that of any other American poet of the time. Within a year his book sold more copies in America and in England than did Milton's *Paradise Lost* in twice that time—a copy for every twenty persons then living in New England. It was such a success (on its relatively small scale, to be sure) as no Book-of-the-Month Club selection of our own day could begin to approach. James Russell Lowell recalled that it "was the solace of every fireside, the flicker of the pine-knots by which it was conned perhaps adding a livelier relish to its premonitions of eternal combustion."

Meanwhile, except for a very few verses, Edward Taylor's poems remained quite unknown to his contemporaries. Whether, had they been published at the time, they would have won anything like the popularity of Wigglesworth's dreary rhymes can only be conjectured. A new generation of colonists, American-born for the most part, was growing to maturity, and their writings show an increasing concern for secular interests. William Bradford had from the beginning foreseen such possible and lamentable developments. Even the fertility of the soil, so ardently prayed for, could become an adversary in the struggle to maintain spiritual values. "For now as their stock increased, and the increase vendible," he wrote in his *History*, "there was no longer any holding them together . . . this benefit turned to their hurt." Long before the close of the seventeenth century, John Josselyn observed that the leading men of Boston were by that time already "damnable rich . . . inexplicably covetous and proud."

Although Josselyn was a critic with little sympathy for most Puritans, he might have found an acceptable Bostonian in Samuel Sewall, who was a man of God and a man of the world. Sewall's long and revealing diary, which he kept from 1674, when he was a youth of twenty-two, almost to his death in 1730, provides the most intimate and the wittiest surviving record of life in seventeenth- and early eighteenth-century New England. In 1676, five years after he was graduated from Harvard College, Sewall married Hannah, daughter of the rich and prestigious goldsmith and mintmaster John Hull. Hannah apparently had set her sights on Sewall when the youth delivered his master's oration at the Harvard commencement ("though I knew nothing of it till after our Marriage," Sewall later recalled). Nathaniel Hawthorne tells the agreeable but apocryphal story that Hull dowered his plump daughter, his only child, with her equivalent weight in pine-tree shillings, putting her on one side of the mint-house scales for the purpose. Actually, the dowry amounted to £500 paid in installments.

In time Sewall became chief justice of Massachusetts. He was among the first to speak out against slavery and in favor of a humane policy toward the Indians, and, as already noted, he conceded women a place in heaven. He was one of the judges who condemned the Salem witches, and the only one to repent and publicly confess his error and guilt. A century and a half later Whittier justly referred to him as "Samuel Sewall, the good and wise."

His diary is an inexhaustible source of delight and of information, tempting to quote at far greater length than space permits. Perhaps the most celebrated entries record his lively pursuit, as a sixty-eight-year-old widower, of the hand of Madame Katharine Winthrop in marriage. On September 8, 1720, he called upon his intended: "Spake to her, saying, my loving wife died so soon and suddenly [that is, his second wife], 'twas hardly convenient for me to think of Marrying again; however I came to this Resolution, that I would not make my Court to any person without first Consulting with her." However, his suit did not altogether prosper. When he called again, he noted:

> Madam Winthrop's Countenance was much changed from what 'twas on Monday, look'd dark and lowering. At last . . . I got my Chair in place, had some Converse, but very Cold and indifferent to what 'twas before. Ask'd her to acquit me of Rudeness if I drew off her Glove. Enquiring the reason, I told her twas great odds between handling a dead Goat, and a living lady. Got it off. . . . In some of our Discourse, I told her I had rather go to the Stone-House adjoining to her, than to come to her against her mind. Told her the reason why I came every other night was lest I should drink too deep draughts of Pleasure. She had talk'd of Canary [wine], her Kisses were to me better than the best Canary.

On the occasion of another visit Sewall recorded:

> I told her I loved her, and was so fond as to think that she loved me: She said had a great respect for me. I told her, I had made her an offer, without asking any advice; she had so many to advise with, that twas a hindrance. The Fire was come to one short Brand besides the Block, which Brand was set up in end; at last it fell to pieces, and no Recruit was made: She gave me a Glass of Wine. I think I repeated again that I would go home and bewail my Rashness in making more haste than good Speed. I would endeavour to contain myself, and not go on to

Judge Samuel Sewall of Boston, shown in this portrait by John Smibert, served the Massachusetts Bay Colony in many capacities, including that of Chief Justice. Sewall's literary fame rests primarily on his invaluable diary, but he also was the author, among other things, of "The Selling of Joseph" (1700), perhaps America's first published antislavery tract.

sollicit her to do that which she could not Consent to. Took leave of her. As came down the steps she bid me have a Care. Treated me Courteously. Told her she had enter'd the 4th year of her Widowhood. . . . I did not bid her draw off her glove as sometime I had done. Her Dress was not so clean as somtime it had been. [Sewall had once before complained to his diary about the lady's soiled linen.] Jehovah jireh!

In the end, after much haggling, the two could not reach a satisfactory understanding concerning either financial or personal arrangements. On November 11 Sewall cursorily noted in his diary: "Went not to M^m Winthrop's."

However, he was not yet finished with his matrimonial pursuits. Fourteen months later he set his cap for another local widow, Mrs. Mary Gibbs. On January 12, 1722, he wrote that lady:

Madam, your removal out of town and the severity of the winter are the reason of my making you this epistolary visit. In times past (as I remember) you were minded that I should marry you, by giving you to your desirable bridegroom. Some sense of this intended respect abides with me still, and puts me upon inquiring whether you be willing that I should marry you now, by becoming your husband; aged, and feeble, and exhausted as I am, your favorable answer to this inquiry, in a few lines, the candor of it will much oblige, Madam, your humble servant.

This time his suit was successful. The two were married on March 29, 1722.

Such selected excerpts from Sewall's writings, amusing as they are, hardly give the full measure of his style as a man and as a writer. He was learned and religious, a man of solid substance. As the son-in-law of the wealthiest man in the colony he became so engrossed in worldly affairs that he abandoned his thoughts of becoming a clergyman. It is fair to say he watched his ledgers as closely as he read his Bible. Elsewhere in his writings he expressed a love of the scenes of his childhood near Newburyport that was, in the words of one historian, "as passionate as that which he held in reserve for the heavenly kingdom":

As long as Plum Island shall faithfully keep the commanded post [he wrote in a lyrical aside to an essay on biblical prophecies], notwithstanding all the hectoring words and hard blows of the proud and boisterous ocean; as long as any salmon or sturgeon shall swim in the streams of Merrimac, or any perch or pickerel in Crane Pond; as long as the seafowl shall know the time of their coming, and not neglect seasonably to visit the places of their acquaintance; as long as any cattle shall be fed with the grass growing in the meadows, which do humbly bow down themselves before Turkey-Hill; as long as any sheep shall walk upon Old-Town Hills, and shall from thence pleasantly look down upon the River Parker, and the fruitful marshes lying beneath; as long as any free and harmless doves shall find a white oak or other tree within the township, to perch, or feed, or build a careless nest upon, and shall voluntarily present themselves to perform the office of gleaners after barley-harvest; as long as Nature shall not grow old and dote, but shall constantly remember to give the rows of Indian corn their education by pairs; so long shall Christians be born there, and being first made meet, shall from thence be translated to be made partakers of the inheritance of the saints in light.

The English Puritan had, hardly with conscious knowledge, become an American, rooted in the American soil.

THE PILGRIM
LEGEND

Plymouth Colony was established in 1620 by a small band of religious radicals known as Separatists, who wanted to restore the Church to "its primitive order, libertie, & bewtie" even if it meant separating from the Anglican communion. Before the rediscovery in 1856 of William Bradford's original account of their experiences, much that was told and believed of the Pilgrims was the more or less fanciful recreation of nineteenth-century romancers, authors and artists alike. There were, for instance, no log cabins at Plymouth such as the one depicted in Jennie Brownscombe's highly imaginative early twentieth-century painting of The First American Thanksgiving, *reproduced below, in which the Elder Brewster is shown giving a benediction.*

PILGRIM HALL, PLYMOUTH

Michael Corné's early 19th-century painting depicts The Landing of the Pilgrims; *no Indians were present at the event.*

A 19th-century engraving provides another fictional version of the landing at Plymouth "after long beating at sea."

THE LANDING

Of the one hundred two Pilgrims who came over on the *Mayflower*, only forty-one were actually Separatists, or "Saints," as they often called themselves; the rest were profane Anglican "Strangers," who were coming to the New World in search of economic betterment. And although there were many outstanding Strangers, including Miles Standish and John Alden (both immortalized in the nineteenth-century by Longfellow), it is the spiritually strong Saints who have left their imprint on American culture in the form of the romantic Pilgrim saga. Contrary to this legend, there was never any formal disembarkation at Plymouth Rock. Cape Cod was first sighted on November 10, 1620, and a reconnoitering party went ashore the next day. It was not until Saturday, December 9, on the "Third Discovery" expedition, that a band from the *Mayflower* anchored their shallop off Clark's Island in Plymouth harbor; the Saints insisted that the Sabbath be kept, and so the explorers did not step ashore until the following Monday, December 11 (December 21, New Style). Nine days later the Pilgrims decided to settle on the high ground in the southern part of the harbor, just behind a ten-ton glacial boulder now known as Plymouth Rock. It is doubtful whether any of the Pilgrims actually stepped ashore onto the Rock; that legend was not popularized until around 1770, when the Pilgrims' landing was first celebrated as Forefathers' Day. Since then the Rock has become a hallowed patriotic symbol, a mecca for endless waves of pilgrims.

Peter F. Rothermel's 1869 engraving presents still another romanticized version of the landing.

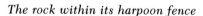

Town Square, Plymouth

The rock within its harpoon fence

ODYSSEY
OF
THE
ROCK

There is no mention of Plymouth Rock in William Bradford's *History*, and indeed little attention was paid to the ten-ton boulder until the eve of the Revolution. In 1741, when plans were made to build a commercial wharf over the rock at the foot of Cole's Hill, six-year-old Ephraim Spooner first heard a tale of the Pilgrims landing at Plymouth Rock from ninety-five-year-old Thomas Faunce; however, it was not until around 1770 that Spooner mentioned the Rock's story to some members of the Old Colony Society. Finally, in 1774, the Sons of Liberty adopted Plymouth Rock as a symbol of American independence. On Forefathers' Day of that fateful year Militia Colonel Theophilus Cotton and a group of Liberty Boys attempted to wrest the rock from its waterfront site, but the granite slab broke in half and the bottom half fell back into its bed on the wharf. The upper portion was ceremoniously moved to Plymouth's Town Square, and gradually the legend of Plymouth Rock began to spread. But the rock's size decreased as its popularity increased (egg-sized chunks were sold to souvenir hunters at $1.50 apiece), and in 1834 it was decided to move the monument to a safer place. During the relocation the already diminished upper portion of Plymouth Rock broke again, and the next year, cemented together and marked with the date, it was put on view within a five-foot-high fence of harpoons and boat hooks in front of Plymouth's Pilgrim Hall. In 1859 the Pilgrim Society purchased Hedge's Wharf in order to rescue the lower portion of the rock from the abuse of wagon wheels. By 1867 the bottom half was gloriously resting under a monumental Victorian canopy with iron gates. In 1880, when the two parts of Plymouth Rock were reunited under this ornate waterfront baldachin, the date 1620 was finally engraved on the rock. However, the whole monument was still 8 or 10 feet above the high-water mark, a state of affairs rectified in 1920 in honor of the 300th anniversary of the Pilgrims' landing. The wharf was removed, the waterfront relandscaped, and the canopy protecting the rock torn down. Plymouth Rock was then hoisted out of its bed (it broke again in the process), and was fixed and replaced 10 feet nearer the water's edge, where it could be lapped by the sea at high tide. To crown the new arrangement McKim, Mead, and White designed a lustrous Grecian temple of white granite (pictured opposite with the *Mayflower II* in the background). And so, shrouded in Grecian glory, Plymouth Rock lies today.

Hedge's Wharf

Canopy under construction, above;
the completed baldachin, left

Grecian temple

GOING TO MEETING

Pilgrims Going to Church, by George H. Boughton, is one of the best-known images of Pilgrim piety. The 1867 painting accurately portrays the forefathers, walking through the snow with their guns and Bibles in hand, but it does not show them climbing Fort Hill, in Plymouth, where their fort meetinghouse actually stood. Although the Pilgrims were devout and would spend most of the Sabbath in church, they were not sour, bloodless individuals, incapable of warm human feelings. The history-book version of the Pilgrim character is largely a Victorian invention: the men and women of Plymouth were not meek and sentimental nineteenth-century pietists; they were zealous, lusty children of the Elizabethan world, who drank heartily and often dressed in lively colors.

A COMING OF AGE

Opposite, Elfreth's Alley in Philadelphia, allegedly the oldest inhabited street in the United States, looks today much as it did when Benjamin Franklin first arrived in the Quaker city from Boston in 1723. Of his early Philadelphia days Franklin wrote: "I began now to have some Acquaintance among the young People of the Town, that were Lovers of Reading with whom I spent my Evenings very pleasantly and gaining Money by my Industry and Frugality, I lived very agreeably...."

Over the years of Samuel Sewall's adult life, roughly the half century between 1675 and 1725, the colonial scene underwent significant changes. By coincidence, at the beginning of that span of time, two portentous events occurred in the same year. In 1676, with Bacon's Rebellion, for the first time Americans took up arms against royal authority—in the person of Sir William Berkeley, the appointed governor of Virginia. (It was a further coincidence that this armed rebellion was enacted an even century before the signing of the Declaration of Independence.)

That same year of 1676 saw the conclusion of King Philip's War in New England, by far the most devastating of the periodic encounters with the Indians that bloodied the annals of Puritan America. A dozen New England towns were destroyed in the course of that conflict, their inhabitants massacred, routed, or captured. The whole frontier was terrorized. (It was during those troubles that Mrs. Mary Rowlandson endured her captivity with the Indians, earlier mentioned.) However, with the peace the Indian problem in southern New England was finally settled. The colonists there had proved their prowess, and made an enduring claim to the land they had taken over from the natives in the name of God.

With the conclusion of that gory business and, particularly, with the recall of the Massachusetts Bay charter eight years later (among other considerations, King Charles II was annoyed by the minting of he pine-tree shillings by John Hull—a usurpation of the king's prerogative) and the appointment of a royal governor in 1685, forces that had been latent in New England for some years past came to active life. Not all colonists approved of the new attitudes that were altering the pattern of American culture. Sewall himself, who, like many of his successful fellow merchants had traveled abroad and knew a wider world than New England, nevertheless viewed with indignation the frivolity and extravagance of those Bostonians who took the royal governor and his intimates for their models. Some such men, he reported in his diary, "come in a Coach from Roxbury about 9. aclock or past, singing as they come, being inflamed with Drink. At Justice Morgan's they stop and drink Healths, curse, swear, talk profanely and baudily to the great disturbance of the Town and grief of good people. Such high-handed wickedness has hardly been heard of before in Boston." At one point Sewall called the local notary severely to task for shaving his head and "wearing a Perriwig of contrary Colour," one of those abominations affected by the new leaders of society. When Mr. Clendon, the Boston barber and periwig maker, died, Sewall considered it a fitting end that the man had been "almost eat up with Lice and stupified with Drink and Cold." Yet even Sewall looked with some awe on Governor Andros in his "scarlet Coat Laced" and behaved with full deference on the memorable occasion when he was introduced to His Excellency.

With the accession of the Dutch William of Orange to the English throne following the Glorious Revolution of 1688, the colonies at large were brought not only into the orbit of world politics and trade but into the main current of world thought as well. Merchants whose vessels found their way from the West Indies to England and from Chesapeake Bay to the Mediterranean, who might traffic with pirates for treasure from the Orient, who were familiar with the sight of buccaneers walking the streets of polyglot New York and Charleston and even of Quaker Philadelphia, had little sympathy with those authorities who would wall in New England against the contagions of such a sinful but flourishing world.

The colonists were now occupying most of the Atlantic coastal plain from the "Arctic braced" forests of northern New England to the wide deltas of southern Carolina. New cities were rising in the wilderness to vie with such older settlements as Boston and New York. Within a generation of its founding in 1670, Charleston (Charles Town as it was earlier known) had flowered into a vital center of trade and culture that attracted a great mixture of peoples— Barbadians, French Calvinists, English dissenters, Scottish Covenanters, Negroes, Dutchmen from New York and from Holland, Quakers, New England Baptists, Irish Catholics, and Jews, among others—all soon to be fused into a unique cosmopolitan society. No urban center in history had ever grown so rapidly and gracefully as Philadelphia in the decades after its founding in 1682. The city had been widely advertized in England and on the Continent by William Penn as the focus of his land of freedom, and became the port of entry for hordes of hopeful immigrants. By 1720 it was so "full of Country business and Sea affairs" that it outdistanced all its colonial rivals but Boston.

By 1713 the population of the twelve colonies (Georgia, the thirteenth, was not established until 1733) was more than a third of a million. This was partly the natural increase of large families, which could always expect full employment in that world where manpower was in such short supply compared with the amount of work that needed doing. The early Puritans heeded the saying of the Hebrew psalmist who hailed the abundance of children: "As arrows are in the hand of a mighty man, so are children of the youth. Happy is the man that hath his quiver full of them." Cotton Mather had fifteen sons and daughters. His contemporary Roger Clap of Dorchester had fourteen, whom he endowed with such names as Experience, Waitstill, Preserved, Hopestill, Wait, Thanks, Desire, Unite, and Supply. William Phips, who became a royal governor of Massachusetts, was one of twenty-six children, all of the same parents. Benjamin Franklin, born in 1706, was one of seventeen; and so on. At one point Franklin accurately predicted that the population of America would double every twenty years. Thus, by 1760 the colonists numbered

An engraving, done about 1729 by Will Burgis, depicts an armed sloop and the Boston Lighthouse —"a high stone building . . . upon the top of which every night they burn·oil to direct and guide the vessels at sea into the harbour." Boston built this first colonial lighthouse in 1716 to protect the heavy traffic in its port, which resulted in part from the increasing passage of men and goods between the proliferating towns and cities along the Eastern seaboard.

more than one-and-a-half million, a fourfold increase over the 1713 figure.

Immigrants added to the rapidly swelling number of colonists. It was about two generations after the landing of the *Mayflower* that the discontented and harassed people of the Rhine Valley, whose homeland had been ruined by French invasions, first heard of the promise of the New World through Penn's promotional tracts. A vast flow of German peasants, craftsmen, and sectarians streamed across the Atlantic to settle on the rich land of Philadelphia's back country. So great was the influx that even Benjamin Franklin, most liberal of Americans, feared that the basic English culture of Pennsylvania would be submerged by these German-speaking newcomers (although he had earlier accommodated them with his short-lived newspaper, the *Philadelphische Zeitung*—the first German-language newspaper in America).

Those Pennsylvania Germans made every effort to preserve their own culture in an otherwise English-speaking world. The first complete Bible issued in America was printed in German on the press of Christopher Sower in 1743, thirty-nine years before the first English-language edition (other than John Eliot's Algonquin translation printed at Cambridge, Massachusetts, in 1661 and 1663) was produced in the colonies. And at Bethlehem, Pennsylvania, a musical tradition was inaugurated that developed into the celebrated annual festival devoted to the works of Johann Sebastian Bach. In his *Autobiography* Benjamin Franklin recalled that he had visited the church there in 1756, where he was entertained with "good Musick, the Organ being accompanied with Violins, Hautboys [oboes], Flutes, Clarinets, &c." (It was in a Pennsylvania-German newspaper that George Washington was first referred to in print as the "Father of His Country.")

Following the revocation of the Edict of Nantes by Louis XIV in 1685, Huguenots, too, sought refuge in America from persecution in France. Among them were such enterprising craftsmen as the silversmith Apollos De Revoire (or Rivoire) from the isle of Guernsey who Americanized his name to Paul Revere and fathered a son and namesake who forever eclipsed his fame (partly as a consequence of Longfellow's poetic and romantic description of his ride to alert the Minutemen). Scotch-Irishmen came from Ulster and fanned out along the colonial frontiers against the threats from the Indians, forming a rugged line of defense that extended from New Hampshire to South Carolina. About two hundred thousand of them had arrived by the time of the Revolution—twelve times the number of Englishmen who had settled Massachusetts. As Thomas Paine later observed, not England but all Europe was the parent country of America.

In many ways colonial society was more varied than is American society in this century. Each of the little "cities in the wilderness," where commercial and cultural activities were concentrated, was born of widely different circumstances and was shaped differently by its separate experiences. The distinctive character of each was marked in its physical appearance, its social customs, and the nature of its enterprise. For some time to come, overland travel from one to another was an adventure not to be lightly undertaken. How true all this was can be read in the delightful journal kept by Sarah Kemble Knight, detailing her trip on horseback from Boston to New York and back in the autumn of 1704 and the early spring of 1705. Her colorful account of this journey is a uniquely informative and lively document that has its

The merry band of dancing musicians, above, decorates a Pennsylvania-German hand-lettered manuscript, or fraktur, *of the 18th century. The first time that George Washington was called the Father of His Country in print was on the title page, reproduced below, of a Pennsylvania-German almanac (Der Gantz Neue Verbesserte Nord-Americanische Calendar), published at Lancaster in 1779.*

William Byrd II, Virginia aristocrat and man of letters, is shown in a portrait done in London by Sir Godfrey Kneller, 1715–20. In the History of the Dividing Line *(not published until 1841) Byrd left a vivid account of the unmapped hinterland between Virginia and North Carolina as he found it during a boundary survey of 1728. His* History, *diaries, and other writings earned him the title of "the American Samuel Pepys."*

special place in the history of American literature.

Madam Knight was a widowed Bostonian who, among other activities, kept a writing school that Benjamin Franklin is said to have attended as a child. She was thirty-eight when she took off through the rural countryside and wilderness, unaccompanied save when she hired a companion or fell in with one en route. "Jogging on with an easy pace," a guide warning her "it was dangero's to Ride hard in the Night," or "riding very hard" with another guide, she sometimes found it thirty miles between habitations. At times the roads were little more than traces, occasionally so narrow she was scratched by the trees and bushes at either side. River crossings were perilous. The canoe in which she made one such crossing seemed (in a modern version of her account) "ready to take in water, which greatly terrified me, and caused me to be very circumspect, sitting with my hands fast on each side, my eyes steady, not daring so much as to lodge my tongue a hair's breadth more on one side of my mouth than t'other, nor so much as think on Lot's wife; for a wry thought would have overset our wherry." The inns were abominable. "Down I laid my poor Carkes (never more tired)," she wrote of one, "and found my Covering as scanty as my Bed was hard. Annon I heard another Russelling noise in Ye Room—called to know the matter—Little miss said shee was making a bed for the men; who, when they were in Bed [in the same room], complained their leggs lay out of it by reason of its shortness—my poor bones complained bitterly not being used to such Lodgings, and so did the man who was with us. . . ." Thus she passed the cold night.

When she finally arrived at New York, where she had business, she noted with a woman's eye the tidy interiors with their Delft tiles and meticulously scoured woodwork and plaster, all "neat to admiration." "The Bricks in some of the Houses," she wrote, "are of divers Coulers and laid in Checkers, being glazed look very agreeable." Almost everything about that little city was to her so different from Boston that she felt she had arrived in some picturesque alien land.

The writings of William Byrd II of Westover, Virginia, a slightly younger contemporary of Madam Knight's, reveal one of the most urbane, witty, and accomplished colonials of his generation. Byrd was a seasoned traveler, a graduate of the Middle Temple and a member of the English bar, and a Fellow of the Royal Society. He was a man of princely fortune and princely ways, the very model of a Virginia aristocrat, and a distinguished and powerful figure in his colony's ruling group. "Westover," the mansion he built in his later years and which housed his enormous and hard-worked library (even larger than that of Cotton Mather, and decidedly more worldly in character), still stands, a superb example of colonial architecture. At his death in 1744 he left an estate of 179,000 acres. On parts of his vast domain he had some years earlier "laid the foundation of two large cities"—Richmond and Petersburg. "Thus," he wrote, "we did not build castles only, but also cities in the air."

As a youth, Byrd had been sent to England to be properly educated. (He also studied in Holland and visited the French court.) There he spent a number of rakehell years in the lingering atmosphere of Restoration gaiety and gallantry. He was the friend of Congreve and Wycherley, those masters of fashionable comedy, and he flirted with thoughts of becoming a man of letters

in his own right. In a sense he did just that, but most of his writings were recorded in a secret shorthand and were not intended for publication. His diaries are remarkably candid. One that he kept when he was in his early forties and back in England for some years as a colonial agent recounts his almost incessant amatory pursuits. His first wife had just died, and he found consolation where he could, be his partner a whore, a chambermaid, or a lady of high station. (He paid one of his mistresses two guineas a visit before he dismissed her for her infidelities.)

In a different vein, other sections of his diaries tell of his methodical reading in Hebrew, Greek, and Latin, sometimes in French, Dutch, or Italian, which often enough he did at five or six in the morning; he then customarily said his prayers. (One morning he awoke to find his head "a little out of order. However," he jotted in his diary, "I read 150 verses in Homer.") Between his many and more serious activities concerned with the care of his plantations and with matters of colonial government, Byrd found time to play billiards, cricket, and whist, watch horse races, throw dice, and drink an ample share of wine and spirits. When he visited the capital at Williamsburg on personal or official business he frequented the coffee houses and the theatre. On one occasion, when he had gone forth to review some troops of dragoons, he wrote with eminent self-satisfaction, "Everybody respected me like a king." Another entry, more somber in mood, reported that he had had his father's grave opened to view the remains, but found the corpse "so wasted there was not anything to be distinguished." And he added laconically, "I ate fish for dinner."

Entertaining and informative as they are, Byrd's diaries are obviously highly personal and informal records. He also produced some translations and verse, which he might have read to his guests, but which he also never bothered to publish. His most important literary contribution is a narrative

"Westover," on the James River about 30 miles upstream from Jamestown, remains one of the finest of colonial mansions. The present brick structure, reproduced here from a sketch made in 1825 by a neighbor, Lucy Harrison, was built in the 1730's by William Byrd II to replace a frame dwelling erected by his father. One of "Westover's" most impressive assets was its library—said to have been the best in the colonies—for which William Byrd II gathered more than 3,600 volumes.

47

journal of the boundary survey between Virginia and North Carolina that he supervised in 1728. This manuscript, at least, he revised and refined, although it was not published until 1841, with the title *History of the Dividing Line betwixt Virginia and North Carolina, Run in the Year of Our Lord 1728.* Here, in a vivacious but more formal fashion, Byrd showed himself to be an observant, witty, and accomplished writer. From his position at the peak of sophisticated Virginia society, he looked with a caustically critical and humorous eye at the indolent inhabitants of "lubberland" along the North Carolina frontier:

> Surely there is no place in the World where the Inhabitants live with less Labour than in N Carolina. It approaches nearer to the Description of Lubberland than any other, by the great felicity of the Climate, the easiness of raising Provisions, and the Slothfulness of the People. . . . The Men, for their Parts, just like the Indians, impose all the Work upon the poor Women. They make their Wives rise out of their Beds early in the Morning, at the same time that they lye and Snore, till the Sun has run one third of his course, and disperst all the unwholesome Damps. Then, after Stretching and Yawning for half an Hour, they light their Pipes, and, under the Protection of a cloud of Smoak, venture out into the open Air; tho', if it happens to be never so little cold, they quickly return Shivering into the Chimney corner. When the weather is mild, they stand leaning with both their arms upon the corn-field fence, and gravely consider whether they had best go and take a Small Heat at the Hough [hoe]: but generally find reasons to put it off till another time. . . . Thus they loiter away their Lives, like Solomon's Sluggard, with their Arms across, and at the Winding up of the year Scarcely have Bread to Eat.

As both Byrd and Madam Knight observed, there were marked differences not only between colonies but also within the separate colonies. Benjamin Franklin pointed out that each colony had "peculiar expressions, familiar to its own people, but strange and unintelligible to others." Some expressions, on the other hand, were couched in an idiom that could be all too easily understood wherever it was used, as when Byrd complained to a friend about the "Banditti" from Massachusetts who anchored on the James River near his home to traffic with his slaves, from whom, he remarked, "they are sure to have good Pennyworths." In a similar spirit of regional hostility the New York merchant Gerardus Beekman referred to Connecticut as "that dam'd country." The discords that sprang up often enough within the boundaries of a single colony were no less acrimonious. Colonists who had ventured into the interior looked back with distant and downright enmity at the effete East whose moneygrubbers, they felt, selfishly exploited Western interests. "Those from the westward," wrote Charles Biddle of Pennsylvania, "look upon the people in any of the commercial towns as little better than swindlers, while those of the east consider the western members of a pack of savages"—as Byrd had found the "lubbers" of the North Carolina hinterland.

In the long run the very rivalries and competition between colony and colony were the result of frequent intercourse; the jealousies aroused were born of interrelated concerns that eventually led to recognition of a common destiny. Along the eastern seaboard, at least, the colonial "gentry" were gradually consolidating their interests through business negotiations, intermarriages, college friendships, and vacations. Ideas along with commodities were exchanged by the small ships manned by Yankee, Knickerbocker, Quaker, and Southern shippers as they plied the coastal waters and the inland waterways.

By land as well as by sea intercolonial traffic was growing in volume. The Indian trails and other traces that led across the countryside were slowly beaten into roads that could be recognized as such. Presumably in response to a need for it, America's first road guide was issued in 1732, *The Vade Mecum for America: Or a Companion for Traders and Travellers.* Among other items of interest to the traveler it listed the taverns from Maine to Virginia and the dates and locations of the principal fairs that were seasonally held in the northern colonies. (English visitors were pleased to note that there were "no highway robbers to interrupt them" along the way as there so often were at home.)

Quickened communication also tended to break down the provincial barriers to understanding among different sections of the country, leading gradually to a general community of shared interests. Some observers detected the emergence of a new and recognizable American strain in the colonial population. Just forty years after Madam Knight's adventurous trip, Dr. Alexander Hamilton of Maryland completed a 1,624-mile journey up and down the coast without undue incident. Hamilton was a sophisticated, keen, and articulate reporter, and the journal of his travels is another of those highly readable personal accounts that deserve a place in the history of American writing. As he passed from one stopping place to another on his long journey, armed with helpful letters of introduction, he made frequent observations on the diversity of appearance of separate localities and of local customs and manners that he encountered. Philadelphia, he thought, was rather shabby, its streets encumbered with rubbish and lumber. This, however, he excused as a consequence of the extensive building operations. It would indeed soon be the largest and most populous urban center in the colonies. At New York he quit a company of two or three "toapers" who seemed to be able to "pour down seas of liquor and remain unconquered while others·sunk under the table," and retired at ten o'clock "pritty well flushed" and depressed by his folly at joining such a company. Albany he found to be still an essentially Dutch town. "The young men here call their sweethearts *luffees*," he wrote with genial interest, "and a young fellow of eighteen is reckoned a simpleton if he has not a *luffee*; but their women are so homely that a man must never have seen any other *luffees* else they will never entrap him." In Boston, on the other hand, the ladies were "free and affable as well as pritty." They appeared conspicuously in public and they dressed elegantly; and, he added, "I saw not one prude while I was here."

No two people reporting on the colonial scene saw it in quite the same way. Some emphasized the colorful variety of life in America. Others, like Hamilton, aware as he was of the differences that existed, concluded at the end of his tour that "as to politeness and humanity, [the colonists] are much alike except in the great towns where the inhabitants are more civilized, especially in Boston."

Hamilton's journal, like that of Madam Knight and the diaries of William Byrd, was not published until long after his death. But around the middle of

Dr. Alexander Hamilton was a gifted, highly articulate diarist who recorded, among other things, the "gentlemanly" carousals he shared on his travels as well as at "The Ancient and Honourable Tuesday Club" of Annapolis, "designed for humor and . . . a sort of farcical drama of Mock Majesty," and which he helped establish in 1745. He embellished the club's records, as above, with sketches of such conviviality. The doctor visited Albany, N.Y., which he found to be essentially Dutch, with Dutch-style houses, as seen in the view below of the city's North Pearl and State streets, drawn by James Eights about 1805.

49

the eighteenth century the works of two other colonials, the Reverend Jonathan Edwards and Benjamin Franklin, were not only being printed but were causing comment overseas. Both men were born in New England in the first decade of the century; both were acknowledged sages of their time; both were literary stylists in their separate ways; and both were concerned for the welfare of mankind. Beyond that, however, two more disparate personalities could hardly be named.

"Edwards of New England," as James Boswell referred to him, was the most profound American theologian of his generation; a man for whom the spiritual discipline involved in vanquishing the horror of the doctrine of hell's eternal torment brought him a peace of mind that was "exceeding pleasant, bright, and sweet." He represented the extreme of New England Calvinism and mysticism; he was a man who could hold his audience spellbound— sobbing and terrified—as he told them with quiet but passionate intensity of the immediate peril of damnation. "There was such a breathing of distress and weeping," it has been said of one of his sermons, "that the preacher was obliged to speak to the people, and desire silence that he might be heard."

Few of us today have the inclination to read Edwards' great treatise on freedom of will, published in 1754 (the full and formidable title is *A Careful and Strict Enquiry into the Modern Prevailing Notions, of that Freedom of Will which is supposed to be Essential to Moral Agency, Vertue and Vice, Reward and Punishment, Praise and Blame*); but this became a primary statement in Calvinist theology and won him the regard of distinguished contemporary readers, especially in Europe. From its inexorable reasoning, wrote Boswell, "the only relief I had was to forget it." Dr. Samuel Johnson was equally impressed by Edwards' intellectual prowess.

Edwards' parishioners sometimes found his blazing rebukes difficult to suffer. "The God that holds you over the pit of hell," he once preached, "much as one holds a spider, or some loathesome insect, over the fire, abhors you, and is dreadfully provoked; his wrath towards you burns like fire; he looks upon you as worthy of nothing else, but to be cast into the fire; he is of purer eyes than to bear to have you in his sight."

The extreme refinement of Edwards' theological views and his insistent admonitions aroused resentment in his congregation, and he was finally relieved of his ministry and, as he wrote, "thrown upon the wide ocean of the world, and know not what will become of me, and my numerous and chargeable family." He became a missionary to the Indians and then, for the last few months of his life, president of Princeton College, where his intellectual leadership was understood and welcomed.

There are passages in Edwards' other works that are less profound than those in his systematized metaphysical polemics, but that make more engaging reading. As a child of about twelve he wrote a paper, remarkable for its force of reasoning and exactness of observation and statement, on "the wondrous way of the working of the spider." "In very calm and serene days in the forementioned time of year," he explained, "standing at some distance behind the end of an house or some other opaque body, so as just to hide the disk of the sun and keep off his dazzling rays, and looking alone close by the side of it, I have seen a vast multitude of little shining webs, and glistening strings, brightly reflecting the sunbeams, and some of them of great length, and of

Jonathan Edwards, metaphysician, theologian, and preacher, and the subject of Joseph Badger's portrait, above, made the final and greatest statement of New England Calvinism. He was the prophet of the "Great Awakening," a movement that began in New England in 1734 and lasted some fifteen years, spreading from Maine to Georgia. For several months before his death in 1758, Edwards was president of Princeton, whose Nassau-Hall is depicted above, left, in an engraving of 1763. Like Harvard, Yale, and other institutions of higher learning, Princeton was a center of intercolonial cultural exchange.

such a height that one would think they were tacked to the vault of the heavens, and would be burnt like tow in the sun. . . . But that which is most astonishing is, that very often appears at the end of these webs, spiders sailing in the air with them. . . ." Throughout his life he noted with surpassing delight and aesthetic joy such natural beauties of earth and sky that were symbols to him of God's absolute perfection.

Edwards was not blind to the beauty of God's creations in human form. When he was twenty he wrote in ecstatic wonder of the thirteen-year-old Sarah Pierrepont, whom he was to choose as his wife: "They say there is a young lady in [New Haven] who is beloved of that Great Being, who made and rules the world . . . that she expects after a while to be received up where he is. . . . There she is to dwell with him, and to be ravished with his love and delight forever. . . . She will sometimes go about from place to place, singing sweetly; and seems to be always full of joy and pleasure; and no one knows for what." Four years after that rapturous description, Edwards entered into an eminently sensible and durable marriage with the most estimable young lady. In 1758, as he lay dying of fever after an inoculation against smallpox, he sent a messenger to her reminding her that "the uncommon union which has so long subsisted between us has been of such a nature as I trust is spiritual, and therefore will continue forever."

With Edwards' career the fire of New England Puritanism burned itself out, but not the influence of his original thoughts. His intense struggle with the questions of good and evil, of human will and predestination, the strange mixture of taut logic and supernaturalism that characterizes his writings, and his ecstatic vision of God's infinite presence in the beauty of nature all foreshadowed views that would be followed and reworked by such Transcendentalists as Emerson and other New England writers of the next century.

Today we do not find it easy to read Edwards' flights of metaphysical speculation. On the other hand, virtually everything that his contemporary Benjamin Franklin wrote can still be read with pleasure, and his writings

51

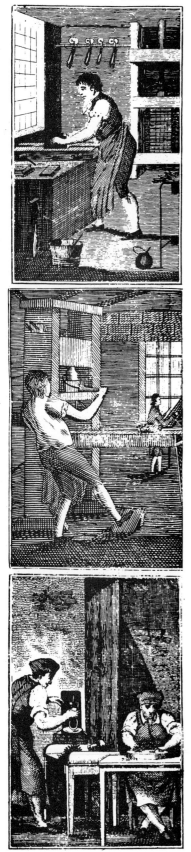

on myriad subjects were voluminous. He was no less philosophical than Edwards, but his concern was more often with worldly affairs. Where Edwards tormented the consciences of his sinning audience, Franklin gave practical and good-humored advice to a young man on the choice of a mistress, or just as shrewdly counseled Great Britain on how to reduce its empire by continuing to mismanage colonial affairs. Where Edwards pondered the salvation of the human soul, Franklin sweetly reasoned with patriarchal wisdom that "human felicity is produced not so much by great pieces of good fortune, that seldom happen, as by little advantages that occur every day; thus if you teach a poor young man to shave himself and keep his razor in order, you may contribute more to the happiness of his life than in giving him a thousand guineas."

Franklin was at once an author, a printer, a publisher, and an editor; a scientist, an inventor, and a philanthropist; a politician, a diplomat, and a statesman—and he was all these things and more to a remarkable degree of excellence and fruitfulness. He was a quintessential example of eighteenth-century enlightenment. The whole world of knowledge and understanding was his province, and he penned his constant flow of thoughts and observations in language that was clear, precise, and salty. Although he carried his *Autobiography* up to 1757, what he wrote therein epitomizes his wise and genial spirit. "In 1732," he recounted, "I first publish'd my Almanack . . . it was continu'd by me about twenty-five years, commonly call'd *Poor Richard's Almanac*. I endeavor'd to make it both entertaining and useful, and it accordingly came to be in such demand, that I reap'd considerable profit from it vending annually near ten thousand." In 1757 he assembled most of the proverbs with which he had "filled all the little spaces that occurr'd between the remarkable days of the calendar" and formed them into a connected discourse "as the harangue of a wise old man to the people attending an auction."

Poor Richard's maxims, which, as Franklin observed, "contained wisdom of many ages and nations," were repeatedly published throughout the colonies. For more than a generation before the Revolution they were something of a common primer for the man in the street. Such memorable adages as "Keep thy shop, and thy shop will keep thee," "Fish and visitors smell after three days," "Three may keep a secret, if two of them are dead," had universal currency. In the trying days of the Revolution such disparate personalities as Abigail Adams and John Paul Jones found comfort in quoting one or another of these maxims. There were at least three separate French translations, and in 1784 a Russian edition was published at St. Petersburg. They are still current.

By his deeds as well as his writings Franklin captured the imagination of the world as had no other American. This self-made republican, a tallow chandler's son, had emerged from the New World "wilderness" to move with grace among the powdered heads of Europe, quipping easily with royalty and conversing and corresponding profoundly with the greatest intellects of the day. His modest garb and unaffected manner masked the most cosmopolitan spirit of his age. What is more, although he never posed as a man of letters, he wrote the King's English with plain words and with utter lucidity.

In his *Autobiography* Franklin recalled that as a youth he was "extramly ambitious" to become "a tolerable English writer." To perfect his style he chose as a model Addison and Steele's London *Spectator,* rewriting its essays from outlines he had made and then repeatedly comparing them with the original to measure his progress. Throughout his long life, in his vast correspondence, both personal and business, as well as in his more formal writing, he assiduously strove to be concise, clear, and cogent.

During his later years in France, Franklin set up a small printing press at his home in Passy and for the amusement of himself and his friends issued a number of his charming light essays that he referred to as *bagatelles.* Some of these were addressed to ladies of the court and intellectual circles, among whom "cher Papa" was a universal favorite. His handwritten notes to these ladies brim with unconcealed, sometimes almost intemperate affection. Toward the close of his stay he wrote his dear friend Madame Brillon a note of parting that typifies his carefully worded endearments:

> Saturday in Passy
>
> Since one day, my dear friend, I will have to leave for America, with no hope of ever seeing you again, I have sometimes had the thought that it would be wise to cut myself off from you by degrees, first to see you just once a week, after that, only once every two weeks, once a month, etc., etc. so as to lessen little by little the inordinate desire that I always feel for your enchanting company, and in this way to avoid the great hurt that I must otherwise suffer at the final separation. But, in testing the experience, I find that instead of diminishing this desire, absence augments it. The hurt that I fear is, thus, incurable, and I will come to visit you this evening.

(According to Dr. John Wakefield Francis, the American son of a German immigrant and a great admirer of Franklin's, Louis XVI became so jealous of Franklin's popularity that he "caused certain *pots de chambre* to be painted at Sèvres with the philosopher's head at the bottom & sent to the ladies.")

Franklin has been called "the first American." This he was in that he spoke and wrote so eloquently and with such authority for the new age and for the New World. He was almost as old as the eighteenth century, and his life touched the developments of that age of enlightenment at practically every point. As a young printer's apprentice in Boston he had heard Increase and Cotton Mather preach; as an old man he stood beside Voltaire in Paris to be proclaimed the incomparable benefactor of mankind. He personified the intellectual revolution of the century that, in one sense, gave birth to the United States of America; for it was the singular fortune of the new nation to emerge as a kind of concrete example of the ideal state philosophers of that age had emissioned.

No other person understood as clearly as did Franklin the sense of destiny and high mission in the world that attended the creation of the new nation. In Franklin all the racial and religious differences, the sectional and intercolonial jealousies and rivalries, and the class prejudices were in some manner comprehended and reconciled. He had a practical grasp of the material and spiritual forces that had transformed the British colonists into a new and independent people. No one knew better or viewed more tolerantly the human imperfections that must be accommodated—and the hazards that must be faced—as this fresh experiment in self-rule was attempted. "We must not

In his Autobiography *the pragmatic Franklin wrote that he considered* Poor Richard's Almanack *"a proper vehicle for conveying instruction among the common people, who bought scarcely any other books." The vignette, reproduced above, is from a broadside engraved in the 1840's to illustrate maxims from the perennially popular* Almanack. *By 1730 Franklin was running his own print shop in the city of Philadelphia—a demanding profession, as the 18th-century printer was also a publisher. The old illustrations, opposite, depict the major activities of the print shop: bookbinding, working the press, and typecasting.*

Upon hearing of General John Burgoyne's surrender at Saratoga in December, 1777, Franklin pressed for and achieved treaties of amity and commerce with the French, which were signed the following February. The porcelain statuette above, of Franklin and his royal ally Louis XVI, commemorates the alliance between the two nations.

expect," Franklin wrote Pierre Samuel Du Pont de Nemours, "that a new government may be formed, as a game of chess may be played, by a skilful hand, without a fault . . . chance has its share in many of the determinations, so that the play is more like *tric-trac* with a box of dice."

Quite understandably, American literature during the period of the Revolution was largely, but not altogether, political in character. Essayists turned pamphleteers, poets turned satirists, philosophers turned statesmen, and all drafted documents in liberty's cause. Occasionally, true talents were debased as they lent themselves in patriotic fervor to scorn and vituperation. At other times, the urgent needs of the time inspired some writings of rare brilliance. We hardly need reminding, for example, that the Declaration of Independence is a superb example of English prose.

Before that famous declaration was made, the idea of American independence was far from universally popular in the colonies. As late as January, 1776, Washington's officers' mess, in the encampment outside Boston, still toasted George III's health—as liberty-loving Englishmen. However, the idea of independence was not then novel either. More than a century earlier, a visiting English sea captain reported that Bostonians were even that early looking upon their community as a free state; and in 1759–60 another traveler from abroad, the Reverend Andrew Burnaby, wrote that Pennsylvanians were "great republicans, and have fallen into the same errors of independency as most of the other colonies have."

By then the colonists had indeed developed a degree of economic and political maturity that fitted them for an independent destiny, free from the restraints Britain attempted to impose upon its colonies. They also enjoyed a sense of security they had never before known. It was in September of 1759 that General James Wolfe, commanding a strong naval and military expeditionary force, vanquished Montcalm's French army on the Plains of Abraham and took Quebec, the keystone of France's American empire. For America that was the climax of the French and Indian War. (That conflict was known in Europe as the Seven Years' War, which had started when young George Washington of the Virginia militia, on July 4, 1754, was forced to surrender the meager defenses of Fort Necessity—near what is now the site of Pittsburgh—to his French adversary. "Such was the complication of political interests," wrote Voltaire of the skirmish, "that a cannon shot fired in America could give the signal that set Europe in a blaze.")

With that victory, for the first time in generations, the colonies felt free of the awful menace that had threatened their frontiers. In his *Short History of the English People* John Richard Green wrote that it was with Wolfe's triumph that the history of the United States began; a victory which was one of the turning points that "determined for ages to come the destinies of the world." When a peace was finally settled in 1763 Franklin urged Britain to extend its empire, with the liberties he then believed it stood for, beyond the western mountains and around the globe. But in that year King George did "strictly forbid, on pain of our displeasure, all our loving subjects from making any purchase or settlements in that region" beyond the Alleghenies. Thwarted in their hopes of influencing British imperial policy, the colonists directed their new confidence to their own ends—to the struggle for independence from the mother country, and to their westward progress.

Founding father Benjamin Franklin, the epitome of 18th-century worldliness, as portrayed by David Martin, 1766

Controversy over the colonists' right to self-determination started as a war of words that raged for a decade on both sides of the Atlantic before the "embattled farmers" took up arms to settle the differences of opinion. Much of the literature came in a flood of pamphlets and letters to the press that in their abundance all but papered over the scene. Among the earliest and perhaps the most brilliant of all these short essays started to appear in a Philadelphia newspaper in December of 1767 under the title "Letters from a Farmer in Pennsylvania." Although unsigned, they were at once recognized as the work of John Dickinson, a prosperous, cultured, and studious Philadelphian who was then thirty-five years old—a man of moderate temper and a consummate pamphleteer.

Dickinson's intent was to compose rather than aggravate the prevailing excitement that had blazed up with the passing of the Townshend Acts earlier in 1767. The meaning of his letters, he carefully explained in the first of them, was "to convince the people of these colonies that they are at this moment exposed to the most imminent dangers; and to persuade them immediately, vigorously, and unanimously, to exert themselves, in the most firm, but most peaceable manner, for obtaining relief." He continued:

> The cause of liberty is a cause of too much dignity, to be sullied by turbulence and tumult. It ought to be maintained in a manner suitable to her nature. Those who engage in it, should breathe a sedate, yet fervent spirit, animating them to actions of prudence, justice, modesty, bravery, humanity, and magnanimity. . . .
>
> I hope, my dear countrymen, that you will, in every colony, be upon your guard against those who may at any time endeavor to stir you up,

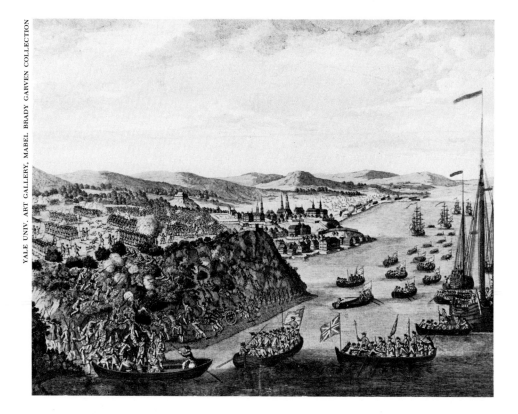

An engraved view of the taking of Quebec, printed in London in 1759, follows an age-old practice in graphic representation; it shows in one scene a sequence of events leading to James Wolfe's brilliant conquest of "impregnable" Quebec on September 13, 1759, the victory by which Britain won dominion over North America. A legend on the print declares that the view depicts "the manner of debarking the English Forces, & of the resolute scrambling of the light Infantry up a Woody Precipice to dislodge the Captains post, which defended a small entrenched path, through which the Troops were to pass. Also a view of the signal Victory [the next day on the Plains of Abraham] obtained over the French regulars, Canadians and Indians which produced the surrender of Quebec."

under pretense of patriotism, to any measures disrespectful to our Sovereign and our mother country. Hot, rash, disorderly proceedings injure the reputation of a people as to wisdom, valor and virtue, without procuring them the least benefit.

Further, he advised his fellow Americans, "we never can be made an independent people, except it be by *Great-Britain* herself, and the only way for her to do it, is to make us frugal, ingenious, united, and discontented." All governments make mistakes, he declared, but these could be corrected and passions cooled. He hoped that it might "be impossible to determine whether an *American's* character is most distinguishable for his loyalty to his Sovereign, his duty to his mother country, his love of freedom, or his affection for his native soil."

Dickinson's letters were instantly reprinted in almost all the colonial newspapers. They were collected and issued separately, and they were published in London, in Dublin, and—in two French versions—at Amsterdam; Voltaire applauded them, and Edmund Burke admired them for their cogent arguments. Except for Benjamin Franklin (who wrote clever prefaces for the first of two London editions), John Dickinson was for a time America's most renowned writer. It was neither the beginning nor the end of his distinguished career. Earlier he had written in protest against the Stamp Act, but opposed any violent resistance to the law. (He had also castigated Franklin for his "inflammatory" opinions, not having Franklin's understanding of the need for political hucksterism.) Later he refused to sign the Declaration of Independence, faithful to what he considered the larger interests of the British Empire. Yet, when war erupted he took up arms in the Colonists' cause. Still later he participated in the Constitutional Convention. Whatever his political slant, Dickinson expressed his thoughts with a polished grace that was a contribution to American letters.

The various colleges that had been established along the Atlantic seaboard provided some real training for hopeful men of letters and, what is more, they were debating grounds where students from the different colonies could try their opinions and exchange their ideas. "I have an Opportunity . . . of acquainting myself with Mankind," wrote one Princeton undergraduate in 1772, "by observing the Conduct & Temper of the Students in this Seminary . . . filled with Young-Men . . . from almost every Province, in this Continent . . . also many from the *West Indies*, & some few from Europe." At the commencement exercises the year before that statement was made, two other Princetonians, Hugh Henry Brackenridge and Philip Freneau, both to become well-known authors, delivered a poem, "The Rising Glory of America," that boldly, if not brilliantly, expressed the spirit of national self-consciousness that was gradually pervading the colonies:

> This is the land of every joyous sound,
> of liberty and life, sweet liberty!
> Without whose aid the nobles genius fails,
> And sciences irretrievable must die.

In its entirety, the poem addresses all parts of the colonies, renounces the prestige and authority of Great Britain, and hails the patriots of America who would find a new imperial destiny of their own and a cultural ascendancy that would outrival the glories of the mother country:

The portrait of John Dickinson, reproduced above, is a later version of Paul Revere's 1771 woodcut; it was made for the title page of Dickinson's influential Letters From a Farmer in Pennsylvania. *In the debate that preceded the Revolution, Dickinson took a moderate stand and earnestly endeavored, especially through these letters, to quell the spirit of rebellion in America and to avoid open conflict with England; however, his articulate writings on liberty and freedom in the colonies helped incite revolutionary activities.*

The intense nature of Thomas Paine, the true radical in the pre-Revolutionary ideological battle, is expressed in a plaster bust by John Wesley Jarvis. Paine began his literary career in America by writing articles for the Pennsylvania Magazine *in support of women's rights, antislavery measures, and kindness to animals. He revealed his genius as an arch-propagandist in* Common Sense *(1776), a fervent exhortation for American liberty, and it was Paine's fiery rhetoric that encouraged the despairing Continental Army at Valley Forge in 1777.*

> I see a Homer and a Milton rise
> In all the pomp and majesty of song . . .
> A second Pope, like that Arabian bird
> Of which no age can boast but one, may yet
> Awake the muse by Schuylkill's silent stream . . .
> And Susquehanna's rocky stream unsung . . .
> Shall yet remurmur to the magic sound
> Of song heroic.

These two young undergraduates also collaborated on the first known work of fiction created in this country, *Father Bombo's Pilgrimage to Mecca*, a true and faithful account of the protagonist's "innumerable ills and disasters."

In the years that followed, Freneau issued a steady stream of satirical poetry, versified pamphlets that were directed against English arrogance and aggression and that earned him the sobriquet "the poet of the American Revolution." The turbulence of the times was not ideal for the creation of poetry, as Freneau's classmate James Madison pointed out, and Freneau's early promise was too often lost in his invective propaganda for America's cause.

Following the ratification of the Constitution, with the active support of Jefferson and Madison, Freneau undertook to establish the *National Gazette* —a newspaper designed to counteract with democratic propaganda another paper, *The Gazette of the United States*, a vehicle used by Alexander Hamilton to promote his own and different policies favoring a more selective and aristocratic form of administration. Freneau did his job well enough to be fairly regarded as "the leading editor in America" during the critical years of the newly established government. "His paper has saved our Constitution," wrote Jefferson with partisan appreciation, "*which was fast galloping into monarchy,* and has been checked by no one means so powerfully as by that paper."

Yet, on occasion and on other less virulent themes, Freneau approached a sensibility to the natural beauties of the American scene that heralds the poems of William Cullen Bryant two generations later. At a different time he might have become a major American poet. As it was, his life was full of adventures, some of them grim experiences, and of heated feelings that hindered what could have been his higher achievement. Even so, such famed English writers as Sir Walter Scott and Thomas Campbell found it helpful to steal some of Freneau's lines for their own poems.

No other voice that cried out for American independence, immediate and complete, aroused such passionate response as Thomas Paine's. Little more than a year after he arrived in Philadelphia from England, at the end of 1774, armed with letters of introduction from Benjamin Franklin, Paine issued his first important pamphlet, *Common Sense.* He wrote in his forty-seven page publication:

> In the following pages I offer nothing more than simple facts, plain arguments, and common sense. . . . The Sun never shined on a cause of greater worth. 'Tis not the affair of a City, a County, a Province, or of a Kingdom; but of a Continent—of at least one eighth part of the habitable Globe. 'Tis not the concern of a day, a year, or an age; posterity are virtually involved in the contest, and will be more or less affected even to the end of time, by the proceedings now. Now is the seed-time of Con-

tinental union, faith and honour. The least fracture now will be like a name engraved with the point of a pin on the tender rind of a young oak; the wound would enlarge with the tree, and posterity read it in full grown characters.

By referring the matter from argument to arms, a new area for politics is struck—a new method of thinking hath arisen. All plans, proposals, &c. prior to the nineteenth of April, *i.e.* to the commencement of hostilities, are like the almanacks of the last year; which tho' proper then, are superceded and useless now. Whatever was advanced by the advocates on either side of the question then, terminated in one and the same point, viz. a union with Great Britain; the only difference between the parties was the method of effecting it; the one proposing force, the other friendship; but it hath so far happened that the first hath failed, and the second hath withdrawn her influence.

Paine's pamphlet was issued, anonymously, at two shillings a copy, on January 10, 1776, while George Washington was pinning down the British forces that had occupied Boston. Before the month was out, Washington had read it and praised its "sound doctrine and unanswerable reasoning," which, he declared, "will not leave numbers at a loss to decide upon the propriety of separation." Paine had quite apparently swayed Washington's mind on this delicate point; within no time copies of *Common Sense* were being bought everywhere in the colonies, by patriots and loyalists alike, sharpening public opinion as they were spread about. It was probably the most immediately popular publication that had ever appeared in the colonies. "I am charmed with the sentiments of 'Common Sense,'" Abigail Adams wrote her husband John while he was attending the Continental Congress in Philadelphia, "and wonder how an honest heart, one who wishes the welfare of his country and the happiness of posterity, can hesitate one moment in adopting them. I want to know how these sentiments are received in Congress. I dare say there would be no difficulty in procuring a vote and instructions from all the Assemblies in New England for Independency."

But six months after the Declaration of Independence, now in his bitter retreat at Valley Forge, Washington had to admit that "the game is pretty near up." His meager troops were defecting in all directions. Then, within the week before the heroic commander made his inspired Christmas-night crossing of the Delaware, Paine launched a series of new pamphlets, the first of them opening with those unforgettable words: "These are the times that try men's souls. The summer soldier and the sunshine patriot will, in this

One of the many hardships endured by Washington's troops at Valley Forge was their lack of shelter. A vignette from a 19th-century bank note depicts the homeless men gathering firewood.

crisis, shrink from the service of their country; but he that stands it *now*, deserves the love and thanks of man and woman. Tyranny, like hell, is not easily conquered; yet we have this consolation with us, that the harder the conflict, the more glorious the triumph."

When the war was finally won, Paine went on to stir up wider revolution overseas, for which efforts he was made an honorary citizen of France and tried *in absentia* for treason in England. When he returned to America in 1802, revolutionary ardor in this country had cooled, and he was reviled from the pulpit and in the press as an atheistic agitator (which he was not), and upon his death his remains were refused burial in any consecrated ground. Ultimately, the very bones of this vital, disturbing man were altogether lost.

Like Franklin, no one of the other leading statesmen who saw the Revolutionary cause to its ultimate conclusion—Thomas Jefferson, John Adams, James Madison, and Alexander Hamilton notably among them—posed as a man of letters; no one of them placed the manner of their writing above the matter, above the need to inform, argue, persuade, and elucidate important concerns. "The simplest style, the most mathemathical precision of words and ideas," wrote John Adams, "is best adapted to discover truth and to convey it to others, in reasoning on this subject [politics]." Yet, however they may have constrained the style of their writing, eschewing flourish and artifice in favor of direct statement, their formal documents are more often than not exemplary models of English prose—"literature" in every sense of the term except that it was not intended to be purely such. In the long run, a good part of the most impressive literature produced in America was not "creative writing, but rather essays of a political nature, travel accounts, reminiscences, biographies, and histories."

Actually, we come closer to the personal spirit and individual style of these men in the enormous quantity of their correspondence that has survived. This mass of material is our invaluable inheritance from an age in which communications had to be labored over rather than hastily given to an air wave for transmission. Here, too, we come somewhat closer to the special American idiom that was shaping the development of our native writing. At one point the *Edinburgh Review* took Jefferson to task for using newly coined American words and corrupting the traditional purity of the English language. Jefferson was unperturbed. "Had the preposterous idea of fixing the language been adopted by our Saxon ancestors," he observed, "of Peirce Plowman, of Chaucer, of Spenser, the progress of ideas must have stopped with that of the language . . . what do we not owe to Shakespeare for the enrichment of the language, by his free and magical creation of words? [to be sure,] uncouth words will sometimes be offered; but the public will judge them, and receive or reject, as sense or sound shall suggest." And who could imagine that this huge new founding nation, with its variant strains and unique experiences, would not find its own characteristic manners of expression without undue reverence for standards of "pure" English?

In any case, the practical literature of ideas as it was presented in the diverse writings of these philosopher-statesmen set a solid foundation for a national literature whose influence, like that of American art and architecture, would in time cross back over the Atlantic and create new adventures in thought and expression overseas.

A PROCESS OF LEARNING

The American drive to self-improvement has been a dominant force in the development of our cultural history. During the 1600's many colonists were collecting books, usually English works devoted to "useful" subjects like religion and history; in the next century, with the proliferation of printing presses, libraries, schools, and other accouterments of urban life, came a blossoming of American letters under the aegis of scholars like the Yale-educated Reverend Ebenezer Devotion of Connecticut, shown in his library in a portrait of 1770.

*Above: the Library Company of Phila-
delphia, Fifth Street, home of the collection from 1790 to 1878; below:
a group of Thomas Jefferson's books*

PRIVATE SUBSCRIPTION

Since the early colonial period American bibliophiles, merchants, ministers, and other concerned individuals have helped advance American scholarship through the endowment of learned institutions and libraries. John Harvard led the way in 1638 by leaving his 320-volume library to a fledgling college at Cambridge, Massachusetts, which has since borne his name, and in 1653 a merchant named Robert Keayne left provisions for a public library in Boston. When the Reverend John Sharpe, chaplain to the governor of New York, died in 1700 he bequeathed his books toward the establishment of a public library in that city; this bequest was given new life in 1754 when a group of citizens, by subscription, purchased about 700 additional volumes and established what would become the New York Society Library, a proprietary institution that is still flourishing. In 1727 Benjamin Franklin organized the Junto Club in Philadelphia for the "mutual improvement" of his "ingenious acquaintances." The club met weekly in a tavern, and its need for books impelled

Above: the New York Institution building, the New-York Historical Society's third home (1816–32); below: New York Society Library bookplate

‍OR PUBLIC EDUCATION

Franklin and his friends in 1731 to establish a subscription library, the Library Company of Philadelphia, which was incorporated in 1742. Out of the Junto Club there also emerged the American Philosophical Society, started by Franklin in 1744. In the 1740's libraries were established in Newport, Rhode Island, and Charleston, South Carolina. The New-York Historical Society, founded in 1804 and noted for its library, was part of an early New York cultural center, the New York Institution in City Hall Park, which also housed the American Academy of Fine Arts, the Lyceum of Natural History, the Literary and Philosophical Society, and the American Museum. Franklin, in his *Autobiography*, sums up the beneficial effects of libraries and other institutions: "Reading became fashionable, and our people having no public amusements to divert their attention from study, became better acquainted with books, and in a few years were observed by strangers, to be better instructed and more intelligent than people of the same rank generally are in other countries."

THEATRE ARTS

Generally speaking, colonial Americans spurned the theatre on the grounds that it was impious, immoral, expensive, and worst of all, a useless distraction from Industry. The Puritans of New England regarded it as a "shameful vanitie," designed by Satan to ensnare the soul in evil, and New York's Dutch burghers as well as the Quakers and Presbyterians of the Middle Colonies were also inclined to view the stage with hostility. The aristocratic Southern planters, on the other hand, were more cordially disposed to play acting, and there was a theatre at Williamsburg, Virginia, as early as 1716. But friends of the drama existed throughout the colonies, and primitive, often furtive, performances took place even where prohibited. The frequent playgoing of a national hero like George Washington endowed the drama with a certain air of propriety, and by the late 1700's respectable citizens of many cities were supporting the theatre. When Philadelphia's Chestnut Street Theatre opened in 1794 a contemporary observed that it "immediately became a place of fashionable resort." By the nineteenth century drama was viewed as an effective means of social improvement.

Top: a scene from the dramatization of James Fenimore Cooper's historical novel, The Spy, *painted in 1823 by William Dunlap, a noted playwright and artist; left: a print of 1807 showing Philadelphia's Chestnut Street Theatre; opposite: New York's elegant 2,500-seat Park Theatre, with its rich and prominent audience, painted by John Searle in 1822*

The graduating ceremonies at a seminary for genteel young ladies in Virginia, 1810–20, depicted by an unknown artist

A music class at the Old Lutheran Schoolhouse at York, Pa., 1805

WIDER HORIZONS

Transylvania University, Ky., founded in 1780

A Harvard man with sporting gear

In the seventeenth century the British governor of Virginia thanked God that there were no free schools or printing presses in his colony, for he viewed both as instruments of "disobedience and heresy and sects." In New England the Puritans enforced school attendance, not so much in the cause of intellectual freedom as to ensure a literate clergy. By the late 1700's denominational academies and colleges were being established in the east as well as along the frontier. And by the early years of the Republic, responsible leaders agreed with Thomas Jefferson that Americans would need "a certain degree of instruction" in order to rule themselves and to preserve their liberty. Adequate schooling, insisted John Adams, would have to be extended to "every class and rank of people, down to the lowest and poorest." It was John's wife, Abigail Adams, who lamented the absence of educational opportunities for women. "If you complain of education in sons," she wrote, "what shall I say in regard to daughters, who every day experience the want of it? . . . If we mean to have heroes, statesmen, and philosophers, we should have learned women." However, it would be several decades before inspired feminists like Emma Willard—whose Troy Female Seminary opened in 1821—proved that girls could survive and even excel in intellectual pursuits. It was the education of men and women, rich and poor, that turned America into "the land of the general reader."

Left: an interview between a poor author and a rich bookseller, as represented by Washington Allston about 1810; below: a mid-18th century trade card; opposite: Henry Sargent's The Dinner Party, *painted about 1821, shows a meeting of the Wednesday Evening Club, an informal gathering of artists and literati that convened weekly at Sargent's Boston home to discuss the literary scene.*

AUTHOR & PUBLISHER

The history of American book publishing began in 1639 when the first printing press was set up in Cambridge, Massachusetts. The following year Boston had a "bookebynder," and the bookseller—as a tradesman distinct from the printer—first appeared in that city around 1647 in the person of Hezekiah Usher, who amassed a comfortable fortune in the book trade. The colonial printer-publisher, who turned out mostly religious works and legal documents, was an extremely important member of the community, especially in the smaller towns, where he was apt to function as editor, binder, bookseller, and even postmaster. It was not until the 1820's, however, that the American printer evolved into a true publisher and began to consider the tastes of the reading public, which was demanding a popular literature that included poetry, drama, and fiction. Until the passage of an international copyright law in 1891, there were no restraints, either legal or ethical, to prevent American publishers from pirating European works (generally English novels) and issuing them in various inexpensive editions. As a result, American authors (for whose works publishers had to pay) were largely ignored until the 1850's, when the literature of the United States reached a high-water mark. Still, many native writers had to rely on magazine publication; only after 1891 did they reap financial profits from book publishers.

FIRST FRUITS
OF INDEPENDENCE

Washington Irving spent his last years at "Sunnyside" (opposite), his "snuggery" on the banks of the Hudson River near Tarrytown, N.Y. The romantic house is noted for its Dutch-style gables.

On September 3, 1783, the United States and Great Britain signed the Treaty of Paris, which formally ended the Revolutionary War and officially established American independence. A preliminary treaty had been signed more than nine months earlier, but complicated international negotiations among America's European allies and England's other foes had delayed a final settlement. Except for some bloody skirmishes in the west during 1782, hostilities between the two countries had long ago ceased. However, British forces were still stationed in New York awaiting evacuation by transport, along with thousands of Loyalist residents preparing to quit the city for new homes elsewhere. It was agreed that Washington would officially take over the city on November 25.

For seven long years—since the summer of 1776 when Sir William Howe forced his way into New York—the city had remained firmly under British control; an important and peaceful haven for those who remained loyal to their king, a police state of sorts for those who favored the Revolutionary cause. Now, with liberation in sight, feelings ran high. The Tories were embittered by the change in their fortune, and thousands were preparing to quit the city for new homes; the British garrison, only grudgingly accepting its defeat by the "rebels," asserted its authority until the last possible moment; and the American patriots were understandably impatient to take command of their own destinies. When word of the preliminary peace treaty reached the city, one New York Tory wrote of this "distressing" news: "I find the Loyalists in this country are most shamefully and traiterously abandoned. . . . Our fears at present surpass all description. Never was there upon the face of the earth a set of wretches in a more deplorable situation. Deprived of all hope of future comfort or safety, either for themselves or their unhappy wives and children, many have lost their senses, and are now in a state of perfect madness." Months later, and a mere three days before Washington's scheduled re-entry into the city, British soldiers tore down American flags that had been prematurely displayed by patriotic citizens.

As he awaited that promised day from his temporary headquarters at Newburgh, George Washington sent a "Circular to the States" of the new

71

nation, reminding them that this was the time of their political probation, "that the eyes of the whole world were upon them, and that, among other things, they must remain firmly united "under one Federal Head." It had to be decided whether the Revolution was ultimately to be considered "a blessing or a curse: a blessing or a curse—not to the present age alone, for with our fate will the destiny of unborn Millions be involved. . . ." The spirit of nationalism that animated that document was a timely warning to those separate states that so often during the struggle for independence had failed to observe their obligations both to the government of the Confederation and to the armies it had managed with such difficulty to keep in the field under Washington's supreme command.

That same year Noah Webster, a young schoolmaster in Goshen, New York, exhorted his countrymen to assert their independence and their nationalism in other ways. In the preface of his famous Blue-backed Speller (first issued in 1783), and later in several of his other publications, Webster called for the liberation of American literature from English authority. The national honor, he insisted, demanded "a system of our own, in language as well as in government." Aside from other publications of Webster's, the Speller alone, in time and in its various editions, sold scores of millions of copies—perhaps as many as one hundred million. The little book was carried across the continent by successive generations of westering Americans and, with its propaganda, even found its way to remote Indian tribes. It was one of the best sellers of all time.

In that same eventful year of 1783 Mrs. William Irving was delivered in New York of her eleventh child, to whom she gave the baptismal name of Washington after the great hero of the hour. By happy chance, when Washington Irving was six years old, the child's Scottish nurse spied the Father of His Country in a Broadway shop and, seizing the opportunity, led her charge in to receive the blessing of his revered namesake. The event remained bright in Irving's memory into the last years of his life when, just before his death in his late seventies, he completed his *Life of George Washington*. Long before that, however, Irving was celebrated as the first American man of letters to win wide international renown.

Actually, in the years following the Revolution and before Irving gained eminence, a fair number of American writers found ready audiences for their work. Some of them won a measure of fame abroad, as well as at home, if not always because of the quality of their prose, then at least because of keen interest in what they were writing about. Their message captivated the imagination of certain European authors and inspired them to new adventures in their own writings.

"Do you know Bartram's 'Travels'?" The Scottish essayist and historian Thomas Carlyle wrote to Ralph Waldo Emerson in 1851. "[It] has a wonderful kind of floundering eloquence in it; and has grown immeasurably old. All American libraries ought to provide themselves with that kind of book. . . ." Carlyle referred to the volume, first published in America in 1791 and in England the next year, by the Philadelphia Quaker and botanist William Bartram, recounting his travels through the southern states, from North Carolina to Florida.

With the publication, in 1783, of The American Spelling Book (often called the Blue-backed Speller), Noah Webster gave his country a uniform and distinctly American system of spelling and pronunciation. The work went through many editions (a page from a 1793 printing is reproduced here), and the crude woodcuts used to illustrate its moralistic fables became a characteristic aspect of the book.

72

Bartram's delineation of the American scene in his *Travels*, with its precise descriptions and colorful evocations of the wilds of America, a world barely imaginable to most European minds, provided a literal stage for their thoughts and dreams. The English poet Samuel Taylor Coleridge read the book, and it fired his hope of founding an ideal colony of poets and philosophers—called pantisocracy—in this unspoiled land, a brotherly community where human virtue would hold sway as it could never do in the Old World. Although he abandoned that implausible scheme, Coleridge turned to Bartram's book for many of the vivid images that he wove into *The Ancient Mariner*, "Kubla Khan," and his other poems. Coleridge's fellow poet Robert Southey shared his fantasy of a New World sanctuary, and also made use of Bartram's book in his own writings—as did another of Coleridge's close friends, William Wordsworth. Vicomte François René de Chateaubriand, the most popular French author of his time, came to America briefly the year Bartram's *Travels* was published (he had supposedly come to search for the Northwest Passage, but he never got beyond Niagara Falls.). He subsequently made imaginative use of the American's material to invent passages in *Atala* and *Les Natchez*, tales of romantic agony set amongst the innocent and virtuous aborigines of America, that thrilled a wide European public.

Even earlier, Michel-Guillaume Jean de Crèvecoeur, a widely traveled French émigré and friend of the Bartrams and of Franklin and Jefferson, had painted an idyllic picture of life in the New World that doubtless persuaded many of his European readers to leave their homelands for America. In his *Letters from an American Farmer*, published under the pseudonym

In 1791 William Bartram, the American naturalist, published his Travels. *This classic work contains Bartram's wildlife drawings, like that of the Florida sandhill crane reproduced above; more important, its text provided foreign writers with a romanticized view of the great American wilderness.*

In writing Atala, *Chateaubriand borrowed heavily from Bartram's description of the American South, with its lush forests and savannas.* Atala *is the tragic love story of the Christian Indian maiden Atala and the Indian Chactas, with whom she escapes into what the author calls an Allegheny "desert." The French thrilled at this tale of the faraway; it inspired Girodet's painting,* The Burial of Atala *(a detail appears at left), depicting Atala's interment by the weeping Chactas and Père Aubrey, a hermit.*

73

J. Hector St. John, he celebrated the simple joys of settling in the wilderness and cultivating the virgin soil. "Men are like plants," he observed; "the goodness and flavor of the fruit proceeds from the peculiar soil and exposition in which they grow. We are nothing but what we derive from the air we breathe, the climate we inhabit, the government we obey, the system of religion we profess, and the mode of our employment." Everything in this burgeoning land, he concluded, tended toward the regeneration of man. Crèvecoeur's book was first published in English in 1782, then in a larger French edition two years later, and was widely read. Washington, Franklin, Jefferson, Madison, and other eminent Americans held it in high regard. Overseas, it was praised by Coleridge, Byron, Southey, Charles Lamb, and other British authors of repute.

Like Bartram, Crèvecoeur wrote—at least for publication—largely of the more smiling aspects of the American scene. He was aware of the social tensions that had accompanied the struggle for independence and, although he did not publish such sentiments, he held strong Tory sympathies. Under the garb of patriotism he detected "a certain impatience of government, by some people called liberty," that tended toward lawlessness. Those doubts about the revolutionary fervor seemed justified by the "popular tumults" that occurred during the days of the Articles of Confederation. In 1786-87 virtual civil war erupted in New England when heavily taxed and debt-ridden farmers, without political means to obtain relief, resorted to violence to correct the wrongs that oppressed them. Shays' Rebellion, so-called after Daniel Shays, a Revolutionary War veteran who was one of the leaders of the uprising, was reported to George Washington as an unfortunate indication of the "leveling principle" and the "desire for change" prevalent among many of the people—characteristics which, forty years later, Alexis de Tocqueville thought were outstanding aspects of a flourishing American democracy.

Jefferson wrote to Abigail Adams from France about the Shays eruption: "I like a little rebellion now and then. It is like a storm in the atmosphere." "The tree of liberty," he further observed, "must be refreshed from time to time with the blood of patriots and tyrants." Washington, however, wrote to James Madison that he thought the new nation was verging on anarchy. The outbreak was suppressed with some difficulty and with bloodshed, but it led many thoughtful citizens to appreciate the need for a stronger federal government that could more effectively deal with such disturbances—as Washington was to do some years later in the case of the Whiskey Insurrection. Exercising his authority under the new Constitution, the president then called out the militia to put a stop to such anarchy and confusion. To the surprise of some, fifteen thousand troops from four different states answered his summons to police their fellow citizen in the name of the central government, and that revolt quickly collapsed.

Unwittingly and in indirect ways Dan Shays made his contribution to the history of American letters. His actions spurred one group of aristocratic and conservative intellectuals, known as the Hartford or Connecticut Wits, to collaborate on a series of mock-heroic verses, the *Anarchiad*, which spoke out against democratic liberalism in any form. With such dignitaries as

Alexander Hamilton, sketched here, composed many Revolutionary War letters that bear George Washington's signature. He is most famous as the chief author of the Federalist *(1787–88), a collection of eighty-five essays in support of the Constitution.*

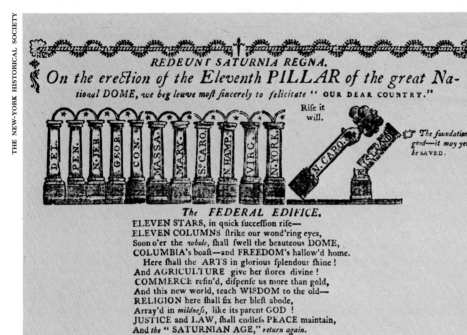

REDEUNT SATURNIA REGNA.

§ On the erection of the Eleventh PILLAR of the great Na- §
tional DOME, we beg leave most sincerely to felicitate " OUR DEAR COUNTRY."

Rise it
will.

☞ The foundation
good—it may yet
be SAVED.

The FEDERAL EDIFICE.

ELEVEN STARS, in quick succession rise—
ELEVEN COLUMNS strike our wond'ring eyes,
Soon o'er the *whole*, shall swell the beauteous DOME,
COLUMBIA's boast—and FREEDOM's hallow'd home.
  Here shall the ARTS in glorious splendour shine !
And AGRICULTURE give her stores divine !
COMMERCE refin'd, dispense us more than gold,
And this new world, teach WISDOM to the old—
RELIGION here shall fix her blest abode,
Array'd in *mildness*, like its parent GOD !
JUSTICE and LAW, shall endless PEACE maintain,
And the " SATURNIAN AGE," *return again.*

New York's ratification of the Federal Constitution on July 26, 1788, inspired this cartoon in the Massachusetts Centinel, *urging North Carolina and Rhode Island to "rise" and accept the Constitution—a document that British statesman William Gladstone would later call "the most wonderful work ever struck off . . . by the brain and purpose of man."*

Timothy Dwight, John Trumbull, Joel Barlow, and Lemuel Hopkins among its contributors—all Federalists at heart who saw democracy as a "wild and fearsome thing," the *Anarchiad* swelled the great stream of polemical writing that heatedly and at times brilliantly debated the question of a new Constitution. As they wrote, a convention was held in Philadelphia to thrash out the issues at stake. From those discussions emerged a series of eighty-five essays written in 1787–88 by James Madison, Alexander Hamilton, and John Jay for New York newspapers—a reasoned plea for the adoption of the Federal Constitution. Thomas Jefferson referred to the *Federalist,* a compilation of those articles, as "the best commentary on the principles of government ever written."

Then after Shays had fled the field, one Royall Tyler, a Harvard graduate and also a veteran of the Revolution (and who later became chief justice of the Vermont supreme court), was sent to New York City in connection with the rebellious veteran's extradition. While there he went to the theatre to see Richard Sheridan's *School for Scandal,* an experience that prompted him to write a play of his own, *The Contrast.* It was the first American play dealing with contemporary social life in this country; a comedy of manners that struck a clearly democratic note—a note conspicuously missing from the *Anarchiad.*

> Exult each patriot heart!—this night is shewn
> A piece, which we may fairly call our own;
> Where the proud titles of "My Lord! Your Grace!"
> To humble Mr. and plain Sir give place.

The play was squarely aimed at a native audience and introduced the character Jonathan, a man of rustic virtues who stands in bright contrast to those affecting "superior" manners and who heads a long file of stage Yankees. When it was first performed at New York's John Street Theatre in 1787,

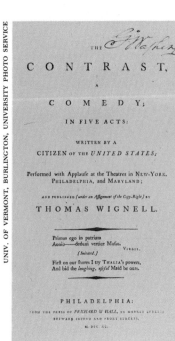

The Contrast, *by Royall Tyler, was the first wholly successful American play performed by professional actors. George Washington attended its first New York performance in 1787, and the* Pennsylvania Herald *rhapsodized that* The Contrast *furnished additional "proof that these new climes are particularly favorable to the cultivation of arts and sciences." When the play was printed in 1790 Washington headed the list of 658 subscribers; the autographed title page of his personal copy is reproduced above.*

George Washington, a devoted theatregoer, was in the audience; he then ensured the play's publication by heading the subscription list. (Unlike the *Anarchiad*, *The Contrast* can still be read for pure pleasure. A musical version of it was only recently staged in New York to critical applause.)

In 1791 another ardent patriot, the English-born Susanna Rowson, published *Charlotte Temple*, a sentimental romance "designed . . . for the perusal of the young and thoughtful of the fair sex," and enticingly subtitled *A Tale of Truth*. Eighteen years after the book first appeared in America, Mrs. Rowson's Philadelphia publisher wrote her that the sales had by then exceeded "those of any of the most celebrated novels that ever appeared in England." Such has been its enduring popularity that it remains in print to this day, having gone through more than two hundred American editions in an untold number of copies. The flow of tears shed over the unhappy fate of the heroine of the story, seduced and then abandoned by her lover (almost inevitably a despicable British lieutenant) can never be measured. Mrs. Rowson wrote numerous other books both before and after the appearance of *Charlotte Temple*, but that novel established her fame. Nevertheless, the author could not make a living from her writing alone. To supplement her income she tried the stage, and then took charge of a Massachusetts boarding school for young ladies.

The first truly professional American man of letters was Charles Brockden Brown, who published his four most accomplished novels in the last two years of the eighteenth century, before he was thirty years old. In his exciting, melodramatic romances (*Wieland; Ormond; Edgar Huntley; Arthur Mervyn*), which are also still in print, Brown used distinctively American materials and American settings, which he felt were far more suitable materials for a native author than the "puerile superstition and exploded manners, Gothic castles and chimeras" usually employed to arouse the interest of readers. Brown's writings won high praise from such eminent English authors as John Keats, Percy Bysshe Shelley, and Sir Walter Scott. In his native land James Fenimore Cooper, Edgar Allan Poe, and Nathaniel Hawthorne, among others, also lauded his writing and were influenced by it. Keats called *Wieland*, an adventure in abnormal psychology and considered Brown's best novel, a "very powerful" book of "accomplish'd horror"; of one frenzied scene in that work, where the protagonist Wieland, inspired by the voice of a ventriloquist, strikes down his wife and children, John Greenleaf Whittier wrote somewhat extravagantly: "In the entire range of English literature there is no more thrilling passage. . . . The masters of the old Greek tragedy have scarcely exceeded the sublime horror of this scene from the American novelist."

A few years before his death, in 1810, Brown called on young Washington Irving to ask him to contribute to a literary magazine he had recently started in Philadelphia. After some modest, quite casual beginnings, Irving's writings were bringing him not only recognition but fame. He had studied for the law and was indeed admitted to the bar, although he never practiced that profession. Rather, he entered the family business. As a youth he had studied drawing and for a time had thought of following art as a profession. Before he was twenty-three he had spent two years in Europe, sent on those travels by his brothers, who were concerned for his health. On that tour he met Madame de Staël, the celebrated sculptor Antonio Canova, the great naturalist Baron Alexander von Humboldt, and, among others, the talented American painter Washington Allston, who praised his sketches and urged him to turn to painting as a career. Throughout his life Irving saw the scenes about him with a painter's vision. He used a pen rather than a brush to record the impressions that formed in his mind's eye, although he also filled his notebooks with delightful drawings.

Allston's suggestion tempted Irving, but his thoughts kept returning to literature, and following his return to America, in 1807–1808, he published some light essays and poems in the *Salmagundi* papers, a book in which he joshingly criticized New York society of the time. Then, in 1809, just two hundred years after Henry Hudson sailed up the river to be named after him, Irving published his first important work, Diedrich Knickerbocker's *History of New York,* a book that had an instant success. Irving described the fictitious author Knickerbocker as "a small, brisk-looking old gentleman, dressed in a rusty black coat, a pair of olive velvet breeches, and a small cocked hat," who vanished up the Hudson after leaving the manuscript of a book to pay the bill of his lodgings. He was "a very inquisitive body . . . although a little queer in his ways." The name has endured and become ubiquitous, as the scores of Knickerbocker societies, clubs, companies, and so on listed in today's New York telephone directory make very clear.

Using historical facts and personages as starting points, Irving created a boisterous but genial satire of life in New Amsterdam under Dutch rule. It was the first fine example of American comic literature, and it created a mythology for his native city that time and all the sober accounts of reliable historians have never overshadowed. His portraits of early Dutch personages transmuted them into mock heroes of endearing absurdity. Wouter Van Twiller, one of New Netherland's early governors, was "exactly five feet six inches in height, and six feet five inches in circumference." His body was "particularly capacious at bottom; which was wisely ordered by Providence, seeing that he was a man of sedentary habits, and very averse to the idle habit of walking." So, too, Irving's obese and beery burghers, enveloped in smoke from their pipes, and their sharp-tongued, waddling wives, swathed in countless petticoats, give infamous but lasting shape to our images of the early Dutch settlers.

As Irving himself admitted, the book immediately "took with the public." One contemporary American critic termed it "certainly the wittiest our press has ever produced," and the author became a literary lion overnight. As he read the antics of Knickerbocker's characters, Sir Walter Scott said his sides ached with laughter. Charles Dickens claimed that he wore out his copy of the *History* by always carrying it about with him. It was part of the book's quick and general success that with his burlesque account of earlier times Irving was satirizing the "follies and blunders" of his own day, as his American readers, at least, clearly realized. In his ridiculous portrait of Wilhelmus Kieft, Van Twiller's successor as governor of the colony, for example, Irving was caricaturing Thomas Jefferson. As a confirmed Federalist and a social conservative, the author detested the policies of the third president and

Father Knickerbocker is depicted in this engraving for an 1812 edition of the History. *His name, recounts Irving, probably comes "from* knicker, *to nod, and* boeken, *books, plainly meaning that [the Knickerbockers] were great nodders or dozers over books."*

scoffed at his democratic person. Thus, he portrayed William the Testy, as he dubbed Kieft in the story, as a bumbling eccentric with his "cocked hat and corduroy small clothes" riding "a raw boned charger"; a man so learned that he was "good for nothing," and who "entangled the government . . . in more knots during his administration, than half a dozen successors could have untied"—in short, like Jefferson, a peculiar, misguided egghead and untrustworthy radical.

Another decade passed before Irving produced anything more of consequence. Then, in 1819–20, he published *The Sketch Book of Geoffrey Crayon, Gent.*, which more firmly and broadly established his reputation on both sides of the Atlantic. He was in England at the time. He had gone there to salvage the family business; but when it went bankrupt and he needed money, his friend Sir Walter Scott encouraged him to resume his writing. Irving had visited the great man at his picturesque home, Abbotsford, in Scotland, and the two had spent days rambling about the countryside, and talking from morning to night.

Van Wyck Brooks observed that *The Sketch Book* was used as a first reader for students of the English language all over the world for almost a century. (It was translated into fifteen languages.) Only a few of the pieces that made up its contents dealt with America, but those included "The Legend of Sleepy Hollow," with its unforgettable headless horseman, and "Rip Van Winkle," which became at once, and forever, precious ingredients of America's folklore. (With these and later tales Irving became the first American writer of short stories.) Aldous Huxley once remarked that a countryside and its people are to a large extent the invention of its poets and its novelists. To the degree that this may be true, the Hudson River valley is the creation of Irving. As he wove its magic into his stories, that river became one of the world's enchanted waterways. To this day one cannot pass the Dunderberg (Thunder Mountain), at the southern entrance to the Highlands, without harking for the voice of Mein Heer, the bulbous-bottomed Dutch goblin with his sugar-loaf hat, bawling his orders for wind and lightning. And who ever visited the Catskills without sensing the abiding presence of the bewitched old Rip and his troop of small folk. It matters little that Irving borrowed European forms for his stories (sometimes to the point of plagiarism), for into them he poured the incident and the fresh spirit of the American world.

Many of the other selections in *The Sketch Book* were devoted to English themes. Irving was charmed by the picturesque past of Europe and by its lore, which he discovered in his voluminous reading and in his wide travels. He spent seventeen years overseas on this visit, moving about in English, German, French, Italian, and Spanish society as an admired celebrity and citizen of the world. He was handsome, personable, and gifted, and he had "a boundless capacity for good fellowship." Early in his sojourn in England he became known as "the most fashionable fellow in London." In Dresden he set his cap for a young lady, Emily Foster, who years later recalled that "he was thoroughly a gentleman . . . to the innermost fibres and core of his heart: sweet-tempered, gentle, fastidious, sensitive, and gifted with the warmest affections; the most delightful and invariably interesting companion. . . ." He had, she also remembered, "a gift of conversation that

The sedentary, monosyllabic governor of New Netherland, Wouter Van Twiller, adopts a customary pose in this 1867 engraving. That "illustrious old gentleman," asserts Knickerbocker, presided over his council "with great state and solemnity. He sat in a huge chair of solid oak. . . . Instead of a sceptre, he swayed a long Turkish pipe."

Washington Irving, the man who "invented" Dutch New York, was a handsome, debonair bachelor of twenty-six when he sat for this portrait by John Jarvis in 1809.

flowed like a full river in sunshine—bright, easy, and abundant." Since Irving seems to have been passionately in love with Emily and she apparently responded to his charm, it is hard to understand why she did not accept the proposal of marriage, which it is said he made. In any event, as they parted for the last time Emily wrote that he "looked up to us, so pale & melancholy I thought I never felt a more painful moment, such starts of regret, a little self-reproach & feelings too quick to analyse." Irving had other such romances, but he never married.

Before he sailed for America in 1832 he had written several other books, including a popular biography of Christopher Columbus and *The Alhambra,* a collection of such tales as could not be told of the New World—of the romantic old palace, of buried Moorish treasures, and of the genius of an ancient past, which generally enhanced his reputation. When he returned to his native land he was hailed as a literary hero.

Amid the general acclaim there were unfavorable remarks that his long exile and his writings on European subjects showed Irving's want of affection for America. Now he almost immediately took off on a trip to the Indian country along the western frontier. Roughing it, as he did, was arduous for the comfort-loving cosmopolite that Irving was; but his countrymen exulted that "our own American Irving" had once again turned his talented eye and pen to describe the picturesque nature of his own country and its denizens. "The ardent patriotism of the author of Columbus," the press reported, "will prompt him to inspire his countrymen with some of his own laudable curiosity about the land we live in; and his pen, invigorated by themes so novel to the rest of the world and so grateful to himself, will trace his impressions with a freshness and force that will rival its happiest exercise in any of his works."

In the published account of his travels, *A Tour on the Prairies,* Irving inevitably refined and romanticized his experiences (he saw aspects of the prairie scene in terms of Gothic cathedrals and Moorish castles). However, the book was a long-lasting success; it has gone through more than thirty editions in English and twenty in translation.

The year the *Tour* was published, Edward Everett of the *North American Review* referred unreservedly to Irving as "the best writer of English prose," which was a very tall claim. Poe, on the contrary, thought that, with "his tame propriety and faultlessness of style," Irving was much overrated. Whatever the measure of critical opinion, by now he had produced his best books; certainly his best-remembered works. He followed up the *Tour* with other accounts of the West and, among other things, after serving four years as United States Minister to Spain, he wrote his multivolume, favorably prejudiced life of Washington, which he completed in his last years.

Irving had introduced writing as an art in America. But, as he observed early in his life, with his writing he "attempted no lofty theme, nor sought to look wise and learned," but rather to address himself to "the feelings and fancy of the reader" rather than to his judgment. "I have always had an opinion," he observed, "that much good might be done by keeping mankind in good humor with one another. I may be wrong in my philosophy, but I shall continue to practise it until convinced of its fallacy." In all this he suc-

ceeded remarkably well. "It has been a matter of marvel, to my European readers," he wrote in 1822 with detached amusement, "that a man from the wilds of America should express himself in tolerable English. I was looked upon as something new and strange in literature, a kind of demi-savage, with a feather in his hand instead of on his head." Irving's success in the eyes of the world delighted his fellow Americans, who had long been irritated by European, notably British, criticism of American writing. Only two years before he wrote the sentences just quoted, the prestigious *Edinburgh Review* had carried Sydney Smith's notorious insult: "In the four quarters of the globe, who reads an American book?" Few American authors have ever been so beloved as Irving was in his time, both at home and abroad. When he died in 1859 at "Sunnyside," his picturesque "little nookery" near Tarrytown, the courts of New York adjourned on the day of his funeral, flags were put at half-mast, and the church bells of the city tolled the grief of multitudes. He was buried in the cemetery at Sleepy Hollow, near where the Headless Horseman heaved his pumpkin-head at the panic-stricken Ichabod Crane.

Sunny Morning on the Hudson, painted about 1827 by Thomas Cole, is an expressive view from the Catskill foothills looking south toward the Hudson Highlands. The varied and undulating Catskills, wrote the poetic Cole, "heave from the valley of the Hudson like the subsiding billows of the ocean after a storm."

81

Bells had not tolled so loudly when James Fenimore Cooper died eight years earlier; however, a memorial service was held in New York, at which, among others, William Cullen Bryant, Daniel Webster, and Irving (whom Cooper had not liked) joined in paying tribute to the novelist. Throughout his career Irving had observed the feelings of his countrymen with consummate tact and charm in all he did and all he wrote. Cooper, on the other hand, had never hesitated to upbraid his fellow Americans when he felt they needed his critical opinions. Irving even went so far as to revise his Knickerbocker history in later editions to reduce any possible offense he might have given to the old Dutch families in his original version. "It was a confounded impudent thing in such a youngster as I was," he wrote, "to be meddling in this way with old family names." He had not meant to offend, he added. Cooper in the course of time earned the resentment of his reading public; his late years were vexed by argument and contention.

Nevertheless, Cooper's stature as a novelist was hardly questioned. For three decades the "glorious Fenimore" had vied with Irving as America's foremost man of letters. In the year of his death, 1851, the *International Monthly* hailed him as "among the foremost of the illustrious authors of the age." That appraisal has been modified over the years, but it indicates the impact Cooper's writings had on his contemporaries. His works, too, were known and celebrated throughout most of the Western world. "They are published as soon as he produces them in thirty-four different places in Europe," observed his friend Samuel F. B. Morse, the artist and inventor. "They had been seen by American travellers in the languages of Turkey and Persia, in Constantinople, in Egypt, at Jerusalem, at Ispahan." In 1828 Franz Schubert pleaded from his deathbed for another of Cooper's novels to distract him in his mortal illness. "I have read [his] *Last of the Mohicans, The Spy, The Pilot,* and *The Pioneers,*" the great composer wrote a friend. "If by any chance you have anything else of his, do please leave it for me. . . ." (It is doubtful that he read much more, for he died within a week.) A generation later Count Leo Tolstoi paid Cooper high tribute in a different way by paraphrasing whole pages from him in writing *The Cossacks.*

There was no early indication that Cooper would write at all. He spent two years at Yale before he was dismissed for some youthful escapade (he was only sixteen at the time). For the next five, and more fruitful, years he shipped before the mast on an ocean-going merchant vessel, and then as a midshipman in the Navy. (Later, those experiences served him well in writing several novels of the sea.) He quit the service to marry—to marry well—and to settle down to enjoy his matrimony as a country gentleman.

Cooper's plunge into authorship was sudden and unpremeditated. One evening he casually remarked that even he could write a better book than the English novel he had been reading aloud to his wife, who, wifelike, after nine years of married life, immediately challenged him to do so. Cooper dashed off a conventional novel of manners, *Precaution,* which was published in 1820, when the author was thirty-one years old. That very modest and dull accomplishment set Cooper virtually into a state of perpetual motion. Within a year he had written *The Spy,* a Revolutionary War romance set in Westchester County where the Coopers were then living. (The aging

The aristocratic James Fenimore Cooper rankled many of his contemporaries with his acid criticisms of Jacksonian America. Nevertheless, the memorial service held for him after his death in 1851 was attended by literary moguls and other luminaries, including William Cullen Bryant, Daniel Webster, and Washington Irving—the trio portrayed in this sketch by Daniel Huntington, executed at the service.

John Jay was an avuncular neighbor of the Coopers and had described for them his wartime efforts to ferret out the British plans by hiring just such a secret agent as Cooper made the hero of his novel.) *The Spy* was a prodigious success, and Cooper's professional career was off to a fast start. In 1822 he moved to New York. He completed more than thirty novels in rapid succession, along with a miscellany of other books and articles (including a classic two-volume *History of the Navy of the United States*) that testified to his gargantuan appetite for work and his formidable powers of invention.

Cooper's name and fame will always be most closely associated with the land beyond the Knickerbocker legends, the wide-angle segment of upper New York state that centers on the Mohawk valley and stretches northward to Lake George and Lake Champlain and westward to the Great Lakes. Here sanguinary battles had been fought during the French and Indian and Revolutionary wars. "The hireling tomahawk struck death on both sides," as one historian has written, and "scarlet coats from Devonshire and Norfolk and tartan kilts from Inverness met white and brass from Béarne and Languedoc, and fell with the life within them." Here, too, the ground was bloodied by the civil strife of friends and neighbors, as at the awful conflict at Oriskany during the Revolution—friends and neighbors who honestly differed as to whether this was rebellion or self-determination.

In the year of the peace George Washington had looked out over this liberated New York countryside and, with a seasoned eye for its beauty and its promise, he bought a piece of it on speculation. So did Alexander Hamilton, Robert Morris, some stolid Dutch bankers, and titled Englishmen. French émigrés vied with Yankees to make their claims. Madame de Staël, the author and one of the most brilliant women of the age, speculated heavily and successfully in New York real estate following Talleyrand's report from America, where he had come for refuge from the Terror in France, that here was "the best place to make money fast." And, at a timely moment, Judge William Cooper, father of James Fenimore, acquired title to a huge tract of these virgin frontier lands and became a border aristocrat, in effect a lord of the manor, in what still remained a semifeudal state and which he ruled from his seat at Cooperstown.

Far above and beyond the lure of profits this, no less than the Hudson valley, was enchanted ground. There was reason to believe the ancient legend that the Great Spirit regarded the region with special favor. The imprint of the hand he once laid upon it in benediction may still be traced in the tapered outlines of the Finger Lakes. It was almost within the span of those clearwatered valleys, according to the Deganawidah story, that Hiawatha dreamed and spoke of a peaceful brotherhood of man. And round about, covering practically all the present state from Lake Erie to the Hudson River, the Iroquois did, in fact, establish the league of Five Nations, the remarkably statesmanlike democratic confederation of aboriginal tribes that was the most powerful combination of Indians on the North American continent. It was that confederacy that suggested Benjamin Franklin's scheme for a union of the colonies. Cooper knew and loved this forested country, and about its real and legendary history he spun the tales for which he is best remembered—America's own "Arabian Nights of the frontier," as they have been called.

James Fenimore Cooper, shown in this oil by John W. Jarvis, was the creator of America's memorable frontier sagas. Cooper shared with Irving and Bryant their great love for the unspoiled wilderness—an affection also expressed in the work of the Hudson River school.

Late in his career Cooper predicted that if anything from his pen were to endure it would be those five frontier romances, written over a period of eighteen years, that he called the Leatherstocking tales. All five stories are woven about the adventures of Natty Bumppo, or Leatherstocking (he also appears in the various books under the names of Deerslayer, Hawkeye, Pathfinder, and Long Rifle), that indomitable frontiersman who has been called "... perhaps the only great original character that American fiction has given to the world." Natty was brave and resourceful, illiterate but sage, kindly but, when need be, deadly with his unerring rifle Killdeer, a true friend of the worthy but an implacable foe of the wicked. Secure in his self-reliance and his higher moral purpose, he lived beyond the need and reach of man-made laws—the completely free individual, the perfect democrat of Jefferson's and Emerson's dream.

In a sense, all Americans are the spiritual heirs of Natty Bumppo, for he remains the symbol of those frontiersmen whose cherished legends have become part of our national inheritance. He has all the individual virtues of Daniel Boone. Davy Crockett, Kit Carson, and the rest, but none of their faults; he is the sublimation of a uniquely American type. He is different from those others, perhaps, in his intimate and frequently expressed love of nature,

Natty Bumppo, hero of Cooper's Leatherstocking tales, appears in this frontispiece of The Last of the Mohicans. *Natty, easily the most famous character in American fiction the world over, was Cooper's symbol of the bravery, gallantry, and courage of the legendary American frontiersman; his death, described in* The Prairie *(1827), occurs only after "the sound of the axes has driven him from his beloved forest to . . . the treeless plains that stretch to the Rocky Mountains."*

84

and in this as in other respects he is the happy product not only of the western movement in American history, but as well of the romantic movement in European literature. He is a type of figure forecast in that image of Daniel Boone created by the earlier reports that pictured this wilderness Adam lying on his back in the forest and singing in sheer delight at being alone and free in his new-found Eden; such an image as prompted Lord Byron, in the eighth canto of *Don Juan,* to interrupt his description of the siege of the Moslems to celebrate Boone, "backwoodsman of Kentucky . . . happiest among mortals anywhere."

Most of Cooper's readers were undoubtedly less interested in Leatherstocking as a symbol of anything than in his breathless adventures among the redskins, whose uncanny forest skills he could more than match. At one point in *The Deerslayer* Natty—Deerslayer in this book—was captured by the Mingos, or Hurons, and bound to a tree while his captors shot at his head to see how close they could come without actually killing him prematurely. As Cooper tells it, so sharp was his eye that by looking into the bore of their rifles Natty could tell precisely where the bullets would hit—"no one could detect even the twitching of a muscle on the part of the captive, or the slightest winking of an eye," and when five or six had discharged their bullets, he taunted his enemies:

> "You may call this shooting, Mingos," he exclaimed, "but we've squaws among the Delawares, and I've known Dutch gals on the Mohawk, that could outdo your greatest indivors. Undo these arms of mine, put a rifle in my hands, and I'll pin the thinnest warlock in your party to any tree you can show me; and this at a hundred yards; ay, or at two hundred, if the object can be seen, nineteen shots in twenty; or for that matter, twenty in twenty, if the piece is creditable and trusty!"

To many Europeans who had never seen an American this resourceful hero was probably more vital and convincing than any of the living mediocrities who were featured in the reports of returned travelers. The Indians, in turn, were a never-ending source of fascination. Even among Europeans otherwise reasonably well informed it was vaguely believed that most if not all inhabitants of North America were redskins. Cooper got his Indians somewhat mixed up and has Natty, innocently unaware of the problems that face the student of such matters, neatly divide them into two groups, the "good" ones and the "bad" ones, the noble savages and the savage fiends. Among Natty's loyal friends and allies were the steadfast young brave Uncas, the last of the Mohicans, and his honorable father, the chieftan Chingachgook— whose name, Mark Twain wrote facetiously, was "pronounced Chicago, I think."

Twain scoffed at Cooper's picture of the frontier, which he remarked was seen as "through a glass eye, darkly"; his Indians belonged to "an extinct tribe which never existed." But on this point his wit was largely wasted. For a hundred years or more the Leatherstocking tales absorbed the reading public of two continents, and beyond, and they determined the way the world was long to regard the American Indian. Those stories remain today among the books we may give up but do not get over. Like Irving, Cooper created a mythology that has been incorporated into the nation's culture and that pro-

jected a particular image of America to far places of the globe.

Beyond their elements of adventure, the Leatherstocking tales trace the inexorable encroachment of civilization on the virgin American wilderness. Natty Bumppo steadily retreats westward "to escape the sound of the ax," until he ends up an aging, solitary trapper (his companions Chingachgook and Uncas have died) on the treeless prairie, a pitiable figure if it were not for his abiding nobility of spirit. An advancing emigrant train, vanguard of the civilization to follow, catches sight of the old man: "The sun had fallen below the crest of the nearest wave of the prairie, leaving the usual, rich and glowing, train on its track. In the centre of this flood of fiery light, a human form appeared, drawn against the gilded background, as distinctly, and seemingly as palpable, as though it would come within the grasp of any extended hand. The figure was colossal; the attitude musing and melancholy, and the situation directly in the route of the travellers." Leatherstocking recedes into the glowing sunset of a heroic past.

In 1833, returning to his home at Cooperstown on the shores of "Glimmerglass" (Lake Ostego) after a long absence, Cooper sadly noted that the nearby woodlands were "lacerated" by the new settlers. His contemporary and neighbor to the south, the landscapist Thomas Cole, lamented about the Hudson valley: "They are cutting down all the trees in the beautiful valley on which I have looked so often with a loving eye." There were many thoughtful Americans who believed that the national virtue which would make all things possible was that lavish gift of nature that was now being so zestfully despoiled. Could one then accept this booming progress that leveled the forests and gouged the hills in the name of some "manifest" destiny? That dilemma tore at the conscience of Cooper and his generation.

It was during those same years, the 1820's and 1830's, that John James Audubon was gathering material with fervent zeal for his monumental volumes on the birds of America, which, with the accompanying text, was to find an honored place in the history of American literature. Audubon, too, was aware that the frontier world was rapidly vanishing. He knew with passionate conviction that no one coming after him would ever have the same opportunity to record the birds of North America in their primeval haunts, and that realization drove him mercilessly to finish his inventory before it was too late. It was the task, as he saw it with almost mystical reverence, "allotted to him by nature." The great auk had already disappeared before he had been able to see a living specimen, and the passenger pigeon was fast vanishing from the forests. On one of his rambles into the suburbs of Manhattan Island William Cullen Bryant visited Audubon in his last home on the shores of the Hudson River. The "American woodsman" was then about sixty years of age, but, Bryant reported, "his form was erect, and his step as light as that of a deer." His writings Bryant described as "vivacious and clear" and suffused with the "poetry of nature." In them there was "an impetuous bounding enthusiasm . . . a strain of exuberant and exulting animal spirits, that carries you whither he wills." And so the world at large found this outpouring of Audubon's experience and spirit.

In 1826, already well launched on his career as an author, Cooper went abroad for seven years, traveling about England and various countries on the

Above, John Audubon, portrayed by his sons Victor and John about 1840. Opposite, Spring—A Girdled "Clearing," *an aquatint of about 1840 after a water color by the English-born artist George Harvey. Americans were then assiduously decimating their forests by girdling the trees (which killed them) and burning the dead timber, leaving, as Harvey blithely explained, "the smiling cheerfulness of the open landscape."*

Continent. His writing continued at its breathless pace (in Paris he finished *The Prairie,* in which the fading Leatherstocking was portrayed) while he viewed the European scene with a critical eye. To correct the misconceptions that the Europeans held of America, he wrote *Notions of the Americans,* and with it offended English and Americans alike. In *A Letter . . . to General Lafayette* he somewhat presumptuously pointed out the superiority of republics to monarchies (this was immediately following the July Revolution in France in which the last Bourbon king was deposed and Louis Philippe, who had once traveled in the backwoods of America, was to be crowned). Cooper had a new concern for political and social problems, and he spoke his mind without compromise.

Cooper had left America in 1826 during the presidency of John Quincy Adams, the last administration whose standards and principles harked back to the earliest days of the Republic. He returned seven years later when the Jackson administration was in full swing, and he was disturbed by the rapid changes he saw developing in American life. "You have been dreaming abroad," remarked a character in one of his novels, "while your country has retrograded, in all that is respectable and good, a century in a dozen years." Cooper was dedicated to the ideals of democracy, but he could not abide the bumptiousness and vulgarity of democracy in action. Most Americans were provincial, he felt, as so many English aristocrats were priggish. As a second-generation member of the landed gentry he was offended by the crass intrusions of capitalistic enterprise in quest of what Irving first called the "Almighty Dollar," and for which the axe was providing an opening wedge in the forest. Like John Adams and other distinguished members of an earlier generation, he did not believe the mass of Americans was qualified to use wisely its right to vote. He did believe that the existence of the landed class he represented was not only compatible with but necessary to a successful and stable democracy.

Against such dangers to society as he saw all about him, Cooper spoke out in tract and story, without restraint, directly and satirically. During the 1840's, when tenant farmers were in virtual rebellion against the old manorial system in antirent riots, the leveling spirit that Cooper deplored came very close to home. In a trilogy of novels, known as the *Littlepage Manuscripts,* he combated these rank heresies. *Satanstoe,* the first of these, has been called one of the most distinguished examples of American historical fiction. (The fact that many of the intrusive and lawless upstarts were emigrant Yankees—those "locusts of the West"—did not endear them to Cooper who, like Irving, had a standing dislike of New England and all its ways.) These outbursts brought instant retaliation in published reviews and comments; Cooper countered with a succession of libel suits—which he won. He also won the bitter resentment of those large numbers whose behavior he so harshly criticized.

Cooper was at his best when he retreated from the vexatious problems of the time to re-creations of the past, into the wilderness and out onto the open sea, a pattern established with the first three books he published after *Precaution;* within two years after *The Spy* he wrote *The Pioneers,* in which he introduced Natty Bumppo, and *The Pilot,* a romance lightly based on the

An anonymous artist, working about 1829, left this view of the Five Points, a notorious New York City slum and spawning ground for crime—a sordid aspect of city life that Cooper decried.

exploits of John Paul Jones during the Revolution. For the last work he drew upon his knowledge of ships and sailormen (with which he had more first-hand experience than he had with Indians), and he produced one of the earliest memorable novels of the sea. The speed with which he prepared these three books set the pace for his lifetime of writing. Unlike Irving, he wasted little of that time in perfecting his style, but rushed through his narratives, far more intent on what he had to tell than how elegantly he might tell it—an option approved by a wide world of readers.

A few years after he died at his home in Cooperstown, with the din of the controversies he had provoked still ringing in his ears, George Sand wrote an appreciation of his work in which she observed that although Cooper had been devoted to his country, he had risen above the life of the America of his time. That statement would have gratified Cooper. Whether he would be pleased by today's translations of his novels into television performances and comic books is more difficult to judge.

Irving shared Cooper's regret at the frenzied pace of progress, though he was far less abrasive in his statements about it, and his nostalgic sadness that the picturesque and adventurous past had given way to the harsh commonplaces of contemporary life. In "The Legend of Sleepy Hollow" Irving remarked that he liked to imagine "a retreat whither I might steal away from the world and its distractions, and dream quickly away the remnant of a troubled life." A multitude of Americans must have sympathized with such sentiments as they witnessed the almost violent change from old values to new that was taking place.

Nowhere was the rapid rate of that change more apparent than in New York City. During Irving's lifetime the friendly little provincial town in which he grew up had become a hectic, teeming metropolis. (In his *Notions of the Americans*, published in 1828, Cooper observed that only a few of the old Dutch dwellings were still standing in the city, distinguishable by "their little bricks, their gables to the street, and those steps on their battlement walls. . . ." He had been told that not more than five hundred buildings of any kind could be dated further back than the peace of 1783.) The city's population had multiplied more than ten times. The once-calm village life had vanished with the upsurge of commerce and industry. Gentlemanly society, as Irving knew it—and as Cooper knew it upstate—had been heavily overlaid by raw democracy.

When the national capital was moved to Philadelphia in 1790, it had been dolefully predicted that New York would be deserted "and become a wilderness, peopled with wolves, its old inhabitants." Then in 1797 the state capital was moved up to Albany. Yet within a brief generation the city became the largest and most bustling urban center in the land, and was growing ever faster. Surveying the scene in 1839, Horace Greeley reported in the *New Yorker* magazine: "New York has become the metropolis, in our country, not only of commerce but of literature and the arts. Like Tyre of old, she has covered the sea with ships, and her merchants are princes. . . . No man well acquainted with the history of Literature and Art in our country during the last ten years, can refuse to acknowledge that New York has towered above her sister cities."

A view of Broad and Wall streets, New York, drawn by John J. Holland in 1797, depicts a group of typical Dutch-style dwellings—with their "gables to the street"—whose disappearance from the city scene was lamented by Cooper.

To this literary capital more and more authors and journalists turned to find a publisher, to further their careers, and to experience the stimulation of the city scene. Thus, the "Southern Cooper," William Gilmore Simms from South Carolina, had to depend largely on the North for publishers and, to a degree, for a public. His first prose tale, *Martin Faber,* and his most important poem, *Atalantis,* were published in New York at the time of a visit to the North in 1832–33. Simms made repeated trips to the city during his immensely productive career, but his love for the South, particularly for Charleston, his birthplace, ruled him with a passion, and he could not long remain away from the peculiar, nostalgic charms of that city.

Simms has been likened to Cooper because he, too, wrote romances of Indians and the frontier and of the Revolutionary past. Like Cooper, oddly enough, in three of his earliest works, written within two years, Simms also started to write on the three different subjects for which he is best remembered. He, too, was a born storyteller, and he, too, wrote with a speed and regularity that left little time for perfecting his style (the typesetters were

Oak Alley at Vacherie, La., typifies the pillared Greek Revival plantation mansions built in the decades preceding the Civil War. Such residences provided the framework for the elegant life obliterated by that bitter conflict.

hard put to keep up with him). *The Yemassee,* one of those early books and his most popular romance, is a thrilling tale of Indian warfare along the South Carolina border in 1715. Here, as in other, similar adventure stories, Simms' Indians have the same pride and courage that Cooper gave to his redmen, albeit Simms characterizes them more realistically. He knew them better in the flesh and blood than Cooper did. As a youth he had ridden through the back country and over the mountains to visit his father, who had gone West during the War of 1812 to fight the Creeks under his friend Andrew Jackson and who had settled in Mississippi as a veritable frontiersman. On his travels young Simms had lived with Indians, and had rubbed elbows with the rough pioneers and the riff-raff of the borderlands.

He was a prolific author in several veins, including verse and the drama, but his preoccupation with Southern traditions and manners worked to his disadvantage in the large market places of the North, where such matters seemed remote and unfamiliar. (Edgar Allan Poe once remarked that Simms would have been more appreciated had he been a Yankee.) With his total affection for and loyalty to South Carolina, as the Civil War approached, Simms could easily rationalize the position of the South. At a time when the Greek Revival style was sweeping the land, with others of like mind he could persuade himself to believe that the South shared the virtues of the ancient Greece democracy, tall-columned white structures, slaves, and all, with Christianity as an added blessing. At the end of the war his life was a shambles. His wife and nine of his fourteen children were dead, and his plantation home, directly on the line of Sherman's march to the sea, was a charred ruin; many of his friends, too, were gone, and his fortune lost. Even so, he resumed writing, but he never emerged from the dark shadows of those later years. Poe had called him, with the exceptions of Brockden Brown and Hawthorne, "immeasurably the best writer of fiction in America." But that accomplishment was largely forgotten.

During the course of his regular visits in the North, Simms formed many warm friendships, notably that with William Cullen Bryant, the prestigious editor of the *Evening Post.* Bryant had come to New York from Great Barrington, Massachusetts, in 1825—one of a number of small-town New England authors (Horace Greeley was another) who turned to New York rather than Boston to seek their literary fortune. Like Irving (and Simms), he had read in the law, but in practice he found it a "wrangling profession" and one that interfered with his creative writing. When he was told on good advice that he could not fail to succeed in New York, "where anybody and everything succeeds," he took off for the metropolis where he was to spend the rest of his long and eminently distinguished life.

In New York he was quickly nominated by Cooper for membership in the "Bread and Cheese Club," which Cooper himself had started with the intention of bringing together in select, informed gatherings the most illustrious literary and artistic talents of the time and place. Members were admitted by a bread and cheese tally. A candidate was rejected if, when his name was proposed in nomination, any cheese was found on the plates of the members. Besides Cooper himself, the members included such distinguished men as the artists Samuel F. B. Morse, Asher B. Durand, and William Dunlap (who

William Cullen Bryant—poet, orator, and abolitionist editor of the New York Evening Post— *was New York City's first citizen for over half a century. He was a smoulderingly handsome man of thirty in 1825 when his longtime friend Samuel Finley Breese Morse did this portrait.*

was also a playwright and a historian of the arts), Fitz-Green Halleck (whom Poe considered second only to Bryant as a poet), and several score other men of accomplishment. (In 1827 the group divided into the Literary Club and the Sketch Club; twenty years later the latter in turn was reformed as the still-active Century Association.)

Bryant's shift to New York was a timely move, for later that same year the Erie Canal was formally opened, which was probably the most important occasion New York has ever known. For the first time the road to and from the West was wide open, and New York was its main terminal. The city's commercial empire was extended far into the back country, to the basins of the western lakes and the Mississippi River. Within barely a score of years the canal business—concentrating at Albany, largely en route to and from New

York—was greater than that derived by New Orleans from the trade of the whole Mississippi River system. By mid-century the population of New York was five times as large as that of Boston or Philadelphia. In the "big city" businesses of every stripe, including publishing, boomed as never before. Such still-familiar names as Harper, Scribner, Appleton, Putnam, and others were all listed in the city directories—testimony to New York's importance to the writing world.

When Bryant arrived in New York his reputation as a poet was already established. He had versified as a child, aiming some of his couplets at that "imbecile slave" Thomas Jefferson, protesting both his politics and his immoralities (it was rumored that Jefferson was enamored of his wife's half-sister, Sally Hemings, a quadroon):

> Go scan, Philosophist, thy [Sally's] charms,
> And sink supinely in her sable arms;
> But quit to abler hands, the helm of state,
> No image ruin on thy country's fate!

With such lines the thirteen-year-old lad, precocious on several counts, won the encouragement of his father (a confirmed Federalist) and, as well, a favorable notice in the *Monthly Anthology*, a literary periodical published in Boston.

Bryant's fame as a true poet, America's first of international stature, came not very long afterward, with the almost accidental publication of an early version of "Thanatopsis." It appeared in 1817 in *The North American Review*, the nation's principal literary journal before the founding of the *Atlantic Monthly* in 1857. Bryant had composed these verses some years earlier, when he was seventeen, but had done nothing with them. His father discovered the manuscript in a desk during his son's absence and left it at the home of an editor of the *Review*. The verses were greeted at first by incredulity. "No one on this side of the Atlantic is capable of writing such verses," expostulated Richard Henry Dana; and it actually took two years to satisfy the last skeptic that young Bryant was indeed the author. (Along with a few other early poems by Bryant, "Thanatopsis" had been published anonymously.)

With the fact of his authorship, and of his unusual talent, well established, in 1821 Bryant published a small volume of his early works, *Poems*; it included "Thanatopsis"—with a newly added beginning—the form in which it has been so fondly remembered by generations of Americans:

> To him who in the love of Nature holds
> Communion with her visible forms, she speaks
> A various language; for his gayer hours
> She has a voice of gladness, and a smile
> And eloquence of beauty, and she glides
> Into his darker musings, with a mild
> And healing sympathy, that steals away
> Their sharpness, ere he is aware. When thoughts
> Of the last bitter hour come like a blight
> Over thy spirit, and sad images
> Of the stern agony, and shroud, and pall,
> And breathless darkness, and the narrow house,

Make thee to shudder, and grow sick at heart;—
Go forth, under the open sky, and list
To Nature's teachings, while from all around—
Earth and her waters, and the depths of air—
Come a still voice.—

He also added a new, equally memorable ending:

As the long train
Of ages glides away, the sons of men,
The youth in life's green spring, and he who goes
In the full strength of years, matron and maid,
The speechless babe, and they gray-headed man—
Shall one by one be gathered to thy side,
By those, who in their turn shall follow them.
So live, that when thy summons comes to join
The innumerable caravan, which moves
To that mysterious realm, where each shall take
His chamber in the silent halls of death,
Thou go not, like the quarry-slave at night,
Scourged to his dungeon, but sustained and soothed
By an unfaltering trust, approach thy grave,
Like one who wraps the drapery of his couch
About him, and lies down to pleasant dreams.

Also included in that slim 44-page book was another early poem. "To a Waterfowl," which was one of the first American poems to be widely praised overseas. Matthew Arnold called it "the most perfect brief poem in the language." Here again, with stoic calm, Bryant sees in nature the enduring handiwork of God, the goodness of the Omnipotent, of which the lives of men and all their works are but fugitive aspects. As the bird disappears in the darkness of night the poet reflects:

Thou'rt gone, the abyss of heaven
Hath swallowed up thy form; yet, on my heart
Deeply hath sunk the lesson thou hast given,
And shall not soon depart.
He who, from zone to zone,
Guides through the boundless sky thy certain flight,
In the long way that I must tread alone,
Will lead my steps aright.

No American poet before him, certainly, had struck such a lyrical note; none had turned so confidently and wholeheartedly to the natural world immediately about him for the subject of his message—to nature pure and simple, as he viewed it. He was the first poet to write of such native birds as the bobolink and the brown thrasher rather than the nightingale and skylark of the English countryside, of the spicebush and the late-blooming fringed gentian rather than England's gorse and primrose, of the wonder of his own country's wild mountains and vast prairies of "the continuous woods where rolls the Oregon, and hears no sound, save his own dashings"—rather than the trimmed and combed neatness of England's landscape.

Such poetry helped to kindle in his friend and walking companion Thomas

A detail from Kindred Spirits, *painted in 1849 by Asher B. Durand, shows Thomas Cole (gesturing with his walking stick) and William Cullen Bryant on a cliff in their beloved Catskills. The work conveys a sense of harmony between cultured man and pristine nature, thus memorializing two "kindred spirits" who celebrated the wonders of the natural scene in America.*

Cole, and in others of the Hudson River school of painting, an appreciation of the native scenery, which they so eloquently expressed in their landscapes. Bryant was an early admirer of Cole's paintings, which he described as carrying the eye "over scenes of wild grandeur peculiar to our country, over our aerial mountain-tops with their mighty growth of forest never touched by the axe, along the banks of streams never deformed by cultures, and into the depth of skies bright with the hues of our own climate; skies such as few but Cole could ever paint, and through the transparent abysses of which it seemed that you might send an arrow out of sight." And when Cole was leaving for a tour of Europe, Bryant admonished him to remember his native land while he observed and admired the ancient grandeurs of the Old World:

> Gaze on them, till the tears shall dim thy sight,
> But keep that earlier, wilder image bright.

Bryant himself made numerous rewarding trips abroad, but in the course of those journeys he always felt the absence of the native wildness of America.

His first little volume had netted Bryant just $15 in five years from the sale of only two hundred seventy copies. He was understandably slow in attempting such a venture again, although in the years following 1821 he wrote more poems than in any other short period of his life. These appeared in literary journals and in newspapers, and with their publication his fame grew. To make his work more readily available to the increasing number of his admirers, in 1832 he brought out a collection of what he deemed his best work up to that time, and his fame spread yet further. Strongly as he felt that American authors should avoid British influences, he wanted to get his later volume published in England, which he did with the friendly help of Irving, who was then in London. ("We do not praise a thing," he once complained, "until we see the seal of transatlantic approbation on it.") Somewhat unexpectedly, the book was spared the harsh words English critics had bestowed on the work of Byron, Keats, Wordsworth, and Shelley. A few years later Edgar Allan Poe reported that Bryant's reputation abroad as well as at home was greater than that of any other American writer.

Earlier in the year that the book was issued, after making a trip to Washington to visit Andrew Jackson in what was then becoming familiarly and vulgarly known as the White House, Bryant journeyed to Illinois to see his brothers who had moved there. During the course of a horseback ride on the prairies he met a group of Illinois militiamen on their way to fight the Indians in the Black Hawk War. "They were a hard-looking set of men," he observed, "unkempt and unshaved, wearing shirts of dark calico. . . ." He spoke with their captain and enjoyed his "quaint and pleasant talk." That officer, he later learned, was the young Abraham Lincoln. From these Western experiences Bryant composed "The Prairies," one of his best poems written in blank verse.

By then Bryant was deeply involved in his responsibilities as editor of the *Evening Post,* a position he assumed in 1829 and held for nearly half a century. Those responsibilities left him little leisure for the literary pursuits he claimed to prefer. By the time his second volume was published, he had completed most of his best work in poetry. In any event, he labored so long and hard revising and perfecting his work that he was not very prolific. That fastidiousness and good taste he carried over to his newspaper activity.

On both sides of his family Bryant was descended from early settlers of the Plymouth Plantation and the Massachusetts Bay Colony. He brought with him from New England to New York the uncompromising honesty and moral strength that was his Puritan birthright. As New York flourished, Bryant prospered, although he was preoccupied by other concerns than money-making. But he never shied from espousing what he considered to be good causes, however unpopular. He influenced public opinion as few editors ever have. At the risk of losing subscribers and advertisers, he supported the nascent labor movement at a time when protest strikes were generally condemned as criminal conspiracies; and for this he was accused of setting class against class and encouraging anarchy. When he felt it just and right to do so he pilloried such eminent national figures as Benjamin Harrison, Henry Clay, and Daniel Webster for their misguided views and political acts. He attacked every threat to free speech, whatever the consequences. "The right

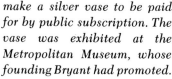

For his eightieth birthday, in 1874, Bryant's friends commissioned Tiffany & Co. to make a silver vase to be paid for by public subscription. The vase was exhibited at the Metropolitan Museum, whose founding Bryant had promoted.

An engraving, from an 1860 Harper's Weekly, *shows a section of New York's Central Park, the planning of which in the 1850's was spurred partly by Bryant's efforts. The poet-editor used the editorial columns of the* Evening Post *to further his campaigns for numerous municipal reforms. In 1845, while on a European tour, he wrote ecstatically about London's extensive parks, and exhorted New Yorkers to set aside land "for a range of parks and public gardens . . . to remain perpetually for the refreshment and recreation of the citizens."*

to discuss freely and openly, by speech, by the pen, by the press, all political questions," he proclaimed in 1837 when he felt an injustice had been done, "and to examine and animadvert upon all political institutions, is a right so clear and certain, so interwoven with our other liberties, so necessary, in fact, to their existence, that without it we shall fall at once into despotism or anarchy." "Liberty" and "Democracy" remained his watchwords.

Bryant threw his abundant energies and his determination into civic as well as national concerns. For more than a decade, at the height of his career, no public affair of any consequence in New York was considered complete unless he spoke, or at least was present on the rostrum. He supported the causes of art and music, as well as of literature. He fought for the creation of Central Park and helped to launch the Metropolitan Museum of Art. He was one of the giants of American journalism, and he was the first citizen of New York, if not of the nation.

The day of his death, on June 12, 1878, at the age of eighty-four, was the occasion for general mourning. His achievements were generously recalled by the press. The *New York Times* pointed to the extraordinary accomplishment of the poet who loved the quietude of nature, but who as editor had to face the "vigorous brutalities of the daily press." The *Tribune* observed that virtually every American was familiar with "Thanatopsis"; "almost every school reader contains it; few students . . . finish their studies without learning it by heart." Longfellow wrote that he constantly kept a copy of that youthful performance on his study table. Bryant, he remarked, was his "master in verse." In the years that followed, the acclaim accorded Bryant's poetry tended to overshadow his enormous editorial contributions.

Some years before he died, in 1865, Bryant had been asked to support a proposal to erect a memorial to Edgar Allan Poe in Baltimore. He refused, remarking that "there should be some decided element of goodness in the character of those to whom a public monument directs the attention of the world." By Bryant's lights Poe had lacked those necessary qualifications. Poe died as he had lived, attended by rumors, suspicions, and anecdotes that were all too true and that cast a long and lasting shadow over his character. On October 3, 1849, he was found lying unconscious in the gutter of a Baltimore street, and a few days later he was dead. He was only forty years old. A commonly told story was that, when found, he was literally almost dead drunk. The stories about Poe's frailties and perversities persist, often without enough evidence to determine the solid truth of the matter.

So many facts are missing from the story of his relatively brief life, so many accounts of it are questioned, that it is not possible to make any final judgments. In a sense Poe's biography was a tale invented by Poe himself. Mark Twain once half-humorously observed that as he grew older he tended to remember only the things that never happened, and Poe shared such a tendency to a disconcerting degree, although he did not live long enough to be old. He told stories of his birth and childhood that are incompatible with the known record; he falsified his age. He did not deny the highly improbable legend—indeed on occasion he helped propagate it—that in 1832 he set off for Greece to help in that country's struggle for freedom; that on such travels he visited Russia and fought a duel in Paris, or was it in Spain, as he also claimed, from which he carried a scar that several persons said they had seen, and so on. He even claimed that in Paris he wrote a novel that was later published under the name of Eugène Sue, the famous French novelist. Ironically, the truth about his life was further confused by the vicious slurs and by the wilfull distortions of the man whom Poe himself chose as his literary executor and early biographer, Reverend Rufus W. Griswold.

Beyond that, there is and always has been large disagreement about his status as a writer. In Poe's own time Emerson dismissed him as "the jingle man," but Tennyson thought he was "the most original genius" America had produced. James Russell Lowell quipped that Poe was "three fifths genius and two fifths sheer fudge," but in France, Charles Baudelaire and Stéphane Mallarmé read Poe's work with fervent admiration and sympathetically translated it into French. In later years he won the praise of such diverse figures as Abraham Lincoln, Theodore Roosevelt, George Bernard Shaw, H. L. Mencken, and, it has been said, Joseph Stalin—and suffered barbs from as many or more equally varied critics. It is probably one measure of the vitality of Poe's work that over the long years its merits are still hotly debated. Even many of those who disapprove of his writing feel they cannot ignore it.

For all the enigmas that confuse the issues of Poe's life there is one grim certainty: he lived in poverty and died in misery. There were only a few relatively brief periods in his mature life when he enjoyed the comfort of security. More often, indeed, he seems to have existed closer to the level of bare subsistence—frequently enough to create the impression that he knew intimately what it meant to suffer from want. Yet, save for intervals of melancholia (during one of which he even unsuccessfully attempted to take his

Edgar Allan Poe, shown here in a Brady daguerreotype, was rarely lauded by his compatriots; he called himself a "magazinist." Today he is regarded as an inspired innovator who influenced the French symbolists, among others.

98

life), for his spells of drunkenness, and for moments of sheer desperation, he labored unremittingly at his literary craft, fired by an almost mystic faith in his own genius. Those labors led in several directions—toward poetry, the short story (to an important extent mystery and horror stories, and some science fiction), and, importantly, literary criticism. In each of these categories he created some models of unusual excellence that had positive influence on other writers about the world at the time and over the years to come.

Poe was born into an uncertain and unstable world. His parents were strolling players who were performing in Boston at the time of his birth. By the time he was two, his dissolute father had disappeared, and his impoverished mother had died in Richmond, Virginia, where she had gone to follow her career on the stage. The infant Edgar was taken into the home of John Allan, a local tobacco merchant, and his wife (whence Poe's adopted middle name). His foster parents gave him a good early education, in England, where they spent five years, and in Richmond. For a time at least they spoiled the handsome, high-spirited, and personable child. Poe never got over the aristocratic pretensions that were formed in his early life. However, as the lad passed through the years of adolescence, Allan, who had inherited a sizable fortune, lost sympathy with him, and tension mounted between the two. When Edgar ran up large gambling debts during his first term at the University of Virginia, Allan refused to pay them, and the youth was obliged to quit the school. (By Poe's lights he had to gamble for the money his wealthy but stingy foster parent would not provide.) In 1827, after a bitter quarrel, Poe left home at the age of eighteen to make his own fortune in the world.

This he found was very far from easy. For the next seven years, while Allan lived, the young runaway intermittently pleaded with him for money to alleviate his poverty and to further his career. From time to time he was grudgingly accommodated with modest sums. There were occasional brief reconciliations between the two, but in the end Poe was cut off from the inheritance which under the circumstances he had no very good reason to expect in the first place, since he had never been legally adopted. During those years he did a hitch in the Army as a means of securing some income, then went on to West Point (with Allan's help) as a cadet and future officer. But when he viewed his diminishing hopes of an inheritance, Poe contrived to have himself dismissed from the academy. The Army was no career for a man without money of his own. (He took his cadet overcoat with him and wore it in years to come, creating with it a picturesque appearance in the eyes of romantic young ladies of his acquaintance.)

Now, instead, he would be a kind of soldier of fortune. In the meantime, also, he struggled for a foothold in the world of letters. In 1831, almost immediately after his dismissal from West Point, he published his first consequential book of poems in New York. Before he left the academy Poe had solicited subscriptions for such a publication from his fellow cadets at 75 cents each, and when the book appeared it was dedicated to The U.S. Corps of Cadets. This collection of just eleven poems included revisions of a select few of Poe's earlier efforts and a half dozen pieces he had composed more recently with painful care—probably between his service in the Army and his admis-

The death of a beloved woman is a recurring theme in Poe's writing. Virginia Clemm, his ill-starred cousin and child-bride, is pictured here. Poe married "Sissy," as he called her, when she was thirteen. Her death in 1847 left him suicidal.

99

sion to West Point, while he was experiencing one of those short periods of reconciliation with Allan. Among the new poems were "Israfel" and "To Helen," two which he later revised (as he was constantly doing with most of his work), and which remain among his most memorable verses. He was then barely twenty-two years old.

When the 124-page volume was issued, some obscure, forgotten publication reported: "Everything in the language betokens poetic inspiration, but it rather resembles the leaves of the sybil when scattered by the winds...." For the rest, it was hardly noticed at the moment. The West Pointers, who duly received their copies, must have felt gulled by the strangely allusive rhymes that confronted them. In a preface to the book Poe tried to explain the principles that guided him in his poetic work. Essentially these pronounced (with an unavowed debt to Samuel Taylor Coleridge) that the immediate object of a poem was "pleasure not truth," that "music, when combined with a pleasurable idea, is poetry." There were no moral implications here such as burdened the work of so many of his contemporaries, particularly in New England. It was poetry for poetry's sake that concerned him— poèsie pure as Baudelaire and Mallarmé would gratefully recognize it and emulate it long before James McNeill Whistler insisted on "art for art's sake."

If Poe had never written another poem he would through this book still

Poe's "tales of ratiocination" (his name for his ingenious murder mysteries) made their debut in 1841 with the publication of The Murders in the Rue Morgue *(a manuscript page from this work is reproduced here).* The Murders *introduced mastermind detective C. Auguste Dupin, prototype for a long line of omniscient criminologists, including Sherlock Holmes.*

be remembered as one of America's great poets. From his reading Poe had learned of Israfel, the angel mentioned in the Koran, "who has the most melodious voice of all God's creatures" and who sang to the accompaniment of his heart which was as a lute. Thus Poe opens his poem:

> In Heaven a spirit doth dwell
> 'Whose heart-strings are a lute';
> None sing so wildly well
> As the angel Israfel,
> And the giddy stars (so legends tell);
> Ceasing their hymns, attend the spell
> Of his voice, all mute

With "To Helen" Poe created one of his masterpieces, whose unforgettable lines possibly recall his grief over the death of the mother of one of his early schoolmates—a woman whom the fifteen-year-old Poe had loved with the ardent but "pure" devotion of an adolescent. (All his life he turned to women for comfort, support, and the security he could not find in his own soul.)

> Helen, thy beauty is to me
> Like those Nicean barks of yore,
> That gently, o'er a perfumed sea,
> The weary, way-worn wanderer bore
> To his own native shore.

And then the lines that have been so incessantly quoted since he first wrote them:

> Thy Naiad airs have brought me home
> To the glory that was Greece
> And the grandeur that was Rome

This older lady love died just as news came of the death of Lord Byron, Poe's poetic hero and idol at the time, while he was helping the cause of Greek independence from the Turks. This may explain the classical setting of the poem.

Poe later observed that to him death was the most melancholy of topics, and that death allied to beauty was the most poetical form that a topic could attain. "The death, then, of a beautiful woman is, unquestionably, the most poetical topic in the world," he wrote, "and equally is it beyond doubt that the lips best suited for such a topic are those of a bereaved lover." That grisly formula dictated the best poems he wrote.

Poe made virtually no money from this publication—nor much from his other, later writings. The time had not yet come when more than a very few American authors could reasonably expect to make a living from their profession. Even Ralph Waldo Emerson took to the lecture circuit to supplement his income from writing—and to reach a wider audience for what he had to say. This was in good part because there were no copyright laws, and American publishers could, and did, pirate British books and articles without paying a cent for them. Poe's case was, as always, special in that the mass of his countrymen were not yet prepared for his message, or his lack of message. Very few of his writings dealt with America or Americans; they treat of other worlds and strangely different, unreal people. It was often an almost

TEXT CONTINUES PAGE 104

POE & THE SYMBOLISTS

In the years 1856–65 Baudelaire, eminent precursor of the symbolists, helped introduce Poe to Europe with a remarkably rich translation of the American's works. Baudelaire recognized in Poe's dictum "The orange ray of the spectrum and the buzz of the gnat . . . affect me with nearly similar sensations" his own theory on the mystic accord of the senses and symbols. Later Baudelaire would write in his poem "Correspondances": "Les parfums, les couleurs, et les sons se répondent (Scents, colors, and sounds interrelate)." The symbolists Verlaine, Mallarmé, and Rimbaud were also in Poe's debt; Mallarmé's translation of "The Raven" appeared in 1875, with striking lithographs by Edouard Manet. Above is Manet's version of "Suddenly there came a tapping"; opposite, his Raven sits "on the pallid bust of Pallas."

Gustave Doré, the French illustrator who excelled in weird and fantastic scenes, was one of the many artists inspired by Poe. His illustrations for "The Raven," like those by Manet, exploit the poem's atmosphere of shadowplay. Here, Doré seems to suggest the lover's futile clasping after Lenore.

supernatural world of horrible incidents. For the most part, in spite of his gnawing poverty, Poe looked for fame rather than popularity. "I love fame—I dote on it—I idolize it—," he once said, "I would drink to the very dregs the glorious intoxication." It was fourteen years before he again attempted to publish a volume of his verse.

All but destitute, he went to live with his widowed aunt, Mrs. Maria Clemm, and her small daughter Virginia. He was now determined to try fiction. In the autumn of 1833, a few months after he had written Allan that he was "absolutely perishing for want of aid," Poe won $50 in a prize contest for the best short story submitted to a local magazine, and then sold another story to *Godey's Lady's Book* for a few additional dollars. As his stories were published he was also winning something of a reputation as a man of letters, sufficient to provide him in 1835 with the first of a series of jobs as a magazine editor in Richmond, Baltimore, Philadelphia, and New York.

Over the next ten years Poe alternated between periods of intense industry and of profound melancholy that led him, almost disastrously at times, to drink. In his first editorial job, with the *Southern Literary Messenger* in Richmond, within eighteen months he wrote eighty-three book reviews and contributed six poems, four essays, and three short stories before he was fired, for a second and last time, for drunkenness. While he held the job he married his thirteen-year-old cousin Virginia. (All his life he referred to his childbride as "Sissy.")

Poe proved to have a keen journalistic sense of what would interest and excite his magazine public. Under his editorship the circulation of the magazine increased sevenfold. He spent even less time five years later as editor of *Graham's Magazine* (where he was paid a magnificent $800 a year plus a small page rate for his own contributions), but even during that short period raised its circulation from 5,500 to an unheard of 40,000 before he quit the job.

By then Poe had become a force in American letters, better known as a critic than as an author. In his reviews he applied personal and rigorous standards that made it seem to one historian as though this department of American literature only began with Poe. He himself criticized the general run of American criticism, which, he wrote in opening one review, had moved from an earlier "servile deference to British critical dicta" to its current "gross paradox of liking a stupid book the better, because, sure enough, its stupidity is American." He had no patience with incompetent or trivial writing, and he used an acid pen in dismissing it as such. He won the reputation of a literary hatchet man, both respected and feared, even hated, for his penetrating judgments. Poe also had his particular prejudices, which were revealed at their sorriest when he waged his private "war" against Henry Wadsworth Longfellow, whom he harshly accused of plagiarism. He also complained of Longfellow's "didactic and conventional habit of thinking," so alien to Poe's own approach to literature. Here, however, he was quarreling with principles, not with the man, which Longfellow himself was one of the few to understand. But, for these criticisms Poe earned the enmity of more than one New England publisher.

The last ten years of Poe's life were filled with accomplishment and misery.

He produced some of his best critical analyses. His review of Nathaniel Hawthorn's *Twice-Told Tales,* which he admired for their purity and their originality, was an early landmark in American criticism. In this he digressed to expound his theory of the short story, a form he developed with such remarkable success. "A skillful literary artist has constructed a tale. If wise, he has not fashioned his thoughts to accommodate his incidents; but having conceived, with deliberate care, a certain unique or single *effect* to be wrought out, he then invents such incidents—he then combines such events as may best aid him in establishing this preconceived effect. If his very initial sentence tend not to the outbringing of this effect, then he has failed in his first step. In the whole composition there should be no word written, of which the tendency, direct or indirect, is not to the one pre-established design. And by such means, with such care and skill, a picture is at length printed which leaves in the mind of him who contemplates it with a kindred art, a sense of the fullest satisfaction." Another of his reviews won him the applause of Charles Dickens. A pirated version of Dickens' *Barnaby Rudge* was appearing in America in installments, heralding a visit by the great Boz himself. Before the last section was printed Poe, to almost everyone's astonishment, had by shrewed deduction untangled the plot and successfully predicted the outcome of the story. When Dickens arrived in America to be lionized and fêted at every hand, he, too, was astonished and took time from his crowded schedule to have a long talk with Poe about the matter, presumably including a discussion of his American critic's technique in divining the conclusion of *Barnaby Rudge.*

It was during the earlier half of that last decade that Poe perfected his own art in the telling of murder mysteries and detective stories. If he did not invent this kind of short story, Poe developed it into a distinct type of fiction in such tales as "The Murders in the Rue Morgue," "The Purloined Letter," "The Pit and the Pendulum," and other thrillers that have an enduring place in the history of American literature. They remain the most popular of Poe's tales, and it was they that to the exclusion of all other fiction Abraham Lincoln liked to read.

Poe's all but infallible detective, C. Auguste Dupin, stands as the prototype of a long line of intellectual amateur sleuths whose activities in today's pocket books, as Leslie A. Fiedler has observed, entertain tired presidents, harried executives, and others "in search of a minor vice with no unpleasant consequences." Years after Poe's death, Sir Arthur Conan Doyle, the "father" of Sherlock Holmes, declared that "if modern authors paid only ten per cent of their debt to Poe for the erection of a statue in his honor he would have a greater monument than the Cheops. He is not only the root, but one of the flowers on his own stem."

Among such tales of ratiocination, as they are called, in which methodical and logical reasoning solves the most intricate mystery, Poe's "The Gold Bug," published in 1843, won the greatest popular success—and a welcome prize of $100. But he was running out of editorial jobs, his wife Virginia had suffered a hemorrhage that foretold her early death, and Poe himself was suffering from bouts with alcohol. With only a few dollars in his pocket he moved to New York to attempt to change his luck. He had contrived his fa-

The English illustrator Aubrey Beardsley, who was once called "The Fra Angelico of Satanism," was master of a perverse, morbid art, remarkably akin to Poe's grotesqueries. Reproduced here is a Beardsley drawing (from an 1898 edition of Poe) of "The Black Cat," with its horrible one-eyed face.

mous—or infamous—"Balloon Hoax," a fictitious account of an aerial crossing of the Atlantic that was published "straight" in the New York *Sun* and that brought mobs of gullible and excited people swarming to the newspaper's offices for further details. There, too, he soon published "The Raven" which, rather oddly, it now seems, created an overnight sensation. As Poe himself observed, "the bird beat the bug . . . all hollow"—and it earned him another $5 or $10.

As do so many of his other poems, "The Raven" tells that old melancholy story, as from the lips of a bereaved lover, of the death of a beautiful woman. At the time Virginia was slowly dying in their little cottage in Fordham, and Poe had never been so desperate. "I have been driven to the very gates of despair more dreadful than death," he wrote a friend in 1846, "and I have not even one friend, out *(side)* my family with whom to advise." That winter the whole Poe family suffered acutely from cold and hunger. Then in January, 1847, his beloved "Sissy" died and Poe's spirit touched the depths. He tried suicide by taking laudanum, but it only served as an emetic. "For more than ten days I was totally deranged," he wrote after another seizure of melancholy. . . . All was hallucination, arising from an attack which I had never before experienced—an attack of *mania-a-potu* [*delirium tremens*]."

Yet, shortly before his death, he still found the means to compose some of his more memorable poems, such as "Ulalume" and "Annabel Lee," in which he returned to his favored theme. It almost seems as if for Poe the only true marriage bed was the grave of those beautiful women whose death he lamented in his poetry, whose mortal lovers await their spectral visits or descend into the tomb to embrace their ghostly remains—as in "Annabel Lee":

> And so, all the night-tide, I lie down by the side
> Of my darling, my darling, my life, and my bride,
> In the sepulcher there by the sea,
> In her tomb by the sounding sea.

Within months of the publication of that poem, and of "The Bells" which appeared in print the same year, Poe went to his own tragic grave. There he lay for twenty-six years before a tombstone was raised to mark the spot—the tombstone of which Bryant in his righteousness could not approve; Walt Whitman was the only prominent American to attend that ceremony.

All his life Poe had been a lonely "aristocrat of the spirit," a living image of the alienated artist, as posterity has regarded him not always kindly. The loneliness he knew in his life attended his death. There were only four shivering mourners at his funeral on that cold October day in 1849. That same day the New York *Journal of Commerce* concluded an editorial on Poe's life and death: "It will not be denied, even by his enemies, that Mr. Poe was a man of great ability,—and all other recollections of him will be lost now, and buried with him in the grave. We hope he has found rest, for he needed it." But all those other recollections were not interred with his corpse. They remain important parts of the durable legend Poe himself helped to make of his life and his career. He never created such a memorable fictional character as Natty Bumppo, but in his own right he filled a comparable role—half man, half myth.

WASHINGTON IRVING'S WORLD

Washington Irving, who once considered making painting his career and who viewed the world through a painter's eyes, was an avid sketcher. However, his greatest visions are those he rendered in his vivid, painterly prose. Irving's writing, because of its extraordinarily pictorial quality, has always appealed to the artist's imagination. It has inspired generations of illustrators, both American and foreign. On the following pages memorable Irving passages are seen through the eyes of some notable nineteenth- and twentieth-century illustrators.

The Wrath of Peter Stuyvesant, *by Asher Durand*

The War Between the Dutch and the Swedes, *by Charles Loring Elliott*

PETER STUYVESANT
&
ANTHONY THE TRUMPETER

The headstrong Peter Stuyvesant and "the jolly, robustious trumpeter named Anthony Van Corlear" have been immortalized on canvas by many American artists:

Opposite, top, Stuyvesant learns from his faithful emissary, Anthony, that New Sweden would not surrender.

The painting opposite, below, shows the battle between the Dutch and the Swedes—"a most horrible battle."

Below, Stuyvesant discovers how Anthony the Trumpeter has "acquired prodigious favor in the eyes of the women." "Marry, sir," replies Anthony, "like many a great man before me, simply by sounding my own trumpet."

Anthony Van Corlear Brought into the Presence of Peter Stuyvesant, *by John Quidor*

A detail from Peter Stuyvesant's Army Entering New Amsterdam, *by the 19th-century Irish genre artist William Mulready, illustrates Knickerbocker's parody of an actual event—the Dutch campaign of 1655 against the Swedish-held forts on the Delaware River. "The lion-hearted Peter" (at far left with peg leg) reviews his "mighty host of warriors." "First of all came the Van Bummels, who . . . were short fat*

men, wearing exceeding large trunk-breeches . . . the first inventors of suppawn, or mush and milk. Close
in their rear marched the Van Vlotens, of Kaatskill, horrible quaffers of new cider, and arrant braggarts
in their liquor. After them came the Van Pelts of Groodt Esopus, dexterous horsemen . . . mighty hunters
of minks and muskrats. . . . Then the Van Nests of Kinderhoeck, valiant robbers of bird's-nests. . . ."

TWO DREAMERS

Maxfield Parrish created this image of the "sage Oloffe" dreaming of New York's glorious future for a 1900 edition of the History. "—And lo, the good St. Nicholas . . . sat himself down and smoked . . . the smoke from his pipe ascended into the air and spread like a cloud overhead. And Oloffe . . . hastened and climbed up to the top of one of the tallest trees . . . he fancied that the great volume of smoke assumed a variety of marvellous forms, where in dim obscurity he saw shadowed out palaces and domes and lofty spires. . . ."

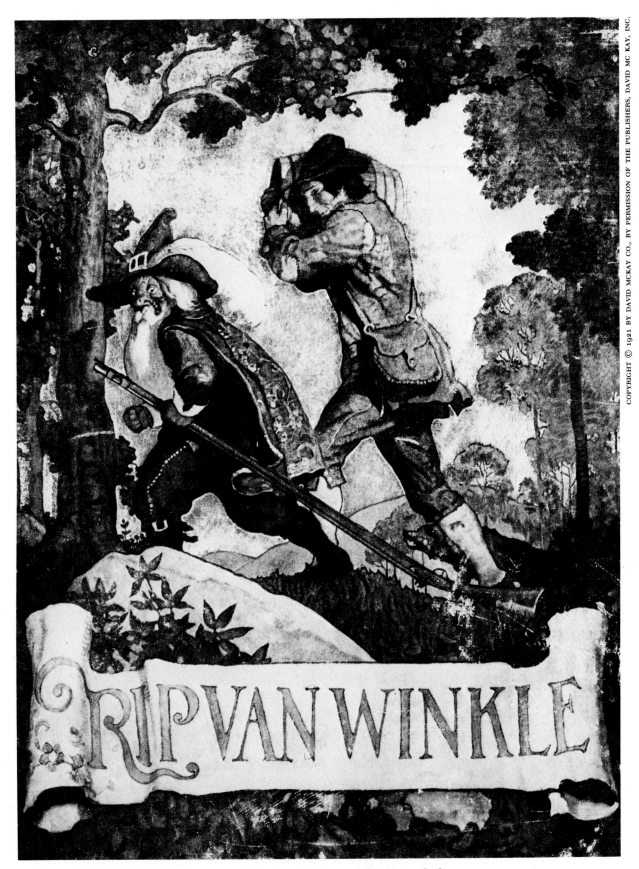

N. C. Wyeth produced this illustration of Rip Van Winkle, ambling through the "Kaatskills" in the company of a stranger—"a short square-built old fellow, with thick bushy hair, and a grizzled beard. His dress was of the antique Dutch fashion:" his breeches "decorated with rows of buttons down the sides. . . . He bore on his shoulder a stout keg, that seemed full of liquor, and made signs for Rip to approach and assist him with the load. . . . Rip complied . . . and mutually relieving one another, they clambered up a narrow gully to a hollow. . . ."

The Headless Horseman, *by George W. Jenkinson*

The above painting depicts the dramatic and famous scene in which the pumpkin-bearing Brom Bones, posing as the "headless horseman," puts to flight Ichabod Crane, his rival for the love of the rich and beautiful Katrina Van Tassel. "Another convulsive kick in the ribs and old Gunpowder sprang upon the bridge; he thundered over the resounding planks; he gained the opposite side; and now Ichabod cast a look behind to see if his pursuer should vanish, according to the rule, in a flash of fire and brimstone. Just then he saw the goblin rising in his stirrups, and in the very act of hurling his head at him."

THE LEGEND
OF
SLEEPY HOLLOW

The courtship of the lovely Katrina by schoolmaster Crane is depicted at right. *"Katrina Van Tassel, the daughter and only child of a substantial Dutch farmer . . . was a blooming lass of fresh eighteen; plump as a partridge; ripe and melting and rosy-cheeked . . . and universally famed, not merely for her beauty, but her vast expectations. She was withal a little of a coquette. . . . She wore . . . a provokingly short petticoat . . . Ichabod Crane had a soft and foolish heart towards the sex; and it is not to be wondered at, that so tempting a morsel soon found favor in his eyes; more especially after he had visited her in her paternal mansion."*

Irving described his beloved Sleepy Hollow as a "sequestered glen" that "is one of the quietest places in the whole world." It is fitting that the genial master of "Sunnyside" is buried in the cemetery of the Old Dutch Church at Sleepy Hollow, Tarrytown, depicted in the late 19th-century water color reproduced below.

Katrina Van Tassel and Ichabod Crane, *by Daniel Huntington*

View of the Old Dutch Church at Sleepy Hollow

Gnomes, *by Arthur Rackham*

116

The Christmas Dinner, *by Cecil Aldin*

The Sketch Book, *which Irving published under the pen name "Geoffrey Crayon, Gent.," was the writer's equivalent of an artist's portfolio or sketch book. It contained favorites such as "Rip Van Winkle" and "The Legend of Sleepy Hollow," as well as many essays on English life. The pictorial capacities of Irving's whimsical description of the gnomes of Rip Van Winkle's dream fired the imagination of Arthur Rackham, the noted English illustrator and water colorist, whose rakish imps are reproduced opposite. "Passing through the ravine, [Rip and the stranger] came to a hollow, like a small amphitheatre, surrounded by perpendicular precipices. . . . On a level spot in the center was a company of odd-looking personages playing at ninepins. They were dressed in a quaint outlandish fashion; some wore short doublets, others jerkins, with long knives in their belts, and most of them had enormous breeches of similar style with that of the guide's. Their visages, too, were peculiar; one had a large beard, broad face, and small piggish eyes, the face of another seemed to consist entirely of nose, and was surmounted by a white sugarloaf hat, set off with a little red cock's tail. They all had beards of various shapes and colors. There was one who seemed to be the commander. He was a stout old gentleman, with a weather-beaten countenance; he wore a laced doublet . . . high-crowned hat and feather, red stockings, and high-heeled shoes, with roses in them. . . ."*

In The Christmas Dinner, *originally published in* The Sketch Book, *Irving described for the American public the bounteous Christmases celebrated in English manor houses. In the drawing opposite, British artist Cecil Aldin has perfectly captured the atmosphere of the country squire's lavish Christmas banquet, as rendered in Irving's prose. "The dinner was served up in the great hall, where the Squire always held his Christmas banquet. A blazing, crackling fire of logs had been heaped on to warm the spacious apartment. . . . We were ushered into this banqueting scene with the sound of minstrelsy, the old harper being seated on a stool beside the fireplace . . . twanging his instrument."*

Anthony the Trumpeter, *of Knickerbocker's* History *fame, inspired English artists, as seen at right.*

Anthony the Trumpeter Drowning, *by George Cruikshank*

Anthony the Trumpeter Setting off to the Wars, *by Leslie*

Fortifying Breed's Hill in the Night, *by F. O. C. Darley*

HISTORY
&
ADVENTURE

The Court of Myrtles.

The Court of Myrtles, *by Joseph Rennell*

Many of Irving's writings were pioneer works devoted to themes and patterns that would be followed by later American romantic writers. For example, he explored the field of biographies of national heroes, and his Life of George Washington *(1855–59) helped develop the popular legend of the first President as the Father of His Country.*

One of the delightful products of Irving's long sojourn in Spain was The Alhambra *(1832), a romantic tale of history and adventure. The writer, who lived in the Alhambra in 1829, wrote: "To the traveler imbued with a feeling for the historical and poetical, so inseparably intertwined in the annals of romantic Spain, the Alhambra is as much an object of devotion as is the Caaba to all true Moslems.... It was the royal abode of the Moorish kings, where, surrounded with the splendors and refinements of Asiatic luxury, they held dominion over what they vaunted as a terrestrial paradise, and made their last stand for empire in Spain.... Externally it is a rude congregation of towers and battlements ... giving little promise of the grace and beauty which prevail within."*

With The Adventures of Captain Bonneville, U.S.A., *Irving became one of the first American writers to "open" the West in a literary sense. Opposite, Bonneville is shown arriving at "a part of the river which filled him with astonishment...."*

118

Captain Bonneville, *by Henry Sandham*

NEW VOICES
IN THE LAND

The Massachusettts State House (opposite), atop Boston's Beacon Hill, was built in 1795–98 after the designs of Charles Bulfinch, Boston's gentleman architect. Oliver Wendell Holmes, with characteristic Brahmin chauvinism, asserted, "Boston State-House is the hub of the solar system." And Henry James described its gilded dome as being "high in the air; poised in the right place over everything that clustered below; the most felicitous object in Boston."

As the nineteenth century advanced, there was no question that New York had become the "great commercial emporium" of the United States, the largest, most populous, busiest, and wealthiest city in the land. However, although Boston lagged in the matter of size, that city had astonishing enterprise of its own. Indeed, until the 1840's Boston merchants still owned more ships than New York's, for example, and a large part of New York's commerce was even then carried upon Massachusetts' account or in Massachusetts' vessels.

Those Yankee vessels were engaged in a global traffic that brought cargoes from distant markets to exchange them for domestic products and to distribute them wherever they were wanted. Sugar from Cuba was carried off to Sweden and Russia; Peruvian bark was transshipped at Boston to Tunis in North Africa; hides from California ("California bank notes") were exchanged for shoes made at Lynn, Massachusetts, to be sold back in California; shirtings made at the Lowell mills were shipped to Montevideo, Uruguay.

In the course of those far-ranging transactions, along with freight, ideas were exchanged—exotic notions, some of them, that fed the Yankee intellect and imagination. As he studied the Indian philosophers in his cabin at Walden Pond, Henry David Thoreau was bemused by the prospect of Irish laborers from Boston come to harvest ice from nearby ponds to be sent for sale here and there about the world (India among them), more often than not to the most outlandish places where such a luxury had been unheard of. (In some of these places it was asked whether ice grew on trees or bushes.) Thoreau reflected in *Walden:*

> Thus it appears that the sweltering inhabitants . . . of Bombay and Calcutta, drink at my well. In the morning I bathe my intellect in the stupendous and cosmogonal philosophy of the Bhagvat-Geeta . . . I lay down the book and go to my well for water, and lo! there I meet the servant of the Bramin . . . come to draw water for his master. . . . The pure Walden water is mingled with the sacred water of the Ganges. With the favoring winds it is wafted past the sight of the fabulous islands of Atlantis and the Hesperides, makes the periplus of Hanno, and, floating

by Ternate and Tidore and the mouth of the Persian Gulf, melts in the tropic gales of the Indian seas, and is landed in ports of which Alexander only heard the names.

For a while, at least, good Bostonians could be persuaded that their city was close to the center of the universe, closer at least than New York was. As Oliver Wendell Holmes genially reminded his readers in *The Autocrat of the Breakfast Table* (1858), the State House on Beacon Hill, was, indeed, "the hub of the solar system." That peculiar cultural eminence was a recent development when Holmes coined his hyperbole. For almost a generation after the Revolution Massachusetts had suffered what Charles Francis Adams in later years called its "ice age"—a period of sterile conservatism in matters of the mind, at least in comparison with earlier accomplishments (and subsequent ones). The region was the bastion of Federalism in a nation moving headlong toward democracy. During that time, Ralph Waldo Emerson recalled, "there was not a book, a speech, or a thought in the State." But then, almost miraculously it seems, followed a generation in which the Yankee genius came suddenly to full flower. At the time Holmes wrote, almost within the shadow of the State House could be found those authors, scholars, poets, and reformers who formed a unique galaxy of talents and temperaments— men and women much given to improving themselves, and by their work, improving others. Neither before nor since has this country seen such a concentration of brilliant intellects.

From New York not Irving or Cooper or Poe could see much good in New Englanders. In his Knickerbocker *History* Irving lampooned his Connecticut Yankee neighbors as crass, unscrupulous traders, men of inferior stature whom the redoubtable Stoffel Brinkerhoff easily bested in the great "Oyster War." Cooper labeled Bostonians sober-sided, self-righteous provincials whose very accent annoyed him and whose "invasion" of the Mohawk valley so defiled that pleasant countryside. Poe referred to Boston, his birthplace, as "Frogpondium," a puddle of a place whose spokesmen, particularly the editors of *The North American Review*, he held guilty of the narrowest regionalism and of egregious self-admiration. Of one of James Russell Lowell's contributions to that periodical, Poe wrote in a critical rage, "All whom he praises are Bostonians; other writers are barbarians." And Poe could not abide the high-mindedness and the "mysticism" of Ralph Waldo Emerson. (In his turn, on the occasion of a visit to New York in 1842, Emerson fancied that he found "lines of latitude & longitude which sever the mind of New York . . . from New England. All our questions seem new to them who live here.")

Those judgments of the New Yorkers may reflect a provincialism of their own, but Poe's animadversions touch on a significant point. The spirit of Puritanism lingered over the New England scene long after the old religious orthodoxies had given way to a more rationalized theology. By the early years of the nineteenth century the Unitarians had delivered man from his burden of total depravity, from the awful predestined fate outlined by Calvinist tenets, and given him a reasonable faith in his own worth, with a promise of Heaven in the bargain. But even with the tyranny of the old theology removed, the moral fervor ingrained in the Yankee character persisted. The

Ralph Waldo Emerson, depicted in an engraving, was an optimist, especially in later life, when his friend Professor Charles Eliot Norton observed: "To him this is the best of all possible worlds, and the best of all possible times. He refuses to believe in disorder or evil. . . . But such inveterate and persistent optimism. . . . is dangerous doctrine for a people."

message was pronounced with different accents better suited to the changing times, but it was delivered in a familiar strain of religious earnestness that was hardly less urgent in its way than the sermons of Jonathan Edwards had been.

For Poe, writing was a special art and an end in itself. To use literature for teaching moral lessons and for spiritual exhortation, as Emerson was doing, was utterly alien to his disposition. Yet it was just this aspect of Emerson's work that made him a major spokesman for his generation. Those who lived their mature lives during the several decades preceding the Civil War found in Emerson's optimism and cheerfulness, his pleas for self-confidence and self-reliance, a perfect prescription for the times. The young democracy was fairly bursting with pride in its accomplishments, eagerly looking to a future of ever greater fulfillments, and with words of gentle wisdom Emerson applauded that spirit and justified it. "One cannot look on the freedom of this country, in connection with its youth," he wrote, "without a presentment that here shall laws and institutions exist in some proportion to the majesty of Nature. . . . It is a country of beginnings, of projects, of vast designs and expectations. It has no past: all has an onward and prospective look."

Emerson spoke as a respected seer; his feet were firmly placed on moral ground, his eyes lifted to the infinite potential for good works that he saw in the nature of man. Emerson's forebears had been Puritan clergymen for generations; his father was a Unitarian minister; and after attending divinity school Emerson himself accepted a Unitarian ministry, only to abandon it when he realized he could not accept the orthodoxies of even that more liberal faith. "It is the best part of the man," he wrote in his journal, "that revolts most against being a minister. His good revolts from official goodness." Emerson would confirm the complete freedom of the soul and of the mind, casting aside all conformity. "Whoso would be a man, must be a nonconformist," he proclaimed. In 1838 he delivered an address at the Harvard Divinity School in which, before an unsuspecting audience, he attacked all formal religion and championed intuitive spiritual experience. The talk aroused so much indignation (it was taken to mean he had repudiated Christianity) that he was not again invited to speak at Harvard until twenty-nine years later. By then his reputation, abroad as well as at home, had grown to a towering height, and in 1866 he had been granted a Doctor of Laws degree.

Although Emerson banished from his thoughts the fear of sin and the terror of the Day of Judgment that had so miserably plagued his ancestors, some strain of essential Puritanism clung to his marrow. On one occasion he went to see the sensational ballet dancer Fanny Elssler perform in Boston. However much he may have enjoyed the entertainment, he reflected that the theatre was not "the safest resort for college boys who have left metaphysics, conic sections, or Tacitus to see these tripping satin slippers." For, he added, "they may not forget this graceful, silvery swimmer when they have retreated again to their baccalaureate cells." As Poe so vehemently assented, Emerson could not always or easily disassociate his artistic criticism from moral criticism.

However, that is an interesting but only incidental sidelight on Emerson's broader views on man, on American democracy, and on the whole universe.

The far-famed Viennese ballerina Fanny Elssler made her American debut in 1840. "The perfection of grace," wrote an admiring critic, "attended every attitude; the airiness of gossamer every step."

123

It is hardly possible to understand nineteenth-century America without coming to terms with Ralph Waldo Emerson. What he wrote could not have been written anywhere else in the world; one needs to know little of America to comprehend his writings. His roots were solidly planted in American soil, but he gathered his inspirations from sources both far and near, and he aimed his thoughts at levels that were beyond time and place. He neither imitated nor rejected European models, but by saying what he felt had to be said, and by saying it in his own way, he turned American literature from its provincial backwaters out into the main current of world literature. His works can be placed on the shelf next to Montaigne's (which were on his own bookshelf) without any sense of disparity.

Emerson was an indefatigable journal-keeper. From his journals he drew material for his lectures and talks, and from these he wrote his essays. In his first formal publication, *Nature*, issued anonymously in 1836 and based on earlier lectures, he outlined the main principles of transcendentalism, a philosophical and partly religious movement that was to flourish in New England for the next quarter of a century and that affected nearly all the important writers of that time and region—and beyond. He was preaching the gospel of a new faith; transcendentalism was religious in that it was both an extension of and a departure from Unitarianism. But it was a movement of varied stripes that formed no simple pattern. Basically, it held the romantic view that individual intuition was the highest form of knowledge and that God, or the Deity, was immanent in nature. Thus it reached an almost mystical belief in individualism and in the complete, inherent harmony of the natural world. "Standing on the bare ground," Emerson wrote, "—my head bathed by the blithe air, and uplifted into infinite space,—all mean egotism vanishes. I become a transparent eyeball; I am nothing; I see all; the currents of the Universal Being circulate through me; I am part or parcel of God." Occasionally, Emerson's mysticism could be mystifying—and not only to Poe. "Father Taylor," as the ex-seafaring minister Edward Thompson Taylor was affectionately known, wrote: "Mr. Emerson is one of the sweetest creatures God every made; there is a screw loose somewhere in the machinery, yet I cannot tell where it is, for I never heard it jar. He must go to heaven when he dies, for if he went to hell, the devil would not know what to do with him. But he knows no more of the religion of the New Testament than Balaam's ass did of the principles of Hebrew grammar."

Although the origins of transcendentalism went back to European philosophy and speculation, in New England it was shaped by the Puritan tradition,

An 1841 drawing of a lyceum lecture at New York's Clinton Hall; according to Mayor Philip Hone, "lectures are all the vogue, and the theatres are flat on their backs."

by the special character of American experience, by the current tide of romanticism, and by the democratic ideal as that had been formulated and observed in America. In his own exposition of transcendentalism, Emerson wove these sometimes contradictory influences into a coherent statement of national aspiration and interest. To many thoughtful persons of his time he seemed to be heading a spiritual and cultural revolution.

In 1837 Emerson amplified the message of *Nature* in a talk before the Harvard chapter of the Phi Beta Kappa Society, calling for America's freedom from European cultural leadership. "The millions that around us are rushing into life," he said, "cannot always be fed on the sere remains of foreign harvests. Events, actions arise, that must be sung, that will sing themselves. Who can doubt that poetry will revive and lead in a new age, as the star in the constellation Harp, which now flames in our zenith, astronomers announce, shall one day be the pole-star for a thousand years? . . . We will walk on our own feet; we will work with our own hands; we will speak our own minds. . . . A nation of men will for the first time exist, because each believes himself inspired by the Divine Soul which also inspires men." Jacksonian democracy could hardly ask for a more sublime apologist. (Emerson preferred the principles of the Democrats, but he thought the Whigs had the best men.)

James Russell Lowell hailed the address as "an event without any former parallel in our literary annals." Oliver Wendell Holmes called it "our intellectual Declaration of Independence." Emerson himself acknowledged "the progress of a revolution" in New England life, but he claimed only to announce it, not to lead it. Long since grown used to concepts of individualism, of equalitarianism, and of chauvinistic Americanism, we cannot easily recapture the freshness of Emerson's message when it was first delivered.

People swarmed to hear him lecture from his carefully prepared manuscripts. His "lapidary" style of composition, as he himself called it, was immensely quotable, and his utterances became watchwords for the day, and for the future: "Hitch your wagon to a star," "Let us be silent—so we may hear the whispers of the gods," "Every man has a call to do something unique," "Give me health and a day, and I will make the pomp of emperors ridiculous," "He builded better than he knew," "A foolish consistency is the hobgoblin of little minds," and so on. Myriad memorable phrases of such nature, rich with affirmation, fell from his lips as he toured about the lyceum circuit, taking the new steam-driven trains as need be to meet his schedule of one-night stands.

His journals remained Emerson's almost inexhaustible source of materials

New York's luxurious Astor House Hotel, which opened its doors in 1836, boasted an elegant reading room (depicted in Nicolino Calyo's painting of 1840) to please its news-hungry clientele. America's addiction to newspapers prompted one English visitor to write: "You are amazed at the energy of the newsboys . . . as they rush hither and thither with their arms full of wisdom, at a penny an instalment." Emerson held that the daily paper, with its "scraps of science, of thought, of poetry," offered an education as well as trash.

for the lectures. "The notes I collect in the course of a year," he explained in a letter to a friend, "are so miscellaneous that when our people grow rabid for lectures, as they do periodically about December, I huddle all my old almanacks together & look in the encyclopaedia for the amplest cloak of a name whose folds will reach unto & cover extreme & fantastic things." At Cincinnati a vast, "lecture hungry" assembly sat for two hours in anticipation of his talk to come. At times, however, the "gate" was a mere $10. Nevertheless, by this fatiguing routine he supplemented his meager income and made ends meet. (Emerson once told a friend that the first money he had received from any of his writings was a check, sent him in 1850, which his publisher had to show him how to endorse.)

To a great majority of Americans of the 1840's Emerson was probably better known as a lyceum lecturer than as a man of letters. The lyceum movement had been organized in 1826 to satisfy a swelling demand for adult education. That zeal for self-improvement amounted to a virtual crusade against ignorance during the mid-years of the century. In 1841 the elegant diarist Philip Hone observed that the theatres of New York were deserted—"flat on their backs"—while overflowing crowds stormed the several large lecture halls of the city. For Americans, wrote one astonished English visitor, going to lectures seemed to be the next most important duty after going to church on Sundays.

At the Lowell textile mills the blooming young ladies from neighboring farms who tended the spindles were offered such cultural opportunities that Anthony Trollope referred to the industrial establishment as "a philanthropical manufacturing college." When one of his countrymen went there to lecture and announced he would cut his fee, he was told by those proud and independent girls that they would come at the regular price—"on the same footing as other ladies"—or not at all.

In his private, individual pursuit of education Elihu Burritt, the "Learned Blacksmith," aimed to "stand in the ranks of the workingmen of New England and beckon them onward and upward to the full stature of intellectual men." He kept a Greek grammar inside his hat to study as he worked at his forge. A sampling from his diary of 1837 reads: "*Monday*, June 18, headache; forty pages Cuvier's Theory of the Earth, sixty-four pages French, eleven hours forging. *Tuesday*, sixty-five lines of Hebrew, thirty pages of French, ten pages Cuvier's Theory, eight lines Syriac, ten ditto Danish, ten ditto Bohemian, nine ditto Polish, fifteen names of stars, ten hours forging. *Wednesday*, twenty-five lines Hebrew, fifty pages of astronomy, eleven hours forging. *Thursday*, fifty-five lines Hebrew, eight ditto Syriac, eleven hours forging. *Friday*, unwell, twelve hours forging." He was twenty-seven years old at the time.

There was little doubt that the American people were becoming increasingly literate. As the century advanced, the spread of educational facilities at all levels gradually turned America into "the land of the general reader." The simplest evidence of this could be found in the American's strong addiction to his newspaper. Journalism became a large and highly competitive enterprise. Emerson thought the ubiquitous newspaper was, at its best, an important instrument in the spread of enlightenment and the safeguarding of liberty. With "scraps of science, of thought, of poetry . . . in the coarsest sheet," he wrote, the daily paper brought the university to every poor man's door. If it also purveyed a fair share of sensational trash, the price was worth it.

In 1834 Emerson had settled in Concord, after a sojourn in Europe where he met Carlyle, Coleridge, Wordsworth, and others. Concord was the home of his forefathers, and there he would spend his remaining productive years. "They who made England, Italy, or Greece venerable in the imagination," he recalled of his homecoming, "did so by sticking fast where they were, like an axis of the earth . . . the soul is no traveller." Concord became his axis. After all, history repeated itself at Concord; Concord could well be one's Rome, one's world. There he enjoyed neighborly association and correspondence with Henry Thoreau, Amos Bronson Alcott, Margaret Fuller, Orestes Brownson, Nathaniel Hawthorne, and others who were more or less engaged in the transcendental movement.

As Emerson was well aware, the transcendental movement and the concomitant excitements that were stirred up within and about it had certain comic aspects. In "Transcendental Wild Oats," from *Silver Pitchers and Independence*, Alcott's daughter Louisa May wrote an entertaining description of her father's cooperative community in Massachusetts, Fruitlands, where, for the brief season they held together, the members led a vegetarian life and strove to achieve "the harmonic development of their physical, intellectual, and moral natures." (The diet at this little utopia was restricted to those "aspiring" vegetables that grow in air; baser ones, like beets and potatoes, that grow downward were forbidden.) "The good Alcott," Carlyle wrote, ". . . bent on saving the world by a return to acorns and the golden age"; and Emerson referred to the older man as a "tedious archangel." On October 30, 1840, Emerson wrote Carlyle, "We are a little wild here with numberless projects of social reform; not a reading man but has a draft of a new Community in his waistcoat pocket. I am gently mad myself."

Another, somewhat less eccentric experiment in cooperative living based on transcendental principles, Brook Farm, near Boston, lasted from 1841 to 1847 before enthusiasm waned and the group dissolved. The formidable blue-stocking author Margaret Fuller participated in that enterprise. Miss Fuller was an extraordinary, aggressive woman under the influence of whose intellect, Emerson conceded, "you stretch your limbs and dilate to your utmost

"Standing on the bare ground, — my head bathed by the blithe air, & uplifted into infinite space, — all mean egotism vanishes. I become a transparent Eyeball." Nature, p. 13.

Poet-painter Christopher Pearse Cranch was an early convert to transcendentalism but never became a devotee of the movement. He poked gentle fun at some transcendental pomposities in a series of caricatures entitled Illustrations of the New Philosophy *and including the literal interpretation of Emerson's "transparent eyeball," shown above. Cranch was a welcome visitor at Brook Farm, shown opposite in a detail from a painting by Josiah Wolcott.*

size." (She herself asserted, "I find no intellect comparable to my own.") In his journal he recorded, "She ever seems to crave somewhat I have not, or have not for her." In the end Margaret contracted a secret marriage in Italy with Marquis Angelo Ossoli and bore him a child before, in 1850, all three were drowned in a shipwreck off Fire Island on the way back to America.

Departures into utopianism, such as Fruitlands and Brook Farm, had little appeal for Emerson. He described Brook Farm as "the Age of Reason in a patty-pan." "I do not wish to remove from my present prison to a prison a little larger," he wrote. "I wish to break all prisons. I have not yet conquered my own house. . . . Shall I raise the siege of this hencoop, and march baffled away to a pretended siege of Babylon?" He would rather keep a bachelor's hall in hell, he said, than luxuriate in a boarding house in heaven. Beyond that he was enough of a Yankee materialist to believe in competitive industry, in trade, in the rights of property, and even in a natural aristocracy. Any conflict between such interests and his stated ideals could be resolved—transcended—by moral sentiment. More than any other American, Emerson was responsible for adapting Jefferson's vision of an agrarian democracy to the rise of technology and a mass society.

In spite of his contemporary fame as a lecturer and the acclaim given to his essays, Emerson's literary reputation would have been secure had he written nothing but poetry. The best of his poems are as profoundly original as Poe's, although in an entirely different way. Poe experimented with melodic rhythms, Emerson with visual symbols (as had so many Puritan writers of an earlier day). Every schoolchild remembers his "Concord Hymn," written to be sung at the dedication, in 1837, of the Minute Man monument memorializing the battle fought at Concord in April, 1775. Henry Thoreau joined the chorus on the occasion. It begins:

> By the rude bridge that arched the flood,
>   Their flag to April's breeze unfurled,
> Here once the embattled farmers stood
>   And fired the shot heard round the world.

The imagery was richer in his poem "The Snow-Storm," written four years later, and this time fresh from his own experience:

> Announced by all the trumpets of the sky,
> Arrives the snow, and, driving o'er the fields,
> Seems nowhere to alight: the whited air
> Hides hills and woods, the river, and the heaven,
> And veils the farm-house at the garden's end.
> The sled and traveller stopped, the courier's feet
> Delayed, all friends shut out, the housemates sit
> Around the radiant fireplace, enclosed
> In a tumultuous privacy of storm.
>
> Come see the north wind's masonry.
> Out of an unseen quarry evermore
> Furnished with tile, the fierce artificer
> Curves his white bastions with projected roof
> Round every windward stake, or tree, or door.
> Speeding, the myriad-handed, his wild work

In 1858 landscape painter William J. Stillman organized the Philosophers' Camp near Follansbee Pond in the Adirondacks, where Emerson and other learned companions enjoyed a haven for reflection and study close to nature. Stillman captured the idyllic atmosphere of the retreat in the painting reproduced above.

So fanciful, so savage, nought cares he
For number or proportion. Mockingly,
On coop or kennel he hangs Parian wreaths;
A swan-like form invests the hidden thorn;
Fills up the farmer's lane from wall to wall,
Maugre the farmer's sighs; and at the gate
A tapering turret overtops the work.
And when his hours are numbered and the world
Is all his own, retiring, as he were not,
Leaves, when the sun appears, astonished Art
To mimic in slow structures, stone by stone,
Built in an age, the mad wind's night-work,
The frolic architecture of the snow.

Once started, reading or quoting Emerson's poetry can become habit-forming. From an abundance of other temptations one further sample must here suffice, the poem "Fable" in its entirety:

The mountain and the squirrel
Had a quarrel,
And the former called the latter "Little Prig";
Bun replied,
"You are doubtless very big;
But all sorts of things and weather
Must be taken in together,
To make up a year
And a sphere.
And I think it no disgrace
To occupy my place.
If I'm not so large as you,
You are not so small as I,
And not half so spry.
I'll not deny you make
A very pretty squirrel track;
Talents differ; all is well and wisely put;

If I cannot carry forests on my back,
Neither can you crack a nut."

Here, as always, but in an unusually light vein, Emerson views the universe as a cosmic seesaw, with contradictory and opposing forces always in the balance and needing to be offset one against the other. It has been said that he built the eternal contradictions of life into a system.

During the Civil War Emerson played a more prominent part in organized social affairs. But his mental powers were waning, as he recognized in his poem "Terminus," written in 1866–67. "It is time to be old," he said, "To take in sail." His memory started to fail him. He could not remember the word for umbrella, but with good humor referred to it as the thing that "strangers take away." At Longfellow's funeral he could not recall the name of his old friend. "That gentleman was a sweet, beautiful soul," he was heard to say, "but I have entirely forgotten his name."

For more than a score of years, during the time of Emerson's major accomplishments, the idyllic little town of Concord was "the intellectual seed pod of the nation." Here Henry David Thoreau was born; here he lived virtually his entire life; and here he died at the age of forty-five, twenty years before Emerson's own death in 1882. When, in his famous Phi Beta Kappa address at Harvard, delivered the year Thoreau was graduated from that college, Emerson defined what the American scholar must be, it almost seems he had the younger man in his thoughts—a man of fearless independence of mind, "without any hindrance that does not arise out of his own constitution."

With his head full of Greek poetry and Oriental wisdom, his studious eye alert to every detail of the natural world about him, Thoreau was a true scholar, and as Alcott remarked, he was "the independent of independents." At Harvard Thoreau went to chapel in a green coat because the rules required him to wear a black one. (He has been called a Huckleberry Finn who went to Harvard.) In later years he asserted his independency by declaring an individual war against the government when he found its demands unconscionable. "Know all men by these presents," he wrote the town clerk when he refused a command to pay for the support of some clergyman whose sermons he never listened to, "that I Henry Thoreau do not wish to be regarded as a member of any incorporated society which I have not joined." Then, as "a majority of one," he in effect seceded from the state by refusing to pay his poll tax when he felt it supported the cause of slavery. "I simply wish to refuse allegiance to the State," he asserted, "to withdraw and stand aloof from it effectually." As a consequence he went to jail for a night, until, against his wishes, one of his aunts paid his tax for him.

Thoreau's rebelliousness became most vehement as he rose publicly to defend John Brown, who was condemned to hang for the raid at Harpers Ferry. His closest friends, even supporters of abolition, urged Thoreau to desist from such imprudence. But Brown was a man cut to Thoreau's measure, a man prepared to act upon his own innermost convictions, regardless of the consequences. Thoreau had to speak out, passionately and loudly, against what he deemed the injustice being done. It was one of his rare public actions, and the ardor of his message helped move Massachusetts toward an anti-slavery stand.

Henry David Thoreau setting out on one of his excursions—as he called his frequent travels and bucolic ramblings—sketched in 1854 by his Quaker artist-friend, Daniel Ricketson of New Bedford.

131

Thoreau was as decidedly against the slavery of thought, custom, and commerce. He has been called a disciple of Emerson's. He lived with Emerson and his family for several years and was their close neighbor during his lifetime. But he was too much his own man to be anyone's disciple. He was a very complicated person who sought to reduce life to its utmost simplicities. (At a dinner table he was once asked what dish he preferred, and he answered, "the nearest.") A man is really rich, Thoreau observed, only in proportion to the number of things he can afford to do without. He insisted on the practicality of the impractical. Man, he thought, becomes the tool of his tools; he invents improved means to unimproved ends. "Our inventions are wont to be pretty toys," he wrote, "which distract our attention from serious things. . . . We are in great haste to construct a magnetic telegraph from Maine to Texas; but Maine and Texas, it may be, have nothing important to communicate. . . . As if the main object were to talk fast and not to talk sensibly." "The nation itself, with all its so-called internal improvements, which, by the way, are all external and superficial," he concluded, was "an unwieldy and overgrown establishment . . . tripped up by its own traps."

The decade immediately following Thoreau's graduation from Harvard was a booming period in America. Railroads were annihilating old notions of distance; timetables were replacing calendars as a measure of time. The trains, in those early days, were as punctual and inexorable as the fates, and Thoreau noted with surprise that even his more dilatory neighbors learned to be on time at the stations. "Getting left," that colloquialism of a timetable era, was a privation few wished to endure. "Thus," Thoreau concluded, "one well conducted institution regulates a whole country."

Railroads also quickened the development of industry, big business, and high finance, and opened the way to vast new fields of speculation in a day when speculations of all sorts ran riot. They were carriers of a surging material prosperity. With new wealth grew new wants, if not new needs. For many, to get rich quick became first a dream then an awakening possibility. Texas land, California gold, and the Western trade opened the doors to larger fortunes. Intellectual and spiritual activities were subtly affected by these rushing advances, in New England as elsewhere.

But trains were for other people; Thoreau would go only so far as he could walk of a day. It was the quickest way of going where he wanted to go: the most immediate next point of interest. When neighbors suggested he join the gold rush to California, he quizzically wondered "why I might not sink a shaft down to the gold within me, and work that mine." He was dedicated to the search for what was truly essential in his life, no more. His one, declared purpose was "so to love wisdom as to live according to its dictates, a life of simplicity, independence, magnanimity, and trust."

At Harvard, Thoreau remarked, they taught all the branches of knowledge, but "none of the roots." In and about the little hut he built near Walden Pond, near Concord, where he spent a retreat from July 4, 1845, to September 6, 1847, he sought to get at the very roots of his own existence and to test his self-reliance. (Perhaps it was no coincidence that he started that solitary adventure on Independence Day.) Most men, he observed, "live lives of

The representation, above, of Henry Thoreau's self-built cabin at Walden Pond is from a sketch by Thoreau's sister Sophie. It embellished the title page of the first edition of Walden *(1854).*

Thoreau, depicted in a daguerreotype of 1856, was characterized in Bronson Alcott's essay "The Forester," which appeared in the Atlantic *shortly before the outdoorsman's death. "I had never thought," wrote Alcott, "of knowing a man so thoroughly of the country as this friend of mine, and so purely a son of nature. . . . One shall not meet with thoughts invigorating like his often: coming so scented of mountain and field breezes and rippling springs. . . . I know of nothing more creditable to his greatness than the thoughtful regard, approaching to reverence, by which he has held for many years some of the best persons of his time . . . a devotion very rare in these times. . . ."*

quiet desperation." In the woods he determined "to live deliberately, to front only the essential facts of life . . . to live deep and suck out all the marrow of life," to reduce life to its lowest, and thus its highest, terms. Out of his experience there he wrote his most famous book, *Walden*, which was published in 1854 and which remains one of the world's most singular and rewarding travel books. In those two years, lived in utmost simplicity (although he was almost within smelling range of his mother's home cooking, which he shared often enough), Thoreau explored a universe of his own about as thoroughly as any man ever has. "I have travelled a good deal in Concord," he wrote. He also explored the natural world about him at Walden Pond with intense curiosity and piercing observation. He learned its most intimate secrets by "conversing" with woodchucks, among other forms of communion. He watched nature, it was said, like a detective who is to go upon the stand in a courtroom. As Emerson observed, by devoting his genius and love to the fields and hills and waters of his native Concord, Thoreau proved them universal in their revelations.

About this time Nathaniel Hawthorne noted in his journal that "Thorow" (as Hawthorne first spelled the name of the man whom he had recently met) was "a young man with much of wild, original nature still remaining in him, and so far as he is sophisticated, it is in a way and method of his own. He is as ugly as sin, long-nosed, queer-mouthed, and with uncouth and somewhat rustic, although courteous manners, corresponding very well with such an exterior. But his ugliness is of an honest and agreeable fashion, and becomes him much better than beauty. . . . For two or three years back, he has repudiated all regular modes of getting a living, and seems inclined to lead a sort

Nathaniel Hawthorne, painted at the age of thirty-six by Charles Osgood, was, in the words of a contemporary, "a splendidly handsome youth, tall and strong." "He was," as Henry James later wrote, "a beautiful, natural, original genius, and his life had been singularly exempt from worldly preoccupations and vulgar efforts. It has been as pure, as simple, as unsophisticated, as his work. He had lived primarily in his domestic affections, which were of the tenderest kind; and then—without eagerness, without pretension, but with a . . . quiet devotion—in his charming art."

of Indian life. . . . He is a good writer . . . giving the spirit as well as letter of what he sees." Listening to the younger man talk, Hawthorne observed, was "like hearing the wind among the boughs of a forest-tree; and with all this wild freedom, there is high and classic cultivation in him too."

Thoreau was pleased when thousands of wasps chose his hut for shelter when the weather turned cool in October; he cherished the demonic laughter of the loon as it rang across the pond and through the woods; he allowed an "uncommon" mouse that haunted his house to run across his shoes and up his clothes. (He summoned it from the woodwork by playing on his flute.) Once he watched a battle to the death between red and black ants—"red republicans" against "black imperialists." Concord had never seen carnage on such a scale, he reflected. He singled out a red one (likening it to Achilles come to avenge his friend Patroclus), locked in combat with his black adversary, and he placed them under a glass tumbler on his table to watch closely their heroic struggle. "I was myself excited somewhat even as if they had been men," he wrote. "The more you think of it, the less the difference. . . . I have no doubt that it was a principle they fought for, as much as our ancestors, and not to avoid a three-penny tax on their tea; and the results of this battle will be as important and memorable to those whom it concerns as those of the battle of Bunker Hill, at least."

Like Emerson, Thoreau was an inveterate journal-keeper. Of the millions of words he wrote into those journals, relatively few got into print during his own lifetime. *A Week on the Concord and Merrimack Rivers* was published in 1849, but won little attention. His lecture "Civil Disobedience" was casually printed that same year, and in its theme, long afterward, Mahatma Gandhi found ways of passive resistance to what he considered a tyrannical government. *Walden* has had an impact in many lands about the world where it has fed protests against materialism and movements toward liberalism.

In whatever he wrote, Thoreau was one of the first Americans to try for a native idiom, although with a highly personal accent. He wrote more straight-forwardly than Emerson and with a warmth the older man could not match. But his criticism of society, his ecological notions, his studied appreciation of nature, were not duly appreciated until nineteenth-century optimism, the vaunted faith in unlimited growth and progress, and the absolute certainty of American's manifest destiny came into question in our own century.

Thoreau's obstinacy was not always endearing. "Henry does not feel him-self except in opposition," Emerson noted in his journal. "He wants a fallacy to expose, a blunder to pillory, requires a little sense of victory, a roll of the drums to call his powers into full exercise." Another friend remarked, "I love Henry, but I cannot like him; and as for taking his arm, I should as soon think of taking the arm of an elm tree." As he lay dying, his pious aunt asked if he had made his peace with God. "Why, Aunt," Thoreau retorted, "I didn't know we had ever quarreled!" When he was gone, Emerson said of his lamented friend that no truer American had ever existed. "The country knows not yet, or in the least part," Emerson wrote, "how great a son it has lost. It seems an injury that he should leave in the midst his broken task which none else can finish, a kind of indignity to so noble a soul that he should depart out of Nature before yet he has been really shown to his peers for what he is. . . . His soul was made for the noblest society; he had in a short life exhausted the capabilities of this world, wherever there is knowledge, wherever there is virtue, wherever there is beauty, he will find a home."

In July, 1842, Nathaniel Hawthorne came to Concord with his wife Sophia Peabody to live in the "Old Manse," the home of Emerson's grandfather and the house where Emerson himself lived for a time and wrote part of *Nature*. As the general "handyman" of the village, Thoreau was charged with helping to put the garden in order for the newcomers. Although the two men were in most respects as different as day and night, Hawthorne and Thoreau enjoyed a sympathetic friendship from the start. Hawthorne's daughter recalled that her father liked Thoreau best of all men in Concord, although their friendship did not have time to ripen fully, for Hawthorne moved away from the village. However, when asked by a New York publisher to approach Thoreau about writing a book, Hawthorne demurred; he thought there was "one chance in a thousand that [Thoreau] might write a most excellent and readable book." His Concord neighbor, Hawthorne averred, was "the most tedious, tiresome, and intolerable—the narrowest and most notional" of persons, whatever his other virtues.

Hawthorne had come to Concord after a year of intermittent residence at Brook Farm, in which he had invested his savings. He had started that experiment in cooperative living with some enthusiasm, which he recorded in his journal. "Could you see us sitting round our table at mealtimes, before the great kitchen fire," he wrote in April, 1841, "you would call it a cheerful sight." Margaret Fuller was also in residence at the time, and Hawthorne reported that she owned a very fractious "transcendental heifer," which was likely to kick over the milk pail and which hooked the other cows and soon made herself ruler of the herd. "This morning I have done wonders," he noted a day later. "Before breakfast, I went out to the barn and began to chop hay for the cattle, and with such 'righteous vehemence,'" he was told, that "in the space of ten minutes I broke the machine." He was then given a "four-pronged instrument" called (as again he was told) a pitchfork. Thus armed, with two other fellow workers he made "a gallant attack upon a heap of manure." (The manure pile was referred to as a gold mine.) "This office being concluded, and I having purified myself," he wrote, "I sit down to finish this letter." However, four months later he concluded, "in a little more than a fortnight I shall be free from my bondage . . . —free to think and feel! . . . Is it a praiseworthy matter that I have spent five golden months in providing food for cows and horses? It is not so." On such a note he awakened from whatever were his utopian dreams.

Hawthorne's earlier sedentary and somewhat solitary life had hardly trained him for such activity under such circumstances. He was born in Salem, Massachusetts, the scion of a long file of New England forebears, the first of whom had arrived in America in 1630—a man, as Hawthorne pictured him, who was "grave, bearded, sable-cloaked and steeple-crowned," and a persecutor of Quakers. That settler's son served as a judge in the Salem witchcraft trials, and upon his head one of his victims pronounced a curse that his descendants blamed for such evils as befell the family thereafter. Hawthorne's own father, a sea captain, died of yellow fever in far-off Surinam when Hawthorne was only four years old. From then on his widowed mother kept largely to her own room in a sort of haunted melancholy, and the child grew up in what he later termed the "cursed habits" of solitude.

In 1825 Hawthorne graduated from Bowdoin College, where he had enjoyed a somewhat convivial undergraduate life, with Henry Wadsworth Longfellow and Franklin Pierce, the future president, as schoolmates. By then Hawthorne had already decided to become a writer. What is considerably more, he intended to write fiction, a form of literary art that did not easily jibe with the Puritan strain that was part of his heritage as well as part of his ambiance. (Speaking of his Puritan ancestors, Hawthorne wrote, "Strong traits of their nature have intertwined themselves with mine.") This was a distinct departure from the New England tradition of writing; novels were still somewhat suspect there at the time. In his preface to *The Scarlet Letter*, his most accomplished work, Hawthorne pays heed to this point: "'What is he?' murmurs one gray shadow of my forefathers to the other. 'A writer of story books! What kind of a business in life,—what mode of glorifying God,

The pretty Sophia Amelia Peabody, painted in 1830 at the age of twenty-one by Chester Harding, was married to Hawthorne in 1842 after a long courtship. "Nothing like our story was ever written—or ever will be—," wrote the ardent suitor to his bride-to-be, "for we shall not feel inclined to make the public our confidant; but if it could be told, methinks it would be such as the angels might delight to hear." Once married, the Hawthornes' life together was paradisiacal—as if they lived in "a perfect Eden."

or being serviceable to mankind in his day and generation,—may that be? Why the degenerate fellow might as well have been a fiddler!'" At another point he asked himself where in his own land, to which he was devoted, he could find the dramatic material that bolsters a good novel. "No author, without a trial," he observed, "can conceive of the difficulty of writing a romance about a country where there is no shadow, no antiquity, no mystery, no picturesque and gloomy wrong, nor anything but a commonplace prosperity, in broad and simple daylight, as is happily the case with my dear native land."

However, Hawthorne overcame such odds, although it took him time to find his way in writing. For a dozen years after his graduation he spent the bulk of his time dreaming, reading, reflecting, and writing small pieces that were sometimes published anonymously. With some exaggeration he told Longfellow, "I have seen so little of the world that I have nothing but thin air to concoct my stories of." At the time, he referred to himself as the most obscure man of letters in America. He also told Longfellow that he had put himself in a dungeon, the key to which he could not find. Even if the door were open, he added, he would be almost afraid to come out into the "living world," as he called it.

He need not have worried, for in those twelve years his peculiar genius gradually ripened and came to flower. In 1837 he published *Twice-Told Tales*, a small collection of stories that had been periodically published over the years and his first important work. He was then thirty-three, and with that publication he realized that he was ready to emerge from his restricted life. Falling in love with Sophia Peabody was a strong incentive for him to come out of the shell he claimed to have made for himself. To better his income he took a job at the Boston Custom House before moving on for the brief spell at Brook Farm. Of his experience at Brook Farm he later reflected, in the words of one of his fictional characters, "no sagacious man will long retain his sagacity, if he live exclusively among reformers and progressive people, without periodically returning into the settled system of things, to correct himself by a new observation from that old standpoint."

It was with such thoughts in mind that he soon moved on for his first, three-year sojourn at Concord, the early years of his idyllic marriage to Sophia, and his quickly formed friendship with Thoreau. He knew Emerson too, of course. At one point the three went skating together, each according to his own style, which in an amusing way reflected the separate nature of these very different individualists. As Hawthorne's daughter remembered the somewhat unlikely scene: "One afternoon, Mr. Emerson and Mr. Thoreau went with [Hawthorne] down the river. Henry Thoreau is an experienced skater, and was figuring dithyrambic dances and Bacchic leaps on the ice—very remarkable, but very ugly, methought. Next him followed Mr. Hawthorne who, wrapped in his cloak, moved like a self-impelled Greek statue, stately and grave. Mr. Emerson closed the line, evidently too weary to hold himself erect, pitching headforemost, half lying on the air."

Hawthorne was not much impressed by Emerson, or by Margaret Fuller and the other transcendentalists of Concord, for that matter. He did not have to go far beyond the threshhold of the "Old Manse," he reflected, to encounter such strange moral cranks as could not be found elsewhere "in a circuit of a

THE OLD MANSE, CONCORD, MASS.

Man's accidents are God's purposes

Sophia & Hawthorne 1843

Nath Hawthorne

This is his study

1843

The smallest twig
leans clear against the sky,
Composed by my wife
and written with her dia-
mond

Inscribed by my
husband at sunset
April 3d 1843
In the gold light   S A H
Sun d

The newlywed Hawthornes went immediately to the "Old Manse" in Concord, Mass., where they lived for three blissful years. Their contentment is expressed in the inscriptions, reproduced above, which they scratched onto one of the tiny window panes in Nathaniel's study with a romantic instrument—Sophia's diamond ring.

thousand miles." Most of them had been attracted to the little village, he wrote, "by the wide-spreading influence of a great original thinker" (meaning Emerson) who lived there. In his turn, Emerson remained blind to Hawthorne's special merits as a writer, and he could not easily penetrate his reserve as a person. "Nathaniel Hawthorne's reputation as a writer is a very pleasing fact," Emerson observed with transcendent complacency, "because his writing is not good for anything, and this is a tribute to the man."

Hawthorne had none of those moral certitudes that Emerson propounded in the bulk of his writing, nor the optimism that led Emerson to see goodness triumphant in the universe about him—that led him to see even evil as but goodness in the making. (Carlyle worried that Emerson could not see the hand of the devil in human affairs.) Hawthorne sensed rather the constant presence of evil as a contending force in human nature. Where Emerson cheerfully reconciled opposites, Hawthorne could find no such harmony as he explored the cavern of the mind; where Emerson made affirmative statements, Hawthorne asked questions he could not answer. It is impossible to conceive of Emerson writing fiction; Hawthorne developed American fiction into a polished literary form of unprecedented originality.

Poe was quick to appreciate Hawthorne's writing. As the Hawthornes were settling down in the "Old Manse" in 1842, *Twice-Told Tales* was reissued with additional material. These, Poe wrote in a long, perceptive critical review, were rich in imagination, invention, creation, and reality. He recognized Hawthorne as a true master of the short story. "Of Mr. Hawthorne's tales," Poe remarked, "we should say, emphatically, that they belong to the highest region of Art—an Art subservient to genius of a very lofty order. . . . The style is purity itself. Force abounds. High imagination gleams from every page. Mr. Hawthorne is a man of truest genius." To a large extent that verdict has been sustained by time.

During this sojourn in Concord, Hawthorne wrote the tales and sketches that were published in 1846 in two volumes as *Mosses from an Old Manse*, a work containing the finest examples of his descriptive prose. In describing the "Old Manse" and its surroundings, Hawthorne refers to the white pond-lilies of a neighboring river:

> It is a marvel whence this perfect flower derives its loveliness and perfume, springing as it does from the black mud over which the river sleeps, and where lurk the slimy eel and speckled frog and the mud turtle, whom continual washing cannot cleanse. It is the very same black mud out of which the yellow lily sucks its obscene life and noisome odor. Thus we see, too, in the world that some persons assimilate only what is ugly and evil from the same moral circumstances which supply good and beautiful results—the fragrances of celestial flowers—to the daily life of others.

But for all his merits as an author, he could not make a living by writing alone, and that year he accepted the post of Surveyor of the Port of Salem, a political appointment that expired in 1849 with a change of administration. The next year he issued his masterpiece, *The Scarlet Letter*. Never entirely satisfied with his tales, Hawthorne had longed "to achieve a novel that should evolve some deep lesson and should possess physical substance enough to stand

alone." With *The Scarlet Letter* he did precisely that.

The theme of the novel was drawn from a tale he had outlined thirteen years earlier, and which, in turn, he had based on a historical incident recorded in John Winthrop's journals. Set in seventeenth-century Salem, it deals with a young woman "with a figure of perfect elegance" and with "dark and abundant hair, so glossy that it threw off the sunshine with a gleam, and a face which, besides being beautiful from regularity of feature and richness of complexion, had the impressiveness belonging to a marked brow and deep black eyes"—a ladylike figure of grace and dignity as she stood before her judges, condemned for the sin of adultery to wear upon her bosom the symbolic, embroidered scarlet letter A; "a woman whose beauty shone out and made a halo of the misfortune and ignominy in which she was enveloped." In a Catholic land, Hawthorne interjected, with her infant at her breast she might have seemed a sacred image of "Divine Maternity, which so many illustrious painters have vied with one another to represent. . . . Here there was a taint of deepest sin in the most sacred quality of human life, working such effect, that the world was only darker for this woman's beauty, and the more lost for the infant that she had borne."

As the tragic story unfolds, its early Puritan setting becomes far less important than the basic moral dilemmas that are common to all times and all places. Here, as in others of his works, the riddles Hawthorne posed were as basic as those put forth by Hamlet, as nettlesome and as unanswerable. Behind the old symbols of Calvinism he looked for some lasting truth. He also sought freedom from the dead hand of the past, from whatever was obsolete and no longer purposeful. *The House of the Seven Gables*, published in 1851, deals with the curse that was laid upon his great-grandfather during the Salem witchcraft trials and that family tradition believed was to plague all the generations of Hawthornes.

The scene of the novel is set in the nineteenth century; here the curse remains on the "House of the Seven Gables." "Shall we never have done with this corpse of the past?" asks Holgrave, a daguerreotyper who is a lodger in the house. "It lies upon the Present like a giant's dead body. In fact, the case is just as if a young giant were compelled to waste all his strength in carrying about the corpse of the old giant, his grandfather, who died a long while ago . . . we must be dead ourselves before we can begin to have our proper influence on our world, which will then be no longer our world, but the world of another generation, with which we shall have no shadow of a right to interfere." To escape that dead hand of the past, Hawthorne somewhat extravagantly recommended that each generation should build anew its houses and its public buildings alike (a practice not uncommon in our own age, but for different reasons).

Hawthorne's literary career was interrupted in 1852 when he sailed for England, his first and only substantial trip outside New England, to serve as American consul at Liverpool. The post was a reward for a campaign biography he had written for Franklin Pierce, now president of the United States. Before returning to a house he had bought in Concord, Hawthorne stayed on for more than a year in Italy and another year in England after his consular term was finished, writing *The Marble Faun*, perhaps his best book after

Scenes from The Scarlet Letter *are here interpreted by two noted 19th-century artists: reproduced above is F. O. C. Darley's drawing of Hester Prynne clutching her infant daughter Pearl to her breast; below is an engraving after George Boughton's painting of Puritan children averting their innocent eyes in the presence of the tragic, beautiful adultress.*

The Scarlet Letter. "New England," he once wrote, "is quite as large a lump of earth as my heart can really take in"; and although the haunting story of *The Marble Faun* is set in contemporary Rome, its relentless inquiry into the nature and problems of sin and evil and their workings on the human conscience intimately relates the romance to Hawthorne's early fiction of the New England scene.

He returned to Concord in 1860 to live four more troubled years, worried by the state of his finances, disturbed by the Civil War then raging, depressed by the death of Thoreau, and dejected by his inability to complete any of his writings in progress. Just before his death he bitterly exclaimed, "I have fallen into a quagmire of disgust and despondency with respect to literary matters. I am tired of my own thoughts and fancies, and my own mode of expressing them." His work was indeed done—and done supremely well. Reviewing Hawthorne's career, Henry James later wrote: "His work will remain; it is too original and exquisite to pass away; among the men of imagination he will always have his niche. No one has had just that vision of life, and no one has had a literary form that more successfully expressed his vision."

In 1850, before his return to Concord, he had lived briefly at Lenox, Massachusetts, in the Berkshire Mountains. There he had had for a neighbor in nearby Pittsfield the New York author Herman Melville. Melville had just read *Mosses from an Old Manse*—apparently his first reading of Hawthorne's works—and was profoundly impressed. In those tales he found the "great power of blackness" that stemmed from the Puritan past and "from whose visitations, in some shape or other, no deeply thinking mind is always and wholly free." His own mind was certainly not free from such blackness, and in this he felt himself a kindred spirit with Hawthorne. Melville was aware that Hawthorne had earlier been blandly admired as "a pleasant writer, with a pleasant style,—a sequestered harmless man, from whom any deep and weighty thing would hardly be anticipated." This was a shallow estimate he could not accept. "Perhaps no writer," Melville wrote in a review for *The Literary World,* "has ever wielded this terrific thought with greater terror than this same harmless Hawthorne."

Melville considered Hawthorne's probings into the mysteries of evil as penetrating as Dante's, his sense of tragic reality comparable to Shakespeare's. If these sound like extravagant compliments, it should be remembered that America was still seeking to demonstrate that its independent native culture was on a level, at least, with those of the world's older societies. Here was the same nationalist spirit that had led to Lowell's exultation over Emerson's Phi Beta Kappa address at Harvard. "Believe me, my friends," Melville wrote in his review, "that men not very much inferior to Shakespeare are this day being born on the banks of the Ohio. . . . It is for the nation's sake, and not for her authors' sake, that I would have America be heedful of the increasing greatness among her writers." At the time Melville was working with agonized intensity to finish his own masterpiece, *Moby Dick* (and Hawthorne was writing *The House of the Seven Gables*). His comments linking Hawthorne with Shakespeare may reflect to a degree Melville's sense of his own creative genius, a vision of the greatness he, too, might achieve. (He had only recently read Shakespeare for the first time and was understandably deeply moved by the experience.)

Melville had not yet met Hawthorne when he wrote his review, but he did meet him, early in August, 1850, before it was in print. The two met under somewhat unusual circumstances. The occasion was a ten-day-long gathering in the Berkshires that included those two authors, Evert Duyckinck, editor of *The Literary World,* Oliver Wendell Holmes, and several others. During a hike up Monument Mountain the distinguished group was caught in a rainstorm, the story goes, and while Holmes opened a bottle of champagne Melville and Hawthorne took shelter under the same rocks. In that brief forced intimacy their shyness with each other gave way to an easier relationship, and for a while thereafter these two stormy souls saw one another frequently. The "soft ravishments" of Hawthorne "spun me round about in a web of dreams," Melville remarked at one point. Here was one man, he thought, who would understand the deep and dark currents that flooded his own thoughts; and he then almost desperately needed the affection of a sympathetic mind. It was a crucial period in his extraordinary career.

Up to that point Melville's life had been rich in adventure, and he had both enjoyed success and suffered failure. He was born in New York City in 1819, a descendant of Dutch and English colonial forebears. His father went bankrupt and died when the boy was twelve years old, leaving Mrs. Melville and her eight children all but destitute. His schooling stopped when he was fifteen, and for a few years thereafter he went to work at various jobs to help support his family. As he approached manhood, Melville took to the sea as a last resort, in 1837 shipping as cabin boy on a crossing to Liverpool and back. The sea, as he later said, was to be his Harvard and Yale. On this first voyage he saw things on shipboard, and he learned things from the streets of Liverpool's squalid slums, that were unheard of in those colleges. His experiences were already carrying him down into the depths of thought that he would continue to explore over the years to come.

About four years after his return from Liverpool, Melville took off for the South Seas on the whaler *Acushnet* out of Fairhaven (opposite New Bedford). In brief outline the story of his travels in the following several years, as he later imaginatively recalled them in his semiautobiographical novels, runs something like this: when, after eighteen months, he tired of the small-scale hell of life on the whaler, Melville jumped ship with a comrade at the Marquesas and there lived for a month in pleasant "captivity" among friendly cannibals in the valley of Typee, an earthly paradise, with a beautiful Polynesian nymph for a companion. "Civilization had given her no veils," Melville reflected, "Christianity had given her no compunctions." He escaped from that romantic bondage by boarding an Australian whaler, which he deserted at Tahiti. There he worked for a while as a laborer in the fields. Next, in Honolulu, he enlisted as an ordinary seaman on the frigate *United States,* from which service he was discharged in Boston in October, 1844, after having witnessed unforgettable brutality and heroism in the course of the fourteen-month voyage.

Melville's education at sea was now complete. He had voyaged as far from his American home as ships could take him. He claimed to have seen things

Herman Melville, portrayed above, was well described by his friend Hawthorne, who wrote: "Melville, as he always does, began to reason of Providence and futurity, and of everything that lies beyond human ken, and informed me that he had 'pretty much made up his mind to be annihilated.' . . . He can neither believe, nor be comfortable in his unbelief; and he is too honest and courageous not to try to do one or the other . . . he has a very high and noble nature. . . ."

An illustration from one of the journals kept by William H. ("Gunner") Meyers—an adventurous artist-seaman who in the 1840's served with the U.S Navy in Pacific waters—depicts a scene of gay abandon between an American sailor and a South Sea maiden. Far from the stern manners and mores of their home towns, whalers and other New England seamen frequently foundered on the temptations of the carefree life in the islands of the South Pacific.

never before seen by white men. He had experienced aspects of hell not known in New York or Boston, and had enjoyed visions of paradise undreamed of in the most exalted views of the transcendentalists. Somewhere between the two, he had known the protracted trials of purgatory, which was closer to his eventual lot in life. Now he would spell out for his countrymen what he had learned on the deep and in "the remotest secret drawers and lockers of the world."

He was only twenty-five, and other than his recent experiences, he had little to go on. Countless American youths had ventured out to sea, or beyond the Western frontier, and come back with tales of dangers undergone and difficulties overcome that made for exciting parlor talk at home. Melville's admiring relatives urged him to write out his own stories, and to everyone's surprise he managed to do that on the first try, in short order and with totally unexpected facility. He named that manuscript, *Typee: A Peep at Polynesian Life*. His older and politically successful brother Gansevoort, off to London on a diplomatic mission, took a draft of the story with him, knowing how important an English imprint could be on the work of an American author and hoping to interest an English publisher. This he did, thanks in part to the helpful persuasion of Washington Irving, fortuitously just back from his mission in Spain. Publication in America followed almost as a matter of course. *Typee* was promoted in New York as "a new work of novel and romantic interest. It abounds with personal adventure, cannibal banquets, groves of coco nuts, coral reefs, tattooed chiefs and bamboo temples; sunny valleys, planted with breadfruit trees, carved canoes dancing on the flashing blue waters, savage woodlands guarded by horrible idols, *heathenish rites and human sacrifices*." That was enough to warm the blood and titillate the fancies of dreaming landmen who, as Melville observed, passed their days "pent up in lath and plaster—tied to counters, nailed to benches, clinched to desks"—except on Sunday, when they posted themselves at the waterfront "fixed in ocean reveries."

The book more than lived up to its notices. Melville told of going swimming with lithe and amphibious native girls who, "like a shoal of dolphins," seized his limbs, tumbled him about, ducked him, and otherwise made sport of his own cumbersome efforts to cope with their wanton wiles—until he had "supernatural visions" dancing before his eyes. At one point Melville hints at his relationship with the seductive pagan nymph Fayaway:

> As I turned the canoe, Fayaway, who was with me, seemed all at once to be struck with some happy idea. With a wild exclamation of delight, she disengaged from her person the ample robe of tappa which was knotted over her shoulder . . . and spreading it out like a sail, stood erect with upraised arms in the head of the canoe. We American sailors pride our-selves upon our straight clean spars, but a prettier little mast than Fay-away made was never shipped aboard of any craft. . . . If the reader have not observed ere this that I was the declared admirer of Miss Fayaway, all I can say is, that he is little conversant with affairs of the heart, and I certainly shall not trouble myself to enlighten him any farther.

Inimical critics accused Melville of gross exaggeration and irresponsible imagination. *Typee* told a somewhat different story in a remarkably different way from other published accounts by American seamen. What were con-sidered salacious passages in the book were quoted in condemnation, and proper people who were shocked by such samples of erotic lore rushed to read more in *Typee* for themselves. In his review Hawthorne, up in Salem, publicly acknowledged that the author was obviously "tolerant of codes of morals that may be little in accordance with our own." Melville, however, suggested that his countrymen had more to learn from the pagan cannibals than they need learn from the pious missionaries who would change their native ways. "In this secluded abode of happiness," he wrote, "there were no cross old women, no cruel step-dames, no withered spinsters, no love-sick maidens, no sour old bachelors, no inattentive husbands, no melancholy young men, no blubbering youngsters, and no squalling brats. All was mirth, fun, and high good humor. Blue devils, hypochondira, and doleful dumps,

"The Marquesas!" wrote Melville of his sojourn in the South Paci-fic, "What strange visions of out-landish things does the very name spirit up! Naked houris—cannibal banquets—groves of coco-nut...." Melville's first book, Typee *(1846), whose title page is reproduced be-low, was inspired by his island adventures. Below, left, is Mead Shaeffer's illustration from an edition of 1920; the legend reads: "Fayaway and I had a delight-ful little party on the lake."*

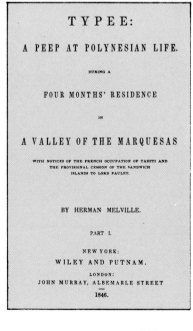

TYPEE:

A PEEP AT POLYNESIAN LIFE.

DURING A

FOUR MONTHS' RESIDENCE

IN

A VALLEY OF THE MARQUESAS

WITH NOTICES OF THE FRENCH OCCUPATION OF TAHITI AND
THE PROVISIONAL CESSION OF THE SANDWICH
ISLANDS TO LORD PAULET.

BY HERMAN MELVILLE.

PART I.

NEW YORK:
WILEY AND PUTNAM.
LONDON:
JOHN MURRAY, ALBEMARLE STREET
1846.

went and hid themselves among the nooks and crannies of the rocks." For such attitudes he was scored by religious and other conventional groups, who thus called further attention to the book. With such wide and controversial coverage in the press, *Typee* was an immediate success—a success of scandal in good part—and Melville became a celebrated author practically overnight.

His reputation so quickly established, Melville produced six more books in as many years—all but one of them inventions fabricated in good part from what he chose to remember of his life at sea and beyond all horizons visible from familiar shores. In the haste of production, and to enrich his narratives, he also borrowed heavily from other men's books about voyages on the ocean-ways and about whaling. It was a rich literature to draw upon, going back to stories of that Leviathan of biblical times, the largest of living creatures, which swallowed Jonah, and continuing over the ages to Melville's day, when the whale's bone and blubber contributed substantially to the American economy; when American ships could be found from one frozen pole to the other, from Africa to Brazil, from Chile to Japan, harvesting the golden profits that came from the crop of monsters they gathered, skinned, and drained wherever the quest led. As Melville was writing *Moby Dick* near Pittsfield, fortunes were literally pouring into New Bedford, Nantucket, and other New England ports that sent out successful whaling fleets. (At New Bedford, Emerson wrote, "they hug an oil-cask like a brother.") At that period the American whaling fleet was three times the size of all Europe's. Whaling exploits had become a national epic.

In writing his version of that heroic quest, Melville named his ship

A lithograph of 1858 after a painting by William Allen Wall depicts New Bedford, Mass., about 1807. By the mid 19th century New Bedford was the whaling capital of the world, its fleet of 329 vessels larger than the fleets of all other whaling towns combined. New Bedford's citizens grew rich; their opulent houses, said Melville, were "One and all . . . harpooned and dragged up hither from the bottom of the sea."

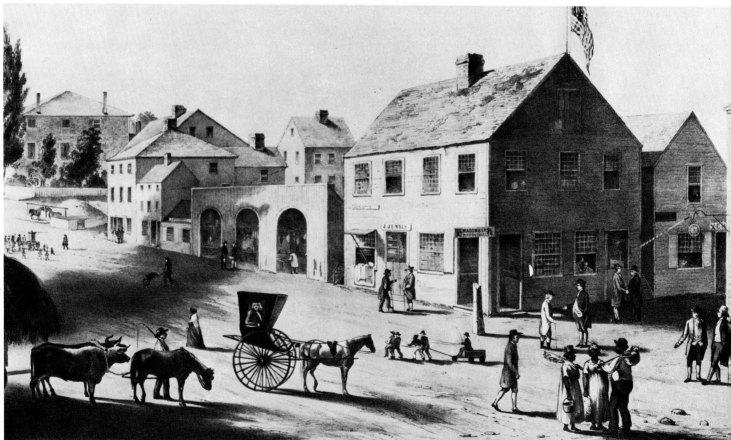

Pequod, after a tribe of savages that had been exterminated by self-righteous intruders from New England, and manned it with a motley, polyglot crew drawn from all corners of the earth. His alter ego in the novel he named Ishmael, after the outcast son of Abraham by his wife's handmaid Hagar, as told in the Bible. For a close companion he invented the savage Queequeg, a Polynesian prince, participating in that cannibal's heathenish rites and pledging him his friendship. He named as skipper of the vessel the monomaniacal Captain Ahab, whose sole, frenzied purpose in life was to capture and kill the great white whale, Moby Dick, who in an earlier encounter had torn away Ahab's leg. (Stories of such a ferocious albino whale were often told in New England seaports.) The story develops into an extraordinary mixture of realistic adventure and complicated symbolism. It is Melville's most significant work. He deals with an epic theme, as basic to man's understanding of his destiny as any to be found in Sophocles or Shakespeare, but here staged on the oil-stained decks of an American whaling ship. The *Pequod* and its crew become a microcosm in which fateful issues are acted out.

Melville dramatizes his message with action-writing that is unsurpassable. As a matter of fact, the routine on a whaler was a stinking business—cutting the whale's blubber into strips, boiling it into oil, and straining that into casks. Melville makes it an inferno as vividly described as Milton's hell:

> Their tawny features, now all begrimed with smoke and sweat, their matted beards, and the contrasting barbaric brilliancy of their teeth . . . their unholy adventures, their tales of terror told in words of mirth; as their uncivilized laughter forked upwards out of them, like the flames from the furnaces; as to and fro the harpooners wildly gesticulated with their huge pronged forks and dippers; as the wind howled on, and the sea leaped, and the ship groaned and dived, and yet steadfastly shot her red hell further and further into the blackness of the sea and the night, and scornfully champed the white bone in her mouth, and viciously spat round her on all sides; then the rushing *Pequod*, freighted with savages, and laden with fire, and burning a corpse, and plunging into that blackness of darkness, seemed the material counterpart of her monomaniac commander's soul.

Not many men chose to repeat a whaling voyage. But neither did many of them soon forget the transporting excitement of the chase and the kill. "It was a sight full of quick wonder and awe!" Melville wrote:

> The vast swells of the omnipotent sea; the singing, hollow roar they made, as they rolled along the eight gunwales, like gigantic bowls in a boundless bowling green; the brief suspended agony of the boat, as it would tip for an instant on the knifelike edge of the sharper waves that almost seemed threatening to cut it in two; the sudden profound dip into watery glens and hollows; the keen spurrings and goadings to gain the top of the opposite hill; the headlong, sledlike slide down its other side—all these, with the cries of the headsmen and harpooners, and the shuddering gasps of the oarsmen, with the wondrous sight of the ivory *Pequod* bearing down upon her boats with outstretched sails, like a wild hen after her screaming brood; all this was thrilling. Not the raw recruit, marching from the bosom of his wife into the fever heat of his first battle; not the dead man's ghost encountering the first unknown phantom in the

The capture of a sperm whale is depicted in a lithograph of the 1850's after a painting by the French artist Ambroise Louis Garneray. Melville, who admired the artist's many representations of whale hunting, declared that he had either been a whaler himself or had been carefully tutored by one. Garneray's work portrays the excitement, danger, and horror of the whale chase as described by Herman Melville in Moby Dick.

other world—neither of these can feel stranger and stronger emotions than that man does, who for the first time finds himself putting into the charmed, churned circle of the hunted sperm whale. . . . A short rushing sound leaped out of the boat; it was the darted iron of Queequeg. Then all in one welded commotion came an invisible push from astern, while forward the boat seemed striking on a ledge; the sail collapsed and exploded; a gush of scalding vapor shot up near by; something rolled and tumbled like an earth-quake beneath us. The whole crew were half suffocated as they were tossed helter-skelter into the white curdling cream of the squall. Squall, whale, and harpoon had all blended together. . . .

As he viewed the scene from ahigh in the crow's-nest, Melville fancied himself striding across the Pacific on giant stilts. He was looking far beyond what his eyes could behold and what he so dramatically described. Ahab's monomania becomes the will of man pitted against infinite evil in the universe, symbolized by the white whale, largest and most defiant of creatures. The entire crew of the *Pequod* becomes involved in this titanic struggle between good and evil, between man and his mysterious destiny; and in the end, as the *Pequod* is destroyed by the whale, maddened by the bristling harpoons that had so long tormented its life, everyone perishes but Ishmael, who lives to tell the story. By means of such symbols, Melville, like Hawthorne (to whom he dedicated the book), poses ultimate questions about heaven and earth for which he could provide no answers.

The tragic epic of *Moby Dick* was the central peak of Melville's career as an author. Today it is widely considered one of the world's greatest novels. At the time, however, the reading public was not prepared for such a complex admixture of hidden meaning with its adventure stories, for a moral allegory dressed in such deceptively colored garb. Melville had gone off into troubled seas of thought that seemed to offer analogies with the nation's painful search for its own identity in those troublous adolescent years preceding the Civil War. His popularity was quite lost with his next novel, *Pierre; or, The Ambiguities*, in which again, with his narrative put ashore this time, he grappled with the equivocal problems of good and evil. Here he was concerned with incest, and even friendly critics were dismayed by this cryptic mind that found no narrow alley too dark or isolated to enter in its search for the underlying truth of life. In *The Confidence Man: His Masquerade*, published in 1857 and the last novel printed during his life, Melville leaves his metaphysical speculations to consider, satirically, the more immediate problems of human relationships. He deals with gullible travelers on a Mississippi steamboat—another different microcosm—who through greed or softheartedness are "conned" into betraying their suspicions of their fellow passengers, even the most pious and earnest of them. Mutual trust, charity, morality, become frauds. Every character is masquerading. Life is a paradox. About this time Hawthorne wrote of Melville, "he can neither believe, nor be comfortable in his unbelief; and he is too honest and courageous not to try to do one or the other." In his perplexity Melville never did finish the novel.

Melville continued to write, verse as well as prose, until he died in 1891, but he was largely ignored by the public and his death went practically unnoticed. For nineteen years he eked out a subsistence as a customs inspector in New York. One of the few discerning contemporary judges who recognized Melville as a great imaginative writer was the English poet and novelist Robert Buchanan. But when he came to New York in 1885 and tried to see Melville—"this Triton," as he referred to him—no one he talked to seemed to know anything about him or where he might be found. Melville's last novel, *Billy Budd*—a long short story actually, completed just before his death and one of his best works—was not published until 1924. By then his extraordinary talent had been rediscovered, or rather, more justly evaluated. With historical perspective it is possible to see that he had asked his countrymen questions which, if they were not prepared to answer, they must at least learn to face, and that he had done it with surpassing literary style and imagination. Once, in a moment of unrestrained optimism, he wrote: "God had predestinated, mankind expects, great things from our race; and great things we feel in our souls. The rest of the nations must soon be in our rear. We are the pioneers of the world; the advance guard, sent on through the wilderness of untried things." However, the questions he posed in his major books put that predestination in some doubt, and this brought Melville closer to the understanding and sympathy of the generations that have survived the wars and tribulations of recent decades.

Buchanan's reason for trying to find Melville in New York was that he considered him the one writer on the North American continent who was "fit to stand shoulder to shoulder" with Walt Whitman. Some years earlier the English poet and essayist James Thomson, author of *The City of Dreadful Night*, among other celebrated works, had written that Melville was the only living American author who approached Whitman "in his sympathy with all ordinary life and vulgar occupations, in his feeling of brotherhood for all rough workers, and at the same time in his sense of beauty and grandeur, and in his power of thought." At the time, that kind of appreciation of Whitman was not quite so rare in this country as was the praise for Melville. Melville's popularity had flared up with his first book and then quickly sputtered out. Whitman started writing just as Melville faded from public attention, and although few people paid much attention to his work at the start, he won fame abroad earlier than in his own country—as has happened to other American authors.

Melville and Whitman were almost exact contemporaries. Both were descended from mixed Dutch and British stock; both were born in 1819 and both lived in New York, within a few miles of each other, for many years; and both died within months of each other. The talents of both men sprouted suddenly and unexpectedly; both continued to write virtually to their dying days in spite of general public indifference to their work. In their entirely different ways, both developed an original and vital approach to the art of writing that was distinctively American in its manner and in its choice of subject matter—as Buchanan and Thomson so clearly realized. And as Thomson remarked, both shared the brotherhood of common men in the course of their experience. For all of that, Melville and Whitman apparently never met, and they paid scant heed to each other's writings. As has often been observed, from Poe's day onward, loneliness and apartness have characterized the American author. For all his announced camaraderie, Whitman had very few friends among literary folk, and no intimate ones. (As already noted, Whitman was the only writer who attended Poe's funeral.)

Like Benjamin Franklin before him and Mark Twain after him, Whitman got much of his essential schooling in printing shops and newspaper offices and in the politics of journalism—an education that is clearly reflected in the peculiar idioms that characterize his most typical works. (Emerson once described Whitman's language as "a remarkable mixture of the *Bhagvat-Geeta* and the *New York Herald*.") He learned, too, from the teeming city itself; its crowds, its theatres (in one of which he heard Shakespeare and Italian opera), its shuttling ferryboats, its lurching carts and omnibuses, its "tumultuous" streets whose noise he once described as a "heavy, low, musical roar, hardly ever intermitted, even at night." He sometimes contributed to that roar, as he told Thoreau, by declaiming Homer at the top of his lungs as he sat beside the driver of an omnibus. He was always to celebrate New York, the poet Mark Van Doren has written, "as a sea of shoulders and faces, a tossing universe of souls that teemed as the sea did with fathomless wonders." In one of his later poems, Whitman himself referred to New York as a "City of Orgies."

By the time he was thirty-six, Whitman had worked as a printer's devil, a journeyman-compositor, a schoolteacher, a carpenter, and a newspaper editor. He had traveled as far from New York as New Orleans, in 1848, and seen something of the near frontier; and he had written and had published some unexceptional, conventional bits of prose and poetry, including one temperance novel. William Cullen Bryant published some of Whitman's earliest prose pieces, but thus far it was an undistinguished and unpromising career that went largely unnoticed—and his life was half over. Then, in 1855, with no forewarning of what proved to be a literary event of large importance,

Whitman published his first version of *Leaves of Grass*, a slender volume of only twelve poems which he would revise and add to all the days of his life and on which in the end his fame would solidly rest.

Whitman set some of the type for that earliest edition with his own hands and published it at his own expense. He even wrote three rhapsodic reviews of his own work, one of them including an anonymous appreciation of the author: "An American bard at last! One of the roughs, large, proud, affectionate, eating, drinking, and breeding, his costume manly and free, his face sunburnt and bearded, his posture strong and erect, his voice bringing hope and prophecy to the generous races of young and old. . . . Right and left he flings his arms, drawing men and women with undeniable love to his close embrace, loving the clasp of their hands, the touch of their neck and breasts, and the sound of their voices. All else seems to burn up under his fierce affection for persons." The author, he claimed, "must recreate poetry with the elements always at hand. He must imbue it with himself as he is, disorderly, fleshly, and sensual, a lover of things, yet a lover of men and women above the whole of the other objects of the universe." Probably no other American writer has better succeeded in creating his own legend, in creating the standards by which he chose to be recognized. However, as a publishing venture *Leaves of Grass* was a complete failure. The poet, not the president, he wrote, would be the common referee for the people of the United States; and, he concluded, "the proof of a poet is that his country absorbs him as affectionately as he has absorbed it."

But the broad public to whom it was addressed either ignored or abused *Leaves of Grass*. Whitman's open allusions to sex and his ambiguous references to homosexuality were unacceptable to most of his generation at every level; the apparent formlessness of his statements seemed shockingly wayward, if original; his vocabulary, drawn from commonplace language—the language of the street and of the daily press and of his own invention—was vulgar by all the formal standards of the day. Then and for years later many qualified critics rejected the work in its successive editions—Longfellow, Lowell, Holmes, Mark Twain, and others, in a long list of distinguished men and women of letters, found little or nothing in *Leaves of Grass* to like or praise. Emily Dickinson never read the book, but she "was told it was disgraceful." Whittier, it was said, cast his copy into the fire. Lowell called it "a solemn humbug." Henry Thoreau wrote to a friend that he found two or three pieces in *Leaves of Grass* "disagreeable, to say the least; simply sensual. He does not celebrate love at all. It is as if the beasts spoke." Yet,

Walt Whitman was a noted celebrator of New York City, which he loved in spite of the unabated cacophony of its tumultuous streets. The above lithograph, after a drawing by Hugh Reinagle, shows St. Paul's Church and the Broadway stages about 1835; one can understand why New York was known as "the City of Omnibuses," and why an English visitor remarked that "the whole length of Broadway is filled with Omnibus Carriages at all hours . . . you might almost say the street was paved with them. . . ."

149

Like many artists, Whitman was often misunderstood, not only in his own day but also after his death. He was caricatured, as in Max Beerbohm's critical comic cartoon of 1904 called Walt Whitman Inciting the Bird of Freedom to Soar; *he was also parodied, as in* Vanity Fair's "poemettina" of 1860 entitled Counter-Jumps. *It begins: "I am the Counter-jumper, weak and effeminate. I love to loaf and lie about dry-goods." It concludes: "I sound my feeble yelp over the woofs of the World."*

Thoreau continued, in these areas, beast or not, Whitman spoke more truth than any other American writer. "Of course," he wrote, "Walt Whitman can communicate to us no experience, and if we are shocked, whose experience is it that we are reminded of? On the whole, it sounds to me very brave and American, after whatever deductions. . . . We ought to rejoice greatly in him. . . . He is a great fellow."

Emerson was the first outstanding American of the time to hail Whitman's talent. When he had read the copy of *Leaves of Grass* Whitman had sent him he wrote the author: "I am not blind to the worth of the wonderful gift of *Leaves of Grass*. I find it the most extraordinary piece of wit and wisdom that American has yet contributed. . . . I find incomparable things, said incomparably well. . . . I greet you at the beginning of a great career." More than a decade earlier, in his essay "The Poet," Emerson had written that he looked in vain for the poet he described. He wrote:

We have yet had no genius in America, with tyrannous eye, which knew the value of our incomparable materials, and saw, in the barbarism and materialism of the times, another carnival of the same gods whose picture he so much admires in Homer. . . . Our log-rolling, our stumps and their politics, our fisheries, our Negroes and Indians, our boats and our repudiations, the wrath of rogues and the pusillanimity of honest men, the northern trade, the southern planting, the western clearing, Oregon and Texas, are yet unsung. Yet America is a poem in our eyes; its ample geography dazzles the imagination, and it will not wait long for metres.

Now came Whitman, who was determined to write just such epic poems as would speak with Olympian perspective of the common aspirations, the abounding faith, the inexhaustible variety of the sprawling and "teeming nation of nations" that was American democracy. He might have stepped right out of the pages of Emerson's essay; and so he did in a figurative sense. The year before *Leaves of Grass* appeared, Whitman was working as a carpenter. In his lunch pail one day he carried a volume of Emerson as food for his thoughts. "I was simmering, simmering, simmering," he once explained; "Emerson brought me to a boil," although he later, unconvincingly, disclaimed any such debt to the Sage of Concord.

There was more to Whitman's efflorescence than the influence of Emerson, to be sure, great as that may have been. Before Emerson wrote "The Poet," that most perceptive of all critics of American democracy, Alexis de Tocqueville, had almost predicted the advent of a Whitman. "I readily admit that the Americans have no poets," Tocqueville wrote in the second volume of his *Democracy in America;* "I cannot allow that they have no poetic ideas . . . the American people views its own march across these wilds—drying swamps, turning the course of rivers, peopling solitudes, and subduing nature. . . . amongst the thoughts which it suggests, there is always one which is full of poetry, and this is the hidden nerve which gives vigor to the whole frame." When America found its true literary spokesman, Tocqueville suggested, that person would use new manners of expression, with little or no regard for the order and regularity that were binding forces on the literature of the Old World. He would celebrate, not the past, but the present and future. His language would close the difference between "refined" and "vulgar" words.

All that proved to be Whitman to the life. He had resolved to be the poet of the New World in the "strange, unloosen'd wondrous time" of the nineteenth century—to put himself "freely, fully and truly on record," as he wrote; "I could not find any similar personal record in current literature that satisfied me." He would, he continued, sound his "barbaric yawp over the roofs of the world." Thoreau forgave him the egoism of his claims. "He may turn out the least of a braggart of all," Henry wrote in a letter, "having a better right to be confident."

Whitman pretended to be at once an average man, a rebel, and a seer—an impossible combination. Actually, he seems to have been assured by a reading he had made of his "bumps" at the celebrated phrenological cabinet of Fowler and Wells that he possessed every human quality in an unusually high degree. In passing, the study of phrenology introduced a number of strange words to his mixed vocabulary.

With all the things that might be said of *Leaves of Grass* as it developed over the years, that volume marked the beginning of a new era in American literary history. "Modern science and democracy," Whitman remarked, "seem'd to be throwing out their challenge to poetry to put them in its statement in contradistinction to the songs and myths of the past." He would be the sensitive instrument through which the march of American progress would be triumphantly recorded; he would be the prophet of the boundless future. Like so much significant American writing, *Leaves of Grass* is social history as well as literature. Qualifying his early estimate of Whitman's work, Emerson at one point commented that in his zeal to leave no aspect of life in America unnoticed, Whitman's poems tended to become inventories, as indeed they do in long parts of his "Song of Myself." Here he ticks off everything from pimpled alligators, hymning katydids, and mother whales to the cheesecloth that hangs in the kitchen and the trip hammers that crash in the factory, from thrusting bulls in the fields and suffering slaves on the run to Yankee clippers scudding the deep and the melting union of human lovers—and so on, without rhyme, and unconventionally organized.

In one of his reviews of his own poems Whitman suggested that the lines never seemed "finished or fixed," but were "always suggesting something beyond." Yet, even in his most cryptic lines the suggestions were often enough rich in imagery. The frequent ambiguity of his references to sex, which confused and disturbed his readers, could give way to passages of intensely lyrical strain, as at one point in his early poem "I Sing the Body Electric," the most "shocking" of such pieces:

> Bridegroom night of love, working surely and softly into the
>   prostrate dawn;
> Undulating into the willing and yielding day,
> Lost in the cleave of the clasping and sweet-flesh'd day.

In protesting against such sensualism, none of his critics apparently recalled that it was hardly as explicit or as fervid as some passages in Shakespeare or, for that matter, in the Song of Songs which is Solomon's. As for his intimations of homosexuality, "the love of comrades," none exceed the overt bonds of affection between David and Jonathan as told in the Old Testament.

Just before the Civil War, Whitman published the third edition of *Leaves of Grass*, including in it his incomparable poem "Out of the Cradle Endlessly Rocking." It tells of a boy who steals out from his home by the sea and hears the plaintive song of a mockingbird whose mate has left the nest, never to return. It begins:

> Out of the cradle endlessly rocking,
> Out of the mocking bird's throat, the musical shuttle,
> Out of the Ninth-month midnight,
> Over the sterile sands, and the fields beyond, where the child, leaving
>   his bed, wander'd alone, bareheaded barefoot,
> Down from the shower'd halo,
> Up from the mystic play of shadows, twining and twisting as if they were
>   were alive,
> Out from the patches of briers and blackberries,
> From the memories of the bird that chanted to me,
> From your memories, sad brother—from the fitful risings and fallings I
>   heard,
> From under that yellow half-moon, late-risen, and swollen as if with
>   tears,
> From those beginning notes of sickness and love, there in the trans-
>   parent mist.
> From the thousand responses of my heart, never to cease,
> From the myriad thence-arous'd words,
> From the word stronger and more delicious than any
> From such, as now they start, the scene revisiting,
> As a flock, twittering, rising, or overhead passing,
> Borne hither—ere all eludes me, hurriedly,
> A man—yet by these tears a little boy again,
> Throwing myself on the sand, confronting the waves,
> I, chanter of pains and joys, uniter of here and hereafter,
> Taking all hints to use them—but swiftly leaping beyond them,
> A reminiscence sing.

In the solitary bird's lament for its dead mate, Whitman found a symbol of the poet's creative urge spiritualizing a physical love that death had forever ended. The sounds of the sea, whispering the theme of death, interpret for the lad the mysterious cadences of the bird's song. The poem is probably autobiographical, a remembrance of a grief long past. In the last verse Whitman writes, "My own songs, awaked from that hour."

The Civil War profoundly affected Whitman's life. He had a Quaker's abhorrence of war, and that kept him out of combat. But the facts and implications of that sanguinary conflict changed his mind about many things, and stirred within him feelings that broke forth in superb poetry—his last and some of his best efforts. News that his younger brother, a volunteer, had been wounded, took Whitman to Washington, where he devoted himself to caring for other wounded soldiers from both North and South, in any way he was needed. He even assisted at operations. For three years he performed such merciful missions in hospitals in and about Washington.

Out of those years of war came *Drum-Taps*, a collection of poems that, in Whitman's own opinion, included his best work. The agony he endured

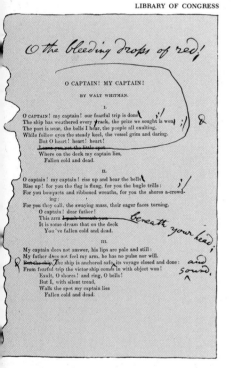

Portrait photographer George Collins Cox took the picture of Walt Whitman, reproduced opposite, in 1887 when the poet was sixty-seven. It was sold to raise money for the aging man of letters, whose pioneer poetry was being ignored by Victorian America. The children are Nigel and Catherine Cholmeley-Jones, whom the photographer visualized as soul-extensions of the poet. Whitman continued to revise his works even after they were published. The page reproduced above includes the celebrated lament, written soon after Abraham Lincoln's assassination.

152

A photograph by Mathew Brady depicts Civil War wounded recuperating at the Carver Hospital, near Washington, D.C. It was at such a hospital that Walt Whitman, the "Good Gray Poet," patiently helped tend the sick.

tending shattered remnants of men can be told in a single stanza from "The Wound-Dresser":

> On, on I go, (open doors of time! open hospital doors!)
> The crush'd head I dress, (poor crazed hand tear not the bandage away,)
> The neck of the cavalry-man with the bullet through and through I
>   examine,
> Hard the breathing rattles, quite glazed already the eye, yet life struggles
>   hard,
> (Come sweet death! be persuaded O beautiful death!
> In mercy come quickly.)
> From the stump of the arm, the amputated hand,
> I undo the clotted lint, remove the slough, wash off the matter and
>   blood,
> Back on his pillow the soldier bends with curv'd neck and side falling
>   head,
> His eyes are closed, his face is pale, he dares not look on the bloody
>   stump,
> And has not yet look'd on it.

As a sequel to *Drum-Taps* he wrote "When Lilacs Last in the Dooryard Bloom'd," an elegy on the death of Abraham Lincoln, whom Whitman had revered. (He once exultantly believed that Lincoln had noticed him and nodded to him while riding through the city streets.) The poem opens with a memorable verse:

> When lilacs last in the dooryard bloom'd,
> And the great star early droop'd in the western sky in the night,
> I mourn'd—and yet shall mourn with ever-returning spring.
>
> O ever-returning spring! trinity sure to me you bring;
> Lilac blooming perennial, and drooping star in the west,
> And thought of him I love.

The unconsolable poet lays a lilac sprig on the passing coffin. Then he hears a carol of death issuing from the throat of a thrush, and finds in this joyous song a comforting reminder of immortality. The dead are at rest; it is only the living who suffer. Whitman moves from the incident of Lincoln's assassination to the sobering remembrance of all the common soldiers who had suffered and died, and had found rest at last. He had moved also from his early egocentric cry of nationalism to a greater and loftier concern for the spirit of mankind. His poetry had reached full maturity.

To eke out the insufficient returns from his writings, while he was in Washington, Whitman took several minor jobs in government offices. He was fired from a clerkship in the Indian Bureau of the Department of the Interior because the secretary of the department considered *Leaves of Grass* a scandalous book. But Whitman had mellowed over the years. In 1871 he published *Democratic Vistas*, a prose pamphlet in which with remarkable candor he discussed the shortcomings of American democracy. The United States was entering its "gilded age," and in the extravagant display of new wealth and the corruption that accompanied unbridled speculation Whitman saw a threat to democracy as he had earlier proclaimed and vaunted it—although he still prophesied a future greatness for the nation.

Then, in 1873, he suffered a paralytic stroke, which he traced to his exposure to gangrene and fever during his hospital days. Although he was still widely censored by the reading public for his vulgarities, by that time a Whitman cult had developed in both America and in England—a cult whose extravagant praise of the "Good Gray Poet," hardly discouraged by Whitman himself, did the man little real service, since it overlaid the solid merits of his work that have accounted for his subsequent fame. However, he was winning international repute; articles about him and his work appeared in England, Germany, France, Denmark, and Hungary. After his death in 1892 his reputation continued to grow. In 1919, the centennial of his birth, even the iconoclastic H. L. Mencken did not hesitate to call Whitman "the greatest poet that America had ever produced." He was finally admitted to the Hall of Fame for Great Americans in 1930.

Had a public opinion poll been taken shortly after the Civil War to determine America's favorite living authors, neither Melville nor Whitman would have ranked very high. The cryptic meanings of the one and the unconventional "yawp" of the other were beyond the appreciation of most readers of the time. In New York, Irving, Cooper, and Poe all died before the war started. Bryant lived on, but in his later years he was considered more important as an editor and a public figure than as an author. To find the likeliest candidates for popular approval it is necessary to turn away from New York and back to New England, particularly to Boston and the nearby village of Cambridge.

Emerson was still writing at Concord, and his stock remained high; he was, indeed, accepted with fresh understanding by a younger generation. But his neighbors Thoreau and Hawthorne had both died before the end of the war, and the immediate Boston area with its Back Bay and Harvard held the greatest concentration of acknowledged and admired literary talent in the land. Such authors as Henry Wadsworth Longfellow, James Russell Lowell, Oliver Wendell Holmes, and John Greenleaf Whittier had been writing their way into the hearts of their fellow Americans for a generation or more, and their widespread popularity was incontestable.

From more southerly precincts the literary output of New England still seemed parochial. In hailing the talents of Bryant, Walt Whitman once observed that only when the New England poet left his native place did he become "a thorough American, and . . . a national poet." But generally speaking, from the eminence of Boston the literary scene to the South and the West simply did not often seem bright. In 1867 one disgruntled Philadelphia writer, George Henry Boker, remarked that "according to the Yankee creed, Longfellow, Lowell, Holmes, Emerson and Whittier are the only poets in America, and also the only poets that New England will permit to exist." This was, of course, an exaggeration. While Poe in New York was waging his "war" against Longfellow, accusing him of unmitigated plagiarism and other literary misdemeanors, that gentle Yankee was delivering appreciative lectures on Poe's poetry to his Harvard classes. "Somebody's a thief," ranted Poe; he claimed that Longfellow's books were "books and no more," lacking any semblance of genius. But Poe's was a one-man war since Longfellow ignored the assault. In his journal for February 24, 1847, Longfellow wrote:

TEXT CONTINUES PAGE 160

155

Longfellow's sketch of his children at table (colored by the children)

SECOND TALENT

The spreading chestnut tree, by Longfellow

Twain's rendering of his carriage ride in Germany

As already noted, the artists and writers of America were often intimately associated in their interests, particularly in New York, where they mingled together in the informal meetings of the Sketch Club. The artist William Dunlap wrote for the stage. Thomas Cole, the eminent landscapist, had a story published in *The Saturday Evening Post* before he won fame as an artist, and all his life he wrote commendable verse. In a friendly spirit James Fenimore Cooper sometimes harassed the artist S. F. B. Morse with criticism of his painting. (While Morse was copying paintings in the Louvre, Cooper looked over his shoulder, exclaiming, "Lay it on here Samuel—more yellow—the nose is too short —the eye too small—damn it if I had been a painter what a picture I should have painteded.") Also, as earlier told, Washington Irving contemplated a career as an artist. His deft sketches, below, have a semiprofessional quality. Drawing was his second talent, an extension of his creative spirit into the graphic arts that won appreciation from the well-known American painter Washington Allston. A number of other writers illuminated their journals and letters with more or less entertaining results. Henry Wadsworth Longfellow, Mark Twain, and Henry James, as the illustrations here indicate, turned their hand to sketching from time to time—with variable results. Twain's drawing of his carriage ride on the Heidelberg road, he jocularly explained, "is not a Work, it is only what artists call a 'study'—a thing to make a finished picture from." (He apologized for the fact that the horse was apparently traveling considerably faster than the wagon.)

Above: Henry James' sketch of his sister Alice; left: two drawings by Irving of Spanish types

157

Poe's drawing of "Sissy"

The pencil portrait of Poe's young wife Virginia, shown above, allegedly drawn by the poet, reveals a special talent. This and other similar studies attributed to Poe are in the style of the celebrated nineteenth-century French artist Dominique Ingres. (He, incidentally, was a fine violinist on the side, and the classic French phrase *le violon d' Ingres* refers to any such excellence in a secondary talent.) As the illustrations on the facing page make clear, Harriet Beecher Stowe was a respectably skilled amateur artist, although she had no formal training. In her European travels she dutifully visited the notable picture galleries, and she was a friend of the English art critic John Ruskin and his group. The paintings shown here were apparently done during her residence in Florida from 1868 to 1884. There were other talents in later years, among them the artist Marsden Hartley, who wrote several booklets of verse, and the writer James Thurber, whose wry wit was successfully carried over to his cartoons.

Paintings by Harriet Beecher Stowe; the house
represented below was her Florida residence.

New Englanders often built replicas of their own home towns as they moved West. Henry Howe's sketch of 1846, depicting the Public Square of Hamilton, Ohio, with its white columned courthouse, recalls a typical New England scene.

In Hexameter sings serenely a Harvard Professor;
In Pentameter him damns censorious Poe.

Meanwhile, large droves of Yankees had joined the great migration to the West, where there were greener pastures and more golden hills than New England could boast of. "How beautiful," Carlyle wrote to Emerson in 1849 as the gold rush loosed a new wave of migrants, "to think of lean tough Yankee settlers, tough as gutta-percha, with most *occult* unsubduable fire in their belly, steering over the Western Mountains to annihilate the jungle, and bring bacon and corn out of it for the posterity of Adam.—There is no *Myth* of Athene or Herakles equal to this *fact.*" With such a remark Carlyle may have been intimating that a good part of that occult fire could have come from reading Emerson's inspiring essays.

At the time that letter was written, New Englanders had already surged into the Middle West, repeating the pattern of tidy villages they had left behind them and establishing schools, libraries, lyceums, and other cultural equipment that were a treasured part of their heritage—and somewhat wistfully recalling that capital of learning they had moved away from. As the historian Henry Steele Commager has suggested, the literary founding fathers of the United States were to a large extent New Englanders who created and imposed a New England image upon the rest of the land. Much that was distinctive about American nationalism, Commager observed, was to be conditioned by the circumstance. The patriotic hymn "America" ("My country, 'tis of Thee") was written in 1831 by the Boston clergyman Samuel Francis Smith and was first sung at a Boston Fourth of July celebration. Thus it was, writes Commager, "that Americans on Iowa prairies or the plains of Texas would sing 'I love thy rocks and rills, thy woods and templed hills' with no sense of incongruity." By similar influences it also came about that Plymouth rather than Jamestown is so widely thought of as the birthplace of America; that Paul Revere would be "the winged horseman of American history and Concord Bridge the American equivalent of the Rubicon"; that Boston's State House, as Holmes claimed, could be thought of as "the hub of the solar system." One other token of that spreading interest in New England writing was that within a year of its publication one tenth of the first edition of Longfellow's *The Song of Hiawatha* had been bought by a single Chicago jobber who was serving the Midwest. In the end, for the rest of the world all Americans came to be called Yankees—although not always flatteringly.

In later years William Dean Howells described an occasion in the early 1860's when as a young man he made a literary pilgrimage from Ohio, where he was born, to Boston, where he was entertained at dinner as something of a young prodigy from the West by Lowell, then editor of the *Atlantic Monthly*. Oliver Wendell Holmes was present, among others, and young Howells reported ecstatically to his father that dinner lasted four hours "and involved an intoxication to me, as entire as that of Rhine wine."

Around 1869, on a return visit to Ohio, Howells stopped overnight at the home of James Garfield, then a congressman, later to become president of the United States. "I was then living in Cambridge," Howells recalled, "in the fullness of my content with my literary circumstance, and as we were sitting with the Garfield family on the verandah that overlooked their lawn I was beginning to speak of the famous poets I knew when Garfield stopped me with 'Just a minute!' He ran down into the grassy space, first to one fence and then to the other at the sides, and waved a wild arm of invitation to the neighbours who were also sitting on their back porches. 'Come over here!' he shouted. 'He's telling about Holmes, and Longfellow, and Lowell, and Whittier!' And at his bidding, dim forms began to mount the fences and followed him up to his verandah. 'Now go on!' he called to me, when we were all seated, and I went on, while the whippoorwills whirred and whistled round, and the hours drew toward midnight."

Longfellow, Holmes, and Lowell were a triumvirate of "classical" Yankee poets. All three were cultured Christian gentleman with long and reputable New England pedigrees. They were, as well, men of scholarly interests, creative talents, and industrious natures; all were associated with Harvard as students or teachers, or both. They were all Brahmins, a term humorously applied to upper-class New England society; "the harmless, inoffensive, untitled aristocracy" of the region, as Holmes once wrote, "which has grown to be a caste by the repetition of the same influences generation after generation." The trio were among the leaders of a group of literary and intellectual lights who frequented much the same social circles over a period of decades, who knew and admired one another's books and poems, and who in the 1850's formed what came to be known as the Saturday Club, at whose periodic meetings they discussed matters of common interest. For fairly transparent reasons that select group early came to be known as a mutual admiration society. However, one practical and lasting result of those discussions was the founding in 1857 of the *Atlantic Monthly*, a magazine to which all the club members and their literary friends made occasional contributions. Emerson describes a meeting of the club at which a new issue of the *Atlantic* was distributed; "Every one rose eagerly to get a copy," he recounted, "and then each sat down, and read *his own* article." (Melville never made the pages of the *Atlantic* and Whitman but twice, but their work was also ignored by almost all the other contemporary periodicals.)

Of the Brahmin poets Longfellow was the most illustrious, the most beloved by his countrymen. More clearly than any other poet, in his works he reflected the popular American taste of the time. He had a peculiar genius for writing, in simple images, in rhymes that could be easily memorized, and with appropriate moral sentiment, precisely what the public wished to read and felt it should read for its cultural betterment. His familiar narrative verses about the village blacksmith, Paul Revere, Priscilla and John Alden, Hiawatha,

A self-portrait of 1847 shows Henry Wadsworth Longfellow reclining in his study at Craigie house in Cambridge. From 1843 until his death in 1882, he worked in the serenity of his study, cut off from the immediate present, intent on writing poetical histories that are more lyrical than factual.

Evangeline, and other heroes of myth and history are unforgettable elements of our American heritage. Indeed, to criticize the author, as Poe did, seems almost unpatriotic.

Also, to consign Longfellow's work to the children's corner, as is done often enough in these later times, is rather arbitrary treatment of a man who enjoyed international renown in his own day. In 1851 he was hailed from France as the foremost American poet. The next year *Blackwood's Edinburgh Magazine* opined that "Mr. Longfellow need not shun comparison with any living writer." Some years later the London *Spectator* foretold that *Hiawatha* would "doubtless live as long as the English language." George Eliot thought that poem and *The Scarlet Letter* were the "two most indigenous and masterly productions in American literature."

The man's praises were sung everywhere. A Chinese mandarin even transcribed Longfellow's "Psalm of Life" on an ivory fan. The "Psalm" was, in fact, one of the best-known poems written in the English language in the nineteenth century. It carried a message of moral earnestness that strongly challenged the melancholy pessimism of Goethe and other contemporary romantic authors with a voice of encouragement that endeared Longfellow to his generation.

> Life is real! Life is earnest!
>   And the grave is not its goal;
> Dust thou art, to dust returnest,
>   Was not spoken of the soul.

That and other verses of the poem have at one time or other probably been memorized by every schoolchild in America—and by numerous people elsewhere. During the Crimean War, it is said, a soldier who lay dying before Sevastopol repeated its stirring lines, possibly and ironically including the final verse:

> Let us, then, be up and doing,
>   With a heart for any fate;
> Still achieving, still pursuing,
>   Learn to labor and to wait.

Longfellow spoke from a rich native inheritance. Four of his ancestors, including John Alden and the elder Brewster, had come to America on the *Mayflower*. His father and grandfather had both gone to Harvard. He himself had been graduated from Bowdoin College in Maine in 1825 at the age of eighteen; as earlier mentioned he was a schoolmate of Hawthorne's. (When he was an undergraduate he had written his father that he did "most eagerly aspire after future eminence in literature.") Subsequently, he taught modern languages there and at Harvard. Between times he made long and extensive visits to Europe. He was indeed a much-traveled man, and to prepare for his professional career he had steeped himself in European lore and languages, especially German and Scandinavian. (On one of his journeys he noted with interest and some shock that in Stockholm clergymen actually smoked in the streets, and that in Uppsala professors were paid in corn.) In his lifetime he served as a two-way agent, on the one hand introducing American themes to Old World audiences and on the other transplanting European cultural traditions in New World soil. His wife, whom he had married in 1831, died in Rotterdam while the couple was on a trip overseas in 1835. Eight years later he married Frances Appleton, whose very wealthy father bought and gave the newlyweds the historic eighteenth-century Craigie house in Cambridge to live in. That was—and still remains—a handsome structure that had served as Washington's headquarters at one point during the Revolutionary War. Whitman described Longfellow's comfortable life in such surroundings: "reminiscent, polish'd, elegant, with the air of finest conventional library, picture-gallery or parlor, with ladies and gentlemen in them, and plush and rosewood, and ground glass lamps, and mahogany and ebony furniture, and a silver inkstand and scented paper to write on." Longfellow customarily dressed in the height of fashion—"almost too much so," according to one observer who described how his "blue frock coat of Parisian cut, a handsome waistcoat, faultless pantaloons, and primrose-colored kids set off his compact figure, which was not for a moment still." Emerson confided to his journal that one could not go to Longfellow's "palace," with its "servants, and a row of bottles of different coloured wines" and other sumptuous accouterments, and talk about things—things, that is, that interested Emerson. The host seemed to be untouched by the issues and questions that disturbed the minds of many of his thoughtful contemporaries. From this pleasant sanctuary Longfellow expressed little concern for the contemporary American scene. For most of his works he borrowed themes from the past and from stories of distant lands, and in them he was far less mindful of historical actualities than he was of poetic effects. He did not revive *the* past so much as he created *a* past. The formidably intellectual Margaret Fuller complained that for Longfellow nature, "whether human or external, is always seen through the windows of literature." (According to one observer, the poet even closed all the shutters of his house to avoid the sight of a thunderstorm.)

Longfellow was always dapper, as shown in the above photograph. He was a gracious host to the many visitors who came to see him at Craigie house, depicted in Benson J. Lossing's sketch, below. The photograph (below, left) shows the poet in his study.

Longfellow's Indian idyll, Hiawatha, is a magical story that captured the imagination of readers throughout the world and made its author the great, popular American poet. The "song" was an instant best seller, selling 50,000 copies in five months. Frederic Remington, noted depictor of frontier life, executed the representation of the Indian hero, reproduced at right, for a Boston edition, first published in 1891.

His famed narrative poem, *The Song of Hiawatha*, published in 1855, was derived both in its spirit and in its facile meter from the Finnish epic *Kalevala*, which he had been reading and which he found "charming." Hiawatha was a historic personage, an Indian medicine man of the sixteenth century who was one of those responsible for organizing the Iroquois Confederacy. But Longfellow used only the name for his poetic purposes, not the available biographical record of the man.

"I have at length hit upon a plan for a poem on the American Indians," he wrote in his journal for June 22, 1854, "which seems to me the right one and the only. It is to weave together their beautiful traditions into a whole. I have hit upon a measure, too, which I think the right and only one for such a theme." For guidance concerning those traditions he turned to the writings of Henry R. Schoolcraft, the well-known American ethnologist who had made a special study of Indian lore and customs. In one of his works Schoolcraft tells of a legendary Indian hero of miraculous birth, who was sent among his people to clear their rivers, forests, and fishing grounds and to teach them the arts of peace; and it was around this theme that Longfellow imaginatively wove his narrative. Thus he started his tale:

> Should you ask me, whence these stories?
> Whence these legends and traditions,
> With the odors of the forest,
> With the dew and damp of meadows,
> With the curling smoke of wigwams,
> With the rushing of great rivers,
> With their frequent repetitions,
> And their wild reverberations,
> As of thunder in the mountains?
> I should answer, I should tell you
> "From the forests and the prairies,
> From the Great Lakes of Northland,
> From the land of the Ojibways,
> From the land of the Dacotahs,
> From the mountains, moors, and fenlands
> Where the heron, the Shuh-shuh-gah,
> Feeds among the reeds and rushes.
> I repeat them as I heard them
> From the lips of Nawadaha,
> The musician, the sweet singer."

Such was the popular success of *Hiawatha* that it became the subject of a series of lithographs by the firm of Currier and Ives. Like others of Longfellow's lyrical verses, it has also been set to music.

For *Evangeline: A Tale of Acadie,* Longfellow also turned to Schoolcraft, and to other writers who knew something of "the forest primeval" and "the murmuring pines and the hemlocks, bearded with moss" and of the Acadian land with its shores and meadows and tranquil villages, all of which, sight unseen, Longfellow chose to describe so colorfully in the long, tragic narrative poem. To brighten the image of these lands in his mind's eye, he went to look at the *Panorama of the Mississippi,* by John Banvard, a half-mile-long scenic painting done in journeyman stage-set style that was unfolded from one roller onto another to simulate a moving picture—a popular device of the time. That showpiece happened to be touring the Boston neighborhood while Longfellow was composing his poem.

The critical reservations of Margaret Fuller and Edgar Allan Poe about Longfellow's "plagiarisms," and his lack of original or profound ideas did nothing to stem his mounting popularity. Nor did Longfellow's more than comfortable circumstances lead him to indolence or sloth. He remained an industrious and meticulous craftsman, a prolific and fluent author. His so-called household poems, lyrical in quality, placid in tone, expertly contrived, continued to sink deep into the national memory. Even for those who feel they have long since put these poems aside, a mere citing of a few sample verses may recall old delights that could well be recovered by a fresh reading. The first and last stanzas of "The Village Blacksmith," published in 1841, are cases in point:

> Under a spreading chestnut-tree
> The village smithy stands;
> The smith, a mighty man is he,
> With large and sinewy hands;
> And the muscles of his brawny arms
> Are strong as iron bands.
>
> Thanks, thanks to thee, my worthy friend,
> For the lesson thou has taught!
> Thus at the flaming forge of life
> Our fortunes must be wrought;
> Thus on its sounding anvil shaped
> Each burning deed and thought.

To *The Courtship of Miles Standish* Longfellow brought a touch of gentle humor unknown in Hawthorne's tales of seventeenth-century New England, as when, acting as surrogate, John Alden presents the case of the doughty little captain to Priscilla:

> But as he warmed and glowed, in his simple and eloquent language,
> Quite forgetful of self, and full of the praise of his rival,
> Archly the maiden smiled, and, with eyes overrunning with laughter,
> Said, in a tremulous voice, "Why don't you speak for yourself, John?"

In *Tales of a Wayside Inn,* published in 1863, Longfellow practically made the lasting reputation of Paul Revere with the inaccurate but appealing reconstruction of his famous ride, a reputation that might otherwise have been all but lost to history. (Later in the century antiquarians discovered Revere's merits as a silversmith, and his fame soared to new heights. Without Longfellow's poem it is a fair guess that examples of Revere silver would not command the towering prices they do on today's market.)

> Listen, my children, and you shall hear
> Of the midnight ride of Paul Revere,
> On the eighteenth of April, in Seventy-Five;
> Hardly a man is now alive
> Who remembers that famous day and year.
>
>   ❖   ❖   ❖   ❖
>
> For, borne on the night-wind of the Past
> Through all our history, to the last,
> In the hour of darkness and peril and need,
> The people will waken and listen to hear
> The hurrying hoof-beats of that steed,
> And the midnight message of Paul Revere.

Many of Longfellow's poems were published as tiny illustrated booklets. Reproduced below are several pages from a gayly decorated edition of "The Village Blacksmith," probably dating from the 1880's.

These poems were among the best sellers of their day. *The Courtship of Miles Standish*, for example, sold more than 15,000 copies in Boston and London on publication day in 1858. Three years earlier, 30,000 copies of *Hiawatha* had been sold within five months. Longfellow all but rivaled Tennyson as the poet laureate of his age. Before the century was out, his work had been translated into at least a dozen different languages, including Russian, Hungarian, and Portuguese.

Remarking upon Longfellow's tranquil and productive life at Craigie House, Hawthorne once observed that the poet appeared to be "no more conscious of any earthly or spiritual trouble than a sunflower is—of which lovely blossom he, I know not why, reminded me." However, in July, 1861, that tranquillity was suddenly and cruelly shattered. On a hot summer day of that month, while she was using hot wax to seal up some locks of her daughters' hair in packages, Longfellow's wife's light summer dress caught fire. Despite Longfellow's attempts to smother the flames, Frances was critically burned and died the next day. In his efforts to help her, the poet himself was so badly burned that he could not attend the funeral services— badly enough burned about the face so that shaving became inadvisable, whereupon he grew the full beard he wore for the rest of his life.

In the wake of that tragedy Longfellow wrote a friend that although he was outwardly calm, he was "inwardly bleeding to death"; and to another correspondent, "I have no heart for anything." But he remained a man of letters. He completed the group of poems that would appear in *Tales of a Wayside Inn* and, among other signal accomplishments, finished his notable translation of Dante's *Divine Comedy*. His fame continued to spread over two continents. When he returned to Europe in 1868–69 he was given a private audience with Queen Victoria, he dined with Gladstone, and he was entertained by Tennyson. James Russell Lowell once wrote from London that to know Longfellow "is to be somebody over here . . . it is as good as knowing a lord." He also talked with Franz Liszt (who then set to music Longfellow's introduction to his *Golden Legend*); he was given honorary degrees at Oxford and Cambridge, and otherwise enjoyed what was, in effect, a triumphal tour. Back home at the Craigie House he welcomed a long file of distinguished visitors that included the emperor of Brazil, the great English historian James Anthony Froude, and Anthony Trollope, among others. Children came to this shrine and, one day, a woman who arrived with all her luggage, under the delusion

that she was Longfellow's wife—she had to be taken away by the police.

Almost everyone who was received at Craigie House remarked on Longfellow's special charm as a host, and all who met him were impressed by the sweetness and gentleness of his nature. The English clergyman and novelist Charles Kingsley thought Longfellow's face was the most beautiful he had ever seen. As a man and as a poet he was beloved around the world. Children, especially, were inevitably drawn to him. On the occasion of his seventy-second birthday the children of Cambridge gave him as a present a chair made of wood from the chestnut tree he had celebrated in "The Village Blacksmith"; and throughout America his birthdays were celebrated in public schools. On March 18, 1882, although he was ill and confined, he kindly showed a group of schoolchildren through his house; six days later he died. After his death a bust of him was unveiled in Poets' Corner at Westminster Abbey, the only American to be so honored.

In 1854, to provide more time for his literary pursuits, Longfellow had given up his teaching post at Harvard. His chair was almost immediately filled by his younger neighbor and friend James Russell Lowell. Like Longfellow, Lowell was descended from seventeenth-century New England settlers, and he also lived in a pre-Revolutionary Georgian house, "Elmwood,"

A photograph taken by Oliver Wendell Holmes catches James Russell Lowell, the romantic young bookman, leaning against a tree at "Elmwood," his Cambridge home. A literary lion by the age of twenty-nine, Lowell was, according to magazine editor Nathaniel Parker Willis, the "best launched man of his time."

that still stands in Cambridge. The house had been first the home of Lieutenant Governor Oliver, last of the royal deputies in Massachusetts, and stood in a part of the community known as "Tory Row." In 1774 Oliver was forced by patriots to sign his resignation and find safety in Boston. The structure, Lowell wrote, "was born a Tory and will die so." (His grandmother wore black on the Fourth of July and lamented "our late unhappy difference with His Most Gracious Majesty.") Lowell was born there and he died there, and he took on some of the color of those surroundings.

He was another Brahmin graduate of Harvard, where he was the class poet—although because of certain indiscretions he was not permitted to deliver his piece in person. Within a few years after he left college (and then law school), and after suffering through one unhappy love affair during which he considered suicide, he married a young woman who was something of a poet in her own right. With her encouragement and inspiration, he launched his literary career—which was to be long and distinguished. In the single year of 1848, when he was twenty-nine, he published four books that firmly established his reputation as a poet, a wit, a social and political satirist, and at times an almost unforgivable punster, displaying a versatility beyond that of any of his contemporaries. It was a remarkable accomplishment for such a young man, enough in itself to constitute a career.

In one of those four publications, *A Fable for Critics*, issued anonymously but immediately recognized as his work, he humorously but very shrewdly offered his criticisms of contemporary American writers. He scrawled the lines, he said, "at full gallop . . . in a style that is neither good verse nor bad prose," wondering whether his readers would think he was making fun *of* them or *with* them. Nevertheless, in most cases posterity has agreed with his estimations (which are much more detailed than the following abbreviations might suggest). Emerson, Lowell wrote, had "A Greek head on right Yankee shoulders." Some of Emerson's poems, he observed, "welled from those rare depths of soul that have ne'er been excelled," and, he continued:

> 'Tis refreshing to old-fashioned people like me
> To meet such a primitive Pagan as he,
> In whose mind all creation is duly respected
> As parts of himself—just a little projected;
> And who's willing to worship the stars and the sun,
> A convert to—nothing but Emerson.

> ✿   ✿   ✿   ✿

> There is Bryant, as quiet, as cool, and as dignified,
> As a smooth, silent iceberg, that never is ignified . . .

> ✿   ✿   ✿   ✿

> There comes Poe, with his raven, like Barnaby Rudge,
> Three fifths of him genius and two fifths sheer fudge . . .

and so on down a long list of other writers, including Thoreau, Irving, Cooper, and Lowell himself:

> There is Lowell, who's striving Parnassus to climb
> With a whole bale of *isms* tied together with rhyme,
> He might get on alone, spite of brambles and boulders,
> But he can't with that bundle he has on his shoulders . . .

The irrepressible Margaret Fuller remarked that Lowell's "great facility at versification has enabled him to fill the ear with a copious stream of pleasant sound." But, she concluded, "his thought sounds no depth, and posterity will not remember him." Here she was not quite right. In fact, posterity will remember Margaret Fuller herself somewhat better for the thinly veiled reference Lowell made to her in his *Fable,* with lines that anticipate Ogden Nash:

> She always keeps asking if I don't observe a
> Particular likeness 'twixt her and Minerva.

However, Miss Fuller had a point. Lowell was a prodigious reader, in six languages; and his mind brimmed and overflowed with literary notions that he sometimes could not get down on paper quickly enough to catch his own thoughts securely. With his great erudition he had more in his mind than he could or did think out in any depth. When he was in his twenties he confessed to Longfellow that he was giving up poetry for a while because he could not write slowly enough. Once he dashed off six pages of verse to a friend simply in praise of a cheese the man had sent to him.

Among Lowell's most memorable and original contributions were the *Biglow Papers,* published in book form in 1848 and 1867. For these he created as narrators several shrewd and comic Yankee characters, idealists in homespun who were descended from Royall Tyler's Jonathan and more immediately from Major Jack Downing, Brother Jonathan, and Sam Slick—all of them popular oracles in contemporary literature, rich in folk wit and wisdom, who spoke in an exaggerated New England vernacular. "In choosing the Yankee dialect," wrote Lowell, "I did not act without forethought. It had long seemed to me that the great vice of American writing and speaking was a studied want of simplicity, that we were in danger of coming to look on our mother-tongue as a dead language, to be sought in the grammar and dictionary rather than in the heart." So for the first series of *Papers* he invented Hosea Biglow and Parson Homer Wilbur, types he derived from what he called the "divinely illiterate." "I reckon myself a good taster of dialects," he remarked, and with these figures he set the whole country laughing.

However, Lowell strongly felt that true humor was never divorced from moral conviction. This first series was inspired by the Mexican War, which he, like Thoreau and others, felt was a shameful maneuver to expand the slaveholding territory. In his mocking exposure of sham and deceit, be it in peace or war, he reflected a broad segment of public opinion, which added to the popularity of these *Papers:*

> 'T wouldn't suit them Southern fellers,
>   They're a dreffle graspin' set,
> We must ollers blow the bellers
>   Wen they want their irons het;
> May be it's all right ez preachin',
>   But *my* narves it kind o' grates,
> Wen I see the overreachin'
>   O' them nigger-driven' States.

One of Lowell's characters, an unmoral trickster named Birdofredum Sawin, is gulled by propaganda into fighting with a Massachusetts regiment in the

Birdofredom Sawin, with only one leg, to stand upon.

Lowell's abolitionist sentiments were manifest in the Biglow Papers, *for which he created—"as a mouthpiece for the mere drollery" —Birdofredom Sawin, shown in this George Cruikshank drawing.*

169

Mexican War. He returns disappointed and disillusioned—and minus a leg, an arm, an eye, and four fingers. Lowell revived his *Papers* (and Sawin) in the second series to deal with the issues of the Civil War. Here the verse is more subdued in tone and deeper in spirit. Lowell was profoundly stirred by the conflict, in the course of which he lost three beloved nephews. At the war's end he composed an ode in honor of the Harvard men who had lost their lives in army service, a poem that was generally regarded as one of the noblest utterances about the war. It may prove to be, as has been said, Lowell's most enduring work. In the course of those verses he pays tribute to Abraham Lincoln. With Whitman, he was among the first men of letters to recognize the greatness of the martyred president, whom he therein called "the first American."

> Such was he, our Martyr-Chief,
>   Whom late the Nation he had led,
>   With ashes on her head,
> Wept with the passion of an angry grief:
> Forgive me, if from present things I turn
> To speak what in my heart will beat and burn,
> And hang my wreath on his world-honored urn.
>   Nature, they say, doth dote,
>   And cannot make a man
>   Save on some worn-out plan,
>   Repeating us by rote:
> For him her Old-World moulds aside she threw,
>   And choosing sweet clay from the breast
>   Of the unexhausted West,
> With stuff untainted shaped a hero new,
> Wise, steadfast in the strength of God, and true.

In 1857, shortly after he assumed his teaching duties at Harvard, Lowell became editor of the newly founded *Atlantic Monthly*. His editing during his four years at that job was brilliant, for he had a richly informed mind and a sure sense of the effective use of language. (He even cautioned Emerson about his diction.) However, his "constructive" emendations of manuscripts occasionally aroused resentment in his contributors. When he deleted a sentence from an article by Thoreau, that strongly opinionated author protested violently—and he never offered the *Atlantic* another piece. Thomas Wentworth Higginson took Lowell severely to task for changes he had made in a manuscript. "I wish to be understood," Higginson wrote Lowell, "as giving a suppressed but audible growl at the chopping knife which has made mincemeat of my sentences. It isn't pleasant to think that my sentences belong to such a low order of organization that they can be chopped in two in the middle and each half wriggle away independently."

In spite of such differences, the magazine flourished as a prestigious publication—without looking far beyond the New England horizon for its authors. There seemed little need to do that with so much talent close at home. From his editorial chair at the *Atlantic*, and then for a while at *The North American Review*, by his own political and literary essays, his sane and sympathetic criticisms, and his editorial judgment, Lowell exercised a powerful influence on public taste and opinion over the period before, during, and after the Civil War.

In 1877, as a reward for his staunch support of the Republican Party, he was appointed United States minister to the court of Spain. On accepting the post he remarked, "I should like to see a play of Calderon," but as he admitted later, he could not stomach bullfights. (Oliver Wendell Holmes once remarked that Lowell's was the first letter he had ever had from Spain that did not mention a bullfight.) The keen mind and the gracious manner of this articulate, learned Yankee were duly appreciated by the cultured society of Madrid, as they were in London when he became minister to the Court of St. James's in 1880—the leading post in the diplomatic service. (Henry James suggested that "the true reward of an English style was to be sent to England" in such a capacity.) Fredrika Bremer, the Swedish writer who had visited the Lowells in Cambridge, observed that when he had what he called his "evening fever," Lowell's gay and witty talk was like an "incessant play of fireworks"; and this gift as well as his polished formal speech kept him in constant demand in social and intellectual circles wherever he was. However, he confessed that trying to write while he fulfilled his diplomatic duties was like trying to be a setting hen that had also to answer the doorbell.

Earlier in his life, in the *Biglow Papers* and elsewhere, Lowell had been critical of Britain's attitudes toward America. But in his later years he found England virtually a second home. Oxford, Cambridge, and Edinburgh universities all gave him honorary degrees; Oxford offered him a chair; and he became godfather to Adeline Stephen, later better known as Virginia Woolf, the distinguished English author. Lowell, like Cooper before him, was critical of the less attractive aspects of democracy in America, and he kept reminding his countrymen of the great traditions of the Old World that he thought they should recognize and appreciate. But he remained an inveterate Yankee to the end. From Spain he wrote that the longer he stayed there the better he liked America. From England he wrote that the well-combed, tidy landscape made him homesick for the more casual and rugged aspects of the scene at home. In spite of the sophistication of the European circles he moved in so amiably and so comfortably, he wrote Henry James that he thought the best society he ever saw, "take it by and large," was in Cambridge, Massachusetts. During all these years Lowell was a mediator between the cultures of the two worlds, as Longfellow was and had been. In his essay "On a Certain Condescension in Foreigners," published in 1871, he reminds Europeans, specifically Englishmen, of their own misguided conceits:

> The only sure way of bringing about a healthy relation between the two countries is for Englishmen to clear their minds of the notion that we are always to be treated as a kind of inferior and deported Englishman whose nature they perfectly understand, and whose back they accordingly stroke the wrong way of the fur with amazing perseverance. Let them learn to treat us naturally on our merits as human beings, as they would a German or a Frenchman, and not as if we were a kind of counterfeit Briton whose crime appeared in every shade of difference, and before long there would come that right feeling which we naturally call a good understanding. The common blood, and still more the common language,

An engraving of about 1875 depicts the home of the Atlantic Monthly *on Tremont Street, Boston. The founding of the magazine in 1857—with Lowell as editor—marked a high point in Boston's cultural development, and the* Atlantic *quickly became a national institution. Throughout America—in small rural towns, western cities, and eastern centers—thousands of subscribers eagerly awaited each new issue and thrilled at the works of its illustrious contributors.*

are fatal instruments of misapprehension. Let them give up *trying* to understand us, still more thinking that they do, and acting in various absurd ways as the necessary consequence, for they will never arrive at that devoutly-to-be-wished consummation, till they learn to look at us as we are and not as they suppose us to be. Dear old long-estranged mother-in-law, it is a great many years since we parted. Since 1660, when you married again, you have been a step-mother to us. Put on your spectacles, dear madam. Yes, we *have* grown, and changed likewise. You would not let us darken your doors, if you could help it. We know that perfectly well. But pray, when we look to be treated as men, don't shake that rattle in our faces, nor talk baby to us any longer.

To the end of Lowell's life he retained his intemperate tendencies to smoke and to read—and his unquenchable youthful exuberance. When he was sixty-nine years of age he wrote his daughter, "I was passing a Home for Incurable Children the other day, and said to my companion, 'I shall go there one of these days.'" He died a very few years later, at "Elmwood," without ever having brought his innumerable talents into any sharp focus, though nevertheless acclaimed as one of America's most accomplished and venerable men of letters. In a memorial, *The Christian Union* observed that although Lowell had never seemed to realize his full potential, "there was always in him a thought deeper than he expressed, a life profounder than he disclosed. This is true only of men of real greatness; such men are always richer and ampler than their work."

Lowell had accepted the editorial job at the *Atlantic Monthly* in 1857 somewhat reluctantly, because he thought his older neighbor Oliver Wendell Holmes was better qualified for the post than he was—and only with the assurance that Holmes would be among the first and steady contributors. Holmes complied on both points, and with his contributions he helped establish at the same time his own literary fame and the magazine's reputation. (It was he who named the periodical.)

Holmes was born in what must be remembered as the magic year of 1809, which saw the births of Poe and Lincoln, of Darwin, Tennyson, Gladstone, Chopin, and Mendelssohn. Like Longfellow and Lowell, he was descended from seventeenth-century New England forebears—among others, from the poet Anne Bradstreet, daughter of Thomas Dudley, governor of the Massachusetts Bay Colony—and, like Melville, also from Dutch ancestors who were among the early settlers of Albany. Holmes, too, lived in an eighteenth-century house in Cambridge, a house that had served as a military headquarters at the outset of the Revolution. It was there, the story goes, that plans were laid for fortifying Bunker Hill, and that the floors were dented by the butts of soldiers' muskets.

Holmes duly went to Harvard and was graduated in the class of 1829. (One of his classmates was Samuel F. Smith, the author of "America.") Within a year of his graduation, when he was barely twenty-one years of age, Holmes

Oliver Wendell Holmes, doctor and literary wit, portrayed himself as an anatomy professor in the self-drawn cartoon, left. In 1886 he was caricatured, far left, by Sir Leslie Ward ("Spy") for London's Vanity Fair.

excited wide public interest with his fiery poem "Old Ironsides," protesting the proposed demolition of the *Constitution*, the frigate that had served first in the Tripolitan War, then in the War of 1812, when, under the command of Isaac Hull, it had beaten the British *Guerrière* in a memorable battle off the coast of Newfoundland. Holmes' poem starts with the rousing verse:

> Ay, tear her tattered ensign down!
>   Long has it waved on high,
> And many an eye has danced to see
>   That banner in the sky;
> Beneath it rung the battle shout,
>   And burst the cannon's roar;—
> The meteor of the ocean air
>   Shall sweep the clouds no more.

Thanks in some measure to Holmes' verse, which he had dashed off in great haste, the restored ship remains one of the tourist attractions of Boston.

Following his graduation from Harvard, Holmes studied medicine at Boston and then in Paris under Napoleon's favorite surgeon. (He also read law, but gave that up after one year.) During the next quarter of a century he produced only occasional literary pieces, along with several important medical treatises. However, his lectures on anatomy and physiology, first at Dartmouth and then at Harvard, were brilliant expositions of his combined wit and scholarship. One of his students recalled that when Holmes entered the lecture hall he was greeted by "a mighty shout and stamp of applause." There followed a "charming hour" in which he made the most difficult study fascinating to his spellbound class. He had equal success lecturing to lyceum audiences on these and other subjects—this "trying and dangerous business of lecture-peddling," as he called it.

Another of his contemporaries observed that Holmes made a study of witticism. Even in the company of the great Boston talkers, his conversation was supreme. With the flow of what he termed his "linguacity," at times he quite simply took over the conversation of his circle, but with such commanding spirit and humor that few found fault with him. Emerson recalled that on a train trip they made together, Holmes talked steadily for twenty miles. At one meeting of the Saturday Club he reportedly told Lowell, "Now, James, let me talk and don't interrupt me."

The sprightly cast of Holmes' mind was already apparent when he was a young student in Europe. At one point in his travels he caught a glimpse of William IV and noted: "The King blew his nose twice, and wiped the royal perspiration repeatedly from a face which is probably the largest uncivilized spot in England." He even viewed the medical profession with a critical, detached, and amused attitude—and an independence that seemed both undignified and controversial to his more serious colleagues. When he first hung out his shingle he chose as a motto, "the smallest fevers thankfully received." He did not actively practice medicine for long. However, he remained a stimulating agent within the profession. In 1860 he read a paper before the Massachusetts Medical Society protesting that the public was being overdosed with drugs, a radical opinion for which the society immediately disclaimed all responsibility, but a criticism that proved with time to be all too

Holmes inaugurated his literary career in 1830 with his fiery ode, "Old Ironsides." The poem inspired a surge of public indignation that helped save the U.S.S. Constitution *from destruction. Old Ironsides has been restored several times; today she lies in the Boston harbor, as shown above, a shrine for American patriots.*

A scene in a fashionable boarding house is depicted in a lithograph of the mid 19th century, when many urban Americans lived in such lodgings. This amazed the acid English critic, Mrs. Trollope, who observed that "a great number of young married persons board by the year, instead of 'going to housekeeping'.... Of course this statement does not include persons of large fortune, but it does include many whose rank in society would make such a mode of life quite impossible with us."

reasonable and just. Almost as radical was his recommendation that women be admitted to the Harvard Medical School. Everything considered, he once remarked, he would prefer a male practitioner; "but a woman's eye," he reflected, "a woman's instinct, and a woman's divining power are special gifts . . . If there were only a well-organized and well trained hermaphrodite physician I am not sure I would not send for him—her . . . as likely to combine more excellence than any unisexual individual." (As an interesting footnote to his professional concerns, in 1846 he had used the word "anaesthesia" in its current sense when he saw a patient for the first time rendered almost insensible to pain, with sulphuric ether, during a dental operation. It was a word that, as he then foretold, would be "repeated by the tongues of every civilized race of mankind" in the years to come.)

Until Lowell asked him to write for the *Atlantic* in 1857, Holmes' literary talents had been largely devoted to pleasing his friends and classmates at social gatherings. (Over the years he wrote almost forty poems for his class reunions.) Later, on the occasion of his seventieth birthday, he recalled that Lowell's request for contributions to the magazine had awakened him "from a kind of literary lethargy in which I was half slumbering to call me to active service. Remembering some crude papers of mine in an old magazine, it occurred to me that their title might serve some pert papers, and so I sat down and wrote of what came into my head under the title, 'The Autocrat of the Breakfast-Table.' This work was not the result of an express premeditation, but was, I may say, dipped from the running stream of my thoughts."

The "crude papers" he referred to had appeared under the same title twenty-five years earlier in the *New England Magazine*. He resumed the series with the opening words, "I was just going to say, when I was interrupted . . . ," as though there had been only a momentary time gap. Then, to the joy of his readers, he went on to describe the imaginary table talk at a boarding house in Boston, interspersing a number of his most memorable poems in the text. Presumably, these conversations and versifications were very much the same as the otherwise unrecorded interchanges at the Saturday Club—with Holmes himself always the most conspicuous performer.

In passing it should be recalled that the boarding house was a very popular American institution about the time Holmes was writing. The proliferation of such accommodations, created by housing shortages, increasing rents, and the chronic servant problem, was phenomenal. It has been estimated that at least 70 per cent of the population during the 1800's lived in boarding houses at some time in their lives. Thus, the scene he set in the *Autocrat* was thoroughly familiar to his audience, and the interest in his story was the greater for that.

The *Autocrat* has been called "one of the most highly civilized books ever written in America." Its success was instant on both sides of the Atlantic. In England Thackeray observed that no man there could then write with the "charming mixture of wit, pathos, and imagination" that Holmes commanded. When it appeared in book form the *Autocrat* sold ten thousand copies during the first three days. In a later comment on Holmes' style the Boston *Daily Advertiser* pointed out that "his writings have the spring of the hickory, the smack of the cider, the tonic of the climate and the vigor of the type of men hardened by the struggle that has formed our national character. . . ." Holmes included in his rambling and miscellaneous discourse two of his most fondly remembered poems, "The Chambered Nautilus" and "The Deacon's Masterpiece." In the former, the chambered nautilus, a mollusk that builds ever larger shells as it grows, symbolizes human aspiration; the poem ends with the familiar verse:

> Build thee more stately mansions, O my soul,
>   As the swift seasons roll!
>   Leave thy low-vaulted past!
> Let each new temple, nobler than the last,
> Shut thee from heaven with a dome more vast,
>   Till thou at length are free,
> Leaving thine outgrown shell by life's unresting sea!

"The Deacon's Masterpiece," subtitled "The Wonderful One-Hoss Shay," is often considered to be a parable of the breakdown of Calvinism, represented by the deacon's carriage, so constructed that it would last precisely a century and then fall apart all at once. The poem might illustrate as well Holmes' distrust of *any* rigid logic that pretended to be everlastingly true and irrefutable.

> You see, of course, if you're not a dunce,
> How it went to pieces all at once,—
> All at once, and nothing first,—
> Just as bubbles do when they burst.

> End of the wonderful one-hoss shay,
> Logic is logic. That's all I say.

Holmes' antipathy to the lingering presence of Calvinistic theology stemmed from his deep faith in science—or Science, as he habitually capitalized the word—which he felt offered a rationally acceptable revelation of the divine mind. Instead of Calvinistic predestination, he preferred to believe that heredity and environment played a large role in the direction of human lives. Three novels he wrote deal with abnormal physiological and psychological conditions for which the characters involved are not responsible— "medicated novels," as they have been termed, that anticipate much of the

In his "logical story" entitled "The Deacon's Masterpiece, or the Wonderful 'One-Hoss Shay,'" Holmes makes a witty, satirical attack on the rigorous logic of old-time Calvinism. He demonstrates that a system based solely on logic goes to pieces all at once, "just as bubbles do when they burst." Howard Pyle's illustration of the "shay" dates from about 1890.

Emerson and Holmes belonged to the same literary circle. They are shown seated together in Boston's public garden in the retouched photograph reproduced above. Holmes, who wrote a biography of Emerson, referred to the latter as "a winged Franklin" and "a soaring nature, ballasted with sense."

fiction of later years. In *Elsie Venner: A Romance of Destiny*, published in 1861, he challenges the concept of original sin and human responsibility, and explains the fate of his heroine (the prototype of whom is said to be Margaret Fuller) in terms of a scientific analysis of her character and of the pattern of her inherited characteristics. Elsie is an evil person in spite of herself, and not to be blamed for doing what her genes and the conditions of life have made her do. This sort of materialistic determinism seems, ironically, hardly less binding than the predestination of the Calvinists, which Holmes ridiculed.

Holmes was a small, slender, asthmatic man, but he was fond of sports and a firm advocate of physical fitness. There were those in his day who felt that physical vigor and spiritual sanctity were incompatible; that in a sporting match the best preacher would be chosen last, since athletic capacity was in inverse ratio to spiritual accomplishment. But Holmes was dismayed by the reluctance of his young countrymen to indulge in body-building activities. "I am satisfied," he wrote in the *Autocrat*, "that such a set of black-coated, stiff-jointed, soft-muscled, paste-complexioned youth as we can boast in our Atlantic cities never before sprang from the loins of Anglo-Saxon lineage . . . and as for any great athletic feat performed by a gentleman in these latitudes, society would drop a man who should run round the [Boston] Common in five minutes." Holmes himself took delight in rowing on the Charles River—and in watching horse races and boxing matches.

He never did stop writing and talking with style until old age and failing eyesight diminished his efforts. As he was approaching eighty he wrote an English friend that he had "a cataract in the kitten state of development," betraying his lifelong and uncontrollable weakness for punning. Nevertheless, in his late seventies, in response to many invitations, he was persuaded to visit England once again. As he sailed away, burdened with going-away presents, he proudly put to use the best of them all, that new gadget the safety razor. In London the round of breakfasts, luncheons, teas, dinners, and receptions made him wish that, like a ruminant, he had a number of stomachs. He met Robert Browning—or rather, Robert Browning met him; he discoursed with Henry James and Oscar Wilde, with whom he had earlier talked in America; he visited Tennyson; he went to the Derby in a royal car with the Prince of Wales and sat with him in the royal box; and, like Longfellow and Lowell, he received degrees from Oxford, Cambridge, and Edinburgh. At Cambridge the students sang "Holmes, sweet Holmes," a variation of the familiar lyric by John Howard Payne, and at Oxford they asked if he had come in the "One-Hoss Shay." He went on to Paris to talk with Louis Pasteur, "one of the truest benefactors of his race," as Holmes called him. He arrived at New York on his seventy-seventh birthday, and returned home to deliver an address on the occasion of Harvard's two hundred and fiftieth anniversary.

To those who asked for an octogenarian's advice on longevity, he suggested they might imagine that they had a mortal disease which no doctor could diagnose. On his eightieth birthday he wrote his friend John Greenleaf Whittier: "Here I am at your side among the octogenarians. At seventy we are objects of veneration, at eighty of curiosity, at ninety of wonder; and if we reach a hundred we are candidates for a sideshow attached to Barnum's great

176

exhibition." (Holmes loved the circus.) That year he wrote "The Broomstick Train; or the Return of the Witches," a yarn in which he tells of witches released from hell who return to earth in the form of the latest wonder of the age, the electric trolley car. He called the book the "wintry products of my freezing wits."

Much earlier in life he had written a poem, "The Last Leaf," a touching lyric about an oldster who had outlived all his contemporaries (he was characterizing Herman Melville's grandfather):

> The mossy marbles rest
> On the lips that he has prest
>   In their bloom,
> And the names he loved to hear
> Have been carved for many a year
>   On the tomb.
>
>   ✻   ✻   ✻   ✻
>
> And if I should live to be
> The last leaf upon the tree
>   In the spring,
> Let them smile, as I do now,
> At the old forsaken bough
>   Where I cling.

He himself was such a "last leaf," outliving Emerson, Hawthorne, Lowell, Longfellow, and most of his other eminent contemporaries. After he died in 1894, at the age of eighty-five, a tablet to his memory was placed in King's Chapel in Boston; the inscription ends with the words, "A true son of New England, his works declare their birthplace and their times, but their influence far transcends these limits." In the next generation his son and namesake reached his own high level of literary skill in his legal papers and letters. The younger Holmes was a professor of law at Harvard, chief justice of the Massachusetts supreme court, and associate justice of the U.S. Supreme Court.

Another of Holmes' talented contemporaries, the beloved poet John Greenleaf Whittier, died at the same age—eighty-five—just two years earlier. In 1885, after a visit from Holmes, Whittier wrote a friend that the two oldsters were like stranded mariners warming themselves at a fire kindled from the wreck of their vessels, their literary shipmates having almost all slipped away. When Lowell died in 1891, Holmes reminded Whittier, using similar imagery, that they were among the few survivors of a wrecked ship, clinging to the spar of a raft and barely keeping their white-bearded chins above the water. A year later Whittier was also dead. His last poem included some lines for Holmes' eighty-third birthday.

Although he too was descended from early settlers of New England, Whittier was no Brahmin. He was born of Quaker parents in rural Massachusetts, in a farmhouse that had been passed down through several generations of the Whittier family. He did not go to Harvard; he was, in fact, self-educated to a large degree. (He made slippers by hand to pay for some of the limited schooling he received.) His boyhood and youth were spent on the ancestral farm, playing and working in the fields, and reading what he could

John Greenleaf Whittier, poet laureate of New England, was a man steeped in "marvelous stories of the denizens of the forest and stream, traditions of witchcraft, and tales of strange happenings."

get his hands on. That childhood was later recalled in "The Barefoot Boy," one of his unforgettable poems:

> Blessings on thee, little man,
> Barefoot boy, with cheek of tan!
> With thy turned-up pantaloons,
> And thy merry whistled tunes;
> With thy red lip, redder still
> Kissed by strawberries on the hill;
> With the sunshine on thy face,
> Through thy torn brim's jaunty grace;
> From my heart I give thee joy,—
> I was once a barefoot boy!
> Prince thou art,—the grown-up man
> Only is republican.
> Let the million-dollared ride!
> Barefoot, trudging at his side,
> Thou hast more than he can buy
> In the reach of ear and eye,—
> Outward sunshine, inward joy:
> Blessings on thee, barefoot boy!

The family homestead was recalled in another memorable poem, perhaps Whittier's best—*Snow-Bound:*

> The moon above the eastern wood
> Shone at its full; the hill-range stood
> Transfigured in the silver flood,

The Country Gallants, painted by John George Brown in 1876 and reproduced below, is similar in spirit to Whittier's poem "The Barefoot Boy," which recalls the poet's own youth in beautiful, rural New England. Brown's canvas, like Whittier's idyll, conveys the innocence and freedom of childhood.

Its blown snows flashing cold and keen,
Dead white, save where some sharp ravine
Too shadow, or the sombre green
Of hemlocks turned to pitchy black
Against the whiteness at their back.
For such a world and such a night
Most fitting that unwarming light,
Which only seemed where'er it fell
To make the coldness visible.

Shut in from all the world without,
We sat the clean-winged hearth about
[That is, brushed clean with a turkey's wing],
Content to let the north-wind roar
In barred rage at pane and door,
While the red logs before us beat
The frost-line back with tropic heat;
And ever, when a louder blast
Shook beam and rafter as it passed,
The merrier up its roaring draught
The great throat of the chimney laughed;
The house-dog on his paws outspread
Laid to the fire his drowsy head,
The cat's dark silhouette on the wall
A couchant tiger's seemed to fall;
And, for the winter fireside meet,
Between the andirons' straddling feet,
The mug of cider simmered slow,
The apples sputtered in a row,
And, close at hand, the basket stood
With nuts from brown October's wood.

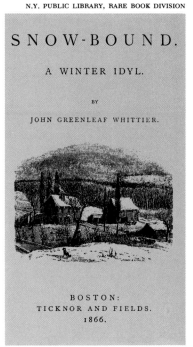

SNOW-BOUND.

A WINTER IDYL.

BY

JOHN GREENLEAF WHITTIER.

BOSTON:
TICKNOR AND FIELDS.
1866.

Snow-Bound was published in 1866 by Boston's leading publishers. Whittier's Yankee idyll, wrote one American literary historian, was a work of "tender devotion. . . . But against the background of a nation fast adapting itself to urban ways the poem appears something more than a cold pastoral. It is a quiet tribute to a form of civilized living that was passing. Here embodied in glowing terms was the Jeffersonian dream of the virtuous small landholder, beholden to no one and winning an honest, laborious livelihood from the soil."

For those who sprang from the soil of New England, wherever they had wandered such verses carried an incomparable nostalgia—the essence of the Yankee legend and spirit and of the landscape where it flourished. Of *Snow-Bound* Thomas Wentworth Higginson wrote: "Here we have absolutely photographed the Puritan Colonial interior, as it existed till within memory of old men still living. No other book, no other picture preserves it to us; all other books, all other pictures combined, leave us still ignorant of the atmosphere which this one page re-creates for us. . . ." It is indeed more than a poem; it is a social document of the highest interest and value.

For much of Whittier's early life, from 1833 to 1860, he was actively engaged in the abolitionist movement, as an editor, a writer, a politician, and an active agent. In some circles he was practically ostracized socially for those antislavery views, unpopular as they were among conservatives who hoped to keep the ship of state from rocking too violently; at other times and places he suffered indignities and even physical peril from antagonistic mobs. However, he claimed he was prouder to have signed the Declaration of Sentiments, which was adopted at the first convention of the American Anti-Slavery Society, than to find his name on the title page of any book.

Whittier's strongest statement in this cause he so wholly supported came when Daniel Webster pleaded in defense of the Compromise of 1850, after

179

a bitter controversy between North and South. The Compromise included among its provisions the Fugitive Slave Act. By this last enactment all citizens were subject to fines and imprisonment for harboring, concealing, or rescuing a runaway slave. For Whittier, and those who shared his views, this was a betrayal of elementary human justice. (Emerson called it a "filthy enactment.") He lashed out at Webster in a poem, "Ichabod," for what Whittier deemed a compromise beyond the limits of conscience. In later years even the poet was disturbed by the vehemence of his attack on Webster, whose moral courage had been strained to the utmost to meet the crisis of the hour and in whose heart these lines must have rankled:

> So fallen! so lost! the light withdrawn
>   Which once he wore!
> The glory from his gray hairs gone
>   Forevermore!
>
> *   *   *   *
>
> Of all we loved and honored, naught
>   Save power remains;
> A fallen angel's pride of thought,
>   Still strong in chains.
>
> All else is gone; from those great eyes
>   The soul has fled:
> When faith is lost, when honor dies,
>   The man is dead!

Whittier lived to regret the harshness of that judgment. The passage of time showed that under the explosive circumstances of the moment, Webster's stand was temperate and statesmanlike. Time has also increased his reputation as an orator whose declamations were themselves literary masterpieces of a kind. In 1830, as a relatively young man, Webster had warned the nation of the horrors of fratricidal strife in replying to the accusation by Senator Hayne of South Carolina that New England was narrowly sectional in her interests and hostile to the South. In the last paragraph of his speech, in which he protested that Hayne's contention led toward disunion and civil war, Webster reached rare heights of eloquence and prophecy, which were more expressive than most of the purely literary creations of the day.

> When my eyes shall be turned to behold for the last time the sun in heaven, may I not see him shining on the broken and dishonored fragments of a once glorious Union; on States dissevered, discordant, belligerent; on a land rent with civil feuds, or drenched, it may be, in fraternal blood! Let their last feeble and lingering glance rather behold the gorgeous ensign of the republic, now known and honored throughout the earth, still full high advanced, its arms and trophies streaming in their original lustre, not a stripe erased or polluted, not a single star obscured, bearing for its motto no such miserable interrogatory as "What is all this worth?"

His exhortation ended with the famous words, "Liberty *and* Union, now and forever, one and inseparable!"

Webster died in 1852, shortly after the Compromise of 1850 was enacted.

Daniel Webster was a man of intense nature, as expressed in the daguerreotype above. He was nicknamed "Black Dan" because of his swarthy complexion; his eyes, according to the English historian Thomas Carlyle, were like "anthracite furnaces." Webster deserves a place in American letters because of the magical literary quality that lifts the speeches he wrote above mere rhetoric.

Whittier lived on. During the Civil War he wrote "Barbara Frietchie," a poem describing a supposedly historic incident that took place as Stonewall Jackson triumphantly entered Frederick, Maryland—and including the familiar lines:

> "Shoot, if you must, this old gray head,
> But spare your country's flag," she said.

When the war was finally fought and finished, Whittier somewhat whimsically recalled that in those earlier years of agitation he had left the haunts of the muses "to turn the crank of an opinion wheel"; that he had made "his rustic reed of song a weapon in the war with wrong." That was only partly true. In the prewar years he had produced a number of works having nothing to do with abolitionist sentiment and politics, including the popular poem "Maude Muller" and, in 1849, the most important prose piece of his career, *Leaves from Margaret Smith's Journal in the Province of Massachusetts Bay, 1678–79.* This imaginary story of life in early New England is so carefully and skillfully documented that it is, in effect, a creative historical reconstruction of the period that witnessed the Salem witchcraft trials. However, it was in the last forty years of his life that Whittier wrote most of the poems for which he is best known.

The historian Francis Parkman, who outlived Whittier by a year, referred to him as "the poet of New England," and as such he was revered by the American people. In Whittier's old age his birthdays were calendared as festivals, greetings were sent to him by young and old alike from across the nation. In 1887 a community of Quakers in California, wishing to honor the poet, named their town after him (a town that became the birthplace of President Nixon.) He was and would continue to be remembered more fondly for his homely verses than for the abolitionist polemics of his earlier years.

Earnest and persistent as he was in those antislavery poems, tracts, and editorials, Whittier never achieved with them the spectacular success that Harriet Beecher Stowe instantly won with *Uncle Tom's Cabin, or Life Among the Lowly* when it appeared in book form in 1852. This sensational novel had a cast of characters who have become immortal figures in American folklore— the devout and faithful Negro slave, Uncle Tom, the mulatto girl, Eliza, who escapes from her bondage by fleeing across the frozen Ohio River, the angelic white child, Little Eva, her mischievous Negro companion, Topsy, and the cruel, degenerate Simon Legree, who was, incidentally, a Vermonter.

During the years she had spent in Cincinnati Mrs. Stowe had seen her father and brother aid runaway slaves from across the river in Kentucky; her deeply religious spirit (she was the daughter, wife, sister, and mother of ministers) was aroused to the pitch of passion by the insufferable consequences of the Fugitive Slave Act. To explain how her modest talent could generate such a potent message, she remarked that God had written her book. Actually, Mrs. Stowe wrote most of the book at her kitchen table after she had put her several children to bed for the night—tears splashing on the manuscript as she penned her story. It was the greatest of American propaganda novels, and it won her nationwide prominence and international attention. With this one book she became a symbol for humanitarians the

TEXT CONTINUES PAGE 184

Harriet Beecher Stowe, the wife and daughter of prominent abolitionists, has been called a volcanic soul served by an "apostolic mission." After writing Uncle Tom's Cabin, *one of the most influential novels of all time, she devoted herself to works about the New England scene—writings that established a point of departure for later New England authors, notably Sarah Orne Jewett.*

181

UNCLE TOM
IN
ART & THEATRE

Soon after the publication of Harriet Beecher Stowe's Uncle Tom's Cabin *in 1852 an American critic observed: "Even the Wizard of the North never so held a world spellbound—never spoke to so many hearts, or excited in each such wondrous enthusiasm." The emotionally charged story was widely translated; from Paris George Sand wrote to Harriet Stowe, saying, "The people devour it, they cover it with tears." In England the* Spectator *commented on "Tom-mania." The best seller inspired scores of works by artists on both sides of the Atlantic, as the sampling here indicates: the French lithograph (above), the theatre poster (above, left), the sculptural group (below, left), and the lithograph of Simon Legree (right). Uncle Tom soon became a stable fixture in theatrical repertories the world over, and by the 1870's literally hundreds of troupes were devoting themselves to the extremely lucrative profession of "tomming." The movies, too, have had their fling with Uncle Tom—witness the extravaganza of the 1920's. There have even been Uncle Tom card games and comic books.*

world over; reformers found in her plot, sharply outlined, the ultimate and most pitiable degradation of the human spirit that went with slavery. *Uncle Tom's Cabin* was translated into almost every language. Tolstoy compared the book with the work of Hugo and Dickens; Heine, Macaulay, and George Sand all seriously reviewed it. Palmerston read *Uncle Tom* three times and Gladstone cried over it. When Mrs. Stowe went overseas in 1853, she met with an enthusiastic reception by her admirers. On a subsequent visit to England, among other tributes to her fame, she was honored by Queen Victoria. At home the abolitionist statesman Charles Sumner thought that Lincoln never would have been elected if Mrs. Stowe had not published her melodramatic fiction. About ten years later, when the Civil War was raging, President Lincoln said to the author, "So you're the little woman who made this great war." It may well have been the most influential novel in all history. This "Iliad of the blacks," as the book has been called, has probably sold almost seven million copies.

Aside from its topical character, *Uncle Tom's Cabin* had a broad sentimental appeal that, among other things, led to its dramatization in the theatre in Europe as well as in America. It remained on the boards in this country for at least sixty-seven years, and it has been revived in recent years as a straight production, as an opera, as a "swing" performance, and as a silent movie. (Inevitably, it was also made into a comic strip.) Her stern upbringing had led Mrs. Stowe to suspect the theatre as a device of the devil. However, when the play based on her book was staged in Boston, she could not resist the temptation to watch a performance. Carefully escorted and "well muffled," she secretly visited the theatre and was enchanted by the spectacle, whatever may have been the damage to her conscience from that sinful adventure. On at least one other occasion she lapsed from the path of righteousness, unwittingly this time, by accepting a refreshing punch before a party in her honor. She was not aware that the drink was alcoholic in content, and when the others arrived, the guest of honor, in her lace mitts and hoop skirts, was sleeping off the effects of the potion.

Like Whittier and Holmes, Harriet Beecher Stowe lived to be eighty-five. During that long life she wrote many other books, some of which—her New England novels, *The Minister's Wooing, The Pearl of Orr's Island*, and *Oldtown Folks*, for instance—can be read today with pleasure. She was as well informed about the Puritan past as was Hawthorne. But her work, like that of some of the greater Yankee contemporary poets, does not now enjoy the appreciation and favor it once did.

While Longfellow, Lowell, Holmes, and other genteel Yankee poets were acquiring laurels on two continents, Emily Dickinson, unbeknownst to all but a privileged few persons, was writing poems by the thousand in almost complete seclusion in her Amherst home. None was published over her name during her lifetime, and but a handful appeared anonymously—and contrary to her wishes. Fame and recognition came to her only years after her death, when a substantial part of her verse found its way into print. In 1939 one responsible critic could claim for her work that "no finer body of lyric poetry by an American author of the nineteenth century can be found."

Emily Dickinson had an unusual life, but nothing about her circumstances explains the development of her unusual talent. She was descended from

Emily Dickinson, the pensive subject of the daguerreotype reproduced above, was, with Walt Whitman, among the most inventive poets in 19th-century America. Thomas Wentworth Higginson, the critic and editor who was one of her few confidants, remarked: "I saw her but twice face to face, and brought away the impression of something as unique and remote as Undine or Mignon or Thekla."

seven generations of solid New Englanders. Her grandfather was largely responsible for the founding of Amherst College, as a check to the "erroneous ideas" being expounded at Harvard. His son, a lawyer, in turn became treasurer of the college. He was an austere man who, Emily recalled, had never played. It was said that he once laughed. ("If Father is asleep on the sofa," Emily wrote, "the house is full.") As a young woman, after a normal girlhood, she fell in love under circumstances that have never been clearly revealed, although overtones of a serious romance can be read into many lines of her poetry.

That was apparently a deep, but in the end hopeless attachment—and there was more than one of these, perhaps. Thereafter, for most of her mature life, Emily lived almost completely withdrawn from society, a wraithlike recluse dressed in white. Her world contracted to the limits of her Amherst house and garden and her family circle from which she very rarely strayed. She never married, although as a determined spinster she had occasional correspondence with several men whom she somewhat naively referred to as her "mentors." (As a schoolgirl she had written, "I am always in love with my teachers.") To one of these, who had asked for her photograph, she sent instead a brief, singular self-portrait. "I . . . am small," she wrote him, "like the wren; and my hair is bold, like the chestnut burr; and my eyes, like the sherry in the glass that the guest leaves." Her unspent passion did not blight her spirit. "I find ecstasy in living," she once wrote; "the mere sense of living is joy enough."

Her principal mentor was Thomas Wentworth Higginson. In appealing for new talent, Higginson had admonished authors to "tolerate no superfluities" in their writing. "There may be," he advised, "years of crowded passion in a word, and half a life in a sentence." This is very close to what Emily did in many of her short poems, but in a style so unconventional and so surprising that Higginson was not prepared for it. He was both mystified and intrigued by the "fiery mist" that, as he said, enshrouded this "gnome" (she sometimes signed her letters to him "your gnome"), and rejoiced in "the rare sparkles of light" that he found in her verse. In any case, she made clear to him that her poems were not for publication. They were her secret "letter to the world." She wanted only counsel and approval for her private benefit.

Her poems were written on scraps of wrapping paper, on anything that came to hand at the moment of inspiration—and there were hundreds and hundreds of them. When an authoritative edition of what could be gathered together of her poems was published in three volumes they numbered 1,775. Almost two-thirds seem to have been written within eight years. Her messages were usually brief, just a few lines, almost telegraphic:

> The bustle in a house
> The morning after death
> Is solemnest of industries
> Enacted upon earth,—
>
> The sweeping up the heart,
> And putting love away
> We shall not want to use again
> Until eternity.

Withdrawn from the world, in the solitude of her room, Emily Dickinson composed poems that "moved like bees upon a raft of air." She usually scribbled her verses on odd scraps of paper, as the fragment above.

The most commonplace words were charged with fresh life as she put them into new contexts, and nothing was too trivial or too sacred for her sharply focused attention—flies and bees and snakes and spiders, heaven and earth and life and death. She flirts with eternity and all but joshes heavenly beings and the Almighty himself:

> A smile suffused Jehovah's face;
> The cherubim withdrew;
> Grave saints stole out to look at me,
> And showed their dimples, too.

Without traditional regard for rule or rhyme, she spun out her lines with changing rhythms and vivid images that lend strange magic to the commonplace as well as to the ethereal, often linking them together in unexpected associations—much as her Puritan predecessors had done in their sermons and verses. Thus she conceived of death as coming with a broom and a dustpan; a journey to the Day of Judgment was to her a "buggy-ride"; eternity "rambled" with her; and so on. The universe she saw from her bedroom window and garden patch was a homely apparition. Of a morning the sun rose in the East "a ribbon at a time," and as day closed, the "housewife in the evening west" came back to "dust the pond . . . till brooms fade softly into stars—and then I come away."

Her lines can be enigmatic to the point of confusing her critics and her public. In 1861 she wrote:

> Wild nights—wild nights!
> Were I with thee,
> Wild nights should be
> Our luxury.
>
> Futile the winds
> To a heart in port
> Done with the compass,
> Done with the chart.
>
> Rowing in Eden—
> Ah, the sea!
> Might I but moor tonight
> In thee.

In 1891, five years after her death, when her early editors were preparing a selection of Emily Dickinson's poems for publication, one wrote another: "One poem only I dread a little to print—that wonderful 'Wild Nights,'—lest the malignant read into it more than that virgin recluse ever dreamed of putting there." The author was little help in such matters. Her ecstasies had been very personal and private concerns. As she transmuted her thoughts into verse, however, she created a body of poetry that in her day only Whitman surpassed in originality. Reviewing her work after her death, Higginson commented on her wayward, irregular use of language. He was then somewhat more indulgent than he had earlier been. "In many cases," he wrote, "these verses will seem to the readers like poetry torn up by the roots." But, he further observed, "when a thought takes one's breath away, a lesson on grammar seems an impertinence." Here, he concluded, were "flashes of

wholly original and profound insight into nature and life." In time his appraisal became broadly accepted.

As earlier remarked, an important part of the best American writing cannot be called "creative literature," and the contributions of Abraham Lincoln are remarkable examples of that fact. His addresses are studded with masterly phrases and thoughts, unmatched in their lucidity and brilliant simplicity. Of all the statements about the Civil War—in verse or prose, in orations or letters, including those made by Whittier, Whitman, Longfellow, and other literary giants of the day—none had more poignancy and force, none were more felicitously expressed, than those of Lincoln, who was without any literary pretensions whatsoever. "I am loathe to close," he said in his first inaugural address, reading from his carefully refined manuscript:

> We are not enemies, but friends. We must not be enemies. Though passion may have strained, it must not break our bonds of affection. The mystic cords of memory, stretching from every battlefield and patriot grave to every living heart and hearth-stone all over this broad land, will yet swell the chorus of the Union when again touched, as surely as they will be, by the better angels of our nature.

Lincoln's second inaugural address was even more memorable, and, well known as they are, his remarks lose nothing with repetition:

> Fondly do we hope—fervently do we pray—that this mighty scourge of war may speedily pass away. Yet, if God wills that it continue until all the wealth piled by the bondman's two hundred and fifty years of unrequited toil shall be sunk, and until every drop of blood drawn with the lash shall be paid by another drawn with the sword, as was said three thousand years ago, so still it must be said "The judgments of the Lord are true and righteous altogether."
>
> With malice toward none; with charity for all; with firmness in the right, as God gives us to see the right, let us strive on to finish the work we are in; to bind up the nation's wounds; to care for him who shall have borne the battle, and for his widow and his orphan—to do all which may achieve and cherish a just and lasting peace, among ourselves, and with all nations.

In the meantime, on November 19, 1863, Lincoln had delivered his noblest utterance of all with the Gettysburg Address before some fifteen thousand persons. As he approached the cemetery, looking ungainly on a horse that was too small for him, souvenir hunters were culling from the battlefield buttons and bullets and other remnants of the gory conflict. In the vicinity there were a scattering of coffins and the skeletons of horses yet unburied. He had ac-

The consecration of the "Great National" military cemetery near Gettysburg on November 19, 1863, is the subject of the illustration reproduced above, which originally appeared in Frank Leslie's Illustrated Newspaper, *New York, on December 5, 1863. The eyewitness sketch was done by Joseph Becker. The town cemetery is at left, and the platform from which Lincoln delivered the Gettysburg Address is left of the flag pole.*

Executive Mansion,

Washington, _____ , 186 .

Four score and seven years ago our fathers brought forth, upon this continent, a new nation, conceived in liberty, and dedicated to the proposition that "all men are created equal"

Now we are engaged in a great civil war, testing whether that nation, or any nation so conceived, and so dedicated, can long endure. We are met on a great battle field of that war. We have come to dedicate a portion of it, as a final resting place for those who died here, that the nation might live. This we may, in all propriety do. But, in a larger sense, we can not dedicate— we can not consecrate— we can not hallow, this ground— The brave men, living and dead, who struggled here, have hallowed it, far above our poor power to add or detract. The world will little note, nor long remember what we say here; while it can never forget what they did here.

It is rather for us, the living, to stand here,

The first draft of the Gettysburg Address, above, does not belie its hasty composition; Lincoln changed some words as he read the speech.

cepted the invitation to make a few "appropriate" remarks in spite of the pressure of official duties and of personal anxieties (his son Tad was gravely ill), and he hastily jotted down his thoughts. For two hours before he spoke, the celebrated Massachusetts orator Edward Everett faultlessly rendered his long, memorized oration. When Lincoln finally rose to speak, he barely glanced at the single sheet of manuscript before him. He finished his "little speech," as he called it, within two minutes, before many in the crowd realized he had begun, before some photographers had adjusted their tripods. The applause was tardy, and the next day most of the big newspapers reported the president's speech inconspicuously, as though it had been a brief addendum to Everett's copious remarks. Some Democratic editors damned the address as completely inadequate to the occasion. "The cheek of every American must tingle with shame," reported the Chicago *Times*, "as he reads the silly, flat and dishwatery utterances of the man who has to be pointed out to intelligent foreigners as the President of the United States."

However, in just two hundred and sixty-eight magnificently composed words Lincoln had delivered one of the most moving and significant expressions of American democracy. Everett was the first to recognize the quality of Lincoln's statement. "I should be glad," he wrote the president the next day, "if I could flatter myself that I came as near to the central idea of the occasion in two hours as you did in two minutes." From England Gladstone reminded the world that with his public utterances Lincoln had demonstrated his extraordinary talents as a literary artist.

It is not easy to reconcile that sort of consummate artistry with Lincoln's addiction to the broad humor of the frontier, which was bred in him from his childhood. Even in the most agonizing moments of his presidency, he relied upon comic relief of the commonest sort to ease the tensions of crucial circumstances. Among his favorite popular humorists was the journalist Charles Farrar Browne, much better known by his pen name Artemus Ward, who, like a Will Rogers of earlier days, in his writings and lectures jibed at the follies, the sentimentalities, and the insincerities of the times. "Artemus Ward's Sayings," couched in misspelled words and curious dialect, have little appeal to modern readers, but they attracted a wide audience in England as well as in America before Ward died of tuberculosis in London in 1867, a lecturer and showman to the last.

The day before he issued the Emancipation Proclamation, on Saturday, September 21, 1862, Lincoln called a meeting to read a draft of that statement to his cabinet for their consideration—and he introduced the grave subject by reading a short chapter of Ward's "High-Handed Outrage at Utica," which had just appeared. It was not one of Ward's funniest pieces, but Lincoln hoped such an introduction might ease his advisers toward the step of enormous consequence, not only to the immediate military and political situation that confronted the Union, but to the social and economic developments that would surely evolve from that proclamation for all time to come. Not all the members of his cabinet were entertained, but it gave the president a chuckle as he reached his fateful decision.

Ward helped secure a publisher for the first book by his contemporary Josh Billings—the pen name of Henry Wheeler Shaw, another humorist whose pithy quips won a wide audience that also included Lincoln. He had spent a year at Hamilton College before he was expelled, probably for some misdemeanor. "Hamilton has turned out a good many fine men," he later remarked, "—it turned me out." "The mule is haf hoss and haf Jackass," Billings observed in a characteristic style, "and then kums to a fullstop, natur diskovering her mistake." In their writings and innumerable lectures both Ward and Billings were paving the way for that supreme humorist Mark Twain.

Sound, scholarly history has not always been written by men with high degrees of literary skill. However, in the nineteenth century New England produced three major historians whose works are still esteemed both for their solid content and range and for the unusual merit of their styles—William Hickling Prescott, John Lothrop Motley, and Francis Parkman. They were Brahmins all, descendants of old and prominent New England families, graduates of Harvard, and men of high social station. All three were men of independent means, under no compulsion to undertake any arduous work; but all three suffered the compulsion to labor mightily at their self-imposed tasks of history-writing, at times under extraordinary difficulties. No doubt the Puritan strain that ran through their blood made industrious activity a necessity in their lives. (When an English visitor complained to a Boston lady that America had no leisure class, she replied, "Oh yes we have, but *we* call them tramps.") All three, it might be added, considered history to be primarily a form of literature.

Born in 1796, Prescott was the oldest of the three. When he was an undergraduate he was accidentally hit in the left eye by a hard crust of bread, which left him without the sight of that eye. Shortly afterward, trouble developed in his other eye—a trouble that grew progressively worse over the rest of his life. He could never again read without extreme and often painful difficulty. At times he was, in effect, totally blind. Even with this tragic prospect apparent so early in his life, and against the admonitions of specialists, he decided to pursue a literary career. On a European tour, when he was about twenty years old, he bought a noctograph, a complicated apparatus that enabled him to write with a pointed stylus on carbonated paper, virtually without seeing what he was doing. With this aid, he observed, he circumvented "the two great difficulties in the way of a blind man's writing . . . his not knowing when the ink is exhausted in his pen, and when his lines run into one another." For the prodigious research he undertook, he had to rely upon paid secretaries to read to him in several languages, and he depended heavily on American foreign service personnel to send him transcripts of basic material. (He had to teach his readers to pronounce Spanish so that he could understand it.)

In spite of these formidable handicaps, Prescott produced a number of very substantial works, distinguished by vast erudition and polished prose. Like other Brahmin writers of his day, he was not professionally interested in the American

Boston Brahmin historian William Hickling Prescott, shown in an engraving of 1861, produced America's first scholarly studies on Spain and Latin America. He never visited Spain or any of the Hispanic lands whose histories he so eloquently retold, yet he always referred to Spain as "the country of my adoption," calling it the land where "old manuscripts and old wines of the noblest kind flourish side by side—the land of the hidalgo—the land that I love."

CULVER

democratic world, but looked to far places and other times for his subjects. He preferred not to "meddle with heroes who had not been under the ground for two centuries, at least." In 1837, somewhat hesitantly, he published his first major book, *A History of the Reign of Ferdinand and Isabella*. Few Bostonians had known he was writing it. As one contemporary remarked, "most of his friends thought that he led rather an idle, unprofitable life, but attributed it to his infirmity, and pardoned and overlooked it as a misfortune, rather than as anything discreditable." Actually, Prescott had been working at an unbelievable rate. Although he hated to get up early, he left instructions for the bedclothes to be pulled off him if he was not up at a prescribed hour. His secretary would read to him for six hours a day in a darkened room as he took notes with his noctograph. (The screens and curtains of the room were readjusted with almost every cloud that passed across the sky.) Then, alone and quietly, he would digest what had been read to him before he started to write. He wagered his secretary that he would complete so many pages in a given time, and imposed penalties on himself when he failed to do so. When the book appeared, not only was Boston captivated by the story as he told it, but with it Prescott quickly won the respect and admiration of the scholarly world abroad as well as at home. Among other honors, he was elected to the Royal Academy of History in Madrid. Public and private archives in Mexico, France, Sicily, and Italy as well as England were opened to this extraordinary American author and scholar.

Almost immediately Prescott started to prepare his next major opus, *A History of the Conquest of Mexico*, which was published in three volumes in 1843, and, following that, his *History of the Conquest of Peru* in two volumes, issued in 1847. Such subjects, as was said, had "the superior advantages of relating to his own quarter of the globe." To this day his accounts of the almost legendary achievements of the conquistadors remain standard authorities, in spite of all subsequent research on the subjects. With these books he also established canons of modern historical writing that deserve the respect they still get.

His strength was failing, however, and in 1850 he went to England for a change of scene and pace. That was, according to George Ticknor, his biographer (who wrote with some exaggeration), "the most brilliant visit ever made . . . by an American citizen not clothed with the *prestige* of official station"—such was Prescott's reputation; such also was his elegant and charming presence and manner. He was the house guest of the dukes of Northumberland and Argyll, of the Earl of Carlisle and the Duchess of Sutherland. He was presented at court. Oxford gave him a degree. There was no end to the respect paid him. Disraeli innocently asked him if he was related to the great American author of the Spanish histories. "I squeezed his arm," Prescott reported, "telling him that I could not answer for the greatness, but I was the man himself."

In 1858 Prescott suffered a slight stroke; but he went on writing industriously. "As to not working, as you kindly recommend," he wrote to one Spanish friend and scholar, "—to use Scott's words [Sir Walter Scott, whose historical romances Prescott deeply admired] on a similar recommendation to him, 'Molly, when she puts the kettle on, might as well say, Don't boil kettle' . . .

Boston-born and Harvard-educated, John Lothrop Motley concentrated on the history of the Netherlands. He was more didactic than Prescott and consciously preached the virtues of Protestant liberty as opposed to "decadent" Catholic absolutism. His heroes were all heroic—either unspeakably evil like the cruel Habsburg, Philip II of Spain, or magnificently good like the beneficent Dutch leader, William of Orange.

in truth long habit makes me find business—that is literary labor—the greatest pleasure." He died the next year. In a tribute to his memory, the historian George Bancroft observed that Prescott "was himself greater and better than his writings." His generosity to the poor and unfortunate was widely recognized and appreciated in Boston. With his handsome appearance and charming manner he had been a universal social favorite. To the end of his life he labored with love at his chosen task.

Like Prescott and Parkman, Motley rejected any thought of writing a political history of his own country. He would have liked to be a novelist, and did, in fact, write two books of fiction that have largely been forgotten. In the end, he chose as his lifelong work the history of the Netherlands, of their successful struggle for independence from Spain. With this theme he hoped to demonstrate how, with William of Orange as a hero and Philip II as a villain, the eventual Protestant victory led toward freedom and democracy as against the decadence of autocratic Catholic rule. (Of Philip II, Motley wrote, "If there are vices—as possibly there are—from which he was exempt, it is because it is not permitted to human nature to be perfect in evil.") He saw in the pattern of these developments events and ideas that determined the course of European and American history over the centuries to come. Motley's first work, *The Rise of the Dutch Republic*, published in three volumes in 1856 after ten years of preparation at Dresden, the Hague, and Brussels, established his high stature as a historian. Although he wrote other substantial books about the Netherlands, the *Dutch Republic* remains his foremost achievement. He was distracted in some degree from his career as a historian by his distinguished diplomatic service, first as secretary of the American legation at St. Petersburg, and later as United States minister to Austria, and, in 1869–70, to Great Britain. He was relieved of both those later posts for purely political reasons, or his work as a diplomat might in the long run have overshadowed his reputation as a historian.

Francis Parkman was the greatest of this trio of superb historians. For most of his mature life he too, like Prescott, was half blind and had to write with the aid of an apparatus that kept the lines of his notes in order as assistants read aloud to him. Worse, he suffered from a nervous disorder that at times made it impossible for him to work at all. (At one point in his later life an eminent French physician warned Parkman that he might go insane.) Yet, before he died in 1893, at the age of seventy, he had completed not only *The Oregon Trail*, a novel, and a book about roses but also his gigantic masterpiece of seven parts in eleven volumes dealing with the long struggle between the French and the British, with their Indian allies, for mastery of the North American continent. With this series he established his fair claim to rank among the leading historians of the age. One enthusiastic fellow historian compared Parkman with Herodotus, Thucydides, and Edward Gibbon. It was, he wrote, a "book for all mankind and all time." However this may be, his fame remains secure in our own day.

When he was a Harvard undergraduate, a classmate later recalled, Parkman already had "'Injuns' on the brain." He made many excursions through the eastern wilderness on foot and by canoe in areas he would one day write about. In 1843 he made the European tour customary among young gentle-

Francis Parkman, shown above, was the historian "of the American forest" and its denizens. "My theme fascinated me," he declared, "and I was haunted with wilderness images day and night."

On one of his forays out of Boston, the young Francis Parkman took his turn standing guard on the Oregon Trail, an adventure he described in The Oregon Trail. *Virtually alone in the stillness of the prairie night, wrapped to the nose in a blanket to ward off the icy dew, Parkman was awed by the majesty of the wilderness. His stance must have been similar to that depicted at left in* The Night Watch, *a lithograph of 1849 after a drawing by John W. Audubon, the naturalist's son. The watch was the inescapable duty of every able westward-bound pioneer.*

men of his class; and after graduation he attended Harvard Law School, and then, in 1846, to improve his health and to study the Indians, he undertook the one great physical adventure of his life, going West to journey along the Oregon Trail. For some weeks he traveled and lived with a band of Sioux Indians, and he got to know the hunters, trappers, half-breeds, and other types of that remote wilderness—types so many worlds apart from his own patrician circle in Boston. He took his turn standing guard, wrapped to his nose in a blanket against the icy dew of the prairie night. At Fort Bridger an Indian chief offered him a native girl in exchange for his horse—a bargain he declined, as a proper Bostonian would. He ate raw buffalo meat and found the liver "excellent," and listened to his native hosts vomit and retch during the night from having gorged themselves. An Indian chief described in detail how he had captured an enemy from another tribe, then scalped him before cutting the tendons of his wrist and flinging his still living body on the great fire that had been prepared.

It was a strenuous experience for the youth. He joined buffalo hunts, perilous as they could be, with uncontrollable zest for the excitement of overtaking and mingling with the vast herds and, with his swift and nimble horse on a dead run, singling out and killing his victims. "In a moment," he wrote of one such escapade, "I was in the midst of the cloud, half suffocated by the dust and by the trampling of the flying herd; but I was drunk with the chase and cared for nothing but the buffalo. . . . In a moment I was so close I could have touched them with my gun. . . . As I passed amid them they would lower their heads, and turning as they ran, attempt to gore my horse. . . . One just in front of me seemed to my liking, and I pushed close to her side. Dropping

The Buffalo Hunt, *reproduced above, was painted in 1861 by Arthur F. Tait. More than a decade earlier, during the trip to the West that resulted in* The Oregon Trail, *Parkman took part in a buffalo chase, a savage "sport" enjoyed by both amateurs and professionals until the once-numerous American bison was extinct.*

the reins I fired, holding the muzzle of the gun within a foot of her shoulder." He then killed a bull and, opening its throat, cut out the tongue, tied it to the back of the saddle, and rode back to camp. Parkman's lust for the kill reflected an attitude toward the wilderness world that was far less benign than that of Emerson and Thoreau; it was closer to his Puritan forebears' hostility to the denizens of the raw land they settled.

He wrote the book that thus described his adventures, *The Oregon Trail,* after he returned from the expedition—a book that has ever since been one of his most popular writings. But he returned from his experiences the worse for wear, his health more precarious than it had been. The physical strain of the trip, in fact, led to a complete breakdown, from which he had to recover before he could write the book. He deplored his progressive illness and weakness as much as he suffered from his various complaints. (He referred to those difficulties as "The Enemy.") Even before *The Oregon Trail* was published as a book (it originally appeared serially in the *Knickerbocker* magazine), he started the first of those eleven volumes that would have the collective title *France and England in North America,* his truly great work that would be completed only in 1892, a year before his death and more than forty years after he began the project. Blind and broken with illness, as a recent critic has written, Parkman fought like a wounded knight to finish his books.

Parkman began outlining the theme that was his lifetime's obsession when he was still in his teens, reading widely and intensively, far beyond the requirements of his college courses. "His thoughts were always in the forest," he later recalled, writing in the third person, "whose features possessed his waking and sleeping dreams, filling him with vague cravings impossible to satisfy." Ironically, in view of his subsequent, incapacitating frailties, he also pursued a program of physical fitness—rowing, boxing, riding, and hiking—to prepare him for work in the field. For he was convinced that it was necessary for him to know the rigors of the wilderness as well as did the heroes of the histories he would write. "Faithfulness to the truth of history," he claimed, "involves far more than research, however patient and scrupulous, into special facts. The narrator must seek to imbue himself with the life and spirit of the time." So, in his youth, between his spells of illness, and until he was reduced to "armchair research," he did manage to visit many scenes of the old Anglo-French frontier, from Canada to Florida, as well as out on the Oregon Trail. "My chief object in coming so far," he wrote of one of his youthful expeditions, "was merely to have a taste of the half-savage kind of life necessary to be led, and to see the wilderness where it was yet uninvaded by the hand of men." In Maine he heard from an ancient brave how his tribe had suffered attacks by the Mohawk, who took captive children and roasted them over the fire on forked sticks. And he learned the legendary history of the Ojibwa, the Iroquois, the Huron, and the Fox.

Parkman was a pioneer in an area of history that had hardly been touched. But he was as much an artist as a historian. He exhausted the resources of the libraries in and about Boston, and at times when he was physically able, he managed to visit archives in London and Paris. He converted the materials he found in dusty books and documents—and his stored-up memories of the frontier world as he had seen it—into texts of extraordinary eloquence. In our day, when literary fashion tends to favor spare and understated prose, Parkman's writing may seem prolix and turgid—as when he describes the Missouri River as "that savage river, descending from its mad career and a vast unknown of barbarism, poured its turbid floods into the bosom of its gentle sister [the Mississippi]." Even so, it is impossible to escape the peculiar magic of the fervid and sonorous phrases of his mature narratives. Thus he describes the occasion when, on April 9, 1682, La Salle, after a prodigious effort that had taken him from Canada down the Mississippi to its mouth, pronounced the claims of France to the great American West:

> The Frenchmen were mustered under arms and while the New England Indians and their squaws looked on in wondering silence, they chanted the *Te Deum*, the *Exaudiat* and the *Domine salvum fac Regum*. Then, amid volleys of musketry and shouts of *Vive le Roi*, La Salle planted the column in its place, and, standing near it, recited a long proclamation.... On that day the realm of France received on parchment a stupendous accession. The fertile plains of Texas; the vast basin of the Mississippi from its frozen northern springs to the sultry borders of the Gulf; from the woody ridges of the Alleghanies to the bare peaks

Parkman's major work, France and England in North America, *includes an account of the martyrdom of the French Jesuit missionaries, Fathers Jean de Brébeuf and Gabriel Lalemant, who were crucified by the Iroquois of New France in 1649. A 17th-century engraving shows the Iroquois pouring boiling water over Brébeuf's naked body, a torture they repeated three times in derision of the sacrament of holy baptism.*

of the Rocky Mountains—a region of savannas and forests, sun-cracked deserts and grassie prairies, watered by a thousand rivers, ranged by a thousand war-like tribes, passed beneath the scepter of the Sultan of Versailles; and all by virtue of a feeble voice, inaudible at half a mile.

At another point in his long story, he told of the French Jesuit priests who labored in the New World for the conversion of the heathen natives, leaving a record of physical heroism and of spiritual adventure rarely paralleled in the annals of history. "Men steeped in antique learning," Parkman wrote of those black-robed fathers who illumined the American wilderness with an apostolic flame and found God's wonder in all they saw, "pale with the close breath of the cloister, here spent the noon and evening of their lives, ruled savage hordes with a mild, parental sway and stood serene before the direst shapes of death. Men of courtly nurture, heirs to the polish of a far-reaching ancestry, here, with their dauntless hardihood, put to shame the boldest sons of toil."

These men had the manliness and stamina that Parkman so much admired and tried so hard to cultivate in himself in spite of his increasing disabilities. Vicariously, he relived the exploits of his various heroes. In a sense he was describing his own inner self when he wrote of those Jesuits, and of Frontenac, La Salle, Howe, Wolfe, and the other commanding figures in his epic. A trapper in the Rocky Mountains once told Parkman that "a gentleman of the right sort will stand hardship better than anybody else," and Parkman would have liked to believe that. He wrote of the great adventurer and pioneer La Salle as a "man of thought, trained amid arts and letters," as Parkman was himself. In his massive "history of the American forest," as he termed his great work, he hoped to "realize a certain ideal of manhood,—a little mediaeval." He did this, but with a scrupulous attention to the truth of the matter. "The full stature of this nearly blind historian, tortured by sickness and imaginings of sickness," one authority has recently observed, "is suggested by the fact that no man has attempted to do again the full story of the struggle for mastery of the North American continent."

Parkman's death marked the virtual end of a long, distinguished era of writing in New England. Holmes survived him by barely a year; Emerson, Longfellow, Lowell, and Whittier had died in the preceding decade or so. Prescott, Thoreau, and Hawthorne were all dead before the end of the Civil War. The famous cemetery at Mount Auburn outside Boston was becoming overcrowded with celebrities. The younger generation of Yankees had produced no equals or rivals of this dying breed of regional giants. More than one thoughtful contemporary agreed with the Bostonian Barrett Wendell, himself a qualified man of letters (among other things he wrote a history of American literature), when he observed in 1893 that "We are vanishing into provincial obscurity. America has swept from our grasp. The future is beyond us." New Yorkers with a pride of their own to favor could laugh when, some years later, one of their wits referred to New England as "the abandoned farm of literature." It was time that the writing of the future should depart from the canons established and cherished in New England. The seeds of those changing values had actually been sown years earlier and had produced ripe fruit long before the New England "founding fathers" of American literature had put down their pens.

THE LITERATURE OF PHOTOGRAPHY

The American writers and poets of the 1820's and 1830's set themselves the task of proving that the United States could rival Europe in literary accomplishments. By the 1850's, when American letters came of age, a generation of writers, clustered in the East, was continuing to find inspiration in nature and the American landscape. Just as the process of urbanization was beginning to overtake the land, the writers of the American renaissance found new meanings in the lush forests and fields and rustic homesteads that dotted their countryside, new joys in the rock-bound shores (such as the Maine setting shown below) and the strong oceans lashing each coast. The photographs on the following pages evoke the scenes that inspired the great flowering of Yankee literary talent.

CULVER

197

"Between two tall gateposts of rough-hewn stone (the gate itself having fallen from its hinges at some unknown epoch) we beheld the gray front of the old parsonage terminating the vista of an avenue of black ash-trees. . . . The glimmering shadows that lay half asleep between the door of the house and the public highway were a kind of spiritual medium, seen through which the edifice had not quite the aspect of belonging to the material world. Certainly it had little in common with those ordinary abodes which stand so imminent upon the road that every passer-by can thrust his head, as it were, into the domestic circle. . . .

How gently, too, did the sight of the Old Manse, best seen from the river, overshadowed with its willow and all environed about with the foliage of its orchard and avenue,—how gently did its gray, homely aspect rebuke the speculative extravagances of the day! It had grown sacred in connection with the artificial life against which we inveighed; it had been a home for many years in spite of all; it was my home too; and with these thoughts, it seemed to me that all the artifice and conventionalism of life was but an impalpable thinness upon its surface, and that the depth below was none the worse for it."

Nathaniel Hawthorne, from *The Old Manse*

"In the woods, too, a man casts off his years, as the snake
his slough, and at what period soever of life, is
always a child. In the woods is perpetual youth. Within
these plantations of God, a decorum and sanctity
reign, a perennial festival is dressed, and the guest
sees not how he should tire of them in a thousand years.
In the woods, we return to reason and faith. There I feel
that nothing can befall me in life,—no disgrace, no
calamity (leaving me my eyes), which nature cannot repair."

Ralph Waldo Emerson, from *Nature*

"So all night long the storm roared on:
The morning broke without a sun;
In tiny spherule traced with lines
Of Nature's geometric signs,
In starry flake, and pellicle,
All day the hoary meteor fell;
And, when the second morning shone,
We looked upon a world unknown,
On nothing we could call our own.
Around the glistening wonder bent
The blue walls of the firmament,
No cloud above, no earth below,—
A universe of sky and snow!
The old familiar sights of ours
Took marvellous shapes; strange domes and towers
Rose up where sty or corn-crib stood,
Or garden wall, or belt of wood;
A smooth white mound the brush-pile showed,
A fenceless drift what once was road;
The bridle-post an old man sat
With loose-flung coat and high cocked hat;
The well-curb had a Chinese roof;
And even the long sweep, high aloof,
In its slant splendor, seemed to tell
Of Pisa's leaning miracle.

❊   ❊   ❊   ❊

All day the gusty north-wind bore
The loosening drift its breath before;
Low circling round its southern zone,
The sun through dazzling snow-mist shone."

John Greenleaf Whittier, from *Snow-Bound*

"For the first week, whenever I looked out on the pond it impressed me like a tarn high up on the side of a mountain, its bottom far above the surface of other lakes, and, as the sun arose, I saw it throwing off its nightly clothing of mist, and here and there, by degrees, its soft ripples or its smooth reflecting surface was revealed, while the mists, like ghosts, were stealthily withdrawing in every direction into the woods, as at the breaking up of some nocturnal conventicle. The very dew seemed to hang upon the trees later into the day than usual, as on the sides of mountains.

This small lake was of most value as a neighbor in the intervals of a gentle rainstorm in August, when, both air and water being perfectly still, but the sky overcast, mid-afternoon had all the serenity of evening, and the wood thrush sang around, and was heard from shore to shore. A lake like this is never smoother than at such a time; and the clear portion of the air above it being shallow and darkened by clouds, the water, full of light and reflections, becomes a lower heaven itself so much the more important."

Henry David Thoreau, from *Walden*

"*Along the northern coast,*
Just back from the rock-bound shore and the caves,
In the saline air from the sea in the Mendocino country,
With the surge for base and accompaniment low and hoarse,
With crackling blows of axes sounding musically driven by
   strong arms,
Riven deep by the sharp tongues of the axes, there in the redwood
   forest dense,
I heard the mighty tree its death-chant chanting;
The choppers heard not, the camp shanties echoed not,
The quick-ear'd teamsters and chain and jack-screw men
   heard not,
As the wood-spirits came from their haunts of a thousand
   years to join the refrain,
But in my soul I plainly heard."

Walt Whitman, from "Song of the Redwood Tree"

"The ship tore on; leaving such a furrow in the sea as when a
cannon-ball, missent, becomes a ploughshare and turns
up the level field. . . . 'There she blows!—she blows!—she blows!—
right ahead!' was now the masthead cry. 'Aye, aye!' cried Stubb,
'I knew it—ye can't escape—blow on and split your
spout, O whale! the mad fiend himself is after ye! blow your trump—
bluster your lung!—Ahab will dam off your blood. . . .' And Stubb
did but speak out for wellnigh all that crew. . . . their wild craft
went plunging toward its flying mark. . . . They were one man,
not thirty. For as the one ship that held them all; though it
was put together of all contrasting things—oak, and maple,
and pine wood; iron, and pitch, and hemp—yet all
these ran into each other in the one concrete hull, which shot on
its way, both balanced and directed by the long central keel;
even so, all the individualities of the crew, this
man's valour, that man's fear; guilt and guiltiness, all varieties
were welded into oneness, and were all 'directed to that fatal
goal which Ahab their one lord and keel did point to.

   The rigging lived. The mast-heads, like the tops of tall
palms, were outspreadingly tufted with arms and legs. Clinging to
a spar with one hand, some reached forth the other with
impatient wavings; others, shading their eyes from
the vivid sunlight, sat far out on the rocking yards; all the
spars in full bearing of mortals, ready and ripe for their fate.
Ah! how they still strove through that infinite
blueness to seek out the thing that might destroy them!"

208   Herman Melville, from *Moby Dick*

REGIONS
& REALISM

Washington Arch in Spring
(opposite), painted by Childe
Hassam in 1890, evokes
Henry James' birthplace and
one of the writer's favorite
New York settings. To James,
the square was "the ideal of
quiet and of genteel retire-
ment . . . . this portion of
New York appears to many
persons the most delectable.
It has a kind of established
repose which is not of frequent occurrence in other
quarters of the long, shrill
city; it has a riper, richer,
more honourable look than
any of the upper ramifica-
tions of the great longi-
tudinal thoroughfare—the
look of having had some-
thing of a social history."

In July, 1868, Charles Francis Adams and John Lothrop Motley arrived in New York with their families aboard the Cunard Line transatlantic steamer *China*. Adams was the grandson of the second president of the United States and the son of the sixth; Motley was the renowned historian turned diplomat. The two men were returning from distinguished service abroad as American ministers to Great Britain and Austria respectively. Both had been appointed to their posts by Abraham Lincoln, and both had been away from their native land throughout the years of the Civil War and its immediate aftermath. They came back to a nation vastly changed by the war and its consequences from the one they had left to undertake their diplomatic missions. Young Henry Adams, who had been serving over those years as his father's secretary in London, was with the returning party. Later in life, reflecting on that homecoming, he wrote that had the group been "Tyrian traders of the years B.C. 1000, landing from a galley fresh from Gibraltar, they could hardly have been stranger on the shore of a world so changed from what it had been ten years before."

The war had loosed titanic forces which the peace had diverted into new channels, forces that were mounting at a prodigious rate in that year 1868. "Probably, the parallel of this is not to be found in the world's history," wrote an English observer of the scene. "All records, of whatsoever period, show, that during fierce and desolating struggles, the populations engaged in them have suffered fearful privations and miseries, and that protracted periods have elapsed before they have been able to recover from their effects. America, which in so many respects had shown herself superior to ordinary rules, has . . . shown that the heaviest and most costly civil conflict can be borne not only without exhaustion, but even with an increase of national prosperity." He was, to be sure, speaking of the triumphant North; for a time to come the South presented a less happy picture. Yet even the South soon recovered from the trials it had so painfully suffered. Within fifteen years of Appomattox the cotton crop was larger than it had ever been before the war. Tobacco assumed an important role in the economy of the Upper South, with such brands as Bull Durham and Duke's Mixture becoming familiar smokes about the world (that inveterate smoker, James Russell Lowell, introduced Alfred, Lord Tennyson to Bull Durham, a tobacco also enjoyed by Thomas Carlyle).

To the reunited nation there seemed to be no limit to the golden opportunities that opened up on a continental scale. As Henry Adams clearly saw in retrospect, the postwar generation of Americans was, in fact, creating virtually a new world—a world powered by great and growing mechanical energies and manned by a fresh army of clerks, mechanics, and laborers. It was a world of bigger, more crowded cities, a world that beckoned to great hordes of immigrants, each with a golden gleam in his eye. Business and industry were reorganized, as mammoth corporations were planned and inaugurated. Political parties were restructured, and new types of leaders assumed power —men of a different breed from the long file of Adamses who had so conscientiously and effectively served their country over the generations past. Speculation was unbounded, great fortunes were amassed, and corruption at all levels of business, society, and politics was clearly manifest. The individualism and self-reliance extolled by the transcendentalists as an expression of the higher self was converted into a concept of that rugged individualism that led to material gain and power. It was a period of unbridled acquisitiveness and corrupt practices that Mark Twain, with his co-author Charles Dudley Warner, branded "the gilded age" in the novel they published in 1873. As one illustration of their account of collusion between politicians and unscrupulous operators, the authors mention the indignation of a notorious burglar who was reported to have served one term in a penitentiary and another in the U.S. Senate. The latter claim, the ex-convict is said to have complained, was untrue and did him a great injustice. Such was the nature of the times that it is hard to tell the heroes from the villains in *The Gilded Age*. Mark Twain was himself a speculator throughout his life, a true son of the age he described in his book, although he ever remained an honest man.

Practically nothing of that turbulent and heterogeneous experience could be learned from the writing of the New England Brahmins and their ilk. By and large they succeeded in keeping the problems and the often raucous excitement of the contemporary American scene at arm's length. But as they spun out their engaging and accomplished tales, essays, and verses, and with these won the plaudits of a large reading public at home and abroad, there were others in the North, East, South, and West who were viewing the world about them from different and critical angles, and who were also winning acclaim with their writings in diverse strains.

The variety of their output reflected the varieties of the land itself. There were calls for the "great American novel"; but it was almost impossible to speak and write with any general outlook, in any single fashion or with any common accent, in a nation of so many very different regions and with such a mixed population. (H. G. Wells once confessed that in trying to report on his travels in America he felt like an ant crawling over the carcass of an elephant.) So there were many separate voices speaking from all points of the compass with views and interests that, put in their proper places, formed a complex mosaic of the national culture.

A substantial portion of the diversified literature that was produced in the

Bull Durham Tobacco, whose internationally known trademark is depicted above, was enjoyed by a wide variety of smokers, including such sophisticated and cosmopolitan literary lions as James Russell Lowell and the Britishers Thomas Carlyle and Alfred, Lord Tennyson.

AMERICAN TOBACCO COMPANY

last several decades of the nineteenth century took the form of the novel, a rising literary form in that period. Writing early in the next century, Frank Norris, a novelist himself, remarked: "To-day is the day of the novel. In no other day and by no other vehicle is contemporaneous life so adequately expressed; and the critics of the twenty-second century, reviewing our times, striving to reconstruct our civilization, will look not to the painters, not to the architects nor dramatists, but to the novelists to find our idiosyncracy." Much of this writing stressed a new note of realism. To a degree rarely practiced in earlier times, an effort was made to delineate the everyday experiences of contemporary American life in terms of the more or less ordinary rather than the exceptional individual, of the immediate and the familiar rather than the rare or the strange circumstance. In that spirit many novels celebrated the regional setting in all its local color and with a cast of characters drawn from life. Generally that material was treated sympathetically, at times humorously, with shameless but transparent exaggerations that in effect sharpened a sense of reality. The spectrum of local colors thus produced was a bright reminder of cherished regional peculiarities at a time when multiplying machines and quickening communication promised, or threatened, an unprecedented standardization of life across the nation. In good part those voices spoke of an innocence and simplicity that was vanishing from American life before the plundering advances of industrialization.

During the great gold fever of 1849, two Cuban artists, Augusto Ferran and José Baturone, executed an album of lithographs called Tipos Californianos, *from which the scenes reproduced below are taken. They depict prospectors at their favorite haunts, the local saloon and the pay desk.*

From the Mother Lode country of the Far West, with such tales as "The Luck of Roaring Camp" and "The Outcasts of Poker Flat," Bret Harte gave the world at large a fresh, vivid image of that raw and lusty land at the remote rim of the American continent. With *The Hoosier Schoolmaster* and other novels Edward Eggleston provided a meticulously detailed picture of life in the backwoods country of Indiana, an area he knew well as a circuit-riding Methodist minister and a pastor of several small churches. Also in Indiana, the beloved Hoosier poet James Whitcomb Riley was turning out such popular verse as *The Old Swimmin'-Hole and 'Leven More Poems,* which

The Maine landscape, typified by the Penobscot Bay scene below, is sympathetically described in the works of Sarah Orne Jewett. She was a master of American regional literature, and her best writing has been characterized as "a miracle in pastel shades."

celebrated the rural Midwestern scene. In New Orleans George Washington Cable wrote of Louisiana life with its complex patterns of mingling cultures and races; wrote with such intimate knowledge and such candor of that mixed, polyglot society that he antagonized many of its members. Cable was a twice-wounded veteran of the Confederate cavalry who had become convinced that slavery had been an evil and that the plight of the free Negro was no less evil. The South could only be solidly reconstructed, he maintained, when racial inequities were eliminated. For such views he was called a traitor to his section, although *he* thought it would be treason to remain silent.

From Georgia, Joel Chandler Harris issued his Uncle Remus stories, still among the greatest works dealing with American Negro folklore, faithfully retold in local dialect. He was among the first to use this material with subtlety and appreciation. Uncle Remus remains a beloved, shrewd, and immortal figure who remembered the time "befo' de war, endurin' de war, en atter de war," and who could philosophically explain to a white boy through such characters as Brer Rabbit and Brer Fox the ability of the weak and harmless to overcome the strong and oppressive. As Harris wrote, in these legends "it is not virtue that triumphs, but helplessness; it is not malice, but mischievousness." Uncle Remus became internationally famous, and some of his tales have been translated even into Bengali and African dialects. Beside Harris' carefully studied, lifelike portrait of Uncle Remus, Harriet Beecher Stowe's depiction of Uncle Tom is more like a caricature, too pious and too faithful to strange codes to be true or believable.

Mrs. Stowe had written *Uncle Tom's Cabin* in Maine, and some of her later fiction, sympathetically depicting life in that northernmost state, served as an inspiration to another Down Easter, Sarah Orne Jewett, who wrote her own tales of the area that she knew so well. "It is difficult," she observed, "to report the great events of New England; expression is so slight, and those few words which escape us in moments of deep feeling look but meagre on the printed page." However, her talent matured as she herself matured, and her masterpiece, *The Country of the Pointed Firs*, has been judged as the best piece of regional fiction produced in America in the nineteenth century. In precise and charming terms, with gentle humor and understated pathos, she here records a vanishing way of life along the Maine coast.

On that coast, she wrote in one of her appealing passages, "where many

In the Uncle Remus stories Joel Chandler Harris (below, right) captured the speech of American blacks. Arthur B. Frost's drawings, like the examples at right and left, are inseparable from the text of the stories.

green islands and salt inlets fringe the deep-cut shore line; where balsam firs and bayberry bushes send their fragrance far seaward, and song-sparrows sing all day, and the tide runs splashing in and out among the weedy ledges; where cowbells tinkle on the hills and herons stand in the shady coves— on the lonely coast of Maine stood a small gray house facing the morning light. All the weather-beaten houses of that region face the sea apprehensively, like the women who live in them." So she spoke of the passing local scene in terms that everlastingly preserved its haunting loveliness.

In his early books, and then again in some of his later ones, Hamlin Garland wrote of life in the raw as he had seen it as a child and young man in Wisconsin, Iowa, and South Dakota during the final decades of the last century. This "Ibsen of the West," as Garland has been called, reviewed that scene with a mind sharpened by a retreat to polite circles in the East and by wide reading, and he was determined to tell of it with a strict accounting of its grim realities. ("Veritism" was Garland's term for the form of realism, flavored with local color, that he practiced.) He wrote in anger, and with spirit and pity. What he described was no conventional rustic idyll. Life on the Middle Border, he reported, could be as confining, unwholesome, and emotion starved as life in any city slum. "All across northwestern Iowa and up through central Dakota," he remarked after a return visit to that area in 1887, "I brooded darkly over the problem presented, and this bitter mood was deepened by the condition in which I found my mother on a treeless farm. . . . It was in that mood of resentment that I began to write (immediately after returning to Boston) the stories which made up the first volume of *Main-Travelled Roads*." (That book was published in 1891.)

Eggleston had already written with disenchantment about life in the West, but Garland's indictment was more severe. Back in New England Whittier could hymn of a snowbound family reciting stories before the blazing hearth in a stout ancestral farmhouse, of the cheerful adventure of daily excursions through the drifts to care for the cattle. Garland wrote of snow driven by an eighty-mile-an-hour wind with the temperature thirty degrees below zero— wind and snow that howled mercilessly about his family's frail shelter; and of his father's desperate sallies toward the stable to feed the imprisoned cows and horses and to replenish the household's fuel, and of his mother's unending drudgery. "There is a mystic quality connected with free land," Garland once told an interviewer, "and it has always allured men into the West. I wanted to show that it is a myth."

Without such evocative, carefully delineated reminders of a vanishing

215

America our understanding of our national experience would be partial and impoverished. In 1894 Edward Everett Hale observed that "everybody writes 'local' stories nowadays; it is as natural as the whooping cough." Much of that literature was written in a minor key. In some of it realism was confused with quaintness and sentimental detail. But the best of it pictured the American civilization at the grassroots level, as the nation emerged from the Civil War and sought a new sense of unity in its divergent strains and far-flung parts. In the end, it announced the decline of the importance of such local accents, rather than their vitality. In time such manifestations of provincialism became collectors' items, like their visual equivalents in Currier and Ives prints.

No other author threw himself into the currents of his time and locale with more gusto than Samuel Langhorne Clemens, so much better known by his pseudonym Mark Twain. His literary style, tuned to the ear as much as to the printed page, was a direct reflection of his highly entertaining manner of speaking. Twain had a love of and a gift for the spoken language, and his public talks were almost as famous as his writings. He was in a sense an international jester, with a strong American accent.

Before the Civil War he had known the large freedom of a small boy in a village on the banks of the Mississippi—a childhood background from which his mature imagination never quite escaped. "It was a heavenly place for a boy," he later remembered, with its swimming hole, wooded outskirts, lively playmates, and the constantly changing and wondrous spectacle of life along the greatest of rivers. As a licensed pilot Twain, in his early twenties, came to know that river as well as any book he had ever read. In those ante-bellum days a Mississippi steamboat pilot followed an exalted calling, to qualify for which, Twain reflected, "a man had got to learn more than any one man ought to be allowed to know; and . . . he must learn it all over again in a different way every twenty-four hours." Everything that nature could contrive to tax the skill and the nerve of the navigator gave the Mississippi the character of a "wicked river." The land seemed to flow in a ceaseless counterpoint to the running water, building up islands that moved upstream as currents of the muddy river added here, subtracted there, to and from a deposit of silty earth; and the river made prodigious jumps across necks of land, radically changing the relative positions of towns and landmarks. As Twain concluded, the whole thirteen hundred miles that La Salle had floated down two centuries earlier was by Twain's time solid, dry land.

Up until the Civil War and until the transcontinental railroads redirected the main lines of traffic, the Mississippi remained the principal highway of America. From a basin larger than the combined areas of Spain, Portugal, Germany, Austria, and Italy, as Twain explained, the great river carried to the Gulf of Mexico the waters of fifty-four subordinate rivers. Every vessel transported a cross section of humanity, people of many tongues and several colors traveling for diverse reasons. As Twain later wrote, "I got personally and familiarly acquainted with all the different types of human nature that are to be found in fiction, biography or history." As a child his schooling had been early interrupted by his father's death, following which he had been apprenticed to a printer's shop—"the poor boy's college," as Lincoln termed

As a stand-up comedian and raconteur, Twain had no peer. In 1868 he joined the Redpath lecture bureau, a booking agency that sent the known and the unknown to town and city lyceums all over the East. After "trying it on the dog," as Twain called his out-of-town rehearsals, he tested his material on the difficult Boston audiences, and then set off annually on four-month-long tours, earning an average $100 per night. The caricature, above, appeared in Puck.

At forty Twain wrote of his years as a steamboat pilot: "I loved the profession far better than any I have followed since, and I took a measureless pride in it. The reason is plain: a pilot, in those days, was the only unfettered and entirely independent human being that lived in the earth." The view from the bridge, as suggested in the 1875 engraving, left, had a lonely grandeur that the writer would long to recapture.

it. Now, on the river, Twain read constantly to improve his education and his mind. And from his stored-up experiences he subsequently wrote one of his classics, *Life on the Mississippi*, a book that has been called "a memorial seemingly as enduring as the river itself."

Twain's career as a writer began in the years shortly after the outbreak of the Civil War. (He was not then quite sure which side of the conflict he was on, although he very briefly served in a Confederate militia band.) With the river closed to all normal traffic, he joined his brother on a journey into the farther West—an experience he later described in his book *Roughing It*. Twain stayed for several years in "the wondrous city of Virginia," perched halfway up the Nevada mountains, where, nearby, the greatest mining bonanza of all Western history was being exploited in a frenzy of speculation. Over a score of years more than $300 million worth of gold and silver was taken out of that country—a country so rugged it could "grow" nothing but precious metals. Twain tried his hand at prospecting, but with meager results—although he never did lose his dream of making a quick fortune one way or other. He made more immediate capital by writing for the Virginia City *Enterprise*, for the first time under the name of Mark Twain—a sobriquet taken from the call of the leadsmen on the river boats when a depth of two fathoms was sounded. Here, and later in San Francisco, he was encouraged in his writing by the Yankee crackerbox philosopher Artemus Ward (the pseudonym of Charles Farrar Browne), whose dry humor Lincoln enjoyed and who was at the time on a popular lecture tour in the West. (When Ward received a telegram from San Francisco asking what he would take for forty nights in California, he replied "Brandy and water.") In San Francisco Twain also was encouraged by Bret Harte, who was already an established author with a national reputation.

Twain's own success now came quickly. In 1865 his fresh version of an old

*The tall tale of wagering Jim
Smiley and his gifted frog was a
favorite with Twain's audiences.
So well known was the story and
its teller that theatre promoters did not think it necessary to
mention Twain's name in this 1869
poster announcing his lecture.*

California tale about the Jumping Frog was published in the New York *Saturday Press*, then in other papers across the land, and two years later when this was published as the title piece of a series of sketches in book form, *The Celebrated Jumping Frog of Calaveras County, and Other Sketches*, his career as a writer was secure. At the same time he discovered his rare talent as a lecturer who could enrapture his audiences with funny stories. He clinched his fame in 1869 with the publication of *The Innocents Abroad*, a frolicsome report of his experiences on a cruise to the Mediterranean and the Holy Land with a group of other American tourists.

That cruise was itself a significant adventure. Twain's shipmates were typical of those ordinary Americans who, in the wake of the war, prospered to the point where they could afford to travel overseas for pleasure. (In 1891, the customs reported, 90,000 tourists returned from abroad through the port of New York alone.) They saw the Old World with its celebrated monuments through eyes very different from those of, let us say, Hawthorne, Irving, and Longfellow. Twain chose to present his narrative through just such eyes of the plain American he pretended to be, a proud native product who was not to be bamboozled by any European claims to cultural superiority. (He once remarked, "there are no common people, except in the highest spheres of society.") "It is popular to admire the Arno," he wrote of his visit to Florence. "It is a great historical creek with four feet of water in the channel and some scows floating around." He observed that Lake Como could not compare with Lake Tahoe in beauty. "We examined modern and ancient statuary with a critical eye," he explained, "in Florence, Rome or anywhere we found it, and praised it if we saw fit, and if we didn't we said we preferred the wooden Indians in front of the cigar stores of America." (In his famous cartoons for the "Miraculous Draught of Fishes" Raphael had made a miracle of his own, Twain observed on a later occasion; he "puts three men into a canoe which wouldn't have held a dog without upsetting.") "Wherever we went," he continued, "in Europe, Asia, or Africa, we made a sensation. . . . None of us had ever been anywhere before; we all hailed from the interior; travel was a wild novelty to us, and we conducted ourselves in accordance with the natural instincts that were in us, and trammeled ourselves with no ceremonies, no conventionalities. We always took care to make it understood that we were Americans—Americans!" And thus he expressed the extravagant but benign nationalism of post-Civil War democracy.

The Innocents Abroad was an immediate best seller, second in sales only to *Uncle Tom's Cabin*. Twain had deliberately written to entertain the masses, and in this he succeeded admirably. He prospered, and he married. On the cruise he had been smitten by a miniature portrait of the sister of one of his shipmates, and when he returned home he wooed and won her. It was shortly thereafter, about 1871, that he moved to Hartford, Connecticut, where he resided the rest of his life. From that haven of domesticity, in the next dozen years he produced, among a number of other books, the three for which he is best remembered: *Tom Sawyer; Life on the Mississippi; Huckleberry Finn*—books which were written from the memories of his earlier life and which saw the development of Twain into one of the rare masters of American language. In these books, like no other American author before him, Twain converted the truth of his own direct experience into a distinctive native idiom. "There is no such thing as 'the Queen's English,'" Twain declared. "The property has gone into the hands of a joint stock company and we own the bulk of the shares." In the early years of this country's independence Noah Webster had appealed for a true American style in literature and speech. Twain finally produced it, although Webster might have been surprised at the results.

Those three Twain classics have enjoyed such enduring popularity that it is fair to assume that their stories are well known to the average American reader. It is an underprivileged boy or girl who has not made the acquaintance of the two unforgettable youngsters Tom Sawyer and Huck Finn. Yet, Twain denied that he was writing for children. Of *Tom Sawyer* he wrote William Dean Howells, "It is not a boy's book at all. It will only be read by adults. It was only written for adults." As for *Huckleberry Finn*, Carl Van Doren named it and *The Scarlet Letter* the two greatest novels created in America— oddly pairing a book of juvenile adventure and one with adultery as its theme. Ernest Hemingway went even further and claimed that all modern American literature comes from *Huckleberry Finn*—and his own prose, which also seeks to convert the truth of actual experience into a style suited to the American ethos, owes a debt to Twain's book. It is of more than passing interest to recall that the library in Concord, Massachusetts, barred *Huckleberry Finn* as unfit for young readers. (Huck was such a wonderfully ingenious liar, among other things, and he and Tom were bent on outwitting the adult world that tended to stifle their youthful enthusiasm.) Twain was delighted. "That will sell 25,000 copies of our book for sure," he gleefully wrote his publisher. (The sales of later editions of Twain's books were given a fresh boost in 1930–31 when Jackie Coogan played the part of Tom Sawyer in the moving pictures.)

At the high tide of his success, with book royalties flooding in and other projects prospering, Twain's fortunes suddenly reversed. Always a hopeful speculator, he had put large sums of money into a typesetting machine. Suspicious of commercial publishers, he had also backed a firm that published his own books. Both projects failed in the panic year of 1893, and Twain was driven into bankruptcy. However, to honor his debts he took off on a lecture tour of the world, and in a few years he had not only paid off his creditors but had accumulated a new fortune. He continued to write until the end of his days, but his best work was already done.

Twain detested humbug and undue pretension. His humor was typically underlaid by pessimism—the pessimism that came from closely observing human folly. "Everything human is pathetic," he wrote. "The secret source of Humor itself is not joy but sorrow. There is no humor in heaven." His mood grew more bitter and cynical in later years. Like other thoughtful contemporaries, he was disillusioned by the "progress" of the gilded age. He loved people, but not the public—the "damned human race," as he more than once termed it, meaning damned in both senses of the word.

However, before he died in 1910, Twain had won the respect and affection of a large part of that human race. "I am persuaded," Bernard Shaw once wrote to him, "that the future historian of America will find your works as indispensable to him as a French historian finds the political tracts of Vol-

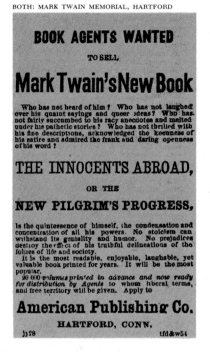

BOOK AGENTS WANTED

TO SELL

Mark Twain's New Book

Who has not heard of him? Who has not laughed over his quaint sayings and queer ideas? Who has not fairly succumbed to his racy anecdotes and melted under his pathetic stories? Who has not thrilled with his fine descriptions, acknowledged the keenness of his satire and admired the frank and daring openness of his word?

THE INNOCENTS ABROAD,

OR THE

NEW PILGRIM'S PROGRESS,

is the quintessence of himself, the condensation and concentration of all his powers. No stoicism can withstand its geniality and humor. No prejudices destroy the effect of his truthful delineations of the follies of life and society.

It is the most readable, enjoyable, laughable, yet valuable book printed for years. It will be the most popular.

30,000 *volumes prin'ed in advance and now ready for distribution by Agents* to whom liberal terms, and free territory will be given. Apply to

American Publishing Co.

HARTFORD, CONN.

j528   tfd&w54

Twain's long connection with the American Publishing Company of Hartford began with his first novel, Innocents Abroad *(1869). The notice of the book, above, appeared in the Hartford* Courant. *Shown below is James Paige's typesetter, a temperamental invention that an enthralled Twain called "an awful mechanical miracle." He then invested years of income and hope in its perfection, only to abandon it in 1889.*

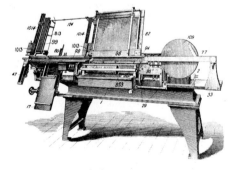

TEXT CONTINUES PAGE 224

219

MARK TWAIN IN HARTFORD

Top: Twain's house in Hartford; above: the author with his wife and daughters

"Of all the beautiful towns it has been my fortune to see," Mark Twain wrote of Hartford, Connecticut, "this is the chief.... You do not know what beauty is if you have not been here." In 1871, shortly after his marriage to Olivia Langdon, Twain moved there. Harriet Beecher Stowe, Charles Dudley Warner, and other literary lights were among his new neighbors. In 1874 he commissioned the architects Edward T. Potter and Alfred H. Thorp to design and build an unusual brick residence in the Victorian style, with high-peaked gables and a profusion of verandas. (The public was inclined to consider the structure one of Twain's practical jokes.) There he lived with his growing family for seventeen happy and industrious years. In this elaborate establishment, staffed with seven servants, the Clemenses played host to a long succession of eminent visitors, including such well-known authors as George Washington Cable, Thomas Bailey Aldrich, and William Dean Howells, the great actors Henry Irving, Lawrence Barrett, and Edwin Booth, and all but endless others of varying talents. Following one of his visits, Howells described the "little semi-circular conservatory" at the west end of the library, which, he wrote, was "of a pattern invented by Mrs. Harriet Beecher Stowe." Twain's three adored daughters, Susan, Clara, and Jean, had talents of their own, and often staged amateur theatricals in the library of their home. "My elder sister, Susy," Clara recalled, "... was altogether the genius among the children. She had marked talent for writing and composed a charming little play when she was not more than fourteen or fifteen. We performed it one Thanksgiving night for a large company of invited friends, and all agreed that it was full of originality." They also staged a dramatization of their father's novel for children, *The Prince and the Pauper,* in which Twain himself took part and convulsed the audience with his pranks. In that performance the conservatory served as the palace garden, complete with plants.

Top, left: scene from a play by Susan Clemens, acted by (left to right) Clara, Charles Dudley Warner's niece Margaret, Jean Clemens, Susan Clemens, and a neighbor, Fanny Friese; top, right: program for The Prince and the Pauper; *above: a rendering of the elaborate conservatory in Twain's house*

221

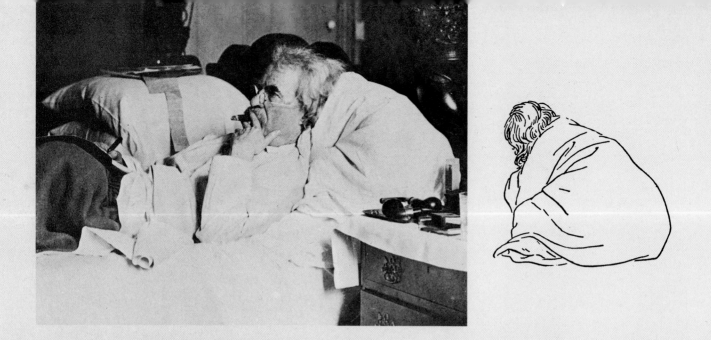

Twain's billiard room was a center of activity in his home. Here he did much of his reading, note taking, and writing. The large billiard table that stood in the middle of the room was sometimes stacked with books; notes he made from them virtually "upholstered" the walls. However, the table was cleared often enough, for Twain was an indefatigable billiard player. He could play all night, with or without the other aficionados he frequently invited to share in his passion for the game—and to share his Scotch, his conversation, and his cigars. He was a late riser and often wrote in bed, propped by his pillows and puffing a cigar. ("More than one cigar at a time," he once observed, "is excessive smoking.") In the photograph shown above, the crumpled pillow and Twain's tousled hair create the illusion of a small figure crouching at his ear. When he viewed the picture, Twain remarked, "People often ask me where I get my ideas. . . . A little imp whispers in my ear and tells me what to say."

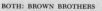

Above: Mark Twain at work in his bed, with a line rendering of his "little imp" whispering in his ear; left: Twain playing billiards with a friend. Sometimes he would invent new rules on the spur of the moment in order to win a game.

Through his writings and his publishing activities, Twain was a man of substantial wealth by the time he was fifty. He hoped to reap another fortune by heavily investing in the development of a new typesetting machine. This venture proved his undoing; the invention was a complete practical failure. Along with other business reverses, he was forced into bankruptcy in 1894. To save money he closed his Hartford house; to make money enough to discharge his debts he left on a worldwide lecture tour. When he was in London he received the news that Susy had died at home at the age of twenty-four. He persevered in his career, a saddened and somewhat embittered man. He died in 1910, predeceased by his wife and daughter Jean.

Above: Mark Twain at ease in the library of his Hartford home smoking a meerschaum pipe; left: a shell-framed portrait of Susy, made shortly before her death; below: a notice from the Hartford Courant, April 19, 1902. Susy had been taken there to die. "To me," Twain wrote of the house, "it was a holy place and beautiful."

"MARK TWAIN'S"
HOME FOR SALE.

One of the most beautiful and valuable residences in this city, located on Farmington Avenue, with a frontage of about 800 feet on the Avenue. Large house with 19 rooms conveniently arranged and beautifully decorated; brick barn with tenement for coachman; green-house. This is a rare opportunity to purchase a magnificent home in the best residential section of the city.

For further particulars regarding price, terms and permit to examine the premises, apply to Franklin G. Whitmore, 700 Main street, Hartford, Conn., or to William H. Hoyt & Co., 15 West 42nd street, New York City.

taire." In Germany his public appearances, and his publisher's promotional campaign, had won him a large audience; translations of his works in that country numbered more than a million. In Soviet Russia, it is said, Twain's translations have sold more than three million. In Latin America he remains the most popular American author. Aside from his broad popularity with the reading public, his writings were seriously reviewed throughout Europe by critics of eminence. Far and wide he had become literary ambassador of the American democratic tradition.

In a memorial tribute, William Dean Howells declared that Mark Twain was "incomparable, the Lincoln of our literature." Howells was qualified to make that judgment on two counts: he was the acknowledged dean of American letters, and he had known Twain and his work as well as any man. The two were warm friends for forty years. They enjoyed one another's company and critically admired one another's talents. On one occasion Howells wrote Twain, "Your visit was a perfect ovation for us; we *never* enjoy anything so much as those visits of yours. The smoke and the Scotch and the late hours almost kill us; but we look each other in the eyes when [you] are gone, and say what a glorious time it was, and air the library, and begin sleeping and dieting, and longing to have you back again." Twain in his turn remained duly grateful for Howells' early encouragement and his usually sound counsel, and considered him a writer "without peer in the English-speaking world."

Howells had a remarkable career. He was, someone has said, "in himself almost an entire literary movement, almost an academy." Born of poor parents in Ohio, he was to a large degree self-taught. He learned to set type almost as soon as he could read, and went on to work and write for Midwestern newspapers. When he was in his early twenties the *Atlantic Monthly* published several of his poems. At about that time he made his first visit East and met Lowell, Holmes, Hawthorne, Emerson, and others of his literary gods. With condescension worthy of the New England literary establishment, Hawthorne sent a note to Emerson, declaring, "I find this young man worthy." During the dinner then given for him by Lowell, Holmes glanced at Howells and, turning to the host, said, "Well, James, this is something like the apostolic succession; this is the laying on of hands." The occasion was quite enough to turn a young man's head, but Holmes' remark was in fact prophetic. Within hardly more than a decade Howells was to become editor in chief of the *Atlantic*, a prestigious, influential post that he assumed when he was not yet thirty-five years old and still without benefit of serious formal education, at Harvard or anywhere else.

Meanwhile, however, Howells had spent four years abroad as American consul in Venice—a reward for having quickly compiled a helpful campaign biography of presidential-aspirant Abraham Lincoln in the summer of 1860. From his experience overseas he wrote, among other things, *Venetian Life* and *Italian Journeys*, both of which won him serious attention when they were published. Lowell professed astonishment that a product of America's "shaggy democracy" from beyond the Alleghanies could achieve such "airy elegance" and "delicacy" in his writing. (For a while Howells carried favorable reviews about with him as if they were love letters.) In those travel sketches he tried to provide true impressions of everyday life in Italy, to ob-

William Dean Howells was a native of Ohio who settled in the East in 1865, after serving five years as American consul in Venice. Howells, who soon found himself at the center of intellectual life in Boston, was, in the words of Alfred Kazin, "the Brahmins' favorite child but the first great champion of the new writers."

serve that realism in his writing that was to distinguish his fictional stories about American life in years to come. The critical applause he earned with these reports served as paving stones to his subsequent fortune.

When he returned to America in 1865, Howells gravitated to Boston, where he served as subeditor of the *Atlantic* for five years under James T. Fields before becoming editor in chief. He did not disguise his delight in joining the intellectual and social life of that community, which he found "so refined, so intelligent, so gracefully simple" that he doubted it could be equaled anywhere on earth. To that life the young Midwesterner adjusted so gracefully and completely that Lowell felt it proper to compliment him.

However, Boston was changing during those postwar years. People alien to old New England traditions—Irish-Catholics and Jews, among others—swarmed into the city and soon far outnumbered those of true Yankee stock. In the North End the city spawned one of the most noisome urban slums in the entire country. Before this wave of polyglot newcomers, those older, Protestant Bostonians who could do so retreated to the Back Bay and the suburbs. Elsewhere in Boston men with large schemes now talked in millions of dollars instead of mere thousands, and, as the business cycle varied, winning or losing vast fortunes. Henry Adams observed that the traditional Bostonian suffered from "a sort of Bostonitis" that came from "knowing too much of his neighbors, and thinking too much of himself." However, he somewhat ruefully observed, "nowhere in America was society so complex or change so rapid" as in postwar Boston. (At least, that is where he noticed those complexities and changes most intimately and personally; they were, in fact, characteristic of the times in all major American cities.)

Howells was mindful of the changes that were taking place, and he was aware of how well insulated from all this his Brahmin friends and associates were in their diminishing cultural world. When he joined the staff of the *Atlantic* in 1866, it was still the leading American literary magazine, and it was still New England oriented. But the appointment of this young outlander was in itself a harbinger of a new cultural outlook; and during Howells' editorship the list of contributors to the *Atlantic* was enlarged and refreshed with new names. "The fact is," he recalled years later, "we were growing, whether we liked it or not, more and more American. Without ceasing to be New England, without ceasing to be Bostonian, at heart, we had become southern, mid-western, and far-western in our sympathies. It seemed to me that the new good things were coming from those regions rather than from our own coasts and hills."

As editor and critic Howells was quick to appreciate promising young talent wherever it came from. Frank Norris, Stephen Crane, and Hamlin Garland were only a few of the rising generation of authors whose work he sponsored. (He also urged upon his readers the works of such European realists as Balzac and Tolstoy.) Howells also held out a helpful, open editorial hand to young Henry James, who later in life gratefully acknowledged the benefits he had received. "You showed me the way," he wrote Howells, "and opened me the door. . . ."

As an author in his own right, Howells further influenced a generation of writers. For more than a half century, indeed, he was a major spokesman of

American literature. His output was prodigious—dozens of novels, thirty-one dramas, eleven books of travels, some volumes of verse, seven collections of short stories, and several autobiographical essays. In the best and most typical of his works Howells was portraying the lives of average Americans in those decades of social and moral transformation that followed the Civil War, and doing so with meticulous artistry. As one critic has written, Howells was convinced that plain American life was not only worthy of literature but that it was the only material worthy of American literature. He was one of the first authors to attempt such a faithful depiction of contemporary, commonplace American experience, and in his own day he was judged new-fashioned, even radical, for doing so. But in perspective he must be seen as a major prophet of the realism that has dominated American fiction to our own day. Howells was, Carl Van Doren wrote, "the intimate historian of his age, who produced the most extended and accurate transcript of American life yet made by one man."

During his years on the *Atlantic* Howells was developing his pioneering creed of realism—a creed that was in harmony with the rising scientific spirit of the age, and with the democratic spirit itself. "I feel more and more persuaded," he wrote, "that we have only to study American life with the naked eye in order to find it infinitely various and entertaining. The trouble has always been that we have looked at it through somebody else's confounded literary telescope. I find it hard work myself to trust my eyes, and I catch myself feeling for the telescope, but I hope to do without it, altogether, by and by." Just how well he could, in fact, trust his eyes and record the realities he observed is suggested by his description of a meeting of two rural neighbors, who, "when they had hornily rattled their callous palms together, stand staring at each other, their dry, serrated lips falling apart, their jaws mutely working up and down, their pale-blue eyes vacantly winking, and their weather-beaten faces as wholly discharged of expression as the gable ends of two barns confronting each other from opposite sides of the road."

Then, in the 1880's, he left the *Atlantic* and moved to New York—a move that has been called "the great symbolic episode in the early history of American realism." As champion of the new writing, Howells found New York, after Boston, "lordly free" in its artistic tolerances, and the undisputed, growing capital of publishing and of mass culture. It was more *real* than Boston: "Boston seems of another planet," he wrote. In New York, in any case, he wrote the most significant of his books, and from the "Editor's Study" and the "Editor's Easy Chair" of *Harper's* magazine his most urgent literary criticism.

Merely to list all Howells' works would require more type than it takes to fill this page. *The Rise of Silas Lapham*, published in 1885, is one of the greatest of his many novels. It was the first study of the self-made businessman in the history of American literature; a story of a man who in his success could afford to build a "mansion" in the Back Bay but who in the end lost the fortune he had accumulated but found his soul. Lapham's rise and fall is not only a commentary on business ethics in the gilded age, it is quite as importantly an account of the failure of a nouveau-riche family to breach the walls of Brahmin society.

In New York Howells became ever more keenly aware of the strains that American society was suffering with the growth of large-scale, speculative,

A Collier's *cover of 1899 shows a night attack by striking railroad workers—a scene that might have inspired Howells.*

competitive capitalism. Life in America, he feared, but had to believe, had become unmercifully complicated. It was, he remarked, "a state of warfare and a game of chance, in which each man fights and bets against fearful odds." In 1886, after the Haymarket Riot in Chicago—a mass protest against the killing of strikers by the police—several "anarchists" were executed on the most dubious evidence. Six years later in the Homestead Strike near Pittsburgh another sanguinary battle broke out between the forces of labor and those of management, and the pattern of industrial brutality was repeated at the expense of the working man. The august president of Harvard, Charles William Eliot, called the strikebreaker the true American hero. But Howells was sickened and shamed by the violence and the injustice of such lacerating episodes, and all they connoted. He was one of the few intellectuals of his time to protest and to plead for mercy and justice—among the first distinguished men of letters to espouse socialism—and it was not a popular attitude.

In *A Hazard of New Fortunes*, issued in 1890, Howells skillfully dramatized those antagonisms and dissensions which he thought reflected the moral degeneration of America. Through the eyes of a couple recently removed from Boston, he surveys the New York scene with a panoramic vision; he describes the life of that "frantic" city in all its complexities and contrasts, its ethnic and social divisions, its commercial and professional rivalries, and its moral conflicts and confusions. It was realistic fiction on a grander scale than any of his other novels, and he looked back on it in later years as his best book "for breadth and depth." To his mind that novel became "the most vital of my fictions; through my quickened interest in the life about me, at a moment of great psychological import. . . . That shedding of blood which is for the remission of sins had been symbolized by the bombs and scaffolds of Chicago, and the hearts of those who felt this bound up with our rights, the slavery implicated in our liberty, were thrilling with griefs and hopes hitherto strange to the average American breast. Opportunely for me there was a great streetcar strike in New York, and the story began to find its way to issues nobler and larger than those of the love-affairs common to fiction." Hamlin Garland called *Hazard* "the greatest, truest, sanest study of a city in fiction."

Howells greatly admired Tolstoy at the time, and that Russian's influence is apparent in his treatment of his theme. (He wrote his sister that he could never again see life in the way he saw it before reading Tolstoy.) He used the streetcar strike to bring the plot of his complex novel to a melodramatic close on a pessimistic note, describing the troubles of 1888, which he had witnessed, in precise detail. Two years earlier he had written Henry James that he thought civilization was "coming out all wrong in the end, unless it bases itself anew on a real equality." However, socialist though he was, he enjoyed the material benefits his own success assured him. "I wear a furlined overcoat," he wrote, "and live in all the luxury money can buy." That success was real enough. From his copious writings, and with his knowledge of the literary marketplace, he enjoyed an income that might have been envied by some of the grasping businessmen he satirized in his novels. James even suggested that Howells' mercenary instincts were distracting his genius into unworthy efforts—and the possibility troubled Howells himself.

Nevertheless, he was abundantly honored for his creative achievements.

Howells, the self-educated printer, is shown above in a photograph of 1909, by which time he was the acknowledged dean of American letters. In summing up Howells' productive career, one critic has observed that he "left the Atlantic Monthly *in 1881 and [took] the literary center of the country with him . . . from Boston to New York."*

The self-taught lad from Ohio, who had won his place among the Boston Brahmins and who had deserted their sanctuary to face the stark challenges of New York's wide-open market, lived out his days as an acknowledged elder statesman of American literature. He received honorary degrees from a half-dozen universities in the United States and England; he was elected the first president of the American Academy of Arts and Letters; he was awarded the gold medal of the National Institute. He had been, as Alfred Kazin has written, "the greatest single force in the literature of his epoch." As a realist in fiction he was succeeded by other writers who went further and deeper along this line, and who became more popular and fashionable—but who owed more to Howells' precedents than they cared to acknowledge.

Nothing more clearly suggests the breadth of Howells' literary interests than that he could at the same time and with equal zest encourage the careers of both Mark Twain and Henry James. It is hard to imagine two American authors more different in their approaches to writing, in their styles and in the substance of their works, than the "Washoe Giant," as Twain was sometimes called, and the fastidious, introspective cosmopolite that James was born to be. (Years later, when the two met in England, James remarked of Twain, "a most excellent pleasant fellow, what they call here very 'quaint.' Quaint he is!") Yet in his earliest days with the *Atlantic* Howells was quick to recognize both their distinctive talents and offer them space in the pages of his magazine. Quite possibly there would have been no *Life on the Mississippi* without Howells, for it was with his hearty support that Twain undertook the writing of this text, and it was with Howells' editorial guidance that he continued to supply the successive installments that first appeared in the *Atlantic*.

With James, as with Twain, Howells maintained a lifelong friendship which, as with Twain, started as soon as Howells joined the *Atlantic*. "Talking of talks," he wrote a friend in 1866 in his first year with the magazine, "young Henry James and I had a famous one last evening, two or three hours long, in which we settled the true principles of literary art. He is a very earnest fellow, and I think him extremely gifted—gifted enough to do better than any one has yet done toward making us a real American novel." Subsequently he qualified that statement by remarking that James' talent was so rare he would probably have to create a special audience to appreciate it. In this he was partly right, because James, in fact, did better than any other American had yet done in creating his novels. Whether they are to be called "real American" novels, however, may be questioned. For, although James was born an American, he died an Englishman, and he lived the greater part of his life overseas. (His older brother William once described Henry as "a native of the James family, and has no other country.") Beyond that, unlike Howells, he thought there was too much missing from the American scene—too much of the deeply rooted traditions and of the ingrained social complexities that he came to believe enriched, even when it corrupted, European life. He once remarked, however, that to be an American was an excellent preparation for culture, and he enjoyed that peculiar advantage.

Henry James was born in New York City in 1843, one of four sons (they had one sister), at 21 Washington Place. (On the occasion of his birth his father's friend Emerson wrote, "Tell Mrs. James that I heartily greet her on the new

A photograph taken at Newport, R.I., shows Henry James, aged twenty, at the time of his Harvard studies. The English novelist Dorothy Richardson once remarked, "it was he after all who had achieved the first completely satisfying way of writing a novel."

friend, though little now, that has come to her hearth.") By any measure his education was unusual. His father hoped that he and his brothers would become citizens of the world and that they might defer forming fixed habits of living and thinking until they were mature enough to make wise decisions in such matters for themselves. Thus, as a child Henry was privately tutored. When he was twelve, the family went abroad for three years. He later recalled having strolled the streets of Paris, visiting the Luxembourg Palace and the Louvre, dressed in a high black hat and wearing gloves and acting like the "little gaping pilgrim" that he was. He also visited London, Geneva, and Boulogne before returning to America in 1858. The next year he was again in Europe, "still changing teachers and localities almost with seasons," as one of his biographers has written.

Again back in America, the family settled briefly in Newport, Rhode Island, and here James renewed an earlier acquaintance with the two noted American artists William Morris Hunt and John La Farge, both of whom had recently returned from years of study abroad. (Henry's brother William was studying painting under Hunt for the time being.) It was La Farge, Henry fondly recalled, who introduced him to the works of Honoré Balzac, Prosper Merimée, and Robert Browning, and who encouraged him to write seriously himself. He went on to enter Harvard Law School in 1862, and it was during his residence in Cambridge that he met Howells, Lowell, and other literary figures of that village and of Boston. His friendship with these men launched James' literary career as a contributor to various American magazines, the *Atlantic*, of course, included; he was then in his early twenties. It was to be one of the most remarkable careers in the history of American letters.

In 1869 James once again sailed for Europe, to spend most of the rest of his life abroad. He revisited Paris, where he met a number of the great French writers—Flaubert, Maupassant, Zola, and, among other realists, the Russian expatriate Ivan Sergeyevich Turgenev, that "beautiful genius," as James described him. James was himself a professed realist, but of a different brand from Howells. "I regard you as the great American naturalist," he once wrote Howells. But, he added, "I don't think you go far enough and you are haunted with romantic phantoms and a tendency to factitious glosses." (Although Howells was the older of the two, he felt himself James' junior in the art of writing. George Moore once quipped that Henry James went abroad and read Turgenev while William Dean Howells stayed at home and read James.) Where Howells described with painstaking detail the American scene as he witnessed it, James probed beneath the surface of the lives of his characters to explain in even more minute detail their psychological motivations—and he did this in a rich, studiously perfected prose that had no real precedent or equivalent in English-language novels.

From 1876 until his death in 1916 James lived principally in England. He was enormously gifted, he had an inner compulsion to excel in his writing, and he was unremittingly industrious. During most of those forty years he produced a staggering number of novels, plays, travel sketches, short stories, and critical essays, with a brilliance he steadfastly sustained. As early as 1883 his collected fiction filled fourteen volumes—and that same year he produced three more works, before proceeding to still more books and articles of various

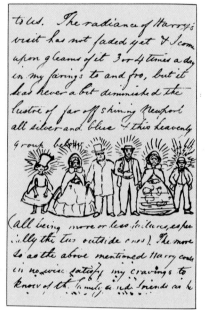

William James was a philosopher and a founder of scientific psychology, as distinguished a contributor to his field as his author-brother Henry was to his. The page, above, with a drawing is reproduced from a letter written by William to his family in 1861.

230

sorts, including some of his most memorable novels.

Whereas Mark Twain aimed his writings squarely at a mass audience, James sought his success in the perfection of his art. For him, the truth of art and the truth of life were the same thing. His unapproached subtlety of phrase and rhythm, his passionate perception of character, and his infinite refinement of particulars—the fastidious taste with which he fashioned every sentence he wrote—irritated or puzzled most of the general public and confounded his lesser critics. At the beginning of 1888 James wrote to Howells of his lack of popular appeal. No one at the time seemed to want his work, he reported. "However, I don't despair," James wrote, "for I think I am now really in better form than I ever have been in my life and I propose yet to do many things." "Very likely too," he concluded, "some day, all my buried prose will kick off its various tombstones at once." And so it is that his reputation today is greater than it was during his lifetime, although even now the casual reader often finds James' intricately constructed prose more difficult than rewarding, more precious than graceful. A fair sampling of his complex and convoluted style might be taken from any number of his writings, as, for example, an excerpt from "Crapy Cornelia":

> The few scattered surviving representatives of a society once 'good'— *rari nantes in gurgite vasto*—were liable, at the pass things had come to, to meet, and even amid old shades once sacred, or what was left of such, every form of social impossibility, and, more irresistibly still, to find these apparitions often carry themselves (often at least in the case of women) with a wondrous wild gallantry, equally imperturbable and inimitable, the sort of thing that reached its maximum in Mrs. Worthingham. Beyond that who ever wanted to look up their annals, to reconstruct their steps and stages, to dot their i's is fine, or to 'go behind' anything that was theirs? One wouldn't do that for the world—a rudimentary discretion forbade it; and yet this check from elementary undiscussable taste quite consorted with a due respect for them, or at any rate with a due respect for oneself in connection with them; as was just exemplified in what would be his own, what would be poor dear old White-Mason's, insurmountable aversion to having, on any pretext, the doubtless very queer spectre of the late Mr. Worthingham presented to him. No question had he asked, or would he ever ask, should his life—that is should the success of his courtship—even intimately depend on it, either about that obscure agent of his mistress's actual affluence or about the happy head-spring itself, and the apparently copious tributaries, of the golden stream.

During the first decade of his expatriation James' writing dealt largely with studies of Americans at home and abroad. Those early novels were largely concerned with the impact of Europe's older civilization upon American life, contrasting America's simplicity and strict moral code and Europe's sophistication and questionable morality—as in *The American* (1877), *Daisy Miller* (1879), and *The Portrait of a Lady* (1881). In the last of these James introduces one of his memorable heroines, Isabel Archer (the "Lady"), an attractive young American girl whom circumstances had taken to Europe, who unexpectedly becomes an heiress and who is taken in by a fortune hunter of shallow character and dubious moral worth. Her own moral sensitivity,

A lithograph depicts James' rich heroine from Schenectady, Daisy Miller, "an inscrutable combination of audacity and innocence."

sharpened and refined by her associations with Europeans, compels her to put up with her bad bargain and her ordained unhappy future.

Edith Wharton, a younger American expatriate author, once observed that for James "every great novel must first of all be based on a profound sense of moral values, and then constructed with a classical unity and economy of means." The story of Isabel Archer satisfied those requirements, as did James' top efforts in the years to come. For a while he turned to analyzing the English character in such novels as *The Princess Casamassima*, published in 1886. That same year, however, he published *The Bostonians*, his only major work with a wholly American setting. Ironically, although these two novels today seem to be among James' more appealing works, they were generally ridiculed by reviewers both in England and America as not being novels at all while other reviewers were giving respectful attention to the ephemeral fiction of the day. It was those hostile comments that led James to write Howells about his failure to please the public with what he considered his best works to date. (He was also writing dramas at the time, with no better popular success.) It took courage and conviction for James to persevere as he did in the face of such blasted expectations; it takes some understanding on our part, over and over again, to realize what remarkable fluctuations of taste contribute to the history of literary reputations. At least one recent, highly esteemed critic, for example, has referred to *Casamissima* as among the most significant novels of its day.

In his last three important novels, *The Wings of the Dove* (1902), *The Ambassadors* (1903), and *The Golden Bowl* (1904), James returned to his earlier theme of contrast between the American and the European character. To the end James remained his own most unsparing critic, and he considered *The Ambassadors* his most perfect work of art. During those later years of his life

When the "New York" edition of The Novels and Tales of Henry James *(1907-17) was being prepared, the novelist himself commissioned Alvin Langdon Coburn to take a series of atmospheric photographs to serve as frontispieces for the various volumes in the collection. Here is Coburn's moody shot of Portland Place, London, intended for the frontispiece of* The Golden Bowl.

he wrote a wide variety of other things, including his famous ghost story, "The Turn of the Screw," which was subsequently dramatized and also made into an opera by the British composer Benjamin Britten, and which revealed just one more facet of James' very special talent.

From 1897 until his death James lived at Lamb House, in Rye, England, and there all his later works were written. He had long since become a citizen of the world, as his father had planned. He had traveled extensively in Europe and knew the Continent and England intimately. Aside from the illustrious French authors already mentioned, in Paris he had known his controversial and brilliant fellow expatriate, the artist James McNeill Whistler, whom he met again in England when both men had removed there. Whistler, James observed, was "a queer little Londonized Southerner, and paints abominably." (He later overcame some of his prejudices against Whistler's particular versions of French impressionism.) In Paris he had also met that other exceptional American expatriate artist, John Singer Sargent, and had provided him with introductions when he, too, removed to England from Paris. At Rye H. G. Wells was a neighbor and visitor, as was Joseph Conrad, an expatriate from Poland. The young American realist Stephen Crane, whose life was so tragically brief, would turn up at Rye, and Edith Wharton—still another American expatriate—paid James her very ladylike tribute. (Although much younger than James, she was at the time making quite a bit more money from her writing than James was from his.)

In 1904 James made a pilgrimage back to America. He had been away for twenty-eight years, and his own country had taken on a romantic cast in his thoughts—as Europe had captured his imagination in the 1870's. He first visited his brother William, now a brilliant and well-known philosopher and psychologist. (Someone has said that whereas Henry wrote fiction with the insights of a philosopher, William wrote of philosophy with the skill of a novelist. "As a wit and humorist," Henry Adams wrote William James in 1908, "I have always said that you were far away the superior to your brother Henry, and that you could have cut him quite out, if you had turned your pen that way.") He then traveled from New Hampshire to Florida and westward to California. At Washington he met President Theodore Roosevelt, who thought him "effete" and "a miserable little snob." James, in turn considered the president "a dangerous and ominous jingo," "the mere monstrous embodiment of unprecedented resounding Noise."

It was a remarkable journey, and out of it came a remarkable travel book, *The American Scene*. (He would have preferred *The Return of the Native* as a title, but Thomas Hardy had already used it.) He found that scene vastly changed since he had last surveyed it, with evidence everywhere of a new vulgarity and power that offended his sensibilities. He questioned whether the old American virtues—moral purity, innocence of spirit, freshness of vision—could be retained amid the vast social and material changes that were taking place; whether America might shake off its provincialism and develop a true civilization worthy of its European heritage. But he did not answer his own questions.

James continued to write until death put an end to his long labors. With the outbreak of war in 1914, he saw the world revealing the moral and cultural

On his seventieth birthday in 1913, some three hundred friends presented Henry James with his portrait, reproduced above, executed by a fellow American, John Singer Sargent. Both the novelist and the painter were among the many American artists of their generation who, repelled by the tumultuous atmosphere of their native land, sought repose and culture in the Old World. In Europe both James and Sargent achieved pre-eminence and technical mastery in their own fields.

Henry and William James, about 1900

Max Beerbohm receives an influential though biased deputation, by "Max"

James and Joseph Conrad, by "Max"

HENRY JAMES IN EUROPE

Henry James lived most of his adult life as an American expatriate in England, where he was drawn by the safety and formalism of English society. He kept in touch with many of the eminent artists and writers of his day, and made only occasional visits to his native land, which served him primarily as a source of reaction for his writing. For James' central theme was the subtle psychological delineation of the innocent American pilgrim in confrontation with the intricacies of European society and manners. The outbreak of World War I was a tragic blow for James, and in 1915 he became a British subject, to show his allegiance to the Allied cause. He died the next year shortly before his Europe—whose society he had so long endeavored to enter and to re-create in his novels—would be reorganized at the Versailles conference tables.

Henry James and J. M. Barrie in London

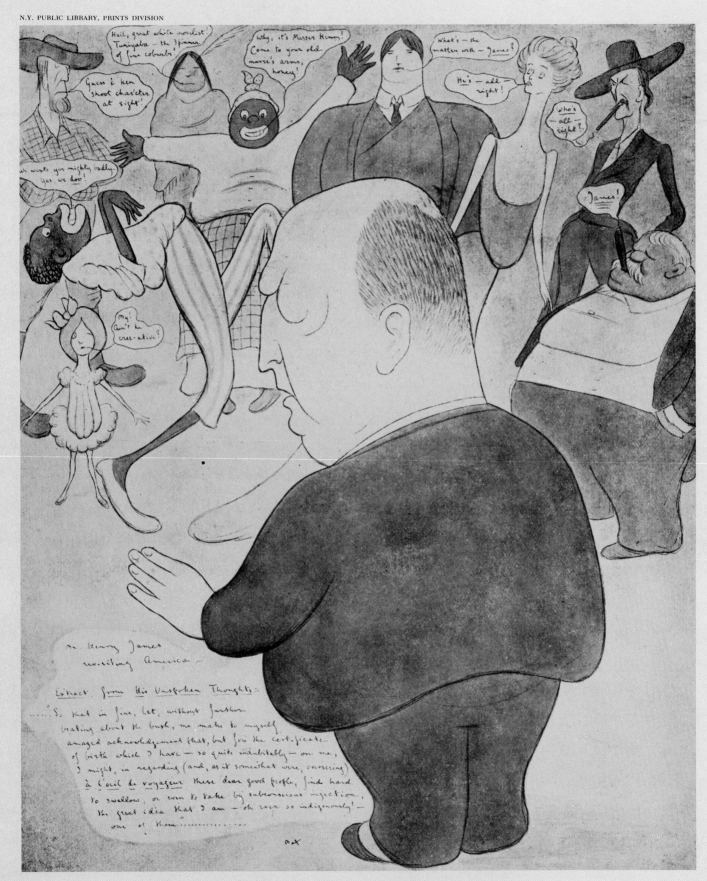

Max Beerbohm's caricature, "Mr. Henry James Revisiting America," 1907

degradation that he had described and sensitively deplored in so many of his novels. "I have the imagination of disaster," he once wrote, "and see life as ferocious and sinister." Now those dark projections of his mind were to be played out on a worldwide stage. "The plunge of civilization into this abyss of blood and darkness by the wanton feat of those two infamous autocrats," he wrote a friend, "is a thing that so gives away the whole long age . . . that to have to take it all now for what the treacherous years were all the while really making for and meaning is too tragic for any words." To show his allegiance to the Allied cause, in 1915 James became a British citizen. He died the next year.

Near the close of the last century, at the height of his career, James went to a lively party in London during the course of which some person poured champagne into his top hat. The young American author Stephen Crane, who was present, tried to repair the damage and quiet the "Master's" indignation. James, Crane wrote, made a "holy show of himself in a situation that—on my honour—would have been simple to an ordinary man." However, Crane added that it was impossible to dislike the older man, "He is so kind to everybody."

In his way James was kind to the Cranes, who for a brief while were his neighbors near Rye, living impecuniously in a rented baronial "castle" where mastiffs roamed at will over floors covered with rushes and where cavernous fireplaces could accommodate whole trees at a time. Crane had fled America, where his quickly won literary reputation had almost as quickly given way to a picture of the drunken, drug-addicted bohemian, a petty criminal—a distorted legend not tempered by the fact that he married an older woman, the "honey-haired" Cora Taylor, who had been the madam of the Hotel de Dream, a Florida whorehouse.

It would be hard to imagine two more different personalities than the extremely proper, celibate, established James, and Crane, almost forty years

A photograph of 1893 shows the twenty-two-year-old Stephen Crane lounging in an artist friend's studio on West 30th Street, New York City—the same flat where Crane wrote his successful novel The Red Badge of Courage. *"In his day," wrote Alfred Kazin, "Crane stood as the 'marvelous boy' in the tradition of Chatterton, Keats, and Beardsley—the fever-ridden, rigidly intense type of genius that dies young, unhappy, and the prey of biographers. Everything that he wrote in his twenty-nine years seemed without precedent."*

his junior, an adventuring newspaper reporter and a refugee from the formalities and proprieties James so earnestly endorsed. Yet, James recognized the younger man's peculiar genius. When Crane died in 1900, in the Black Forest where he had gone hoping to cure his tuberculosis, James wrote Cora, "What a brutal, needless extinction!—what an unmitigated unredeemed catastrophe! I think of him with such a sense of possibilities and powers!"

Crane was not yet thirty when he died. He had suddenly leaped to fame in 1895 with the publication of his novel of the Civil War, *The Red Badge of Courage,* when he was twenty-four and working as a free-lance journalist in New York. Crane had not then seen a battlefield; he was born some years after the Civil War ended. However, he had studied the realistic campaign pictures of Winslow Homer and found in them commonplace details of the soldier's life never mentioned in official reports. But he accurately sensed more than he could possibly have known—among other things that as a trying ground for man's cowardice or courage, war merely intensified basic human problems. His soldier-hero was a very ordinary American farmboy (the novel is half finished before his name is mentioned), a raw recruit who experiences both the pangs of cowardice and the elation of new-found courage before his adventure is over. In either case he did what he had to do, instinctively and in the way his environment had trained him to respond to whatever the situation, without the intervention of moral principle. In tracing the destiny of his character through this sort of determinism Crane, following the lead of Holmes' "medicated" novels, was anticipating the principles of the behaviorist psychologists and opening a new path to the novelist.

In any event, he wrote such a book as had not been written before in America. He inscribed a copy to Howells in gratitude for what he had learned from that older man. But he brought realism to a higher emotional pitch than Howells ever did, and explored areas of human feeling and conduct with an earthy candor that was alien to James' dignified reserve. He was, in a sense, with Twain, creating modern American fiction. Crane was neither well-educated nor well-read, but he was a sharp journalist, and he turned out *The Red Badge* in ten days and nights of writing—for it is a relatively short novel. (He had read Tolstoy's *War and Peace,* which he thought was much too long. The Russian author "could have done the whole business in one-third of the time," Crane observed, "and made it just as wonderful." "It goes on and on like Texas," he laughingly concluded—and thought of writing a book called *Peace and War* to show that the job could be better done.)

With *The Red Badge* Crane struck a rich vein. For many Americans the Civil War remains *the* war. It is still a sure-fire subject for fiction and movies. Round it legend of all kinds have clustered. Its battlefields and cemeteries are sacred in a special way. The effect of the war on American life was immeasurably deep and lasting. In *The Red Badge* Crane gave it intimate significance for Everyman in a prose that bristled with colorful imagery. "The bugles called to each other like brazen gamecocks. . . ." "The sun was pasted in the sky like a wafer." He described the "cat-spit" sound of bullets that "kept pecking" at the soldiers. "Each distant thicket seemed a strange porcupine with quills of flame" as rifles spluttered.

At one frenzied moment of combat it seemed to the young warrior that he

When Crane wrote The Red Badge of Courage *in 1895 he had not yet had any direct experience in war; before beginning his naturalistic masterpiece, he studied old books and magazines and pored over Winslow Homer's Civil War campaign sketches, like that of the Yankee soldier reproduced above.*

saw everything about him with an almost supernatural vision. "Each blade of the green grass was bold and clear. He thought that he was aware of every change in the thin, transparent vapor that floated idly in sheets. The brown or gray trunks of the trees showed each roughness of their surfaces. And the men of the regiment, with their starting eyes and sweating faces, running madly, or falling, as if thrown headlong, to queer, heaped-up corpses—all were comprehended. His mind took a mechanical but firm impression, so that afterward everything was pictured and explained to him save why he himself was there."

H. G. Wells called Crane "beyond dispute, the best writer of our generation." *The Red Badge of Courage*, Wells wrote, "was a new thing, in a new school . . . entirely original and novel. To a certain extent, of course, that was the new man as . . . a typical young American, free at last, as no generation of Americans have been free before, of any regard for English criticism, comment, or tradition, and applying to literary work the conception and theories of the cosmopolitan studio with a quite American directness and vigor . . . there is Whistler even more than there is Tolstoy in the *Red Badge of Courage*."

Crane's first book, *Maggie: A Girl of the Streets*, written when he was twenty-two, was too sordid to find a regular publisher. (It was a story of seduction, prostitution, and suicide—episodes with the like of which Crane had become familiar during his early days as a reporter when he prowled the streets of New York's lower East Side. He later claimed that he got his "artistic education" on the Bowery.) Crane published it privately with money borrowed from his brother, but virtually no one noticed its appearance. In his discouragement Crane thought seriously of giving up writing altogether. But Hamlin Garland had seen the book and recommended it to Howells—and someone told Crane that Howells had likened it to the writings of Tolstoy and that he would say as much in print from his critical eminence. According to one eyewitness, Crane "gulped something down his throat, grinned like a woman in hysterics, and . . . went off to take up his writing again." (Later, Howells told Crane he could do things that Mark Twain could not.) When *The Badge* became an instant success, *Maggie* was reissued for an audience now eager to read Crane's work.

For the rest of his few years on earth Crane lived hard. He wrote incessantly. Because of the rare talent he had shown in *The Red Badge* he was repeatedly commissioned as a war correspondent, a profession then being made glamorous by Richard Harding Davis. On a gun-running expedition to Cuba in 1896 his ship was sunk off the Florida coast. His days'-long struggle against drowning in a dinghy with his several comrades was dramatized in the best of his short stories, "The Open Boat," which starts with the memorable lines, "None of them knew the color of the sky. Their eyes glanced level, and were fastened upon the waves that swept toward them. These waves were of the hue of slate, save for the tops, which were of foaming white, and all of the men knew the colors of the sea."

He covered the war between Greece and Turkey, and when he came out of it, having finally seen war at first hand, he remarked, *"The Red Badge* is all right!"* He seems to have taken delight in facing danger; it brought his sense of life to the highest pitch. When he was under fire with Davis reporting the

Crane, shown as a war correspondent on horseback, courted danger and described with insight man's fears in the presence of death.

238

Spanish-American War, he insisted on walking about until Davis had to pull him down while bullets knocked off his own hat and chipped his field glass. Among many other stories, Crane wrote sentimental reminiscences of his boyhood, he did too much hackwork, and he composed ironic free verses that showed the influence of Emily Dickinson—and he burned himself out before he had fully matured. Even so, he knew the meaning of fear and death, and gave it naked expression in unforgettable form before he met his own early, quiet death in Germany. As Alfred Kazin has written, "he was the first great tragic figure in the modern American generation."

Crane was just one, if the most brilliant, of a number of precocious young newspapermen of the 1890's who won recognition with their special reporting and who also wrote novels that attracted public attention. Their journalistic rounds brought these youthful authors close to the raw materials of life—to the crass, sordid, and violent aspects of the local world, as well as to the picturesque and exciting features of worlds far removed from the American scene; their writings mixed the starkest realism—"naturalism," as it has come to be called—with swashbuckling romanticism that provided vicarious excitement for those fastened in humdrum workaday lives.

The paragon of those roving adventurer-newsmen was Crane's sometime pressmate in Cuba, Richard Harding Davis, the most celebrated reporter of his generation. The publisher William Randolph Hearst paid Davis extravagantly just to report a Princeton-Yale football game, and in his gallery of glamorous types and celebrities the illustrator Charles Dana Gibson featured him as a dashing, handsome youth, along with the incomparable Gibson Girl. His words from far-flung battlefields were what gave the wars of his time meaning, importance, and interest to most Americans—and it was a time of many wars. As correspondent for New York and London newspapers and magazines, Davis covered the Spanish-American War, the Greco-Turkish War, the Boer War, the war between Russia and Japan—and, later, World War I. He reported Indian outbreaks in the American West, he had known well scheming soldiers of fortune in Latin America, he had covered the millennial celebration at Budapest, and Queen Victoria's Jubilee in London, and he had scooped the coronation of Nicholas II in St. Petersburg.

Davis knew everyone, or, rather, everyone knew Davis—headwaiters, princes, actors, presidents, vagabonds, and captains of commerce. Between newspaper assignments he turned out novels, plays, short stories, and collections of his papers that added little of lasting substance to the nation's literary heritage, but that clearly reflected public interest in the international adventures he dramatized with the adept craftsmanship of a practiced journalist. In addition, his legend fired the imagination of a rising generation of aspiring writers, including such men as H. L. Mencken, Sinclair Lewis, and Ernest Hemingway. "The vision of himself as a Richard Harding Davis hero had returned wistfully . . . ," wrote Lewis in his novel *Dodsworth*, "riding a mountain trail, two thousand sheer feet above a steaming valley; sun-helmet and whipcord breaks; tropical rain on a tin-roofed shack; a shot in the darkness as he sat over a square-face of gin with a ragged tramp of noble ancestry."

Frank Norris and Jack London, two closer contemporaries of Davis'—and of Crane's—came out of the West to write down-to-earth accounts about the

With his fast-paced reportage of world events and his daredevil attitude, Richard Harding Davis fired the imagination of his generation; he was its symbol of the "young man's epoch." Davis was at ease in society, as suggested by Charles Dana Gibson's sketch of him at top; he was also at home in the rough-and-ready life of a war correspondent, as shown in Frederic Remington's drawing.

hard facts of life as they witnessed them, and mingling the tough cynicism of the reporter with the romantic fervor of the youthful adventurer. Indebted as they both were to the path-breaking realism of Howells, they felt this represented a too narrow segment of American life as they knew it. In spite of the older man's grave concern with social problems and the unhappy plight of the working man, Norris felt that Howells told his stories largely in terms of what transpired in an affluent urban world "between lunch and dinner, small passions, restricted emotions, dramas of the reception-room, tragedies of an afternoon call, crises involving cups of tea." Norris' "naturalism" probed beneath and beyond those restricted and conventional surfaces of society— "down deep into the red, living heart of things"—as Crane had done, in search of the truth, even when it was ugly.

Along with Garland and Howells, Norris had read *Maggie* and recognized Crane's talent, although he felt its author was more concerned with style than with life. "Who cares for fine style!" he wrote a few years later. "Tell your yarn and let your style go to the devil. We don't want literature, we want life." Like other young men of his day, he suffered an "almost fatal attack of Richard Harding Davis," and, following Davis, he went to South Africa as a war correspondent for *Collier's* and the San Francisco *Chronicle*. There he enlisted with the British army and was captured by the Boers and forced to leave the country. (He sailed way on the same ship with Cecil Rhodes.) A few years later he was in Cuba, where he briefly met Crane who, Norris observed, with respect, had "been in peril of his life on a filibustering expedition," and "was tanned to the color of a well-worn saddle."

Like Crane, he had only a few more years to accomplish his mission in life; he died in 1902 at the age of thirty-one, two years after Crane's untimely death at the age of twenty-nine. As a youth Norris had studied art for a short while with Bouguereau at the Académie Julien in Paris, then returned to his home in San Francisco to spend four years at the University of California before enrolling at Harvard for an additional year of study. He was from an early age a disciple of Emile Zola, "the first and greatest of the naturalists." "The world of M. Zola," he observed, "is a world of big things. The enormous, the formidable, the terrible, is what counts; no teacup tragedies here."

Norris started his first consequential novel, *McTeague*, when he was still in college, although it was not completed and published until 1899, after he had returned from Cuba. Like Bret Harte before him, he knew the color and character of the San Francisco streets and the mean and ordinary life that took place there—along the Barbary Coast and on Telegraph Hill, in Chinatown and other haunts of that pulsing, storied city. He knew the drunkards and the prostitutes along with the petty tradesmen and the shop girls. He also knew the back country of California—the mining regions and the vast wheat fields. Before he finished *McTeague* he had seen far parts of the world as well. His purpose went beyond painting local color, and beyond the confining interests of the New England school that he felt had "dominated . . . the entire range of American fiction . . . narrowing it down to a veritable cult." He found the Far West of his day, with the freshness of its recent pioneer days still upon it, an ample and appropriate stage for the play of the elemental forces that, for better or worse, determine the fate of man—economic forces, as well

Frank Norris, a pioneer in American naturalism, was a suave, elegantly dressed college man, as suggested by the above photograph. Norris was primarily a writer of fiction; he believed that the novel "expresses modern life better than architecture, better than painting, better than poetry."

as those of nature, and internal emotional forces.

In *McTeague* Norris followed his own prescription when he pleaded, "Give us stories now; give us men, strong, brutal men, with red-hot blood in 'em, blood and bones and viscera in 'em, and women, too, that move and have their being." It is a story of violence and passion that starts in the San Francisco office of a charlatan dentist and ends with murder and a grisly death scene in the scorched remoteness of Death Valley; it is a romance dealing with ugly realities amid scenes that were new to most of his readers. The brute nature within his principal characters erodes their finer instincts and leads to their depravity. Life follows the Darwinian pattern of the "survival of the fittest."

Theodore Dreiser, whose own career as an author was just beginning, thought *McTeague* was "as somber and yet true a representation of reality as has been conceived by any writer in the land." Norris' most ambitious work, *The Octopus: A Story of California*, was published the year before he died. (It was the first volume of an intended trilogy, *The Epic of the Wheat*, demonstrating again how implacable and personal forces shape human destiny. A second volume, *The Pit: A Story of Chicago*, was printed posthumously; the third was never written.) Now, at last, his editors agreed, the big American novel would come out of the West—"an idea that's as big as all outdoors." The theme is a struggle between California wheat growers and the railroad operators, between the antagonistic forces of wheat ("It was there, everywhere from margin to margin of the horizon.") and the railroad ("That huge sprawling organism, with its ruddy arteries . . . swollen with life-blood, reaching out to infinity, gorged to bursting, an excrescence, a gigantic parasite fattening upon the life-blood of an entire commonwealth.")

In that struggle men became "mere nothings": the wheat ranchers are defeated, reduced to poverty and suffering, the agent of the railroad is accidentally smothered to death by the wheat he had dishonestly gained, as he watched it being loaded onto his own ship. Yet, in the end, the wheat remains, and as the spokesman of those bonanza California days, Norris describes it, "untouched, unassailable, undefiled, that mighty life-force, that nourisher of nations, wrapped in a Nirvanic calm, indifferent to the human swarm, gigantic, resistless, moved onward in its appointed grooves. . . ." Here he writes lyrically as though men had never before seen such sights as those endless wheat fields. And he writes also in protest. *The Octopus*, published as Theodore Roosevelt became president, was one of the most articulate of the

In his trilogy, The Epic of the Wheat, *Norris intended to describe the growth, marketing, and exporting of wheat. The first part,* The Octopus (1901), *deals with the struggles between California wheat growers and the heartless railroad, which, octopuslike, strangles and ruins them. The photograph below shows a twenty-six-horse-team harvester cutting, threshing, and sacking wheat in Washington state in 1902. The epic's second book,* The Pit (1903), *is an account of the Chicago meat market; the third,* The Wolf, *was never written.*

Jack London, prophet of the strenuous life, was, according to one observer, "a bugle, an awakener, an annunciator, a wall shatterer, a herald of the dawn." A restless, reckless soul whose wanderings took him from California to Europe to Alaska, and even to the Orient, he translated his experiences into vivid, violence-filled fiction.

populist tracts that voiced the agrarian unrest of the time. It has been called "the most ambitious novel of its generation." He was not as accomplished a stylist as Crane—had no intention of being such—but his work has a rude strength that prefigures the writing of Jack London and Theodore Dreiser.

During his own relatively brief life Jack London became the best known of all the younger American writers and, it is said, the most highly paid author in the world. Probably no other writer squandered his talent so prodigally as he did. Within the bare sixteen years of his headlong career he produced about fifty books of fiction, drama, and essays. "I have no unfinished stories," he once remarked. "Invariably I complete every one I start. If it's good, I sign it and send it out. If it isn't good, I sign it and send it out." In spite of that, his popularity was widespread and enduring. It has been reported that in later years in Russia "Yacklunnen" was the most admired of American authors and that Lenin's last days were brightened by reading London's books.

Most of London's output, his fiction at least, was a direct outgrowth of his personal experiences—of circumstances and adventures that gave little early promise of a reputable literary career. It is said that he was the natural son of a wandering astrologer and a spiritualist mother. However true that may be, the lad grew up a waterfront hoodlum on one side or other of San Francisco Bay. Shortly after he graduated from grammar school he became an oyster pirate, robbing the oyster beds of the area so effectively he was dubbed Prince of the Oyster Pirates, as his girl companion on these escapades was called Queen of the Oyster Pirates. He was a hard-drinking, reckless, lawless teenager. When he was seventeen he sailed before the mast as a tough-fisted able-bodied seaman on a sealing ship bound for the Siberian coast and Japan. For a while thereafter he turned tramp and wandered about the eastern states, and at one point was sent to a penitentiary for thirty days.

After a short spell of fairly conventional behavior back in Oakland (he even spent a semester at the University of California), in 1897, when he had just turned twenty-one, he joined the gold rush to the Alaska Klondike. He did not strike pay dirt and became so ill with scurvy he had to give up his quest and head homeward.

Now he started to write in earnest and sold his first story, "To the Man on Trail," a yarn about the Yukon, to the *Overland Monthly* for $5. His life was already more than half over. From then on, however, he produced and sold short stories, verse, and other writings at a formidable rate. He was also writing novels. With the second of these that he attempted, *The Call of the Wild*, published in 1903, he immediately won worldwide recognition; his fortune was assured.

The Call of the Wild, the story of a dog who, taken to Alaska, reverts to type and travels with a wolf pack, follows a theme that runs through much of London's fiction—a theme that reveals the latent savagery that underlies civilized appearances and attitudes. Man himself is little better than an animal. "Civilization has spread a veneer over the soft shelled animal known as man," he wrote. "It is a very thin veneer. . . . Starve him, let him miss six meals, and see gape through the veneer the hungry maw of the animal beneath. Get between him and the female of his kind upon whom his mating instinct is bent, and see his eyes blaze like an angry cat's, hear in his throat the scream of wild stallions, and watch his fist clench like an orang-outang's. . . . Touch his silly vanity, which he exults into high-sounding pride, call him a liar, and behold the red animal in him that makes a hand clutching that is quick like the tensing of a tiger's claw, or an eagle's talon, incarnate with desire to rip and destroy."

That insistence on the importance of brute force is repeated over and again in London's works, as the titles of his books often indicate: *The Son of the Wolf; White Fang; The Strength of the Strong; The Sea Wolf;* and so on. The theme was never more clearly or better stated than in *The Call of the Wild*—considered among his best works. Buck, the dog-hero, remains a well-known and fascinating character wherever adventure stories are read, with an enduring popular audience among the young. It is easy to recall the excitement in first reading how "Buck got a frothing adversary by the throat, and was sprayed with blood when his teeth sank through the jugular!" "This," as the Russian poet Ilya Sulvinsky wrote of London's stories in general, "is the first cigar we smoke in our youth."

London wrote more than adventure stories, to be sure. Although his formal schooling was extremely limited, he had, from childhood, read voraciously. Like Norris and so many of his other contemporaries, he was strongly influenced by the writing of Rudyard Kipling, whose romantic bent set him a model of sorts. Once, in the Klondike, he walked seven miles to borrow a copy of Kipling's *Seven Seas* from a miner camped up the river. He had taken with him to Alaska copies of Darwin's *Origin of Species* and Marx's *Das Kapital* (along with Milton's *Paradise Lost*, Spencer's *Philosophy of Style*, among still other books), and he was steeped in the writings of Nietzsche, with their acclamation of the Superman—with whom he surely identified himself in his

Philip R. Goodwin's illustration for a 1905 edition of London's Call of the Wild *shows Buck, the novel's dog-hero, on the attack. The legend reads: "Straight at the man he launched his one hundred and forty pounds of fury."*

heroic moods, although he claimed to reject such a concept.

Out of that mixed bag of reading he developed his belief that the world belonged to the strong, along with his incongruous but fervent dedication to the cause of socialism and its concern for the weak and the ignorant. He was a "bully" fellow, in Theodore Roosevelt's sense of that word, and he also preached the social interdependence that was so alien to Roosevelt's concept of the rugged individual. Meanwhile, while his life lasted, he found time to report the Russo-Japanese War for the Hearst papers as well as the Mexican campaigns of a decade later, and undertook other exciting adventures with his second wife (he called her his "mate-woman") on distant seas. Socialist though he was, he lived handsomely on his patriarchal California estate in the Valley of the Moon until he died in 1916—apparently a suicide. With his work he had helped to uncover a submerged American world, as Carl Van Doren observed, "instinctive and undisciplined," that our earlier literature had largely passed over. His contemporaries in his yarns of adventure which bespoke the "strenuous life" extolled by Teddy Roosevelt. We rejoice in those stories in our own day, although we can also see them as expressions of the struggle and revolt, of the clashes between the individual and society, that were symptoms of a changing world of ideas.

No American writer of the time was a more perceptive and articulate witness to that changing world of ideas than Henry Adams. Throughout the half century that followed the Civil War, while Twain, Howells, James, Crane, Norris, and others were writing out their messages of realism and naturalism, Adams was observing the American scene from his own special point of vantage. It is better to say that he was observing the human scene, for his perspective was broadened and lengthened by exhaustive studies in history and by travel to virtually all parts of the world, from the Arctic to the South Seas, from the Rocky Mountains to Japan and India, from St. Petersburg and Athens to Mexico City and other capitals and to villages about the globe. He understood with unusual clarity that mature and worthy American literature must deal with universal and timeless issues and interpret these in terms of contemporary American life.

The elegant Adams homestead (above) in Quincy, Mass., was the home of four generations of Adamses, including the two presidents, John and John Quincy. It was a favorite with John Quincy's grandson, Henry Adams, who declared, "The Old House at Quincy was eighteenth century."

As an Adams, Henry had the further advantage of having been exposed since childhood to the conversation of learned and thoughtful men and women, and to libraries of rich variety (and, of course, he went to Harvard). He was the first of his long, eminent family line who was born to be a writer rather than a public servant. (When he visited the White House as a child he thought of it as a home of the Adamses.) The pen was his predestined instrument, and he wielded it with unflagging energy for more than sixty years.

Adams was a superb historian, perhaps excelled in this country only by Francis Parkman. Over a period of nine years, and requiring nine volumes, he wrote his celebrated *History of the United States of America During the Administrations of Thomas Jefferson and James Madison*, dealing with a period when the new republic was undergoing its first major tests (and carefully skirting the years when an Adams was in the presidency).

His principal interest, however, was in the ideas that might explain the course of history, especially as it was being enacted in America. Those ideas he kept revolving in his mind throughout his life in his quest of some plausible and basic explanation of historical developments. "I have never loved or taught facts, if I could help it," he once remarked, "having that antipathy to facts which only idiots and philosophers attain."

Adams shared the pessimism that Mark Twain expressed in his references to "the damned human race" and that also chilled Howells' observations about American society. Like others of his time Adams also was a determinist who saw mankind being maneuvered toward its destiny by implacable forces it could not control. But his determinism went deeper than that of his contemporaries, as he struggled with its implications to society and history. More sensibly than any other American writer of his age he was aware of the increasingly important role of science in shaping human affairs. In 1862, as a young man serving his father at the American embassy in London, he wrote his brother, "Man has mounted science, and is now run away with. . . . Some day science may have the existence of mankind in its power, and the human race commit suicide by blowing up the world." As he grew older he saw little reason to alter that opinion. In 1902 he felt even more immediate concern about such possibilities. "Power leaped from every atom," he reflected, "and enough of it to supply the stellar universe." Man, he felt, could no longer hold off the forces that he had unleashed, especially after the discovery of radium. "It is mathematically certain to me," Adams stated, "that another thirty years of energy-development at the rate of the last century must reach an *impasse*" —an impasse that seemed to have been catastrophically reached at Hiroshima less than thirty years after his own death in 1918.

In his writings Adams translated the doubts and speculations that plagued thoughtful men of his generation into highly informed and disciplined literature. He wrote two creditable novels, *Democracy* and *Esther*, neither of which he published under his name. However, another two books, *Mont-Saint-Michel and Chartres* and *The Education of Henry Adams*, were the capstones of his literary career. These volumes were complementary; both were originally printed privately. In them he contrasted the age of cultural unity, the thirteenth century, with the age of multiplicity, the twentieth, that related to his own experience as an American.

The books were, in effect, summations of his conjecture that all life and thought might be measured in terms of Force. In the thirteenth century, he reflected, the Virgin represented "the greatest force the western world ever felt"; in his own day the eternal mystery of force was represented by the dynamo, which he had marveled at when he visited the fairs at Chicago in 1893 and Paris in 1900. The Virgin Mary, he felt, had "concentrated in herself the whole rebellion of man against fate. . . . She was above law; she took feminine pleasure in turning hell into an ornament; she delighted in trampling on every social distinction in this world and the next." She judged by love alone, and love may triumph over science in the end.

Seven centuries later, Adams conjectured, the dynamo had become the symbol of infinity; he began to see it as a moral force. "Before the end," he wrote, "one began to pray to it; inherited instinct taught the natural expression of man before silent and infinite force. Among the thousand symbols of ultimate energy, the dynamo was not so human as some, but it was the most expressive." The movement that led from the Virgin to the dynamo, from

Henry Adams, shown above in his study, became an assistant professor of history at Harvard in 1870. One of his students described him at that time as "a small man, blue eyes, brown hair, pointed beard auburn verging to red, perfectly but inconspicuously dressed in brownish gray tweeds as I remember, of easy and quiet movement and distinct but quiet speech."

Adams divided world history into three phases. The Electric Age, the third period, was suggested to him by the dynamos he saw at the expositions in Chicago (1893) and in Paris (1900). The drawing at right shows one of these dynamos—the great Allis-Corliss engine—on exhibit at the Chicago Fair. According to Adams' calculations, the Electric Age would last from 1900 until 1917, and, he added, there might be a fourth or Ethereal phase that would "bring Thought to the limit of its possibilities in the year 1921."

unity to multiplicity over the course of centuries, formed an unbroken sequence that was rapidly accelerating. In another generation, were there to be one, a new social mind would have to evolve. "The period from 1900 to 1930 is in full swing," he wrote his friend John Hay from Paris in 1900, "and, gee-whacky! how it is going! It will break its damned neck long before it gets through, if it tries to keep up the speed. . . . I,—a monk of St. Dominic, absorbed in the Beatitudes of the Virgin Mother—go down to the Champ de Mars and sit by the hour over the great dynamos [at the Paris fair], watching them run as noiselessly and as smoothly as the planets, and asking them—with infinite courtesy—where in Hell they are going."

Nevertheless, Adams concluded that if the laws of history could ever be formulated, they would have to be based in good measure on American experience. In the face of all his pessimism it seemed to him likely that America, more than any other country, would shape the uncertain future in the course of the twentieth century. He also concluded that there would have to be some close correspondence between the laws of history and the principles of science as far as these could be determined. The revelation of a scientific basis for history, he concluded, would reduce traditional history to an anachronism; it would mean, he thought, the creation of a new religion.

Adams had been led into the complexities of scientific speculation through his friendship with Clarence King, the leading American geologist of his time. Following his graduation from Yale in 1862, King made a horseback trip across the continent to work in the Nevada and California mines. Shortly thereafter, while in government service, he helped make a geological survey of the Cordilleran ranges from eastern Colorado to California. He knew the western mountains as intimately as Adams knew the streets of Boston and Washington. Adams first met King, "saturated with the sunshine of the Sierras," in Estes Park, Colorado, when Adams himself was all but lost one evening on muleback in those wilderness heights, and he immediately succumbed to his new friend's charm and vast intelligence. The two spent the night, sharing room and bed, talking "till far towards dawn." In his *Education*

Adams wrote of King, "None of his contemporaries had done so much, single-handed, or were likely to leave so deep a trail. . . . He had organized, as a civil—not military—measure, a Government Survey. He had paralleled the Continental Railway in Geology; a feat as yet unequalled by other governments which had as a rule no continents to survey. He was creating one of the classic scientific works of the century." King's writings were not only scientifically accurate, they were unprecedented, eloquent descriptions of pioneering adventures in the West he knew so well and loved so ardently. He was the first of the Western nature writers to win a wide reading public. His *Mountaineering in the Sierra Nevada*, published in 1872, remains a wonderfully readable and fresh classic. Only John Muir surpassed King in powerful and brilliant descriptions of what the grandeur of the virgin West was really like, for all that has been written about it over the past century.

"History," Adams remarked, "will die if not irritated. The only service I can do to my profession is to serve as a flea." He did more than that, to be sure. His well-grounded pessimism subtly illustrated the transition of America during his mature years from an age of confidence to an age of doubt, and that, ironically, at a time the nation was reaching new peaks of material prosperity and scientific achievement. He was suggesting what has long since become clearly evident, that such "advances" solved few of the fundamental problems of human existence or of American democracy as a form of government.

Writing in the third person as he did, and publishing his books anonymously, Adams created an image of an aloof, cautious, intellectually austere man. Actually, a substantial proportion of his literary gift found outlet in his continuous and voluminous and brilliant correspondence. Here his first-rate mind and quick wit were released from the formal restraints the printed word imposed. Few travel letters can compare with those he wrote from odd parts of the world as he restlessly moved from place to place, alone or in the company of others—particularly of the painter and stained-glass artist John La

In 1890 Adams fled to the South Seas with his friend and mentor, John La Farge, whose water color of Polynesian kava makers is reproduced at left. La Farge, who awakened Adams' interest in art, stated that the writer's "historic sense amounted to poetry."

247

Farge. His quick character-sketches of people he met are deft and colorful. "Imagine a man so thin and emaciated," he wrote of his meeting with Robert Louis Stevenson in his vagabondage at Samoa, "that he looked like a bundle of sticks in a bag, with a head and eyes morbidly intelligent and restless. . . . I half expected to see him drop with a hemorrhage at any moment, for he cannot be quiet, but sits down, jumps up, darts off and flies back, at every sentence he utters, and his eyes and features gleam with a hectic glow."

In his letters, he was also a landscape painter in prose, as when he described the volcanoes of a Hawaiian island, the mountains that lined the fjords of northern Scandinavia, or the forests of Ceylon. From Hawaii he wrote, "I am looking, from the porch of the inn, down on the black floor of the crater, and its streaming and smoking lake, now chilled over, some two or three miles away, at the crater's further end. More impressive to me is the broad sloping mass of Mauna Loa which rises beyond, ten thousand feet above us, a mass of rugged red lava, scored by deeper red or black streaks down its sides, but looking softer than babies' flesh in this lovely morning sunlight, and tinged above its red with the faintest violet vapor. I adore mountains—from below. Like other deities they should not be trodden upon." He described the sad, solemn mountains of Norway, which "never knew what it was to be a volcano" as lying "one after another, like corpses, with their toes up, and you pass by them, and look five or ten miles up the fiords between them, and see their noses, tipped by cloud or snow, high in behind, with one corpse occasionally lying on another, and a skull or a thigh-bone chucked about, and hundreds of glaciers and snow-patches hanging to them, as though it was a winter battle-field; and a weird after-glow light. . . . They never can have really enjoyed themselves." Thus he poses the Scandinavian pantheon against the Polynesian, as Newton Arvin has observed. In Ceylon he traveled in an ox cart, "a real cart with two wheels, and two slow, meditative, humped oxen, who are also sacred cattle, and who have the most Buddhistic expression in their humps and horns that ever was reached by God's creatures. . . . We put two chairs inside, and were slowly driven by a naked Tamil, as though we were priests or even Hindu deities, through the woods, every now and then clambering out to inspect some stone tank or temple among the trees, and in secret deadly terror of ticks, leeches and cobras, not to speak of centipedes and scorpions."

Adams had many friends of varied interest, and in his letters to them his own wide-ranging mind and his talents as a writer found their most certain and natural expression. He outlived most of his contemporaries. His dearest friends, John Hay, once Lincoln's private secretary and later U.S. Secretary of State, and Clarence King, both died before Adams' own death in 1918, "The three friends had begun life together," he wrote in concluding his *Education*, "and the last of the three had no motive—no attraction—to carry it on after the others had gone. . . . Perhaps some day—say 1938, their centenary— they might be allowed to return together for a holiday, to see the mistakes of their own lives made clear in the light of the mistakes of their successors; and perhaps then, for the first time since man began his education among the carnivores, they would find a world that sensitive and timid natures could regard without a shudder." His earlier, youthful estimates of what that world might be like were less hopeful but turned out to be more accurate.

ILLUSTRATION UNLIMITED

In William Dean Howells' novel A Hazard of New Fortunes *(1890), Basil March asks Fulkerson if he plans to have illustrations in the new magazine he is launching in New York. Astonished by the question, Fulkerson replies: "My dear boy! What are you giving me? Do I look like the sort of lunatic who would start a thing in the twilight of the nineteenth century without illustrations? Come off!" This passage was written in the course of what is now called the golden age of American illustration (1880–1914). Inventions such as the high-speed press, halftone plate, and color printing led to a phenomenal explosion of high quality illustrated material and a burgeoning of artistic talent under the leadership of masters like Howard Pyle, N. C. Wyeth, and Maxfield Parrish (depicted in the wry self-portrait below).*

"The Vaudeville Theater," by William Glackens, Scribner's, *1909*

Book illustration has sometimes been looked down on as a minor art; yet, in spite of this prejudicial attitude, the book has become a major vehicle for artistic expression during the last hundred years. Throughout the late nineteenth century many notable American artists worked regularly at illustration. The long list includes Winslow Homer, John Sloan, William Glackens, Thomas Eakins, and Frederic Remington. These painters worked with an outlook quite different from that of the artists of the 1970's. Today it is often considered unfashionable to admire a work that tells a story, and the qualities that are usually thought to be meaningful in art are abstract ones—color, structure, and relationship; subject matter is nearly always of secondary importance. However, just the reverse was true in the nineteenth century, when the public as well as the most gifted artists considered the story to be of prime concern. Many painters, even if they were not illustrating, created narrative scenes in which they reconstructed an incident, a legend, or an allegory. Howard Pyle, for example, often contributed canvases originally done as illustrations to exhibits of easel paintings, changing only the title.

"A Gander-Pull" in Virginia, by Frederic Remington, Harper's Weekly, *1894*

THE ARTIST AS ILLUSTRATOR

"Thar's such a thing as calls in this world," by Thomas Eakins, Scribner's Monthly, *1879*

"Last Glimpse of Martha's Vineyard," Charles S. Reinhart's illustration for Harper's New Monthly Magazine, *1886*

"Poor Little One," Elizabeth Shippen Green's charcoal illustration for Harper's New Monthly Magazine, *1911*

Around 1900, when Henry Adams observed that American artists "used sex for sentiment, never for force," he was reflecting the prevailing American attitude that idealized women into bloodless, sexless, personifications of purity. Whether portrayed in the yellowest press or the most dignified magazine, the American madonna remained "unassailable and untouchable on her marble pedestal," with never a trace of unrestrained passion or sensuality. She was a virginal girl or a tender mother, never the independent woman of today. She was, writes art critic Barbara Rose, a "flower to be protected, cordoned off from the world of real events in cozy drawing rooms, and levered as an object with its own esthetic delights (translucent skin, huge luminous eyes, heaving bosoms). . . ."

PURE
&
PRETTY
LADIES

James Montgomery Flagg's "If Wishes Were Figures," pen and ink, Harper's Weekly, *1907*

Charles Dana Gibson's spread for Collier's, 1903

HARPER'S

MARCH

Edward Penfield

Robert J. Wildhack

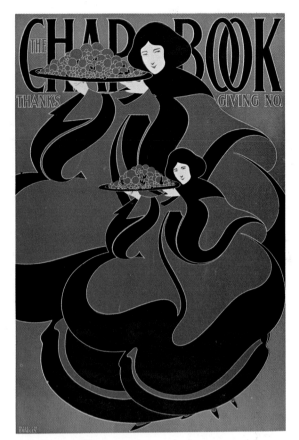

Will H. Bradley

John Sloan

The illustrators of the golden age were sub-
jected to various new and liberating influences
from abroad. For instance, Japanese art, first
shown in London in 1862, introduced the use
of flat colors, asymmetrical composition, and
shallow spaces—modes of expression that were
adopted by the European masters of art nou-
veau. Eventually, Japanese art-cum-art nou-
veau exploded upon the American scene in the
guise of the poster style of the 1890's. The
poster movement was actually initiated in
America in 1889 by the house of Harper, which
commissioned the Swiss poster artist Eugene
Grasset to do magazine covers and posters
advertising Harper periodicals. Other magazines, like *Scribner*'s and *Century* followed suit,
discovering that the art-nouveau poster style
was eye-catching, whether used for a magazine
cover or an advertisement. The main American
practitioners of the poster style included Will
Bradley, Edward Penfield, and John Sloan.

THE
POSTER
STYLE
OF THE
1890's

257

"Catching the 'Limited,'" by William Harnden Foster, Scribner's, *1911*

A MAN'S

WORLD

A Philip Goodwin illustration for Theodore Roosevelt's African Game Trails *(1909)*

The period between the turn of the century and the outbreak of World War I is often called the age of confidence in reference to America's unquestioning belief in its power, its faith in a brilliant and better future. Men were still the master sex. "There is something mentally enervating in feminine companionship," proclaimed *Cosmopolitan* in 1905. "The genuine man feels that he must go off alone or with other men; out in the open air, as it were, roughing it among the rough, as a mental tonic." The man who most embodied this mood of optimism and militant muscularity was the American colossus himself, President Theodore Roosevelt—soldier, writer, statesman, adventurer, and advocate of the strenuous life. The magazines served the manly tastes of the era with adventure stories of swashbuckling heroes who enjoyed drama, big-game hunting, flying, and other activities and deeds of derring-do worthy of T.R. or Richard Harding Davis.

"The Second Installation of Oliver Cromwell as Protector," by Yohn, Scribner's, 1900

American illustration matured during the period from 1880 to 1900 largely because of the development in the 1880's of half-tone photoengraving (a mechanical process for reproducing drawing and painting), and the improvements in four-color printing in the late 1890's. These technical advances opened up a whole new range of expression for illustrators, who could now use water colors or oils to create works whose every stroke could be captured by the four-color printing process. Naturally, periodical illustration became quite lavish. This era also witnessed the rise of the novel, which was often vividly illustrated in a manner almost unknown today except for limited editions. The changes in the illustrator's art are evident in the career of William Thomas Smedley, who began working as a draftsman in New York City in 1878. He drew in pen and ink until the advent of photoengraving, when he switched to water color. Smedley's illustrations, like those of Clifford Carelton, reflect the American scene of the 1890's, especially the genteel middle-class life.

"Will you be my friend indeed?"
painted by Alice Barber Stephens
for Hawthorne's The Marble Faun

THE
ILLUSTRATED
NOVEL

"Each letter slowly consumed to ashes," painted in 1909 by
William Smedley for Twain and Warner's The Gilded Age

"In the Grand Parlor," drawn in 1894 by Clifford Carelton for Howells' Their Wedding Journey

A TASTE OF PARRISH

"The Idiot," Parrish's oddly op cover for Collier's, *1910*

The work of Maxfield Parrish—that prolific, pre-pop master of mass-appeal art—enjoyed a revival in the mid-1960's after two decades of oblivion. Parrish's career was launched in 1895 with a *Harper's Weekly* cover depicting a roly-poly chef holding a plum pudding. For the next three decades he held America spellbound with his world of fairy-tale settings peopled with diaphanously gowned maidens, strange wizened creatures, or mischievous gnomes; the public loved his wit and his lurid, theatrical sense of color. Parrish brought the same charm and technical mastery to whatever work he was commissioned to do: magazine and book illustrations, murals, commercial subjects. British-born art critic Lawrence Alloway summed up Parrish's niche in American culture as follows: "[He] is an artist who lives in the memories of American's rather than in the Museums. His activity was immense and he possessed a flair for coining images that stick in the mind years after the original work has been seen. . . . In his time he was regarded very much as a fine artist."

"The Pool, Villa d'Este, Tivoli," by Parrish for Edith Wharton's Italian Villas and Their Gardens (1904)

FRESH STARTS

Brooklyn Bridge: Variation on an Old Theme (opposite), painted in 1939 by Joseph Stella, evokes the bridge that Walt Whitman envisioned as "singing the strong, light works of engineers...." The bridge was celebrated by many others, including Maxwell Anderson, who made it the setting of his play Winterset. *Hart Crane saw it as the "symbol of our constructive future, our unique identity, in which is also included our scientific hopes and achievements of the future."*

The last decade of the nineteenth century constitutes a watershed of American history. On one side of the divide, the Civil War and all that had gone before were slipping into the storied and legendary past. In 1890 the Superintendent of the Census reported that to all intents the frontier was closed, thus ending a long, dramatic, and significant phase of the country's development. Just a few years earlier Geronimo and his Apache braves had surrendered to a combination of American and Mexican military forces. This was the end of armed resistance by the Indians; the original natives of the land, it seemed, would now slowly fade away. A few straggling buffalo remained on the Western plains, where once they had blackened the landscape in countless herds. Several territories still awaited statehood, but the good free land that had so long and compellingly lured Americans westward was practically all staked out. The "interminable" forests were well on their way to destruction, and proud, growing cities were rising in their stead. The first forest reserves were created in 1891 in an effort to save what was left of the trees. In the course of their plundering advance across the continent Americans had done more damage to the land in "a century of progress" than the combined forces of man and nature could repair in hundreds of years to come.

On the other side of the dividing line of the 1890's, America would plunge into a future of accelerating changes. Forces that had been at work for years past reached a crescendo of large accomplishment at the end of the century. The nation that of old was predominantly agricultural and largely concerned with domestic problems had clearly emerged as a modern urbanized and industrialized state, progressively involved in a world economy and international concerns. The "great experiment" of democracy had generated a national government whose sovereign powers increased with the passing years. Barely more than a generation after the Civil War, America witnessed the twice-remarkable phenomenon of "Fighting Joe" Wheeler: at one time an officer of the Confederate Army, he was now commanding Yankee soldiers in an imperialistic war in Cuba and the Philippines. That brief but "splendid little war" with Spain was followed just a few years later by President Theodore Roosevelt's successful peacemaking intervention in the conflict between Russia and Japan. The United States was well into the currents of international affairs.

Within its own boundaries the country took on an international character as immigrants by the millions thronged to its shores from all about the world. As Whitman wrote, the United States was becoming "a teeming nation of nations." Emerson's professed ideal of a "real American" had been an alloy to be cast up from this human melting pot in future years. Let them all come, he wrote, "The energy of Irish, Germans, Swedes, Poles, and Cossacks, and all the European tribes,—and of the Africans, and of the Polynesians,—will construct a new race, a new religion, a new state, a new literature, which will be as vigorous as the new Europe which came out of the smelting-pot of the Dark Ages. . . ." There were others, however, like Senator Henry Cabot Lodge of Massachusetts, who saw in this invasion of "the wretched refuse, the homeless, tempest-tost" peoples from outlandish places a menace to American destiny—that "wild motley throng, Men from the Volga and the Tartar steppes," as the dismayed poet Thomas Bailey Aldrich referred to this foreign invasion. In their numbers and with their alien traditions they could corrupt or even extinguish the "pure" native breed that had fused in earlier years of immigration. Yet, as far as could be discerned, up until the first serious exclusion of immigrants in the 1920's the American stock had not been impaired by the infusion of these strange and variant elements.

By the turn of the century the United States faced a situation unlike any that had gone before. To Henry Adams the country in 1900 was totally different from what it had been in his youth. "I am wholly a stranger in it," he wrote. "Neither I, nor anyone else, understands it. The turning of a nebula into a star may somewhat resemble the change. All I can see is that it is one of compression, concentration, and consequent development of terrific energy, represented not by souls, but by coal and iron and steam."

The nation as a whole could not wait until the birth of a new century to celebrate its command of its formidable energies and to take measure of those achievements that were leading it into a prominent role on the world stage. Seven years in advance, in 1893, the World's Columbian Exposition opened at Chicago. Here, at the site of what a mere two generations earlier was a tiny frontier hamlet on the prairie, stood an astonishing, lusty metropolis—a metropolis that took tribute from most of the West. Foreign visitors classified the city's vital growth, along with the phenomenon of Niagara Falls, as one of the wonders of the New World. The vigor of the place was almost frightening. After twice burning nearly to the ground in its short history, the city was reborn, as the poet Carl Sandburg later described it, the "City of the Big Shoulders":

> Hog Butcher for the World,
> Tool Maker, Stacker of Wheat,
> Player with Railroads and the Nation's Freight Handler . . .
> Laughing the stormy, husky, brawling laughter of Youth . . .

The buildings of the White City, as the fairground was called, housed a spectacular display of industrial and scientific demonstrations that foretold a future of accelerating advances—of "progress," a word in very high favor at the time. The young writer Theodore Dreiser compared the glistening

A cartoon from a Leslie's Weekly of 1888 depicts what many Americans feared would be the disastrous result of unrestricted immigration: the "last Yankee" stands surrounded by a motley gang of immigrants who have annihilated "the native stock of America."

"A New Divertisement for Summer—A Trolley-Car Excursion," so reads the caption of an illustration, reproduced at left, that appeared in a Harper's Weekly of 1896. During the nineties, thanks to the ubiquitous availability of electricity, the trolley car became an irresistible caravan of joy for anyone with a few cents in his pocket. Cheap to operate and cheap to illuminate with the still relatively new incandescent bulbs, the vehicle became the pleasure wagon of the masses.

structures and their landscaped grounds along the shores of Lake Ontario to a fairyland, created "as though some brooding spirit of beauty, inherent possibly in some directing over-soul, had waved a magic wand." Another rising author, Hamlin Garland, wrote his parents on their Dakota farm, "Sell the cook stove if necessary and come. You *must* see this fair." Henry Adams paid a visit to learn what he could. He thought the neoclassic fair buildings, designed as most of them were in "the pure ideal of the ancients," an "inconceivable" architectural display. To impose such refined academic standards on the raw Midwestern world seemed to him a "rupture in historical sequence." But he found the scientific exhibits fascinating, and he "lingered among the dynamos" thoughtfully.

With its electrical demonstrations the fair made it apparent that the years to come would indeed, and quite literally, be brighter. The lights that bathed the grounds and buildings miraculously turned night into day. Here, for the first time, many people could visualize the untold wonders electricity could perform. For some, like Garland's parents, who were unfamiliar with any device brighter than a kerosene lamp—or at best, gaslight—the fair was illuminating in every sense of the word. "Electricity," boasted one enthusiastic contemporary, "is the half of an American . . . no nation has displayed such aptness in adapting [it] to practical use." As just one example, by 1895 ten thousand miles of electric transit lines were in operation in the nation. Soon a passenger could ride in electric trolleys all the way from Portland, Maine, via New York to Sheboygan, Wisconsin, if any such idea entered his head. Aside from extensive jaunts, the city dweller could get out of the city and back in again quicker and more cheaply on trolleys than ever before, and cities began to build up their outskirts.

Early in the present century the English author H. G. Wells visited Niagara Falls, whose magnificent torrents had recently been harnessed to produce electric power; and he admired that scenic wonder not for its sheer beauty, as travelers usually do, but for its immeasurable serviceability. As much potential power flowed over those falls in a single day as was contained in all the coal mined throughout the world in the same amount of time. Wells looked forward to the happy day when all that "froth and hurry . . . all of it, dying into the hungry canals of intake, should rise again in light and power, in ordered and equipped and proud and beautiful humanity, in cities and palaces and the emancipated souls and hearts of men."

There was another, darker side to the contemporary scene. One would not have guessed from all the dazzling magic projected at the Chicago Fair that the nation was then in the midst of a severe economic depression and financial panic that cast black shadows across the lives of a multitude of Americans. As those shadows lengthened, early in 1894 numbers of unemployed men, called Coxey's Army, tramped off to Washington to protest their plight. Their march was in vain, and for lack of adequate social legislation or effective labor organization the unfortunates had to take such comfort as they could from the pronouncement of the governor of Massachusetts, who advised them that unemployment was an act of God.

One would not have guessed the sorry state of things, either, from the spectacular mansions being raised by the very wealthy along New York's Fifth Avenue, in Newport, and in other purlieus of the privileged classes. Never in history had American society displayed such extreme contrasts between the rich and the poor, the high and the lowly. The panic eased before the century ended, but social discontent and labor unrest continued. Class antagonisms, such as the country had never before known, created a growing breach in the national structure. Violence in industry became practically chronic, and deeply disturbing. Between 1881 and 1906 some thirty-eight thousand strikes and lockouts took place, involving almost ten million workmen and precipitating ever more violence.

Many of the important issues that came to a head in the 1890's are still with us, and the doctrines formulated at that time to examine these issues are still being explored. The problems of progress and poverty, isolation and internationalism, the realization of social security within democracy, urban blight, the conservation of natural resources—these and other matters that seemed so new and nettlesome at the end of the last century have not yet been satisfactorily resolved.

Those problems gave rise to a literature of social reform that won wide attention and that included books of lasting distinction. As early as 1880 Henry George published *Progress and Poverty*, one of the great books of the century, in which he urged a single tax that would eliminate unearned increment on land, provide equal access to the nation's resources, thus wiping out monopoly and speculation and ensuring economic equality to all classes of the country's society. For a generation to come, advanced thinkers acknowledged a debt to this "Bayard of the Poor," as George was called. His writings were read appreciatively not only by many of his progressive American contemporaries but also by such varied and notable thinkers as George Bernard Shaw, Sun Yat-sen, and Tolstoy. Millions of his books were sold in distant and unlikely places about the globe, as well as in the cities and farmlands of this country.

In 1888 Edward Bellamy produced his memorable utopian novel, *Looking Backward, or 2000–1887*. Conceived as "a mere literary fantasy, a fairy tale of social felicity," the book is actually a sharply pointed and skillfully directed exposure of the inadequacies of the private-enterprise system, of the inefficiency and material waste to which that system leads, and, worse, of the attrition of human values that results from it.

The story concerns a young Bostonian who awakens in the year 2000

The iniquitously wide gap between the rich and the poor—the almost inevitable sign of the rapid urban development of the late 19th century—inspired a spate of social protest books. The title page of one such work, Sunshine and Shadow in New York *(1869), by Matthew H. Smith, contrasts a pretentious mansion (top) with a squalid slum tenement (bottom).*

from a sleep of more than a century to find that his familiar world has been utterly transformed. He awakens to a futuristic Brook Farm, so to speak, organized on a national scale. Under a new system of democratic collectivism, private enterprise has been abolished; state capitalism has replaced the great business monopolies of earlier times; social injustices, crime, poverty, and warfare have been eradicated. Everything has been accomplished by orderly, democratic process. Under such benign and rational socialism, public intelligence and ethics have been raised to almost incredible heights. Man has conquered the machine, and all share equally in the abundant economy they have together helped to create. When rain falls, the new Boston streets are automatically covered with protective awnings. The heroine of the novel explains this to her newly aroused friend: "The private umbrella is Father's favourite figure to illustrate the old way when everybody lived for himself and his family. There is a nineteenth-century painting at the art gallery representing a crowd of people in the rain, each one holding his umbrella over himself and his wife, and giving his neighbors the drippings, which he claims must have been meant by the artist as a satire on his times."

Bellamy's novel was a great success and led to the founding of Bellamy clubs throughout the nation and to a Nationalist Party to spread the author's gospel—although from abroad the English reformer William Morris called it "a horrible cockney dream." (In passing, it is interesting to speculate that Bellamy may have got some of his notions from his study of the Inca civilization of old Peru, as Sir Thomas More may have done when he wrote his great classic *Utopia* more than three centuries earlier. In More's story a companion of Amerigo Vespucci's journeys to the west in South America and discovers a government remarkably different from anything then known in contemporary Europe: a co-operative society; an eight-hour workday; a system of justice that needs no lawyers; and a people who enjoy "free liberty of mind," with education for all.)

Bellamy's book helped edge Howells toward the socialism he professed. He called himself a "theoretical Socialist and a practical aristocrat." In 1890 he wrote his father, somewhat apologetically, "it is a comfort to be right theoretically and to be ashamed of oneself practically." Mark Twain was among the multitude who read and admired *Looking Backward*. Both Twain and Howells lived into the twentieth century, but Twain's disillusionment had deepened, and Howells had long passed the peak of his popularity before he died in 1920. "I am comparatively a dead cult," he wrote Henry James in 1915, "with my statues cut down and the grass growing over them in the pale moonlight." James lived on in England till 1916, saddened by the changing literary standards of the time. "A new generation that I know not and mainly prize not," he reflected, "has taken universal possession."

James did, however, leave a literary heir in Edith Wharton, who in her early career as a writer was much influenced by the artistic austerity of James' work. Like James, Mrs. Wharton was well born. Years earlier, Washington Irving described the stately mansions that had been raised along the Hudson River by "the Jones, the Schermerhornes and the Rhinelanders," in

Editor and political economist Henry George (above) and novelist Edward Bellamy (below) were reformers whose works helped to change traditional social theories.

all three of which families Edith Wharton (born Edith Newbold Jones) could trace her ancestors. As a member of the old New York aristocracy she was welcome in the social circles of Newport, Long Island, the Berkshire Hills, and, of course, those of her native city. In 1885 she married Edward Wharton, a wealthy Boston banker with impeccable social credentials.

Edith Wharton's fiction, like that of James, was typically concerned with the leisure class into which she had been born. She cherished the vanishing old Knickerbocker aristocracy, but she was bored by it—as she was offended by the vulgarities of the *nouveaux riches* who were crowding into the social scene. "The people about me were so indifferent to everything I really cared for," she once recalled of her early life, "that complying with the tastes of others had become a habit, and it was only some years later, when I had written several books, that I finally rebelled and pleaded for the right to something better." In short, it was tedium that led her to writing.

Much as she respected the genteel traditions of her class, as an unusually intelligent and sensitive young lady she recognized its foibles. In her fiction she often satirized—gently but firmly—its rigid codes, its social absurdities, and its limited intellectual awareness. She was one of the first of the new critics of American society, a perceptive analyst of those people, as she wrote in one of her books, "who dreaded scandal more than disease, who placed decency above courage, and who considered that nothing was more ill-bred than scenes except the behaviour of those who gave rise to them." Yet, these were her people, whom she knew from intimate experience and could write about with understanding. She could not abide the intrusion of the new caste of brokers and captains of industry, the graceless and alien parvenus who were taking over control of society—and, it seemed, more ominous, of the nation itself—as inevitable as she saw that transfer of power and influence to be. In some of her best novels, *The House of Mirth* (1905), *Ethan Frome* (1911), and *The Age of Innocence* (1920), as a result of which she was awarded the Pulitzer Prize, she was writing with expert craftmanship and deep-felt sympathy the obituary of that order of American gentlemen and gentlewomen she had known so well. The takeover of the new order filled her with dismay. For her, all this was no comedy of manners but a portentous and unfortunate social revolution. In 1907 she left her now invalid husband in the care of others and sailed for France. There she remained for the rest of her life, recalling and viewing the American scene with the eyes of an expatriate.

Thus, too, Ellen Glasgow, a younger contemporary of Edith Wharton's who was also well born, viewed the patrician world about her with a penetrating and satirical eye. Her world was the Old South of Virginia, with its deep-rooted chivalric traditions and its declining gentry, which was the custodian of those feudal virtues. "I grew up," she recollected in later life, "in a charming society, where ideas were accepted as naturally as the universe or the weather, and cards for the old, dancing for the young, and conversation flavored with personalities for the middle-aged, were the only arts practised." In her writings she covered that society with ridicule and wit, although, like Edith Wharton in the North, she, too, witnessed the emergence of a new society with foreboding. "Although in the beginning I had intended to deal ironically with both the Southern Lady and the Victorian tradition,"

Well-born and stately, Edith Wharton chronicled New York society "in all its flatness and futility," to use her own words.

270

she wrote in a preface to one of her books, "I discovered, as I went on, that my irony grew fainter, while it yielded at last to sympathetic compassion."

Also like Edith Wharton, Ellen Glasgow published her first work late in the nineteenth century—a book called *The Descendant,* which she had to hide from her family and her Southern friends because of its ironic cast— and continued to produce novels until well into the twentieth. Again like Edith Wharton, she was awarded a Pulitzer Prize later in life—for the novel *In This Our Life,* published when she was in her late sixties. Although she chose for a motto, "What the South needs now is—blood and irony," with her understanding of the good along with the ridiculous traits of her characters, and her familiarity with her subject, she provided an incomparable social history of the South. In this her writing was wholesomely different from the spate of contemporary "historical" novels, in which the past was re-created with calculated artifice and cloying romance.

Willa Cather was also born in Virginia, a year before Ellen Glasgow; but in 1882, when she was nine years old, she was taken to Nebraska, and it was in the wide, open prairie that she found the spiritual nourishment that sustained so much of her writing. "It's a queer thing about the flat country," she reflected, "it takes hold of you, or leaves you perfectly cold. . . . I go everywhere—I admire all kinds of country. I tried to live in France. But when I strike the open plains, something happens. I'm home. I breathe differently. That love of great spaces, of rolling open country like the sea —it's the grand passion of my life." (Somewhat oddly, she wrote many of her stories of that land from the sanctuary of a New York apartment.)

The Cathers moved to Nebraska during the greatest land boom in America's history. During the 1870's and 1880's migrant hordes were sweeping in huge waves over the country west of the Missouri River. They came from everywhere—from lands only recently settled just to the east of the "boom belt," from Virginia and New England, and from Denmark, Norway, Germany, Poland, and Bohemia. They were urged on by reports of rich black soil, by the persuasion of the government and of the railroads, and by their own natural mobility. Early in 1871 Nebraska's salesman in Scandinavia wrote home: "The fall emigration to Nebraska of people with sufficient capital to commence work on our prairies will be very large. On Monday I go to Sweden and Norway, and will have easy work there. . . . All the papers here will now come out in favor of our state. . . ." Following the completion of the Union Pacific Railroad, within one decade half a million people came to settle in the state.

As a young girl in this polyglot world Willa Cather would listen to sermons in Danish, Norwegian, and French. (There were towns where one might hear no English spoken during a day.) Neighbors taught her Latin, she read the English classics with her two grandmothers, and became familiar with the works of Henry James, read Greek with one of her teachers, and went on to graduate from the University of Nebraska in 1895. She also learned to know and appreciate the moral qualities of those pioneers from different lands who were her neighbors. They became the heroes and heroines of many of her books—the last pioneers of the unconquered West. No one before her had recognized the aesthetic resource of the growing West and the burgeoning talents of the new immigrant strains that were peopling it. And

Ellen Glasgow, who defined fiction as "experience illuminated," wrote novels of social history that deal with the patrician world of Old Virginia or the efforts of tidewater aristocracy to seek its fortune in New York. She began with Virginia history prior to and after the Civil War; in her later writing two themes preoccupied her: the struggle to renew a barren land and the endeavor to survive spiritually in a materialistic city.

Willa Cather grew up on a wind-swept Nebraska farm in the 1880's, when the prairie lands were still thinly populated, mostly with foreign settlers. Although it is the hardy pioneer folk whom Miss Cather had known as a girl that figure in some of her best stories and novels, she is much more than a regional writer; she is a complex spinner of tales who believed that "the higher processes of art are all processes of simplification." Willa Cather's finest works are characterized by strict simplicity, achieved by her quiet style and use of symbols, overtones, and suggestion.

she was a consummate artist in re-creating this world of her girlhood. Like Edith Wharton and Ellen Glasgow, she, too, won a Pulitzer Prize—in 1922 with *One of Ours*, though this was not one of her best books.

Although Willa Cather had published poems and short stories early in the century, her first important novel, *O Pioneers!*, appeared in 1913, when she was forty years old. With this and her two next books, *The Song of the Lark* (1915) and *My Ántonia* (1918), she struck the major theme of her writing —the reaction of men and women to their natural environment, as that revealed heroic and creative qualities of pioneers along the passing Nebraska frontier. Her stories are not *of* the frontier so much as they are cast *in* a frontier setting; they deal with basic human problems of universal import as they were faced in the raw American West by people who had been drawn there from alien lands and who shared the American dream. These first-comers were an aristocracy of sorts—a distinctive aristocracy, which was still close to the elemental struggle for survival but which put moral and spiritual values before material values. As Henry Steele Commager has observed, in her writings Willa Cather returned again and again to that frontier world because there the essential problems of life were simplified, clarified, and dramatized. From that soil came the strength and the courage to meet those problems with fortitude and serenity. "It fortified her," she wrote of one of her characters, "to reflect upon the great operations of nature, and when she thought of the law behind them she felt a sense of personal security."

Willa Cather viewed the passing of the pioneer generation with the same nostalgic regret that Edith Wharton and Ellen Glasgow felt in the decline of the older aristocracies of the East. Succeeding generations did not share the same hardy and lofty spirit of the firstcomers. When the predators of industry and the great marketplaces moved onto the scene an era had passed. In *A Lost Lady*, one of her later novels, Willa Cather wrote:

> The Old West had been settled by dreamers, great-hearted adventurers who were unpractical to the point of magnificence; a courteous brotherhood strong in attack but weak in defense, who would conquer but not hold. Now all the vast territory they had won was to be at the mercy of men like Ivy Peters who had never dared anything, never risked anything. They would drink up the mirage, dispel the morning freshness, root out the great brooding spirit of freedom, the generous, easy life of the great landholders. The space, the colour, the princely carelessness of the pioneer they would destroy and cut up into profitable bits, as the match factory splinters up the primeval forest. All the way from the Missouri to the mountains this generation of shrewd young men, trained to petty economies by hard times, would do exactly what Ivy Peters had done when he drained the Forrester marsh.

Before devoting herself entirely to creative writing, Willa Cather worked for six years (from 1906 to 1912) on the staff of *McClure's Magazine*, one of a rash of inexpensive periodicals that were reaching out to a vast new audience in the closing years of the last century and the opening years of the present one. Her first nationally circulated short stories appeared in the pages of *McClure's*, as did fiction by such well-known authors as Robert Louis

Stevenson, Rudyard Kipling, Arthur Conan Doyle, and others; their stories were illustrated by Howard Chandler Christy, A. B. Frost, Charles Dana Gibson, and other prominent graphic artists. (The development of halftone engravings that reproduced photographs mechanically gave a strong impetus to both book and magazine illustration.) With the proliferation of such magazines and their wide circulation, increased by energetic and skillful promotion, the United States was becoming a nation of magazine readers; and authors of various talents were finding new outlets for their writing.

Early in the present century those popular periodicals—principally *Mc-Clure's, Everybody's, The Independent, Collier's, Cosmopolitan*—became the medium for the more or less sensational exposure of unscrupulous practices in government, business, and industry. In 1902 *McClure's* began publication of Ida Tarbell's critical *History of the Standard Oil Company;* Lincoln Steffens' *The Shame of the Cities* started the next year in the same publication; and these were followed by a flood of such literature of exposure and protest. The publisher McClure's policy came, he explained, "from no formulated plan to attack existing institutions, but was the result of merely taking up in the magazine some of the problems that were beginning to interest the people a little before the newspapers and the other magazines took them up." Many of those who contributed to that literature were skilled writers and critics—novelists as well as journalists, historians and philosophers as well as economists and sociologists. The best of them produced exhaustive studies of high quality. Ida Tarbell took more than four years of investigation and preparation to conclude the fifteen articles for *McClure's* (they subsequently came out in book form). McClure believed in paying his writers for the depth of their studies rather than the amount of copy they turned out. For her efforts she received close to $50,000. To all those probing social critics, however, President Roosevelt applied the epithet "muckrakers." "In Bunyan's *Pilgrim's Progress,*" he wrote in explanation, "you

During the late 19th century, European immigrants—Norwegians, Swedes, Bohemians, Germans, Czechs, Russians, French, and others—swarmed into the still-wild, inhospitable plains of the American West to master the land in the face of droughts, storms, and prairie fires. These polyglot emigrants (like the family shown moving into Loup Valley, Nebr., in a photograph of 1886) people the novels of Willa Cather.

273

may recall the description of the Man with the Muck-rake, the man who could look no way but downward with the muck-rake in his hands; who was offered the celestial crown for his muck-rake, but would neither look up nor regard the crown he was offered, but continued to rake the filth of the floor."

During his two terms as president, Roosevelt himself led an attack on the "malefactors of great wealth" in his trust-busting policies, supported reforms of various sorts to protect the public from careless and nefarious business operations generally, and worked for social justice and for the conservation of natural resources. These were very close to the aims of the muckrakers themselves, and in time, like such other epithets as Yankee, Puritan, and Democrat, the word Roosevelt first used as a term of abuse became almost a title of nobility. In the end, the muckrakers aroused public opinion against the inequities that afflicted life in America to the point where many of the progressive reforms sponsored by Roosevelt, and after him by Woodrow Wilson, came to pass. It was, for instance, Upton Sinclair's novel *The Jungle*, published in 1906, with its exposé of the Chicago meat-packing industry, that prompted Roosevelt's investigation, which in turn led to the pure-food legislation of the same year.

Many of those who applied their pens or pecked at their typewriters in the cause of reform were indebted to the piercing and brilliant analyses of business and the price system published by the Midwestern Norwegian-American Thorstein Veblen. His social and economic theories were startlingly original—iconoclastic to a degree that vexed his academic colleagues and puzzled most of the public. He was an "intellectual wayfaring man and a disturber of the intellectual peace"; but his theories have worn well (he foretold the collapse of the economic system in 1929), and he later became a hero to the intelligentsia. "Where others saw progress, Veblen saw merely change," wrote Henry Steele Commager, ". . . where, to Adams, force was impersonal and mechanical, to Veblen it was personal and psychological." Adams looked for some grand design to the course of civilization; Veblen asked just how do human institutions really work.

In his first three books, *The Theory of the Leisure Class* (1899), *The Theory of Business Enterprise* (1904), and *The Instinct of Workmanship* (1914), Veblen proposed his unorthodox answers to this question. His explorations of the question are too long and complicated to detail in these pages. His most important contribution was to point out the essential antagonism between industry and business, between the production of goods and the quest of pecuniary gain—between technology and ownership, between those who perform a social function through their workmanship and those who squander the benefits in their zeal for profits in the marketplace. "Conspicuous Waste," the title of Veblen's memorable essay, has become a commonplace phrase in our language, and his adroit twists of old adages, such as his observation that "invention is the mother of necessity," still hold an element of agreeable surprise to the unexpecting reader.

Although Veblen never appealed to a popular audience, his basic theories influenced younger writers, notably the muckrakers among them, whether they recognized it or not. In the end it was the novelists who most persuasively made the general public aware of the social problems of the day. Before his untimely death Frank Norris worked at *McClure's* along with Ida

McClure's Magazine, *a leading muckraking periodical of the nineties, sought to expose scandals in politics and business, and gave its full support to the trust-busting efforts of the Theodore Roosevelt administration. The cartoon, below, which comments on the bloated monopolistic trusts of William McKinley's administration, features an indignant T.R. in the lower right-hand corner.*

WILLIE AND HIS PAPA.

274

Tarbell, Lincoln Steffens, and Ray Stannard Baker. Norris' novels *The Octopus* and *The Pit*, already mentioned, were written in the muckraking vein, as were Stephen Crane's *Maggie* and the later works of Jack London, such as *The Iron Heel* and *The Valley of the Moon*, in which economic problems are solved by a return to the land.

Frank Norris, at the time a reader for the Doubleday Publishing Company, was the first to recognize the writing of Theodore Dreiser. Dreiser had come to New York via Chicago from Indiana to make his fortune. On a friend's dare he started the novel that was to be his first published work, *Sister Carrie*, which had aroused Norris' enthusiasm when he read it in manuscript. The story tells how a girl, Carrie Meeber, "full of the illusions of ignorance and youth," leaves her rural home to find love and security in the city. She is seduced by a traveling drummer in Chicago, then elopes with a middle-aged married man to New York. As his fortunes wane, Carrie takes to the stage, and then deserts him, to become a musical-comedy star. Forsaken and impoverished, her lover takes to beggary, and he ends a suicide.

The story is developed, in all its sordid and disagreeable circumstance, with enormously detailed realism and without any moral inhibition—and it came all but directly out of Dreiser's own experiences in life. He was brought up in poverty, his brother's mistress was the town's prostitute, and as a child he witnessed thievery, alcoholism, prostitution, and sordid death. *Sister Carrie* demonstrated in an advanced form the sort of naturalism that Norris himself, and also Crane and London, had tried to urge on the American novel, and that seemed to come almost reflexively to Dreiser's pen; but it was a bit too strong for public tolerance—too ugly and unfit for the drawing rooms where Edith Wharton's ladylike satires and Ellen Glasgow's moralizing fictions were considered to be the proper limits of social exposure. (In Dreiser's story, however, Carrie remains essentially untouched by the lives of those around her.) In 1900 the ground had not yet been sufficiently plowed to receive Dreiser's raw accounts of the tragedies he recognized in American life. Doubleday published the book in 1900, but immediately withdrew it because, as the story goes, Mrs. Doubleday read an advance copy and was shocked. It remained virtually unknown until it was re-issued in 1912.

As one of Dreiser's recent biographers has said, it was "the literary joke of the century" that, as he patiently awaited public acceptance of his straightforward, grim tales, Dreiser served as the successful editor of the Butterick Publishing Company's several periodicals addressed to prim and proper ladies and their daughters, and devoted essentially to selling dress patterns. He who would write most tellingly in his novels of whores, murderers, and otherwise questionable members of society served as a whoremaster of letters, posing as the understanding mentor of prudent ladies bent on sustaining righteousness in the world—cut to Butterick patterns. "Our theme," he wrote in one of his editorials, "is one that a woman may carry into her home, her church, and her social affairs—the theme of the ungrudging helping hand."

When Teddy bears became the vogue during T. R. Roosevelt's heyday, threatening the sale of doll-clothes patterns, he warned the mothers of the land, "Take away the little girl's dolly and you have interfered with the nascent expression of motherhood. . . . You have implanted the race suicide

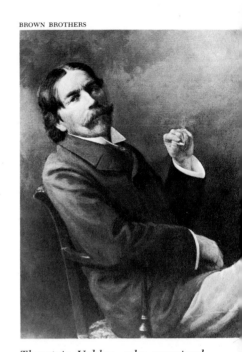

Thorstein Veblen, who examined the workings of capitalism from evolutionary, psychological, and anthropological points of view, was one of the most original economists of the early 20th century. His literary style (unlike that of most of his breed) is powerful, despite its heaviness and awkwardness. Veblen's case against production for profit never revolutionized orthodox academic theory, but it did influence the next generation of social theorists.

Teddy bear

Theodore Dreiser, 1912

Clyde in prison, *by Reginald Marsh for* An American Tragedy

idea where it will work the most harm—in the very heart of the babies themselves." "Bring your babies back to dollies," he pleaded, "or you will have weaned the grownups of the future from the babies that will never be," and so on. To compound the irony he hired the young H. L. Mencken to ghostwrite a series of articles for Dr. Leonard K. Hirshberg on the care and feeding of babies.

Yet it was this same Dreiser who in crude and often careless manner persisted in writing novels that carried realism far beyond anything Howells had imagined. (Howells could not abide Dreiser's work.) Dreiser saw the ruthlessness and the amorality of the world as aspects of a fundamental natural law that inexorably dictated the lives of men and women. There was in nature, he wrote, "no such thing as the right to do, or the right not to do." "We suffer for our temperaments," he also wrote, "which we did not make, and for our weaknesses and lacks, which are no part of our willing or doing." In his insistence that an author be permitted to write what he chooses to write, he broke through the conventional American rhetoric of a moral law to which all should subscribe or duly suffer the consequences. In Dreiser's world "nothing is proved, all is permitted." In time he tore away the barriers of genteel criticism that Henry James struggled so hard to maintain and made a shambles of traditional censorship. He brought a new freedom to American literature. "Heavy, heavy the feet of Theodore," wrote Sherwood Anderson. "How easy to pick some of his books to pieces, to laugh at him for much of his heavy prose. These feet are making a path, and the children who follow after will run quickly and nimbly because the path has been made." That path Dreiser made alone.

Dreiser's success as a novelist was slow in coming. His style was often cumbersome, and the structure of his works careless. But he wrote with utter conviction and with a passionate, instinctive feeling for his material. As has been said, in his writing he lacked everything but genius. In 1925 he published *An American Tragedy*, his most carefully planned novel and his best. The story is based on the actual murder of a young girl by the boy who had made her pregnant and who felt that this mishap might spoil his chances for a successful career. Dreiser could draw upon memories of his own young manhood to understand the feelings and circumstances that might lead to such a crime. In this tragedy he succeeded to a degree he had not earlier attained in using his life experience to show the crisis of a society and an era.

While Dreiser awaited the recognition of his peculiar genius (and meanwhile, to all appearances, devoted his time to hack journalism), with Crane and Norris both dead and Howells in limbo, American fiction endured a relatively dull period during the early years of the present century. William Sydney Porter, better known as O. Henry, came out of several years in jail (for alleged embezzlement) to spin the swift little vignettes of life in New York, his "Bagdad-on-the-Subway," with their sudden, ironic, and surprise endings. (Soviet writers were to study his technique and ape it in Russian stories with an "O. Henry twist.") But no significant voices were heard that advanced the novel to new dimensions until Dreiser's work was recognized and appreciated.

However, other developments in the cultural scene were opening fresh vistas to the imagination. James Gibbons Huneker was writing art, music, and literary criticism for the New York *Sun* (and books about such matters on the side) with a gusto, appreciation, and wit that in this area had no equal in contemporary American journalism. As a Philadelphia schoolboy he had gone with Walt Whitman to concerts; he had studied the piano intensively in Paris for some years; he had closely observed the modern currents that were stirring Europe to new expression in all the arts. His enormous energy and infectious enthusiasm spilled over into his newspaper columns, providing a liberal cultural education for the readers of his generation, telling them of Debussy, Stravinsky, and the Ballet Russe, and of the bohemian artists and writers Huneker had known and admired. He was an effusive and eloquent agent of European modernism as that tide moved westward across the Atlantic.

America experienced the full shock of modernism in the arts when the Armory Show opened its doors at New York in 1913 to reveal examples of postimpressionism, fauvism, cubism, expressionism, and other movements that had developed in the advanced art circles of Europe over past decades. The show moved on to Chicago and Boston, causing excitement that ranged from wide-eyed wonderment to utter revulsion. Meanwhile, at his famous salon at 291 Fifth Avenue in New York the photographer Alfred Stieglitz had already bravely begun to introduce to his compatriots the work of Europe's and America's avant-garde artists.

Winds of change were gusting all through America, leading to fervent if nebulous expectations. "Looking back upon it now," wrote Mabel Dodge Luhan (in 1923 she married her fourth husband, Antonio Luhan, a Taos Indian), "it seems as though everywhere, in that year of 1913, barriers went down and people reached each other who had never been in touch before; there were all sorts of new ways to communicate, as well as new communications." After a ten-year sojourn in Italy as Mrs. Dodge, she had come to New York determined to serve as patron of a new cultural enlightenment. This rebellious daughter of a socially prominent family, "alive like fire," opened her Fifth Avenue salon downtown from Stieglitz's "291," soon rivaling it as a gathering place for the new illuminati. There, at her "evenings," she hoped that artists and agitators, authors, feminists, and others would abet her plan to "upset America . . . with fatal disaster to the old order of things." Nearby Greenwich Village became the center of a new, bohemian society, the first important literary colony in America since Emerson's Concord. In this small and intimate quarter of the city a liberated young generation prepared its protest against the archaic standards of its elders —against all traces of American provincialism—and set out to conquer the wide world of the arts and letters. Here the early plays of Eugene O'Neill were staged, the Provincetown Players performed, and Edna St. Vincent Millay penned her first lyrics. John Reed, who was contributing to *The Masses* at the time, wrote exultingly of New York, "Within a block of my house was all the adventure in the world; within a mile was every foreign country."

Mrs. Dodge was a propagandist for Gertrude Stein, who remained in Paris to work her wonders with words, with telling effect on a rising generation of American writers who sought her out and sat at her feet. Gertrude Stein's one-time San Francisco childhood acquaintance, Isadora Duncan, was developing her theories of interpretive dancing (based in part on the sculp-

Mabel Dodge Luhan, femme fatale and feminist, was an expatriate in Florence, a New York revolutionary, and, finally, the center of the Western writers' group at Taos, N.M. In each city her house was a gathering place for the leading illuminati of the day. It was to Taos that she summoned D. H. Lawrence "from across the world." Her major work, Intimate Memories, *comprises four volumes of literary reminiscences covering the period from 1900 to 1935.*

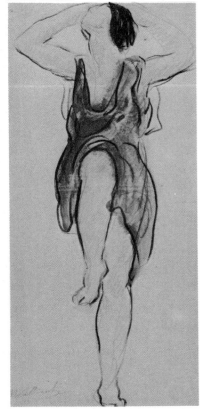

Isadora Duncan is depicted above in a water color by Abraham Walkowitz. "It's positively splendid!" wrote painter John Sloan when he saw her dance in 1909. "I feel that she dances a symbol of human animal happiness as it should be, free from unnatural trammels."

HOUGHTON MIFFLIN AND CO.

Amy Lowell, who campaigned to "put poetry on the map," scorned the "phonograph poets, the caged warblers," of the Victorian era.

tures of the Parthenon and the figures on Greek vases) with a success that made her something of a cult in Europe and a prophet in America. Edith Wharton saw her, garbed in a classical tunic, performing in Paris and wrote that this was "the dance I had dreamed of."

Back in America there were other women—and men, to be sure—who contributed their considerable talents to the renaissance of arts and letters. In Brookline, Massachusetts, Amy Lowell, a collateral descendant of James Russell Lowell, attracted wide attention with her experimental poetry— and with her prestigious name, her wealth, and her sheer physical bulk. (At one point she had considered a career on the stage, but her unwieldy proportions balked any such aspiration.) She was, in addition, the sister of a Harvard president. On a visit to England Amy Lowell became fascinated by the new poetic idiom called imagism, and particularly by the work of the French poet Paul Fort. One of her best-known poems, "Patterns," set in the eighteenth century, tells of a young woman who, as she walks along a garden path, is ardently embraced by her lover and is bruised by his military buttons. He goes off to war and is killed in action. The first and last verses read:

> I walk down the garden paths,
> And all the daffodils
> Are blowing, and the bright blue squills.
> I walk down the patterned garden-paths
> In my stiff, brocaded gown.
> With my powdered hair and jewelled fan,
> I too am a rare
> Pattern. As I wander down
> The garden paths.
>
> In Summer and in Winter I shall walk
> Up and down
> The patterned garden-paths
> In my stiff, brocaded gown.
> The squills and daffodils
> Will give place to pillared roses, and to asters, and to snow.
> I shall go
> Up and down,
> In my gown.
> Gorgeously arrayed,
> Boned and stayed.
> And the softness of my body will be guarded from embrace
> By each button, hook, and lace.
> For the man who should loose me is dead,
> Fighting with the Duke in Flanders,
> In a pattern called a war.
> Christ! What are patterns for?

The poem is often cited as an example of the free-verse movement in America at the time. Her fervent espousal of the new poetry led Amy Lowell to the lecture platform, where she faced ridicule with unfailing good humor as she exhorted her audiences to welcome the "new and striking images, delightful and unexpected forms" of the imagist poetry and the "polyphonic prose" she recommended to them.

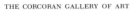

During those years, as John Butler Yeats, the Irish artist who was then living in New York, remarked in 1912, the fiddles were "tuning as it were all over America." H. L. Mencken and George Jean Nathan were about to become editors of *The Smart Set*, an established periodical with intended snob appeal that for a while ranked among the nation's leading magazines. (Three of Eugene O'Neill's early plays were printed in *The Smart Set*.) In 1912 Max Eastman became editor of *The Masses*, a weekly journal which, with its emphasis on a liberal literature and its concern with European fiction, the masses did not read. Also in 1912 Dreiser's *Sister Carrie* had its first, full-dress American publication. It was an *annus mirabilis*. That same year, in Chicago, Harriet Monroe, a poet and a devotee of poetry, founded *Poetry: A Magazine of Verse*. This she launched almost single-handed, soliciting

Yeats at Petitpas', painted in 1910 by John Sloan, depicts a typical gathering at Petitpas' restaurant, a literary hangout on New York's West Side. Van Wyck Brooks is seated at the far left of the canvas; next to him is John Butler Yeats, the Irish painter, and father of the poet William Butler Yeats. The elder Yeats was a second father to Sloan, who described him as "a very interesting old gentleman with a white beard."

279

contributions from friends and acquaintances, from poets and patrons of the arts. To start with, her plan had been to ask for "an audacious advance vote of confidence"; in the end, such was her persuasion and conviction that it became fashionable to support her undertaking. The periodical is still being published, and over the years it has "discovered" a wealth of poetic talent.

It became almost at once a herald of the poetry renaissance that was taking place. During the first several years of publication the pages of *Poetry* included work by some of the most advanced talents of the time—by Ezra Pound, Vachel Lindsay, T. S. Eliot, Carl Sandburg, Robert Frost, Edwin Arlington Robinson, Amy Lowell, and Marianne Moore, among others. Many of these men and women were no longer very young, but they were still to make their reputations. Virtually all of them continued to write for more than a score of years. They formed a bridge between the sophisticated experiments going on overseas and the "yawp" of Whitman. With their rich outpouring, Americans came for the first time to dominate poetry written in the English language, at least according to some reputable American critics.

Harriet Monroe had the good editorial sense to learn from her contributors. Among the youngest and most radical of them in the first years of the magazine was Ezra Pound. Pound was then living in London, and he served the vital little magazine as "foreign correspondent." With youthful zest he wrote that the "American Risorgimento," referring to the rebirth of poetry as represented by the magazine, would make "the Italian Renaissance look like a tempest in a teapot." He then proceeded to write for the early issues about as much editorial matter as did Harriet Monroe herself.

Pound has been fairly judged one of the half-dozen most important figures in the English literature of this century. He was also one of the most eccentric and controversial poets and critics of his time. Until his dying day in 1972 at the age of eighty-seven, debate continued to rage over his capricious behavior and his uneven, extraordinary performance as a writer. His friends became apologists for everything he had done; his enemies dismissed everything he had done. The middle ground between those extremes was all but empty.

Pound's long, colorful life can here be only very briefly summarized. He was born in Hailey, Idaho, in 1885 of parents who were both of prominent American families. He recalled that when he entered the University of Pennsylvania at the age of fifteen, "whey-faced and lanky" with "piercing green eyes," he already knew pretty much what he wanted to do. He then resolved that by the time he was thirty he would know more about poetry than any man on earth. Toward this end he learned more or less of nine foreign languages, including the medieval tongue of the Provençal troubadours, and read writings of the Orient in translation. Meanwhile, he diligently developed his own writing technique. After graduating from Hamilton College, where he had transferred, and taking a Master's degree at Pennsylvania, he taught for a few years at the latter and at Wabash College in Indiana. He lost his post at that last institution when his landlady discovered a prostitute in his rooms.

In 1908 he shipped as a deck hand on a cattle boat and sailed to England. Although he spent most of the rest of his life in Europe, he remained ever an American at heart. ("There are so many things which I, as an American,

The Smart Set *magazine (a cover of 1921 is reproduced above) was founded in 1890; but its heyday came later, from 1914 to 1923, during the co-editorship of the acidic H. L. Mencken (caricatured below) and George Jean Nathan. A magazine of snob appeal, wit, and humor,* The Smart Set *was aimed at a sophisticated, though not necessarily intellectual audience.*

cannot say to a European with any hope of being understood," he observed late in his life. "Somebody said that I am the last American living the tragedy of Europe.") Within a year his literary career was launched, and he quickly became a well-known figure in the London literary world, with friends of all sorts, including Henry James, John Galsworthy, H. G. Wells, Wyndham Lewis, and, particularly, William Butler Yeats, among many other prominent writers. He seems to have made a point of being conspicuous, with his pince-nez, a single turquoise earring, and Byronic collars to set off his red beard. One acquaintance described him garbed in "trousers made of billiard cloth, pink coat, a blue shirt, a tie hand-painted by a Japanese friend, an immense sombrero."

In 1910, after a brief return to America, he went back to London, intent on reforming English poetry. Like Picasso, he was both critic and artist. "Poetry," he wrote, "is a sort of inspired mathematics, which gives us equations . . . for the human emotions"; it is, he said, "the statement of overwhelming emotional values." Verse must be concrete, with no superfluous words; technique was the test of a man's sincerity. He remembered a day in Paris when he saw a flood of beautiful faces amid the hurrying crowds in the metro, and was filled with a sudden emotion. He first wrote a thirty-line poem, and destroyed it because it was a work of "second intensity." Then, a year and a half later, the poetic expression of his feeling, he wrote, came to him as an "equation . . . in little splotches of colour," as a single sentence

According to Carl Sandburg, the controversial Ezra Pound (pictured above) "was the greatest single influence in American poetry." From London, in the early 1900's, Pound urged the new generation of poets to break away from the "glutinous imitations of Keats, diaphanous dilutations of Shelley, wooly Wordsworthian paraphrases, or swishful Swinburniana." By 1917 he was predicting that 20th-century poetry would be harder and saner. . . . as much like granite as it can be. . . . I want it so, austere, direct, free from emotional slither."

TEXT CONTINUES PAGE 284

281

Bob's Party Number One, *by Wood Gaylor, captures the tolerant amorality of a village party of the 1900's.*

Julius' Annex, *a seedy Village speakeasy, by Reginald Marsh*

THE
BOHEMIAN
LIFE

Then There was a Lively Little Fight, *by William J. Glackens*

In 1912 *Poetry* magazine was launched in Chicago, heralding the advent of an American poetic renaissance. The next year New York was host to the memorable Armory Show, which introduced a whole gamut of "shocking" and "revolutionary" modernistic styles, including fauvism, cubism, and expressionism. Since the turn of the century many creatively minded Americans had been flocking to New York's Greenwich Village, where they could live cheaply, anonymously, and uninhibitedly; by the time of the Armory Show, the Village was firmly established as America's center of *la vie de Bohéme.* It was the gathering place for writers and artists with or without talent, for dancers and musicians, and for assorted hangers-on. Among its denizens could be found exponents of a whole galaxy of new freedoms: anarchism, socialism, woman suffrage, free love, birth control, psychoanalysis, and various "isms" destined to dispose of lingering traces of Victorian convention and intellectual provincialism. The Village atmosphere of relaxed manners and morals attracted such writers as Theodore Dreiser, Willa Cather, and Sherwood Anderson, the playwright Eugene O'Neill, and artists like John Sloan and William Glackens. Edna St. Vincent Millay was the district's poet-in-residence; magazines like *The Quill* and *The Masses* were its house organs and intellectual outlets. With the dawning of the jazz age in the twenties the flapper made her appearance at Village cocktail parties and speakeasies. During this decade rising rents forced many Village artists and writers to seek expatriate life in Paris.

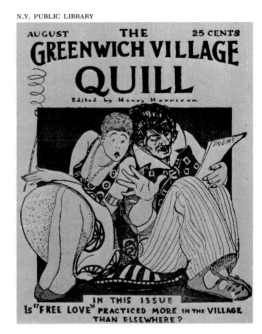

A Quill cover satirizing the Village's image

Bleecker Street, Saturday Night, *by John Sloan*

From 1921 to 1924 Ezra Pound was in Paris working as "foreign correspondent" for Chicago-based Poetry *magazine and helping other writers gain recognition. A photograph taken there in 1923 recaptures a gathering of expatriate intellectuals; seated, from left to right, are Pound, Ford Madox Ford, and James Joyce; art patron John Quinn stands behind Pound.*

in the manner of a Japanese haiku. Thus the "one-image" poem "In a Station of the Metro" in its entirety:

> The apparition of these faces in the crowd;
> Petals on a wet, black bough.

It was about this time that Pound began his collaboration with Harriet Monroe. He was by then also an entrepreneur for the talents of others. Robert Frost was writing in England, all but unnoticed until Pound wrote a review that in effect introduced Frost's work to the world—a decisive moment in his career that Frost never forgot. In 1914 Pound wrote Harriet Monroe: "An American called Eliot called this P.M. I think he has some sense. . . ." A week later he wrote her again: "I was jolly well right about Eliot. He has sent in the best poem I have yet had or seen from an American. . . ." This was T. S. Eliot, who with critical help from Pound went on to fame as one of America's most distinguished poets. Subsequently, Pound became largely responsible for the publication of James Joyce's *Ulysses*, widely acclaimed as the greatest English novel of this century.

Pound abandoned imagism, which he had done so much to introduce— or passed it on, one might rather say, to Amy Lowell, in whose hands it became known as Amygism—sharpening his technique in other ways. His reading was so wide and deep that whatever he did was underlaid by a sense of traditional values, albeit he felt that everything should be reconsidered and "new" in its expression. Also, he believed that poetry could only be properly judged when heard spoken—the exact tone and rhythm of verse must be understood, almost in the manner of music. Form, color, and sound constituted a language of their own, independent of any literal message the words might convey. Thus, in 1916, he wrote "The Game of Chess":

> Red knights, brown bishops, bright queens,
> Striking the board, falling in strong 'L's of colour.

Reaching and striking in angles, holding lines in one colour.
The board is alive with light; these pieces are living in form,
Their moves break and reform the pattern: luminous greens from
   the rooks,
Clashing with 'X's of queens, looped with knight-leaps.

Y' pawns, clearing, embanking!
Whirl! Centripetal! Mate! King down in the vortex,
Clash, leaping of bands, straight strips of hard colour,
Blocked lights working in. Escapes.
   Renewal of contest.

During the rest of his productive life Pound's poetic writing was devoted
to his *Cantos,* a long, loosely linked series of verses, or stanzas, modeled
on Dante's *Divine Comedy.* Part autobiography, part anecdote with obscure
scholarly references, and increasingly reflecting the poet's disturbed mind,
they finally stopped short at Canto CXVII. Those fifty long years were filled
with bizarre incident and tragic circumstance. He was dismayed and embittered by the merciless trench warfare of World War I in which a number of
his friends lost their lives:

There died a myriad,
And of the best, among them
For an old bitch [England] gone in the teeth,
For a botched civilization. . . .

In 1921 he left for Paris, where he promptly moved to the center of a
literary circle, arguing with Gertrude Stein and boxing with young Ernest
Hemingway. Four years later he moved to Rapallo on the Italian Riviera,
which was to be his home for a score of years to come, years during which
he became a crank and a bigot, a vicious anti-Semite and a Fascist. What
poetry he wrote was virtually undecipherable—for example:

(interlude entitled: periplum by camion)
and Awoi's *hennia*   plays hob in the tent flaps
   k-lakk . . . . . thuuuuuu
     making rain
         uuuh
2,   7,   hooo
   der im Baluba

During World War II he made paid broadcasts for the Italian government
—"Europe callin'—Pound speakin'"—in which he advised his American
countrymen that their participation in the conflict was "plain downright damn
nonsense." After Mussolini's fall Pound was brought to America, judged
insane and incompetent to stand trial on nineteen counts of treason, and
jailed for twelve years in a Washington hospital. Robert Frost petitioned for
Pound's release, speaking for himself, Ernest Hemingway, T. S. Eliot, and
others. "None of us can bear the disgrace of letting Ezra Pound come to an
end where he is," wrote Frost. Declared "permanently and incurably insane,"
but harmless, Pound was released. He returned to Italy, where he continued
to wrestle with the problem of ending his *Cantos*—of finding a "paradise"

with which he could conclude his long, rambling message to the world. In Canto CXVI he wrote:

> I have brought the great ball of crystal,
>   who can lift it?
> Can you enter the great acorn of light?
>   but the beauty is not the madness
> Tho my errors and wrecks lie about me
>   and I cannot make it
>   cohere

When Pound died he was again at the center of a controversy because, after heated debate, the American Academy of Arts and Sciences decided not to award him its Emerson-Thoreau medal. His moral aberrations were held against him. There was little doubt that he had been a poet and critic who had helped mightily to turn the tide of Victorianism to modernism. In 1922, when T. S. Eliot received the Dial Award, and in 1954, when Ernest Hemingway was given the Nobel Prize, each of these men in turn affirmed that Pound had a prior claim to such distinctions.

Pound was a relatively young member of the generation of American poets whose work was recognized in the early issues of Harriet Monroe's magazine and whose reputation rose with the years. These men and women displayed a broad spectrum of diverse talents. Edwin Arlington Robinson, sixteen years older than Pound, had small interest in new experiments or in theories of what poetry should be. All he could do, he observed, was to write, and all his life he wrote in a constant vein, immune to novelties and to criticism. As once he wrote:

> Dear friends, reproach me not for what I do,
> Nor counsel me, nor pity me nor say
> That I am wearing half my life away
> For bubble-work that only fools pursue.

He clung to the past as steadfastly as he faced the future, undistracted by innovators and their "movements." As his friend Robert Frost remarked, Robinson "stayed content with the old way to be new."

Robinson was a New Englander, a Down Easter who passed his childhood in Gardiner, Maine. He was the spiritual heir of his Puritan ancestor Anne Bradstreet—somber, introspective, almost morbidly shy (he broke off an early love affair and remained a lifelong bachelor, devoted to his poetry). His early works went virtually unnoticed. To stave off poverty he worked as an inspector of subway construction; to stave off desperation he drank heavily. Then in 1903 Theodore Roosevelt read Robinson's *Captain Craig*, recommended by the president's son Kermit, and wrote an article about the poet for a popular weekly. He also gave Robinson a clerkship in the New York Custom House, where the poet struggled unhappily for four years. Robinson was next granted a summer haven at the MacDowell colony in Peterborough, New Hampshire, and in time he found public recognition and won a succession of Pulitzer prizes.

Many of Robinson's early poems were subtle portraits of vagabond, lonely men etched in a dry New England idiom—of a solitary man climbing a hill at sunset "as if he were the last god going home to his last desire." His

"Miniver Cheevy," published in 1910, is in some respects a comic poem, but it underlines the sense of futility and pessimism that characterizes so much of Robinson's writings.

Miniver Cheevy, child of scorn,
   Grew lean while he assailed the seasons;
He wept that he was ever born,
   And he had reasons.

❖ ❖ ❖ ❖

Miniver loved the Medici,
   Albeit he had never seen one;
He would have sinned incessantly
   Could he have been one.

❖ ❖ ❖ ❖

Miniver Cheevy, born too late,
   Scratched his head and kept on thinking;
Miniver coughed, and called it fate,
   And kept on drinking.

At another time he wrote that the world was "a hell of a place," adding, "that's why it must mean something." Robinson's later and longer poems are often psychological studies in the form of narratives, reflections on human nature and on the complex problems of human relationships, as in his revivification of the Arthurian saga in *Merlin, Lancelot,* and *Tristram.* Here the characters are presented as purely human case histories. Tristram is a man engulfed in his passionate love, not a figure of remote legend; his brief moment of rapturous fulfillment is revealed by Robinson with an intensity of feeling rare in his work:

He saw dark laughter sparkling
Out of her eyes, but only until her face
Found his, and on his mouth a moving fire
Told him why there was death, and what lost song
Ulysses heard, and would have given his hands
And friends to follow and to die for. Slowly,
At last, the power of helplessness there was
In all that beauty of hers that was for him,
Breathing and burning there alone with him,
Until it was almost a part of him,
Suffused his passion with a tenderness
Attesting a sealed certainty not his
To cozen or wrench from fate, and one withheld
In waiting mercy from oblivious eyes—
His eyes and hers, that over darker water,
Where darker things than shadows would be coming,
Saw now no more than more stars in the sky.
He felt her throbbing softly in his arms,
And held her closer still—with half a fear
Returning that she might not be Isolt,
And might yet vanish where she sat with him,
Leaving him there alone, with only devils
Of hell supplanting her.

Edwin Arlington Robinson, wrote poet James Dickey, "is perhaps the greatest master of the speculative or conjectural approach to the writing of poetry." Robinson, depicted above, was a true son of New England—austere, reticent, detached—whose work represents a flowering of Yankee poetry.

But in the end, even such love proves powerless in the face of time and the insoluble mysteries of the universe. With *Tristram* (1928) Robinson won his third Pulitzer Prize. The poem was the selection of a major book club, and Robinson found a wider audience than any important poet had enjoyed since Longfellow.

Robinson and Robert Frost were fellow New Englanders, and held one another in mutual esteem. Although Frost was born in San Francisco, his roots were sunk nine generations deep in rural New England. He was brought back there in his early boyhood, and there he lived for most of his long life. He was a dedicated poet from his youth; he was writing verse when he was in his teens. However, his first works caused little stir. Yet, like Robinson, he had the fortitude to make a success out of what long seemed to be worldly failure. He ended one of his later poems, "Two Tramps in Mud Time," with a statement of the principle that guided his efforts:

> But yield who will to their separation,
> My object in living is to unite
> My avocation and my vocation
> As my two eyes make one in sight.
> Only where love and need are one,
> And the work is play for mortal stakes,
> Is the deed ever really done
> For Heaven and the future's sakes.

Robert Frost, America's best-loved poet of the 20th century, has been described as "a mystical democrat, compassionately filled with a deep regard for the dignity of ordinary living." Opposite and on the following page are a selection of wood engravings, executed by Thomas W. Nason and inspired by lines from Frost poems.

To earn some sort of a living while he honed his developing skills, he taught school, worked as a bobbin boy in the mills and as a cobbler, and edited a weekly paper. From 1900 to 1905 he lived on a farm near Derry, New Hampshire. At best it was a scant living. Then, in 1912, with his wife and children, Frost left for England, where he hoped he might "write and be poor without further scandal in the family." In London his fortunes quickly shifted; he found a publisher for his first book, *A Boy's Will* (1913), the book that, as already remarked, Ezra Pound reviewed so favorably in Harriet Monroe's *Poetry*. Frost was then thirty-nine years old. In 1914 his *North of Boston* appeared in print. When he returned to America the following year he brought with him a growing reputation.

It is quite possible that the work of no other serious American poet is so well known to the reading public of the present generation as is Frost's. (Robinson's earlier popularity has subsided.) For a full half century he produced and published an abundance of verse that remained remarkably consistent in its quality, but which from book to book gradually developed in content and technique. "Few modern poets," writes one contemporary critic, "have shown such a capacity for growth, on into old age." With its very deceptive simplicity, its eminent quotability, much of Frost's poetry has almost assumed the status of American folklore. Virtually from the beginning of his career he mastered the art of suggesting the laconic vernacular of his neighbors "north of Boston," folk of solid integrity, as he viewed them, who lived close to the soil, the rocks, and the hills and streams of their rural countryside. In their monologues and dialogues he invents for them a wisdom wrung from long experience of living—a wisdom sometimes spiced with mischievous wit and irony. "The style is the man," Frost once said, quoting Buffon. "Rather say the style is the way the man takes himself; and to be at all

"He has dust in his eyes and a fan for a wing,
A leg akimbo with which he can sing,
And a mouthful of dye stuff instead of a sting."
"One Guess"

"I often see flowers from a passing
car
That are gone before I can tell what
they are."
from "A Passing Glimpse"

charming or even bearable, the way is almost rigidly prescribed. If it is with outer seriousness, it must be with inner humor. If it is with outer humor, it must be with inner seriousness."

Even Frost's shorter, meditative poems are dramatic, sometimes starting with a person or thing that stirs his wonder and quickly moving to a climactic statement. It is as though he were looking for a thought that he finally discovers in his last sentence, leaving it with us as a challenge to our imagination—as in "The Oven Bird":

> There is a singer everyone has heard,
> Loud, a mid-summer and a mid-wood bird,
> Who makes the solid tree trunks sound again.
> He says that leaves are old and that for flowers
> Mid-summer is to spring as one to ten.
> He says the early petal-fall is past,
> When pear and cherry bloom went down in showers
> On sunny days a moment overcast;
> And comes that other fall we name the fall.
> He says the highway dust is over all.
> The bird would cease and be as other birds
> But that he knows in singing not to sing.
> The question that he frames in all but words
> Is what to make of a diminished thing.

To that question Frost had the answer within himself, as in his poem "Fire and Ice":

> Some say the world will end in fire,
> Some say in ice.
> From what I've tasted of desire
> I hold with those who favor fire.
> But if it had to perish twice,
> I think I know enough of hate
> To say that for destruction ice
> Is also great
> And would suffice.

"We love the things we love for what they are."
from "Hyla Brook"

289

The pastoral vein that runs through most of Frost's poems is clearly suggested by their titles: "The Pasture," "Mowing," "Mending Wall," "After Apple-Picking," "Birches," "West-running Brook," and so on at length. In his earlier poems he describes the sometimes uneasy but always meaningful relation of man to nature. Man has need of nature, but nature has no need of man. Later he came to view the indifference of nature more as a hostile force with which man must struggle as heroically as he can. He regarded man in his earthly predicament with a detachment that ruled out any degree of compassion.

In his lifetime Frost was awarded four Pulitzer prizes, more than any other author. Although in his youth he was twice a dropout from college, in his later years he was heaped with academic honors, which he took quite casually. It will long be remembered that on a chill, windy day at President John F. Kennedy's inauguration Frost, in an unprecedented occasion, recited his poem "The Gift Outright":

> The land was ours before we were the land's.
> She was our land more than a hundred years
> Before we were her people. She was ours
> In Massachusetts, in Virginia,
> But we were England's, still colonials,
> Possessing what we still were unpossessed by,
> Possessed by what we now no more possessed.
> Something we were withholding made us weak
> Until we found out that it was ourselves
> We were withholding from our land of living,
> And forthwith found salvation in surrender.
> Such as we were we gave ourselves outright
> (The deed of gift was many deeds of war)
> To the land vaguely realizing westward,
> But still unstoried, artless, unenhanced,
> Such as she was, such as she would become.

It has been said that the poem he had actually prepared for the occasion was far from his best work, and at the last moment Frost conceded this to himself. He pretended to be unable to read it as the sun glared on the paper before him, and although Vice President Johnson held his hat so as to cast a shadow, Frost instead recited "The Gift Outright" from memory.

Frost has been criticized by some for retreating from the complex problems of the modern world in his preoccupation with pastoral verse. However that

"The woods are lovely, dark and deep,
But I have promises to keep,
And miles to go before I sleep,
And miles to go before I sleep."
          from "Stopping by Woods on a Snowy Evening"

may be, no such statement could possibly apply to his slightly younger contemporary William Carlos Williams. After his graduation from the University of Pennsylvania medical school, Williams practiced medicine to the end of his active life in his home town of Rutherford, New Jersey, "doctoring" largely to the working class of that community—and incessantly writing poetry on the side. For him the poet's task was "to write, as a physician works, upon the things before him," however ordinary or even sordid those might be; and his unusual, often brilliant verse reflects the forms and pressures of modern American life as transformed by his poetic vision.

When he was a medical student Williams had met Pound, and shared his interest in imagism. However, although he was influenced by Pound ("Before meeting Ezra Pound," Williams observed, "is like B.C. and A.D."), he achieved his own characteristic style by using the everyday stuff of his daily life and presenting it, with extreme economy in phrasing, at a rapid pace and in a startling succession of sensations. Consider, for example, "The Red Wheelbarrow":

> so much depends
> upon
>
> a red wheel
> barrow
>
> glazed with rain
> water
>
> beside the white
> chickens

Somewhat longer, "The Crowd at the Ball Game" describes the occasion in quick, incisive flashes of observations. The opening and closing lines provide an adequate impression of the whole poem:

> The crowd at the ball game
> is moved uniformly
>
> by a spirit of uselessness
> which delights them—
>
>   ❖   ❖   ❖   ❖
>
> It is summer, it is the solstice
> the crowd is
>
> cheering, the crowd is laughing
> in detail
>
> permanently, seriously
> without thought

Thus the homeliest images of the common life around him became the elements of Williams' stripped-down verses. The words he so sparingly uses are so meticulously chosen and are so charged with immediate sensation that,

TEXT CONTINUES PAGE 294

A SPECTRUM
OF
SPECTRIC VERSE

The plain face of the magazine
that gave American poetry a jolt

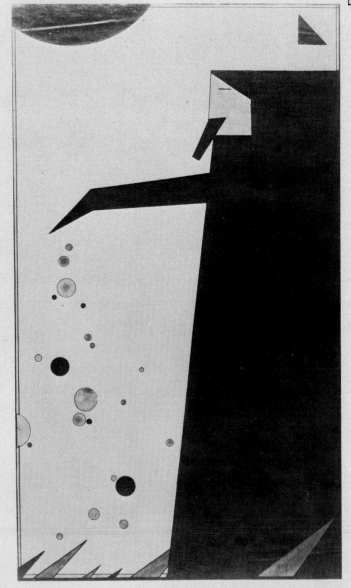

Arthur Davison Ficke's futurist sketch of Emanuel Morgan

In 1916 a new and unheralded constellation of poets appeared in the American firmament—out of Pittsburgh had come Anne Knish and Emanuel Morgan, proclaiming the credo of spectrism, by which they claimed "to push the possibilities of poetic expression" beyond that attempted by the imagists, futurists, chorists, vortacists, the lot. In a slender volume of some sixty pages entitled *Spectra, A Book of Poetic Experiments*, the collaborators presented fifty works, some free verse, some crisply cadenced rhymes, in which were demonstrated poetic prisms "upon which the colorless white light of infinite existence falls and is broken up into glowing, beautiful, and intelligible hues." In the incandescent, not to say voracious world of literary fashion, this was greeted as sensational news. Here was something fresh to build a movement on. A new disciple, one Elijah Hay, became the third spectric poet about this time. Now the three writers, though their corporeal presence would continue to elude admirers for the next eighteen months, became *forces majeurs* in the little poetry magazines. Their poems, their pronouncements, were studied and paid homage to by such luminaries as Harriet Monroe, Edgar Lee Masters, and William Carlos Williams. When the game began to pall and the noise of a few skeptics to rise above the applause, Morgan and Knish removed their masks to reveal the laughing faces of poets Witter Bynner and Arthur Davison Ficke. What had begun as a little joke between two friends had worked far beyond their imagination. An overeager publisher, a rapid inflation of opus numbers that made the spectrics seem productive as only the inspired can be, a few friends brought into the hoax as honorary press agents, had done the rest. In the end Ficke and Bynner were not sure that they had done themselves a good turn. There were those who believed neither man wrote as well under his own name.

"Opus 118

If bathing were a virtue, not a lust,
   I would be dirtiest.

   To some, housecleaning is a holy rite.
For myself, houses would be empty
But for the golden motes dancing in sunbeams.

   Tax-assessors frequently overlook valuables.
Today they noted my jade.
But my memory of you escaped them."
Anne Knish

"Opus 15

Despair comes when all comedy
   Is tame
And there is left no tragedy
   In any name,
When the round and wounded breathing
   Of love upon the breast
Is not so glad a sheathing
   As an old brown vest.

Asparagus is feathery and tall,
And the hose lies rotting by the garden-wall."
Emanuel Morgan

"Opus 6

If I were only dafter
   I might be making hymns
To the liquor of your laughter
   And the lacquer of your limbs.

But you turn across the table
   A telescope of eyes,
And it lights a Russian sable
   Running circles in the skies. . . .

Till I go running after,
   Obeying all your whims—
For the liquor of your laughter
   And the lacquer of your limbs."
Emanuel Morgan

"Elijah Cerebrates for Emanuel

If only my thoughts were dolphins, fat and free,
Untaught by morals and uncurbed by speech,
Fresh as the waves that tumble on the beach,
I could be gay, inconsequentially.
My thoughts are more like anchovies, I see
How rigid, tail in mouth, linked each to each
Immutably and logically they reach,
The present, past and future thoughts of me!"
Elijah Hay

"Portrait" of Anne Knish, by Ficke

A caricature of William Carlos Williams, done by the spectrist poet Emanuel Morgan in 1920, plays up Williams' two divergent careers: that of dedicated physician (symbolized by the stethoscope) and that of assiduous writer of poetry (symbolized by the lyre).

in a sense, they themselves become the subject of his poems. With the imagists, it could be said, he believed that "a poem should not mean but be."

Meanwhile, in the Middle West—the region centering on the rousing city of Chicago—the new spirit in poetry had assumed a particular American bent. Even before Harriet Monroe's vital little magazine was first issued in 1912, there were fresh voices clamoring to be heard in that "heartland" of the nation. She herself had written, among other poems, an ode to celebrate the great exhibition of 1893 in her native city. But her accomplishments as a writer were overshadowed by the rising talents of such Midwestern poets as Edgar Lee Masters, Carl Sandburg, and Vachel Lindsay—and she promptly found room in the pages of *Poetry* for all three, along with the works of Easterners, expatriates, and Europeans, as the quality of their performances dictated. Chicago itself was at once a meeting place, a point of departure, a major crossroads, and a permanent settlement for the unheard of variety of people that were filling up the continent and giving the country its special character among the nations of the world. The city was a thousand miles from the Atlantic coast, where the tradition of American letters had been nurtured for generations past. But, as Masters, Sandburg, and Lindsay instinctively felt, it was the more American for that—closer to the present realities and the future prospects of the nation. Moreover, it was the land of Abraham Lincoln, the apotheosis of the plain man on whose solid, sensible character American democracy would have to depend if it were to prove itself to the world in the long run. (Lindsay was born in Springfield, Illinois, where Lincoln had lived and practiced; Masters' father had been a law partner of one of Lincoln's professional associates; Sandburg wrote a six-volume biography of Lincoln that won a Pulitzer Prize.)

Lindsay recalled that as a child he had never even heard of New England, and Sandburg and Masters were essentially as remote in spirit from Eastern influences in their approach to poetry. For these men the hub of the universe was not the dome of the Boston State House, but a point closer to Chicago, as Sandburg described that city in 1914:

> They tell me you are wicked and I believe them, for I have seen your painted women under the gas lamps luring the farm boys,
> And they tell me you are crooked and I answer: Yes, it is true I have seen the gunman kill and go free to kill again
> And they tell me you are brutal and my reply is: On the faces of women and children I have seen the marks of wanton hunger. . . .

But here, Sandburg added, was "a tall bold slugger set vivid against the little soft cities," bragging and laughing because its vitality was in the heartbeat of the people:

> Laughing the stormy, husky, brawling laughter of Youth, half-naked, sweating, proud to be Hog Butcher, Tool Maker, Stacker of Wheat, Player with Railroads and Freight Handler to the Nation.

Sandburg himself was very much of the people, and he took his language out of the mouths of the people rather than from the voices of past or present poets. He was the son of poor and illiterate Swedish immigrant parents. While he was still a teen-ager, a lad with very little schooling, he had learned about common folk by riding freight trains as a hobo, by working at such odd jobs as barbershop porter, bricklayer, farm hand, dishwasher, and the like. When he was twenty he served as a recruit in the Spanish-American War, reporting his experiences on the side, and returned to work his way through Lombard College in his home town, Galesburg, Illinois. For a dozen years thereafter he worked at higher levels—preparing advertising copy, working on newspapers, and serving as secretary to Milwaukee's socialist mayor. He married the sister of the famous photographer Edward Steichen—and he wrote poetry.

It was in 1912 that he found his way to Chicago and to full recognition as a poet with the publication of "Chicago," quoted in part above and earlier. His free-verse forms—poetry without any fixed metrical pattern and having a loosely organized rhythm—his choice of subjects from among the crude, commonplace, and "unpoetic" aspects of life, and his ordinary American diction all aroused critical discussion. Walt Whitman had written of common people in free, flowing verse, as Sandburg well knew. But Whitman wrote with visionary, prophetic imagination, whereas Sandburg wrote with close attention to the real and often unhappy detailed facts of the matter. Still, Sandburg had his own lyric imagination that crops up in his verses in short passages of characteristic fancy—as in his very brief poem "Fog":

> The fog comes
> on little cat feet.
>
> It sits looking
> over harbor and city
> on silent haunches
> and then moves on.

It was in such a vein that he wrote his *Rootabaga Stories* and other tales of "days that never happened," to the delight of children—stories of Jason Quiff, whose hat, mittens, and shoes were made of popcorn, and other "nonsense tales with American fooling in them."

Robert Frost once remarked that writing free verse was like playing tennis with the net down. But the modern movement in poetry was sympathetic to such excursions into new forms of expression. More than that, the bold colloquialisms Sandburg used came from a popular native speech of singular vitality and vigor. And even further, as the English critic and historian Marcus Cunliffe has remarked, Sandburg appreciated and was affected by the special contribution of the Negro, "with his exuberant-sad philosophy of the underling and his exceptional gift for rhythmic expression"—for such rhythms as were rhapsodically improvised in jazz music. Jazz, Cunliffe continues, quoting one Negro, emerged not from the world of wine, women, and song, but out of "booze, brothels, and blues."

Sandburg collected Negro spirituals, along with other folk music of cowboys, tramps, and workingmen and, accompanying himself on a guitar, sang them at his "readings." He became something of a latter-day troubadour as he sang his way from performance to performance. (In 1927 he published a collection of such music in *The American Songbag*.) Walt Whitman once wrote that "to have great poets there must be great audiences too." With his verse and his music Sandburg reached out to such mass audiences, to

Carl Sandburg, "laureate of industrial America," was, in the words of poet Louis Untermeyer, "the muscular, heavy-fisted, hard-hitting son of the streets," as well as "the shadow-painter, the haunter of mists, the lover of implications and overtones."

295

poetize and lyricize for them their common bond of feelings. As he wrote in his major work on this theme, *The People, Yes:*

> Between the finite limitations of the five senses
> and the endless yearnings of man for the beyond
> the people hold to the humdrum bidding of work and food
> while reaching out when it comes their way
> for lights beyond the prison of the five senses,
> for keepsakes lasting beyond any hunger or death
>   This reaching is alive.
> The panderers and liars have violated and smutted it.
>   Yet this reaching is alive yet
>   for lights and keepsakes.

The People, Yes, written during the dark days of the Great Depression, has been called "one of the great American books"; at the very least it is a quintessential document of the time and place of its creation, written with passionate earnestness by a gifted man who belonged no other place on earth than where he was. The common bond of all Sandburg's works is suggested by his reference to this book as "a footnote to the Gettysburg Address"—his poems were of the people, for the people, and, in a sense, by the people.

Sandburg's Illinois contemporary, Vachel Lindsay, is one of the strangest and saddest figures in the annals of American poetry. Like Sandburg, Lindsay was also a tramp for a time, and a bard—a bard who gave extraordinary, circuslike performances. His poetry ranged from inspired messages to pathetic doggerel. Different as he was from Sandburg, he, too, was very much a man of his time and place.

Lindsay was born of highly religious parents, devout Campbellites, or Disciples of Christ, an evangelical and millennarian sect. As a youth he studied art in Chicago, with no intention of being a poet. (He was already trying to save souls, in part through his art.) However, he found no market for his artistic wares, and with no other means of livelihood he turned to writing poetry—not a likely source of revenue in itself. Bad artist and poet that he was in those early years, after peddling his poems for an asking price of two cents apiece along Third Avenue in New York, he took to the open road, trading his verses and their illustrations for bread and some form of lodging, in the manner of a medieval troubadour. Still he thought of himself as an evangelist rather than a poet, carrying on his "warfare for Beauty and Democracy" by reading such lines as:

> Go plant the arts that woo the weariest,
> Bold arts that simple workmen understand,
> That make no poor men and keep all men rich,
> And throne our Lady Beauty in the land!

During one such expedition Lindsay sent Harriet Monroe his poem "General William Booth Enters into Heaven," intended to be sung to the music of the hymn "The Blood of the Lamb," describing with drum-beat rhythms the apotheosis of the founder of the Salvation Army as he leads a troop of criminals and slum dwellers through the pearly gates:

> Christ came gently with a robe and crown
> For Booth the soldier, while the throng knelt down.

Actual drums, flutes, tambourines, and other instruments were used to accompany his delivery. Harriet Monroe considered Lindsay one of her first discoveries, and published "General Booth" as the lead poem in her issue of January, 1913. In the preceding issue of her magazine she had first presented to an American audience the work of the Bengal poet Rabindranath Tagore, who was to enjoy a great vogue in this country. "It may not be without significance," she wrote, ". . . that these two antipodal poets soon appeared among the earliest visitors to the editor. For the coming together of East and West may prove to be the great event of the approaching era, and if the poetry of the now famous Bengali laureate garners the richest wisdom and highest spirituality of his ancient race, so one may venture to believe that the young Illinois troubadour brings from Lincoln's city an authentic strain of the lyric message of this newer world."

For a while following that publication Lindsay enjoyed considerable popularity. Almost unwittingly he had become one of the "new" poets, hailed by Amy Lowell and Lindsay's home-town friend and fellow poet Edgar Lee Masters, among others. By popular demand he appeared before rapt audiences, reciting, chanting, and whispering such favorite poems as "The Congo," gesticulating ecstatically and closing his eyes as if in a trance.

In 1900, when the stereoscopic view, opposite, of Chicago's Great Union Stockyards was taken, Chicago, "Hog Butcher for the World," was fast becoming a center of literature and avant-garde poetry. Harriet Monroe's Poetry: A Magazine of Verse *was launched there in 1912. One of the magazine's first "discoveries" was the young poet of the Middle West, Vachel Lindsay, who believed that verse should be recited as well as read. A photograph of 1928, below, depicts Lindsay giving a characteristic histrionic reading of his work. The works of two other Chicago folk-poets, Carl Sandburg and Edgar Lee Masters, were also featured in* Poetry.

HERBERT GEORG STUDIO

His written verse was annotated with such guides to delivery as "Shrilly and with a heavily accented metre," "Like the wind in the chimney," "All the 'o' sounds very golden," and so forth. He referred to these performances as "the higher vaudeville," and for the time, the place, and his appreciative public it was good theatre. The following lines from "The Congo," a memorial to a heroic Disciple missionary who died in Africa, convey the flavor of such acts:

> A good old negro in the slums of the town
> Preached at a sister for her velvet gown.
> Howled at a brother for his low-down ways,
> His prowling, guzzling, sneak-thief days.
> Beat on the Bible till he wore it out
> Starting the jubilee revival shout.
> And some had visions, as they stood on chairs,
> And sang of Jacob, and the golden stairs,
> And they all repented, a thousand strong
> From their stupor and savagery and sin and wrong
> And slammed with their hymn books till they shook the room
> With "glory, glory, glory,"
> And "Boom, boom, BOOM."
> THEN I SAW THE CONGO, CREEPING THROUGH THE BLACK,
> CUTTING THROUGH THE JUNGLE WITH A GOLDEN TRACK. . . .

"Heavy bass," reads the script. "With a literal imitation of camp-meeting racket, and trance."

In the end Lindsay came to hate the constant repetition of his "shows." He died in bitterness and despair, by poison according to Masters; he was one of the strange mutations of American culture. For all the bad verse he wrote, his most successful efforts are echoed somewhat surprisingly in some sophisticated modern poetry.

Edgar Lee Masters was the oldest of this trio of Illinois poets. Actually, he was born in Kansas but was brought to Lewistown, Illinois, as a child. For many years of his adult life he practiced law in Chicago, with poetry as his avocation. His greatest contribution to American letters was the *Spoon River Anthology*, published in book form in 1915, which brought him immediate and wide recognition.

Written in free verse, *Spoon River* portrays the secret lives of almost two hundred and fifty members of a small Midwestern community—their hopes and frustrations, their petty intrigues and occasional exaltations, their sins and modest triumphs—all in the form of individual confessions emanating from the burial mounds of the local cemetery. Through these candid, invented epitaphs Masters exposed the meanness and hypocrisy of a small Illinois village. The muckrakers had already aroused interest in social scrutiny, and in his separate, highly individual fashion Masters was echoing their plaints with his intimate and imaginative sketches. As Sherwood Anderson and Sinclair Lewis would soon be protesting in their novels, the corruption of the big cities was spreading its stain across the land, penetrating even those villages where democratic virtues were supposedly so deeply rooted. Within a few years the experiences of World War I would add a new dimension to that spirit of disillusionment, leading American literature toward distinctively modern attitudes and manners of expression.

THE CHILDREN'S WORLD

Writing books specifically for children is a relatively modern practice. The hornbook, devised in the sixteenth century, was the first lesson book in the English language. During the Puritan age a spate of gloomy admonitory volumes was published in both England and America, a typical example being A Token for the Children of New-England. Or Some Examples of Children to whom the Fear of God was Remarkably Budding, before they Dyed *(1700). By the 1740's the London shop of John Newbery was producing "reckless" juveniles in which the desire to furnish amusement together with instruction was evident. It was not until the golden age of illustration in post-Civil War America that the American writers and illustrators of juveniles began dedicating themselves to wholesome gaiety and light-hearted amusement rather than to pure moralizing, and the era of great American children's classics was born; it has never ended.*

"When I was sick and lay a-bed,
I had two pillows at my head,
And all my toys beside me lay
To keep me happy all the day."

Robert Louis Stevenson, from "The Land of the Counterpane"

A CHILD'S GARDEN

Many young children (and young-at-heart adults) have delighted in Robert Louis Stevenson's *Child's Garden of Verses*, which conjures up the nonself-conscious, imaginative world of childhood. In the poem "To Any Reader" Stevenson hints at the loss of spontaneity that often accompanies maturity: "So you may see, if you will look/ Through the windows of this book,/Another child, far, far away,/And in another garden, play./But do not think you can at all,/By knocking on the window, call/That child to hear you. . . ./He has grown up and gone away. . . ." Another poem that evokes the lost joys of childhood is Eugene Field's "Little Boy Blue." Equally appealing are the Brownie books of the 1880's and 1890's, written and illustrated by Palmer Cox, and endowed with a quality dear to children: each spritelike brownie "was easily recognizable in every drawing, and was always consistent in behavior. Thus children could . . . identify each of the characters with someone they knew in real life. . . ."

The Brownies: Their Book, BY PALMER COX, 1887

"*Time was when the little toy dog was new,*
And the soldier was passing fair;
And that was the time when our Little Boy Blue
Kissed them and put them there."

Eugene Field, from "Little Boy Blue"

"*But trouble, as you understand,*
Oft moves with pleasure, hand in hand,
And even Brownies were not free
From evil snag or stubborn tree
That split toboggans like a quill,
And scattered riders down the hill."

From "The Brownies Tobogganing,"
in *The Brownies: Their Book*

On the yellow brick way, by W. W. Denslow

Lyman Frank Baum's Oz books have delighted children of many countries ever since *The Wonderful Wizard of Oz* first appeared in 1900. Baum's tale of Dorothy, a little farm girl from Kansas who is carried by a cyclone to the strange and magical land of Oz, was an instant success. It was illustrated by W. W. Denslow, whose drawing of Dorothy and her dog Toto is reproduced above; also shown are the Cowardly Lion, the Tin Woodman, who longs for a heart, and the Scarecrow, who yearns for brains. Popular demand forced Baum to write thirteen other books; *The Marvelous Land of Oz* (1904) is the only one of the series in which Dorothy does not appear. For this book, Baum's publisher found a new illustrator, John R. Neill, whose pictures have become as identified with the Oz stories as Sir John Tenniel's have with Carroll's *Alice's Adventures in Wonderland*. The Neill drawing, opposite, from the third Oz book, *Ozma of Oz*, shows Dorothy (who now appears as a pretty, wavy-haired blond) and Tiktok, a "Patent Double-Action, Extra-Responsive, Thought-Creating, Perfect-Talking Mechanical Man."

THE MARVELOUS PEOPLE OF OZ

Dorothy and Tiktok, by John R. Neill

MAROONED

"Why is it that the pirate has, and always has had, a certain lurid glamour of the heroical enveloping him round about? . . . Would not every boy . . . of any account . . .

*rather be a pirate captain than a Member of Parliament?"
So wrote Howard Pyle, artist, author, and dean of
American illustrators, about one of his favorite subjects,*
*pirates. Pyle's painting, Marooned, reproduced above,
pictures an abject pirate who has been abandoned on a
desolate sand spit and who awaits his fate in despair.*

THE ART
OF N. C. WYETH

"There is a heroic treatment of anatomy, for example, that makes a Wyeth masculine-type so gloriously strong and virile, —you look for a new discovery and technique. Then that romance of color, of wave, of cloud. Of those authentic, yet fascinating ships that toss or float over seas, fabulously stormy or credibly calm. In the affections of the adolescent boy, there will be few to replace N. C. Wyeth. To the very human critic Wyeth has an insured niche. When one is wearied a bit it is pleasant relaxation to rediscover the sheer color ecstasy and eternal decorative beauty of an illustration by N. C. Wyeth." This accolade, written in 1927, still holds true today. From the early years of the twentieth century, when he studied with the illustrious Howard Pyle, until his tragic death in an auto accident in 1945, Newell Convers Wyeth was one of America's leading artists. He worked in several mediums—illustration for books and magazines, murals, easel painting, and commerical art; but the robust canvases he did for children's classics, bringing to life such idols as Robin Hood, Hans Brinker, Natty Bumppo, and Heidi, are his crowning achievement. And perhaps most famous of all are the illustrations "N.C." executed for sixteen volumes of the Scribner Illustrated Classics series, beginning in 1911 with Robert Louis Stevenson's incomparable *Treasure Island*. It is according to Wyeth's rendering that tens of thousands of Americans have visualized Long John Silver, Blind Pew, and other of Stevenson's bold pirates. Wyeth's world lives on in the classics he illustrated and in the dynasty of artists he sired, notably son Andrew and grandson James Wyeth.

Opposite: the Giant, *1923*

Old Pew calling for his comrades, 1911

An early Wyeth Tarzan, 1913

Dr. Dolittle, Gub-Gub, Dab-Dab, and Boy, from Dr. Dolittle's Puddleby Adventures, *by Hugh Lofting*

LIKES AND DISLIKES

The most popular children's classics are honest works with which a young reader can easily identify. Mary Mapes Dodge's *Hans Brinker, or the Silver Skates* (1865), for example, was a uniquely realistic book for its time. All the episodes ring true, from the brutal scenes in which Raff Brinker treats his family atrociously to the unforgetable race for the silver skates. Animal stories are also appealing. The Doctor Dolittle books, written and illustrated by Hugh Lofting, an Englishman who settled in America, are the result of the author's disgust with man's inhumanity to animals. In the first of the series, *The Story of Dr. Dolittle* (1920), the kind doctor learns animal language from Polynesia the Parrot and becomes the best animal doctor in the world; he is the perfect go-between for children and animals. Frances Hodgson Burnett's *Little Lord Fauntleroy* (1886), however, has been maligned by thousands of grubby-handed little boys who resented being dressed in velvets and laces. Eugene Field expressed their resentment when he wrote: "Mighty glad I aint a girl— ruther be a boy, without them sashes, curls an things that's worn by Fauntleroy." In truth, the foppish Fauntleroy is not the paragon of priggery he is thought to be.

Hans Brinker and his sister, by George Wharton Edwards

Little Lord Fauntleroy before his Grandfather, the Earl, by Reginald Birch

Whitewashing the fence, by Worth Brehm

Mark Twain once wrote in a letter that "the *right* way to write a story for boys is to write so that it will not only interest boys but will also strongly interest any man who *has ever* been a boy." Twain succeeded admirably; his two great boys' classics, *Tom Sawyer* (1876) and *Huckleberry Finn* (1885), long ignored by librarians and parents, became perennial favorites. "Huckleberry," declared the author, "was cordially hated and dreaded by all mothers of the town, because he was idle and lawless and vulgar and bad—and because all their children admired him so, and delighted in his forbidden society, and wished they dared to be like him. Tom was like the rest of the respectable boys, in that he envied Huckleberry his gaudy outcast condition, and was under strict orders not to play with him. So he played with him every time he got a chance." It is the rare reader who cannot identify with the delightful scene, illustrated at left, in which the contriving Tom Sawyer persuades his friend Ben to take over the dull job of whitewashing a fence, observing that "In order to make . . . a boy covet a thing, it is only necessary to make the thing difficult to attain." Louisa May Alcott's *Little Women* is another book that appeals to grownups and children alike; the March sisters work at being good, but they are never prudes.

Mrs. March and the Little Women—Margaret, Jo, Beth, and Amy, by Jessie Willcox Smith

Beginning with the publication of *Ragged Dick* in 1867, more than one hundred eighteen Horatio Alger books fired the imaginations of two generations of American boys. Nearly all Alger books tell the same story: a poor, usually fatherless teen-age boy leaves home to seek fame and fortune in the big city. Through intelligence, good clean living, courage, thrift, and other assorted virtues (plus a fortuitous admixture of pluck and luck), the hero finally attains the dizzy heights of success. The sameness of plot and seldom-varied formula for achieving financial security and social acceptability did not bother the millions of fans who followed the careers of Tattered Tom, Phil the Fiddler, Ragged Dick, and other heroes who star in volumes with such pleasantly alliterative titles as *Brave and Bold*, *Slow and Sure*, and *Strive and Succeed*. The Wild, Wild West was another popular boys' topic, and dime novels and nickle weeklies titillated their readers with romantic claptrap about outlaws and desperados like Jesse James and Billy the Kid, whom they transformed into superheroes. In April, 1896, American youths welcomed a new idol, Frank Merriwell, who made his bow in the first issue of *Tip Top Weekly*. The creation of Gilbert Patten, writing under the pen name of Burt L. Standish, Frank (unlike the pious, plodding rags-to-riches Alger hero) is a clean-cut upper-class Yale man—"gentlemanly, adventurous, brave, handsome, brilliant, athletic, wealthy."

Frontispieces to Alger books

A gunslinging bandit-hero

LARGEST WEEKLY CIRCULATION IN AMERICA

TIP TOP WEEKLY

AN
IDEAL PUBLICATION
FOR THE AMERICAN YOUTH

Issued Weekly. By subscription $2.50 per year. Entered as Second-class Matter at the N. Y. Post Office, by STREET & SMITH, 79-89 Seventh Ave., N. Y.

No. 542   NEW YORK, SEPTEMBER 1, 1906.   Price, Five Cents

FRANK MERRIWELL'S NEW AUTO
OR, THE LURE TO DESTRUCTION

By BURT L. STANDISH

A gasp of horror came from the girl's lips as she saw the machine swerve, plunge headlong over the brink, and came shooting down the face of the cliff.

A typical Frank Merriwell cover: Frank always triumphs in the end.

BETWEEN WARS

A *detail (opposite) from a mural of 1930, by Thomas Hart Benton, highlights some superficial elements of twenties' culture: bootleg booze and bathtub gin, ticker-tape euphoria, gangster movies, and sugar daddies with their girlfriends. Historian Bruce Catton has written that the jazz age was "at one and the same time the gaudiest, the saddest, and the most misinterpreted era in modern American history. It was gaudy because it was full of restless vitality burgeoning in a field where all of the old rules seemed to be gone, and it was sad because it was an empty place between two eras. . . ."*

Within barely a score of years after it was so confidently forecast at the World's Columbian Exposition, the world of the future seemed already to have arrived. As anticipated, electricity quickly became a general source of energy as the century advanced. Not only could it be "piped" into large industrial plants in heavy loads, and motivate trolley cars, it also could be threaded into homes in more modest allotments for individual and family use. At relatively low cost, the common American—the city dweller, at least—could tap at will through slender wires such power as no monarch of the past ever commanded for his personal service. With the throw of a switch or the push of a button, in effect, Niagara Falls would do the necessary work.

As steel, made by the open-hearth process, became increasingly available at practical prices, its uses multiplied accordingly. Skyscrapers were towering ever higher in the major cities. In 1912 the Woolworth Building rose to sixty stories about its steel skeleton. Again, electricity made possible vital elevator service and provided the current for indispensible telephones.

Mass-circulation magazines, as already noted, were presenting the American public, through editorial matter and advertisements and illustrations, with an almost indigestible miscellany of information and advice, breaking down old parochialisms as they carried their messages out of the cities into the farthest reaches of the countryside. However trivial those messages may often have been, the net educational effect upon people whose horizons had been closed in by circumstances was of immeasurable importance.

More novel, more unexpected, was the rapid development of the motion picture as a channel for visual communication. From a side business of the penny arcades and billiard parlors, movies rapidly came into their own and developed a dynamic new language which, even in its stuttering beginnings, spoke directly to the man in the street. "Between 1906 and 1908," reported one contemporary publication, "moving picture theatres . . . have opened in nearly every town and village in the country . . . every city from the Klondike to Florida and from Maine to California supports from two or three to several hundred." It was claimed that many men were even neglecting the saloon

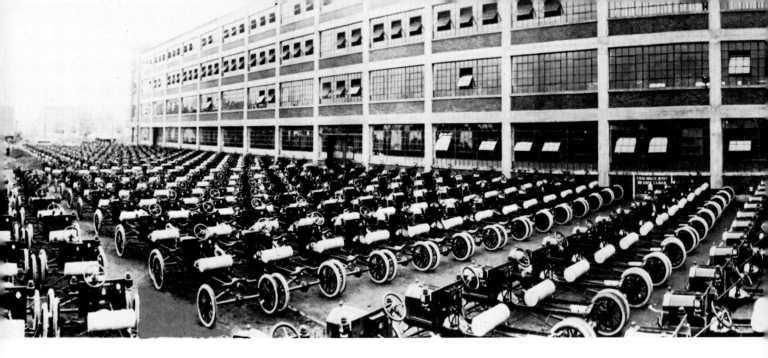

Ford cars, exemplified by the Model T's, above, and inexpensive picture shows, personified by Charlie Chaplin, below, mobilized and mesmerized the masses in the mechanized "Roaring Twenties."

for this new and flickering form of "madness." D. W. Griffith's *The Birth of a Nation* was shown at the White House for President Woodrow Wilson, his Cabinet, and their families; it was the first film permitted within those august precincts. Vast masses of people who were completely unfamiliar with the names and achievements of the greatest figures in history or literature came to know every gesture and antic of Charlie Chaplin, who quickly became an American folk hero of indisputable stature—far better known to the world at large than Daniel Boone had ever been a century earlier, when in the eighth canto of *Don Juan* Lord Byron celebrated the legend of that heroic American frontiersman.

Another mechanical marvel that reshaped the American way of life with comparable speed and consequence was the automobile. Whereas the motion picture was an art form in history that originated as a popular diversion before advancing to more sophisticated and refined levels, automobiling first won favor with the well-to-do as a genteel pastime. It was reported from Paris in 1901 that the king of the Belgians used his motorcar instead of the train on his trips between Brussels and Paris. It seemed, indeed, as *Vogue* magazine suggested at the time, "a royal way of getting about."

The affluent Edith Wharton could easily afford her car and early became an ardent automobilist; she referred to her frequent excursions as her "motor flights." However, in 1906 the association of the automobile with ostentation and privilege led Woodrow Wilson to observe that "nothing has spread socialistic feeling in this country more than the use of the automobile . . . to the countryman they are a picture of the arrogance of wealth, with all its independence and carelessness." His concern was needless. Only a year later one magazine reported that the auto had become a necessity in American life. To support that claim, by 1913 Model T Fords were streaming off the assembly lines at the rate of a thousand a day. The joke that a Ford could go anywhere except in society was well put. The man who could not afford a tin lizzie was poor indeed; the man who owned one enjoyed no distinction on that score over multitudes of his fellow citizens. A revolution in transportation was well under way.

That same year, 1913, Woodrow Wilson succeeded to the presidency of the United States, intent on launching his crusade for the New Freedom in

America. His program was designed "to cheer and inspirit our people with the sure prospects of social justice and due reward, with the vision of the open gates of opportunity for all." In this he was continuing the policies Theodore Roosevelt had vigorously pronounced in the previous administration. Wilson was a scholar and an intellectual, a rare figure in the presidency, and he pursued his ideals with almost reverent dedication. He was acutely aware of the dynamic potential of American democracy in his day, and he displayed bold willingness to accommodate traditional constitutional dogma to the social needs of the country as he saw them. "The Nation has been deeply stirred," he announced, "stirred by a solemn passion, stirred by the knowledge of wrong, of ideals lost, of government too often debauched and made an instrument of evil. The feelings with which we face this new age of right and opportunity sweep across our heartstrings like some air out of God's own presence, where justice and mercy are reconciled and the judge and the brother are one."

Then, the following summer, war broke out in Europe. At the moment the United States was as unwarlike a nation as could be imagined. The "splendid little war" with Spain sixteen years earlier had begun to seem to most Americans like a temporary aberration, an ill-advised excursion into troubled waters. Now there was general agreement that the conflict overseas was no business of ours. This country had no "entangling alliances" with those foreign nations that were preparing to bloody the fields of Europe, chiefly of France. Wilson viewed the carnage that had started there as "a distant event, terrible and tragic, but one which did not concern us closely in the political sense." He advised all Americans to be "impartial in thought as well as in action . . . neutral in fact as well as in name." Thus, in August, 1914, it seemed hardly likely that the United States would soon play a decisive role in the mounting world struggle that, in the end, would materially and spiritually change the tenor of American life.

Within less than three years, by force of inexorable circumstance, Wilson's crusade for the New Freedom was converted into a crusade to make the world "safe for democracy," to finish "the war to end wars." The nation was at once too powerful and too vulnerable to international events to remain isolated from the widespread chaos. In April, 1917, America entered the war on the side of the Allies. "It is a fearful thing to lead this great peaceful nation into war," Wilson announced with characteristic eloquence, "into the most terrible and disastrous of all wars, civilization itself seeming to be in the balance. But the right is more precious than peace, and we shall fight for the things we have always carried nearest our hearts,—for democracy, for the right of those who submit to authority to have a voice in their own governments, for the rights and liberties of small nations, for a universal dominion of right by such a concert of free peoples as shall bring peace and safety to all nations and make the world itself at last free."

To that sort of idealistic appeal the American people at large responded in a spirit of moral fervor. Although great numbers of those called to arms with the conscription of 1917–18 were foreign-born men and their sons, people with strong surviving attachments to the various hostile countries of Europe, there were few who placed the interest of their fatherland before that of their adopted country—or above the ideals propounded by Wilson. After more than a half century of disillusioning experience, it is not easy to recall the ardor with which the Yanks went so far away to war, shipload after shipload of them, with real faith that this could be the last war.

As a popular song put it, when the doughboys arrived in the trenches the war would soon be "over over there"—and so it was. It is no discredit to the brief but essential performance of the American troops to realize that the real history of America's part in the war was, as historians have pointed out, not so much the story of heroic actions at Belleau Wood, St.-Mihiel, and Château-Thierry as of mobilizing the industrial resources at home that supported the Allied armies with the necessary implements and supplies of war. The formal treaty of peace was signed on June 28, 1919. However, the crusading spirit that had earlier led to domestic reforms and then to war lasted long enough to complete the ratification of a constitutional amendment giving American women the right of suffrage—and, almost implausibly, it seems in retrospect, to the addition of the Prohibition amendment, which went into effect at the beginning of 1920.

Then, quite suddenly, the zeal to make over the nation and the world seemed to be exhausted. There still were idealists who continued the quest of lofty objectives, but they were outnumbered. In general, the people had had enough of great causes and noble sacrifices; a spirit of self-indulgence took over. A very substantial number of citizens quickly began to regret the heroic gesture that had instituted Prohibition, and along with those who had in the first place resented such a restriction of their personal liberty, they helped usher in a period of law evasion and corruption without precedent in American history.

Senator Warren G. Harding announced in 1920 that America's immediate need was not for heroics or nostrums, but for healing and what he termed "normalcy." However, there was little that was normal about the postwar period. It was a time of shocking intolerance and hysterical Americanism. In the early 1920's the Ku Klux Klan boasted a membership of about five million persons, dedicated to keeping the Negro in his place, along with other minorities arbitrarily selected for persecution—the list includes Catholics, Jews, immigrants of certain nationalities, "radicals," and other "un-Ameri-

A characteristic World War I U.S. Navy recruitment poster reflects the idealistic fervor of a whole nation swept up in the "war to end all wars." American patriots glorified the effort with such songs as "Over There" and "The Long, Long Trail"; it was the last conflict in which soldiers would sing with unrestrained enthusiasm.

can" folk who did not conform to the ideal of "native, white, Protestant" supremacy. In 1921, 1924, and 1929 Congress placed rigid restrictions on immigration, thus ending an era of deep significance in human history. After a protracted trial and review, Nicola Sacco and Bartolomeo Vanzetti, two philosophical anarchists of foreign birth, were condemned to death on what seemed to many highly dubious evidence. In retrospect they appear to have been executed for their thoughts rather than their deeds. Other aliens with radical notions were deported by the thousand. History books were revised to suit the D.A.R. and the American Legion, and so on. Such hysteria was summarized in an astonishing statement by Walter H. Page, American ambassador to Great Britain: "We Americans have got to . . . hang our Irish agitators," Page ranted, "and shoot our hyphenates and bring up our children with reverence for English history and in the awe of English literature."

All in all, the revolt of the American conscience was over. The crusading spirit of Wilson's administration had dissolved in cynicism and disillusionment. Looking back, it seemed that the Great War had been a great mistake; it had apparently proved nothing and settled nothing. Almost precisely echoing the sentiments Henry James had expressed while the battles still raged (see page 236), in 1923 John Dos Passos wrote: "So was civilization nothing but a vast edifice of sham, and the war, instead of its crumbling, was its fullest and most ultimate expression." Dos Passos had served in the war, as had a number of other American writers, including Ernest Hemingway. "I was always embarrassed by the words sacred, glorious, and sacrifice and the expression in vain," Hemingway wrote in a similar vein in *A Farewell to Arms*. ". . . I had seen nothing sacred, and the things that were glorious had no glory and the sacrifices were like the stockyards at Chicago if nothing was done with the meat except to bury it."

A comparable note of disenchantment ran through much of the literature of the postwar period, not all of it stirred by thoughts of the war. Before the country dreamed of going to war, H. L. Mencken had begun his cynical attacks on the hypocrisy, provincialism, and the sham of American democratic society —against the vulgarities and follies of the "booboisie," as he termed the general run of his fellow citizens in high places or low. Mencken used the word "puritanism" almost as a swearword, an epithet to characterize all those inhibitions suffered by a generation seeking emancipation. He continued to voice his almost rabid iconoclasm through much of the twenties and beyond in the pages of *The American Mercury*, a periodical that he edited from 1924 to 1933, and in his books. The first issue of the *Mercury* announced, in an authentic Mencken manner, that "it will be an agreeable duty to track down some of the worst nonsense prevailing and to do execution upon it —not indignantly, of course, but nevertheless with a sufficient play of malice to give the business a Christian and philanthropic air." Today his boisterous parodies of life in America and his unremitting skepticism seem sophomoric, his wit shallow; but in their time they were a tonic for young authors in revolt against earlier generations and the delight of rebellious undergraduates aspiring to sophistication. (It must be added that his *The American Language*, with its supplements, was a work of serious scholarship that outdid the professors, whom he taunted for their academic pomposities, at their own game.)

During Prohibition thousands of illegal booze palaces sprang up all over America. Many were seedy; some were quite elegant, like the one depicted in Evolution of the Speakeasy *(above), a lithograph of 1929 by J. W. Golinkin. Another manifestation of the lawlessness and corruption of the era was the trial and electrocution of Nicola Sacco and Bartolomeo Vanzetti (portrayed in the Ben Shahn sketch below), who were convicted and sentenced on the basis of controversial evidence.*

In 1919 a handful of exuberant young literary wits began lunching together at New York's Algonquin Hotel, gathering at what came to be known as the Round Table. The Al Hirschfeld cartoon above depicts some of the habitués: at the table in the foreground (the Round Table sometimes overflowed to two or three tables) are pictured, clockwise from lower left: Robert Sherwood, Dorothy Parker, Robert Benchley, Alexander Woollcott, Heywood Broun, Marc Connelly, Franklin Pierce Adams, Edna Ferber, and George S. Kaufman; Algonquin host Frank Case is behind Connelly; the rear table is occupied by Alfred Lunt, his wife Lynn Fontanne, and Frank Crowninshield.

Wits and essayists of the time found a fresh outlet for their talents when, in 1925, Harold Ross founded the very durable *New Yorker* magazine—a periodical, as it was stated, intended for "caviar sophisticates," and "not for the old lady in Dubuque." That weekly's contributors included the most urbane, literate, and stylish writers of the twenties, most of whom continued to add distinction to its pages over the years to come. Much of the material there published over the names of E. B. White, James Thurber, Robert Benchley, Ring Lardner, Dorothy Parker, Alexander Woollcott, and others ultimately came out in book form. Such a galaxy of contemporary talents had not been brought together in an American periodical since the early years of the *Atlantic Monthly*.

In 1943, to celebrate the twentieth anniversary of the *Mercury*, that magazine published a reader consisting of selected articles that had appeared in its pages over the years. The place of honor was given to "The Man Who Knew Coolidge," a piece by Sinclair Lewis, which had first appeared in the issue of January, 1928. "Sinclair Lewis," it was explained, "during the twenties and thirties, said in lusty fiction what *The American Mercury* was saying in many of its articles and sketches." Lewis, indeed, spoke more truly and significantly for the twenties than did Mencken. Critics have called him the major American novelist of the decade, a claim underlined by the fact that at the close of 1930 he was awarded the Nobel Prize for distinction in world literature, the first American to be so honored.

Lewis came out of the Midwest (he was born in Sauk Center, Minnesota), "a gangling, pink-skinned, freckled, red-haired boy." He entered Yale and graduated from that university with the class of 1907. He spent the following dozen years in various activities—doing hack writing, traveling, filling some editorial jobs in New York, and publishing a few minor novels. (Mencken was one of his early supporters.) Then, in 1920, he produced his first important novel, *Main Street*, a book that was at once and widely recognized as a fictional document that superbly fit the critical mood of the time. With it Lewis struck what seemed to be his first mortal blow at the smug and narrow conceits of the American middle class—and in its contented prosperity the middle class had become broadly representative of the nation at large.

320

Although the scene of *Main Street* was placed in a town in Minnesota Lewis called Gopher Prairie, only minor qualifications were required to make his message true of any American community from Los Angeles to New York. "This is America," Lewis wrote with rather heavy irony, "... Main Street is the continuation of Main Streets everywhere. . . . Main Street is the climax of civilization. That this Ford car might stand in front of the Bon Ton Store, Hannibal invaded Rome and Erasmus wrote in Oxford cloisters." American novels had been "debunking" history for about forty years, but no earlier novel had so shattered the myth of the friendly village or the pretenses of middle-class complacency. Five years earlier, in his *Spoon River Anthology*, Edgar Lee Masters had given voice to the hidden faults that underlaid the structure of American life; but he spoke reflectively, through spooks resurrected from a local graveyard and from the village past. Lewis spoke of the immediate, living reality in accents utterly faithful to contemporary, common speech. For all his satire and caricature, thanks to his mimetic gifts Lewis provided an uncannily accurate reproduction of the surface reality of life as importantly as he offered any criticism or revelation. Carl Van Doren wrote him, quoting a colleague at Columbia University as saying, "your book is the most truthful novel ever written." In some ways Lewis' novels were closer to first-rate journalism than to creative writing.

Main Street stirred America from one coast to the other, and even attracted attention overseas. Lewis received letters of appreciation and congratulation from such diverse writers as H. G. Wells and John Galsworthy in England, and in America from the young F. Scott Fitzgerald (whose popular novel *This Side of Paradise* was published the same year) and Annie Oakley (the almost legendary sharpshooter who had some years earlier toured the vaudeville circuit with Buffalo Bill). More surprisingly, the public at large, with an invincible curiosity concerning its own image, responded to the book with such interest that the printers could not keep up with the orders. In the first six months of 1921, 180,000 copies were sold—and the total finally went into the millions. It was the most sensational publishing event of the century up to that point.

The reasons for the success of *Main Street* were not—or do not now seem to be—obscure. By 1920 the American village had become something of a backwater in the national economy, and its traditional life and moral attitudes had become fixed in obsolescent patterns. Although in 1900 Woodrow Wilson had pronounced that "the history of a nation is only the history of its villages written large," for decades thousands of enterprising young people had been fleeing the countryside to find new lives in the large cities. The war had provided a jolt that made this all too obvious. "How're you going to keep them down on the farm after they've seen *Paree*," a popular wartime lyric queried. For a very large audience of those who had not escaped the frustrations and limitations of small-town life, as well as for those who had only recently been freed from that restricted world, *Main Street* defined the situation in relentless detail.

The plot of *Main Street* centers around Carol Milford, a village girl who has gone to college, acquiring a smattering of learning, and who then marries the local doctor in Gopher Prairie. With her limited cultural resources she attempts to reform the aesthetics and ethics of the village—bravely, patheti-

Sinclair Lewis, caricatured above, is shown taking off from "Main Street" U.S.A. in a Model T Ford in a photograph of 1916, below.

BROWN BROTHERS

321

cally, and unsuccessfully. An example of her plight is the meeting of Thana-topsis, the local women's study club:

> Mrs. Dawson opened the meeting by sighing, "I'm sure I'm glad to see you all here today, and I understand that the ladies have prepared a number of very interesting papers, this is such an interesting subject, the poets, they have been an inspiration for higher thought, in fact wasn't it Reverend Benlick who said that some of the poets have been as much an inspiration as a good many of the ministers, and so we shall be glad to hear—"
>
> The poor lady smiled neuralgically, panted with fright, scrabbled about the small oak table to find her eye-glasses, and continued, "We will first have the pleasure of hearing Mrs. Jenson on the subject 'Shakespeare and Milton'."
>
> Mrs. Ole Jenson said that Shakespeare was born in 1564 and died in 1616. He lived in London, England, and in Stratford-on-Avon, which many American tourists loved to visit, a lovely town with many curios and old houses well worth examination. Many people believed that Shakespeare was the greatest playwright who ever lived, also a fine poet. Not much was known about his life, but after all that did not really make so much difference, because they loved to read his numerous plays, several of the best known of which she would now criticize.
>
> Perhaps the best known of his plays was "The Merchant of Venice," having a beautiful love story and a fine appreciation of a woman's brains, which a woman's club, even those who did not care to commit themselves on the question of suffrage, ought to appreciate. (Laughter.) Mrs. Jenson was sure that she, for one, would love to be like Portia. The play was about a Jew named Shylock, and he didn't want his daughter to marry a Venice gentleman named Antonio——

Lewis continued his satires in a succession of other novels. In 1922 he published *Babbitt*, the story of a little man who is trapped by the worship of success and by the materialism of the city world about him, and who in the end becomes a pathetic victim of his shallow illusions. (As one indication of the book's impact, its title added a new word to the American language: "Babbitt" has become a term of disparagement for a narrow-minded, self-centered individual.) One after another Lewis castigated separate elements of contemporary society: in *Arrowsmith* (1925) it is the medical profession; in *Elmer Gantry* (1927) the clergy; in *It Can't Happen Here* (1935) the political world; and so on. After these books appeared, it was impossible to consider the American scene and the American character as these had earlier been viewed.

In his Nobel Prize acceptance speech at Stockholm, Lewis announced that American literature had come of age. It is true that in the period between the two world wars American literature assumed a new importance in the eyes of the world; it was a renascence of sorts, studded with a variety of fresh talent. As Lewis spoke, most of the modern American books he mentioned were available to his audience in all European languages. Many of the older writers, men and women who had in their different ways led revolts before the war, were still actively writing—and writing better, for the most part, in their later maturity. Theodore Dreiser's *American Tragedy* appeared in 1925 and became one of the literary landmarks of the decade. Ellen Glasgow's *Barren Ground* and Willa Cather's *The Professor's House*, both representative of the best work of these now middle-aged women, were published that same year. Robert Frost, Edwin Arlington Robinson, and Amy Lowell were winning Pulitzer prizes with their poems. As Robert E. Spiller has observed, this was a crossroad in time at which two generations met.

William Dean Howells died the year that *Main Street* was published. The era Howells had represented with such authority was gone beyond recall, the realism he had introduced so earnestly and with such telling effect had been replaced by the newer realism of Lewis and his contemporaries: a realism less concerned with great social causes than with the freedom of the average individual to make his own choices in life in his quest of fulfillment—a quest that might lead in many experimental directions.

Sherwood Anderson, still another Midwesterner, was Lewis' exact contemporary. Both wrote principally of small-town people; but here the similarity between the two ends. Anderson had practically no education. His family was "a wandering, gypsy sort of tribe"; when he grew up he served in the Spanish-American War; and he returned to Ohio to marry (for the first of four times) and to become a successful paint manufacturer. Then, at the age of thirty-six, one day, in the very middle of a sentence he was dictating, he walked out of his factory, quit his family, and went to Chicago to become a writer. After some years of discouragement, he made a reputation with *Winesburg, Ohio*, a collection of short stories published in 1919. He was then fifty-seven.

Lewis candidly pictured life as he observed its patterns, transcribing sights and sounds with mirrorlike fidelity. Anderson, however, puzzled over life, looking into the concealed depths of his characters for the emotional and spiritual strivings that he felt must lie suppressed beneath the dull and inarticulate surface of their lives. "I would like to write a book of the life of the mind and of the imagination," he wrote in his memoirs. "Facts elude me. I cannot remember dates. When I deal in facts, at once I begin to lie. I can't help it." He deplored the corrupting influence of the machine as it ordered life, thwarting the primal forces in man's nature.

Anderson was among the first American writers to bring to the novel some awareness of the disturbing influence of the subconscious, with the sexual drive as a clear example. His admission that sex played a vital role in life seemed a bold advance in literature to many of his countrymen. It was a thought alien to Howells' realism. Someone once remarked that a visitor from Mars would learn less about life from Ralph Waldo Emerson than from Italian opera, for the opera at least suggested there were two sexes. In Anderson's stories that fact is clearly established. It was one of his contributions to the new realism.

In 1921 Anderson visited Gertrude Stein in Paris and became her firm friend. He was intrigued by her experiments in "separating words from sense." After reading her book *Tender Buttons*, published in 1914, he recalled: "It was a wonderful medley of words. Words seemed to glance in a new light, to stand away from one another, play games together, roll and tumble about, laugh at me from the page." Stein's message was important, he

Sherwood Anderson, portrayed in the photograph above, experienced life from various viewpoints, including that of race-track enthusiast, factory worker, soldier, house painter, and salesman, before becoming president of a successful paint company and a family man—a role he abruptly gave up to pursue a writing career. Anderson called his literary theme the "starved side of small town life"; his characters are the misfits and the "little people."

thought, "for the artist who happens to work with words as his material"; but he was shrewd enough to realize that she failed to communicate. Anderson was after the truth of things—and telling or writing the truth is a very complicated business. In the preface to *Winesburg, Ohio* he wrote a little story about an old man writing what he called "The Book of the Grotesque":

> That in the beginning when the world was young there were a great many thoughts but no such thing as a truth. Man made the truths himself and each truth was a composite of a great many vague thoughts. All about in the world were truths and they were all beautiful.
>
> The old man listed hundreds of the truths in his book. I will not try to tell you all of them. There was the truth of virginity and the truth of passion, the truth of wealth and of poverty, of thrift and of profligacy, of carelessness and abandon. Hundreds and hundreds were the truths and they were all beautiful.
>
> And then the people came along. Each as he appeared snatched up one of the truths and some who were quite strong snatched up a dozen of them.
>
> It was the truths that made the people grotesques. The old man had quite an elaborate theory concerning the matter. It was his notion that the moment one of the people took one of the truths to himself, called it his truth, and tried to live his life by it, he became a grotesque and the truth he embraced became a falsehood.

In sum, Anderson was a visionary in search of his own self, which he never quite discovered. Gertrude Stein proclaimed him one of the few American authors who could write acceptable sentences; but such sentences as occurred in his writing did not add up to the accomplishment he dreamed of. "Having made a few bicycles in factories," he wrote of his own life, "having written some thousands of rather senseless advertisements, having rubbed affectionately the legs of a few race horses, having tried blunderingly to love a few women and having written a few novels that did not satisfy," he retired to Virginia and became editor of two newspapers, one Republican and one Democratic. He continued to produce novels, but he never escaped from the traps he had set for his characters and for himself.

Anderson was only one of a number of aspiring American writers who went to school, so to speak, to Gertrude Stein in her Paris salon after the First World War. That "stolid and apparently sexless" maiden lady, "who looked and walked like a corpulent monk," as Van Wyck Brooks described her, had begun to convince herself that her work was "really the beginning of modern writing"—that her mission was to move writing out of the nineteenth century into the twentieth, as her close friends Picasso, Matisse, and Braque were converting art into fresh and distinctive idioms. (Miss Stein faithfully read the Paris *Herald-Tribune*, rather than French newspapers, and gave young Picasso a taste for the Katzenjammer Kids.)

Born to wealth, Gertrude Stein went to Radcliffe College, where she was exposed to the brilliant teaching of that eloquent psychologist William James. For a while thereafter she studied the anatomy of the brain at Johns Hopkins University in Baltimore, and as part of her medical routine, took her turn delivering babies. In 1902 she removed to Paris, where she lived the remainder of her life. Her experiments in writing were radically innovative, as became apparent in 1909 with her first published book, *Three Lives*, and more emphatically so in the other works she issued over the decades to come. Her sentences are made to flicker along like the frames of a moving picture, each partly repetitive statement making a limited advance in the development of her theme until the whole presents a continuous series of instantaneous images.

Unfortunately, looking at each individual frame of a motion picture would be a tiresome process, and this is what Gertrude Stein so often tries to make her readers do with her images. On the whole, she is concerned with the process of writing at the expense of the product; and she can be repetitious, boring, and obscure as a result. Nouns are names, she pronounced, and "things once they are named the name does not go on doing anything to them and so why write in nouns." Verbs are what count in a prose sentence. Punctuation gets in the way of a sentence and can be eliminated. "If writing should go on what had colons and semicolons to do with it," she asked—without a question mark. Names, however, are acceptable in verse, for "you can love a name and if you love a name then saying that name any number of times makes you love it more"—and poetry is "really loving the name of anything." So, she wrote, "When I said, A rose is a rose is a rose, and then later made that into a ring, I made poetry and what did I do I caressed completely caressed and addressed a noun." In any case, single words must be liberated from formal contexts and from the rules of grammar and syntax so that they may serve as independent plastic agents of direct expression.

Although she succeeded all too often in baffling some of her audience, her technical innovations startled others into a new awareness of the hidden riches of language. Her massive self-confidence in her technical developments, her sympathetic understanding of the writer's problems, and her critical sense were all sources of guidance and inspiration to many younger American authors, including F. Scott Fitzgerald, Ernest Hemingway, Eugene O'Neill, and as already remarked, Sherwood Anderson. Along with Mark Twain, she was a major formative influence upon modern American prose. She was a trailblazer with her own work. "Sure, she said, as Pablo [Picasso] once remarked, when you make a thing, it is so complicated making it that it is bound to be ugly, but those that do it after you they don't have to worry about making it and they can make it pretty, and so everybody can like it when the others make it."

During World War I Gertrude Stein was unabashedly sentimental over the American doughboys who came to France so cheerfully determined, for the most part, to get the bloody business "over there" done with, come what might. In 1917 there happened to be a surprising number of young writers still in American colleges or recently graduated—at just the age for active service. Some enlisted in the English, French, or Canadian armies before America's entry into the war; some enlisted when the United States entered the struggle. Very few of them waited to be drafted. They all were eager for experience and quick to write about it. Some even entertained the prospect of death on the battlefield as a romantic experience to be faced with spirit. As Malcolm Cowley has written, the most popular American poem of the war was

TEXT CONTINUES PAGE 328

The formidable and legendary Gertrude Stein was aptly eulogized by the American composer and critic Virgil Thomson: "To have become a Founding Father of her century is her own reward for having long ago, and completely, dominated her language."

325

Portrait by Picasso, 1905–06

Portrait by William Cotton

"Gertrude Stein," wrote Carl Van Vechten, "rings bells, loves baskets, and wears handsome waistcoats. . . . In the matter of fans you can only compare her with a motion picture star in Hollywood and three generations of young writers have sat at her feet. . . ." She was an American of Paris, a collector of modern art, a writer of experimental prose, and a legend in her own time. After 1903 her salon at 27 rue de Fleurus, Paris, was a gathering place for Picasso, Matisse, Cézanne, Braque, and other artists. Later she became dean of the group of disaffected writers who were in Paris waiting out America's cultural drought. Ernest Hemingway, a member of this lost generation, loved to visit Miss Stein in her big studio, filled with great paintings. "It was," he recounts in *A Moveable Feast,* "like one of the best rooms in the finest museum except there was a big fireplace and it was warm and comfortable and they gave you good things to eat and tea. . . ."

THE MANY FACES
OF
GERTRUDE STEIN

Portrait by Tal Coat

Stein posing for Jo Davidson; opposite, sketch by Carl Erickson

A collection of photographs, above, portrays members of the lost generation who, out of their disenchantment with the postwar world (all were World War I veterans), created a new literary style. Clockwise, from lower left: Ernest Hemingway as a wounded hero in Milan, 1918; E. E. Cummings as a Harvard senior, 1915; Archibald MacLeish at Yale, 1914; Alan Seeger in the French foreign legion, 1916; John Dos Passos in the 1920's; F. Scott Fitzgerald in officer's training at Fort Leavenworth; and William Faulkner in his RCAF uniform after the war.

"I Have a Rendezvous with Death," in which the author "looks forward to being killed as if he were planning an assignation with a strange new mistress." The poet, Alan Seeger, a young Harvard graduate, enlisted early in the war in the Foreign Legion, a particularly hazardous branch of the French army, and kept his own tragic rendezvous on July 4, 1916.

Malcolm Cowley himself was one of those young men, as were F. Scott Fitzgerald, Ernest Hemingway, E. E. Cummings, Archibald MacLeish, William Faulkner, and John Dos Passos, among others—all of whom would add significantly to the American literary tradition in the decades after the peace. These were highly articulate representatives of what Gertrude Stein, in a conversation with Ernest Hemingway, named the "lost generation"— the intellectuals and aesthetes who survived the slaughter of the war, who were in the end disillusioned by the needlessness of that butchery and by the disheartening, crass politics of the peacemakers, and who then rebelled against the authority of those older men ("swagbellied old fogies," Dos Passos called them) who had ordered such catastrophes. The ideals and values that had led them so willingly into uniform were replaced by a sort of despair or by a cynical hedonism. Many of these men had lived more intensely during their brief military experience than they would ever live again, and they groped for some peacetime equivalent of that excitement which would recapture for them its heroics and its pathos. Some sought to expatriate themselves for a time from America, where postwar life was not especially edifying. And those who chose to do so found Gertrude Stein in Paris, "benign, omniscient, and pleasantly American," as one historian has described her. "America is my country," she explained, "and Paris is my home town." In those words was the welcome suggestion that Americans might try, at least, to have the best of both worlds.

Among those young American authors who after the war "leapt released, on Paris," as Ford Madox Ford said, were F. Scott Fitzgerald and Ernest Hemingway. Fitzgerald was already a celebrity following the publication of his early novels, and Gertrude Stein, whose salon he frequented, reportedly said that he had more talent than all the rest of the lost generation put together. Like Sherwood Anderson and Sinclair Lewis, Fitzgerald came out of the Midwest. He entered Princeton, where he strove to be a social, athletic, and intellectual success among his well-to-do Eastern classmates. When the war came he enlisted and, as soon as he had donned his lieutenant's uniform, convinced himself that he was marked for death on the battlefield, like Seeger and others of the young volunteers. On weekends while he was in training camp he worked feverishly on his first novel, *This Side of Paradise*. "I was certain," he recalled, "that all the young people were going to be killed in the war, and I wanted to put on paper a record of the strange life they had lived in their time." Whatever wounds he suffered were imaginary, for he had just marched aboard a transport that would take him to the front when he was marched off again—Germany had called for an armistice. He was deprived of the climactic adventure he had envisioned, and he resented not having had to face the dangers or the glory of the trenches.

However, there were other roads to glory, and these he had already started to explore in *This Side of Paradise*. That book was a largely autobiographical account of his years at Princeton, during which Fitzgerald had begun his in-

A cartoon by Gene Markey, above, caricatures F. Scott Fitzgerald, enfant terrible of and spokesman for the jazz age. A photograph of 1925, left, shows Scott, his wife Zelda (who according to Scott started the flapper movement in America), and daughter Frances (Scottie) celebrating Christmas with a joyous dance in their elegantly appointed Paris apartment.

329

quiry into the world and the ways of the very rich. The very rich "are different from you and me. They possess and enjoy early, and it does something to them, makes them soft where we are hard, and cynical where we are trustful, in a way that, unless you were born rich, it is very difficult to understand. They think, deep in their hearts, that they are better than we are because we had to discover the compensations and refuges of life for ourselves. . . . They are different." The fact that the aristocrats of wealth (the nearest thing to a true aristocracy in America) could and did lead spurious and futile lives did not diminish Fitzgerald's fascinated interest in them. As money rolled in from his early books and stories, he himself took to spendthrift and dissolute ways in his quest of new excitements. He and his wife Zelda threw themselves into "the greatest, gaudiest spree in history." As he spent his money in Paris or on the Riviera, carousing and generally having "fun," Fitzgerald recalled: "I had everything I wanted and knew I would never be so happy again." He never was.

To be young, handsome, and socially privileged mattered desperately. In his own relatively brief life Fitzgerald acted out the legend of the lost generation to perfection, and tragically. He spoke for "all the sad young men" of his time—the restive, disillusioned youths who flouted the ancient traditions and taboos cherished by their elders. To grow old was not inevitable, it was unthinkable to these flappers and cake eaters of the jazz age. To burn a candle at both ends, as Edna St. Vincent Millay wrote from Greenwich Village in her widely quoted quatrain, gave a lovely light. No less than in the 1960's, there was an abysmal generation gap in the 1920's.

Compared to his later work, *This Side of Paradise* and his other early stories are immature productions (*Flappers and Philosophers, Tales of the Jazz Age, The Beautiful and the Damned*). But Fitzgerald's talent was indisputable, and evident even here. With *The Great Gatsby*, published in 1925, he created a brilliant short novel, a story about the love and death of an immensely wealthy bootlegger who was murdered by a man who then committed suicide, as told by a curious young cousin who was a spectator of those tragic developments of the Prohibition era.

John Held's cartoon of 1926 emphasizes the ever-ready hip flask, which made its appearance during the Prohibition, when flappers frequented speakeasies and attended cocktail parties, danced the Charleston, and drank hooch.

330

Fitzgerald was to write more short stories and such good novels as *Tender is the Night*, but his vogue was already passing in the 1930's. The reviewers wrote him off as a novelist whose talent had dried up. This was less true than that the times were changing; the dark days of the Great Depression had succeeded the frivolous, party days of the twenties. Poor and in debt, with Zelda now confined in an asylum, Fitzgerald drifted to Hollywood to write scenarios for a living. Then, in 1936, he spent some time in a Southern nursing home. Several times he attempted unsuccessfully to take his life, but in 1940 he died of a heart attack. He was aware that he had misused his exceptional gifts as a writer. "I had been only a mediocre caretaker . . . of my talent," he reflected. "His talent was as natural as the pattern that was made by the dust on a butterfly's wings," Ernest Hemingway recalled. "At one time he understood it no more than the butterfly did and he did not know when it was brushed or marred. Later he became conscious of his damaged wings and of their construction and he learned to think and could not fly any more because the love of flight was gone and he could only remember when it had been effortless." But that his technical gift had not diminished is clear from his unfinished manuscript for *The Last Tycoon*, which was published posthumously and which might have been his best work.

Back in his Paris days Fitzgerald had written to Maxwell Perkins, his editor at Scribner's: ". . . This is to tell you about a young man named Ernest Hemingway, who lives in Paris (an American), writes for the *Transatlantic Review* and has a brilliant future. Ezra Pound published a collection of his short pieces in Paris, at some place like the Egotist Press. I haven't it here now but it's remarkable and I'd look him up right away. He's the real thing. . . ."

Perkins did look up Hemingway, and the result was a succession of short stories and novels that made history. Those early novels and stories had an enormous influence on other writers, to the point where the innumerable imitations of Hemingway almost spoil our taste for the real thing. More than that, his fiction shaped the experience and the sensibility of an entire reading generation. Hemingway's expressed intention "to put down what really happened in action . . . the sequence of motion and fact which made the emotion" in concrete words became a distinguishing feature of the dawning literary age. Here was a kind of prose fiction that had not been seen before in America, or, for that matter, anywhere else.

Hemingway was still another Midwesterner. As a youth he had fished the streams and hunted in the woods of northern Michigan with his sportsman-physician father. While still in his teens he worked as a cub reporter on the Kansas City *Star* until he left for the war to join the Red Cross ambulance corps serving on the Italian front. Within three months he was badly wounded and hospitalized before returning home. The enduring shock of that wound can be discerned in much of his writing; it became a central symbol in his fiction, although it is never specifically mentioned. The impact of the experience was no doubt intensified by other incidents in his life. Hemingway was probably the most accident-prone literary celebrity in American history. Glass skylights crashed on his head; small boys stuck fingers into his eyes; sharp branches tore jagged wounds in his face; in November, 1930, he drove himself and John Dos Passos off a Montana road into a ditch, and he emerged with a badly broken arm; and so on, until his death by suicide.

When Edna St. Vincent Millay, above, published her second volume of verse, A Few Figs from Thistles *(1920), she became a symbol of social upheaval. The collection includes the oft-quoted quatrain beginning "My candle burns at both ends," about which critic Vincent Sheean has written: "Scott Fitzgerald's stories bestowed a self-consciousness upon the young people of the 1920's . . . but Edna in that one quatrain supplied them with a* point d'appui, *an aesthetic justification for kicking over the traces. . . ."*

Sherwood Anderson's letter, reproduced at right, in which he introduces Ernest Hemingway to the American bookseller Sylvia Beach, helped launch Hemingway on his expatriate life. Miss Beach's Paris shop, Shakespeare & Co., served the lost generation as bookstore and library; it even became a publishing house when no publisher could be found for James Joyce's Ulysses. *Sylvia Beach's memoirs,* Shakespeare and Company *(1959), provide a vivid record of Paris in the 1920's.*

For a year or so, while he was gainfully employed as a reporter and a writer of advertising copy, he tried his hand at poetry and fiction, encouraged by Sherwood Anderson. Then, in 1921, he married and left for Paris, provided by Anderson with a letter to Gertrude Stein. As he came to know her, Hemingway thought Stein "got to look like a Roman emperor and that was fine if you liked your women to look like Roman emperors. But Picasso painted her, and I could remember her when she looked like a woman from Friuli [in northeastern Italy]." He also knew F. Scott Fitzgerald, Ezra Pound, James Joyce, and other members of the British and American avant garde who frequented the cafés and bistros of Paris in the twenties—and who also worked in that city, to be sure.

In Paris—that "moveable feast," as he later called the years he lived there —Hemingway began to collect the impressions that would become a permanent part of American literature as he sifted them into his novels and his short stories. Gertrude Stein and Ezra Pound blue-penciled his first efforts, paring away his adjectives and his "literary" redundancies and helping him to arrive at the hard style, the terse description, and the spare dialogue that became basic ingredients of his best and most influential work; as when he described a wounded hero returning from the front in an ambulance beneath the stretcher of a dying soldier whose blood dripped down on him—"The drops fell very slowly, as they fall from an icicle after the sun has gone." Here, as in all Hemingway's writing, emotion is held at a distance; only the bare happening is recorded, to affect the reader as it may.

Early in 1924 a small volume of fifteen short stories by Hemingway, entitled *in our time*, was issued in Paris as a limited edition. With this, his writing began to attract attention. (It was the book Fitzgerald had mentioned to Perkins.) The eminent American critic Edmund Wilson admiringly called these short pieces "Mr. Hemingway's dry-points." In one of the first issues of *The American Mercury* Mencken at least noticed the appearance of the stories, although with some detachment. Here was, he reported, "the sort of brave, bold stuff that all atheistic young newspaper reporters write. Jesus Christ in lower case. A hanging, a carnal love, and disembowellings. Here it is, set forth solemnly on Rives handmade paper, in an edition limited to 170 copies, and with the imprimatur of Ezra Pound." (The following year the book was published, with additions, as *In Our Time* in the United States.) With the appearance of the novel *The Sun Also Rises* in 1926, and of *A Farewell to Arms* in 1929, Hemingway was generally accepted as a leading interpreter of that age of disillusion. His key characters were principally men who put their faith only in violence, sexual passion, and the ritual of such sports as bullfighting —and in food and drink, certainly. Most of them did, indeed, drink too much. But the war had taught them to anticipate doom with such composure as they could contrive. They had flirted with death and felt its presence so intimately that afterward nothing else seemed quite so real and imminent, so much to be taken for granted. In *A Farewell to Arms* Hemingway describes a pile of corpses he viewed after an Italian counterattack almost as dispassionately as if he were reading from a laboratory report:

> Until the dead are buried they change somewhat in appearance each day. The color change in Caucasian races is from white to yellow, to yellow-green, to black. If left long enough in the heat the flesh comes to resemble coal-tar, especially where it has been broken or torn, and it has quite a visible tarlike iridescence. The dead grow larger each day until sometimes they become quite too big for their uniforms, filling these until they seem blown tight enough to burst. The individual members may increase in girth to an unbelievable extent and faces fill as taut and globular as balloons.

When it was published in 1929, *A Farewell to Arms* immediately jumped to the head of the best-seller lists. More than one eminent reviewer felt obliged to refer to it as a masterpiece. To many readers the story seemed a tragedy of broken hopes, a farewell to almost everything. It was built on the theme of universal loneliness in the midst of war, and it left the impression of overwhelming emotion severely controlled, conveyed with the fewest possible words. That was typical of the best of Hemingway's writing. His style is stripped clean for action and terse dialogue (he had a keen ear for characteristic patterns of speech), leaving everything else to implication.

He was now only thirty years old. He would continue to write and publish for another thirty years, but more than half of his best work was already done. He rested from his storytelling for a while after the publication of *A Farewell to Arms*. The royalties he earned only increased the affluence he was enjoying from his second marriage to a relatively wealthy young woman who had purposefully pursued him about Europe. (Like Anderson, he married four times before retiring from the lists.) He could now more easily afford to live just such a life as he provided for his fictional heroes. The typical Hemingway hero is a virile, sophisticated world traveler, an accomplished sportsman who courts danger with calm self-assurance and pursues beautiful women with zest. Good food, fine wine, and an abundance of liquor are his fare. Like the bullfighters Hemingway admired so much, the hero lives his life "all the way up." So Hemingway did, with energy to spare, for the next twenty years. Fixed in the public eye, he became his own hero. There had never before been a celebrated American author whose extraliterary exploits were so rich in adventure.

However, he continued to write (and to remarry). He was among the most ardent *aficionados* of bullfighting. He saw in the ritual of the bullring a kind of microcosm of life and death, and in 1932 he published *Death in the Afternoon*, dealing with this subject. In other books and stories, densely packed with action, he wrote of the innumerable wild beasts he had slain on safari in Africa or in the Rockies, and he used his deep-sea fishing exploits off the coasts of Florida and Cuba to color other tales of adventure. Several of such stories were made into moving pictures. But he was more and more yielding to self-indulgence and self-imitation.

Nevertheless, in 1940, Hemingway published *For Whom the Bell Tolls*, his longest and most ambitious novel—and his most popular if not his best work. (Paramount Pictures bought the story for $150,000 as a vehicle for Ingrid Bergman and Gary Cooper.) He had participated in the Spanish Civil War as a press correspondent, and he used his experiences in that service to weave a romance of love and death in the land he had learned to love and whose agony was for him a personal wound. He wrote with unwonted compassion of the courage and martyrdom of the Spanish people, through which he came to terms with his own ideal as he stood with them shoulder to shoulder. His title, of course, came from the sermon of John Donne: "No man is an Ilande, intire of it selfe. . . . every man is a peece of the Continent, a part of the maine . . . ; any man's death diminishes me, because I am involved in Mankinde; And therefore never send to know for whom the bell tolls; It tolls for thee."

With this work Hemingway returned to a common humanity, to a reconsideration of man and society. For most of the next decade he produced nothing more. With his third wife, early in 1941, he went to the Orient to cover the conflict between the Chinese and Japanese. In a mood of depression he wrote Maxwell Perkins that his fellow writers were now "dying like flies": Thomas Wolfe in 1938; Ford Madox Ford in 1939; F. Scott Fitzgerald in 1940; Sherwood Anderson and Virginia Woolf in 1941. Then he went off to London as a war correspondent, still acting out the legend that he had himself so largely created. Gray-haired and bearded, he was known to his familiars as Papa Hemingway or, as he sometimes insisted with crude wit, "Old Ernie Hemorrhoid, the poor man's Ernie Pyle."

However, Hemingway joined the American forces that had invaded Europe, and although he fearlessly exposed himself to enemy gunfire, he was not again wounded. He was immensely popular with officers and enlisted men alike, and with members of the French resistance. Their story of his "assault" on Paris—roaring in ahead of the French and American troops in a jeep to "liberate" the liquor stores of the Ritz Hotel, his old hangout of the 1920's —became one of the great tales of the war, still told by old-time attendants at the Ritz.

He resumed writing, with variable results, until 1952, when he produced a long short story, *The Old Man and the Sea*, that won wide acclaim and persuaded the Pulitzer Prize committee to award him the prize for fiction. Two years later he won the Nobel Prize for literature. The same year, 1954, on another African safari he was again badly injured, this time in an airplane accident. His adventurous life was running out, and, ill and discouraged, he wrote little more. He finished a short book, *A Moveable Feast*, which recounted in typical Hemingway prose his early days in Paris, with sketches of Gertrude Stein, Fitzgerald, Pound, and his other friends of those years—remembrances that are less than charitable. His condescension, especially toward Fitzgerald, betrayed the arrogance with which he now bolstered his ego; it was unbecoming in a man of such indisputable accomplishment. (The little volume was published posthumously.) But his powers were waning with his health. On Sunday morning, July 2, 1961, he arose before dawn, picked up a double-barreled shotgun and blew off the top of his head. The novelist John O'Hara once termed Hemingway the greatest writer since Shakespeare. That amazing pronouncement may indicate the impact of Hemingway's work on some of his contemporaries, but it is hardly a lasting judgment of his talent. He was indeed, as Alfred Kazin has remarked, "the bronze god of the whole contemporary literary experience in America . . . the whole lost generation conception of art and society reached its climax in him . . . [a] conception that was the brilliant and narrow concentration of the individualism and alienation from society felt by the artist in the twenties. . . ." But, as Kazin also observed, although Hemingway's view of life summed up the immediate postwar era, it did not reach toward the future as did that of some of his contemporaries. When Hemingway was writing his later books the lost generation was passing into history. With changing times new problems arose that overlaid memories of World War I and its immediate consequences. Other writers faced these different concerns with varying points of view, but generally with an eye to the large new issues that loomed on the American scene with the advent of the 1930's.

The prevailing temper of the twenties had not quite lasted out the decade. In 1929, with the thunderous crash of the stock market, the mood of the country changed quickly and radically. For another ten years, until preparations for war gave the nation another severe jolt of a different kind, America endured a period of economic depression that at first seemed unreal, then intolerable, and finally endless. These were also years of portentous developments abroad. The Japanese invaded Manchuria in 1931; Italians marched into

Ernest Hemingway, spokesman for the disillusioned lost generation, expressed in his prose "a robustly masculine temperament and . . . a mood issuing out of the war." Aside from writing, he cared most about action. The photographs, below, depict him in various activities: from left to right, they show the author-sportsman proudly holding a trout he caught in Sun Valley, Idaho, in 1939; on a hunting trip in 1934; as a correspondent in World War II; with a huge game fish.

BETTMANN ARCHIVES

BETTMANN ARCHIVES

BETTMANN ARCHIVES

BROWN BROTHERS

335

Ethiopia in 1935; Hitler entered the Rhineland in 1936; and also in 1936 civil war broke out in Spain. But the large majority of Americans, although they may have disapproved of those foreign depradations, felt that they could and should do nothing about the situation. The country was in an overwhelmingly isolationist mood, convinced that it could continue to exist safely behind a wall of neutrality. There were more immediate problems at home, grim enough in themselves, to be concerned about.

In spite of the Depression and the growing threat of war, the decade of the thirties was a rich period in the history of American letters—in poetry and the drama as well as in fiction and literary criticism. Among the writers of the older generation already discussed, Frost, Sandburg, Anderson, Robinson, and Lewis, among others still to be mentioned, were continuing to create works of undiminished quality for the most part. Other authors who had established their reputations in the 1920's, like Fitzgerald and Hemingway, also contributed to the steady flow of American literature. Younger authors emerged to describe the darkened image of America, to write of a new kind of malaise that was worse than that suffered by the lost generation.

But there was another side to the matter. Feeling the pinch of the Depression, expatriates returned home to find unexpected values in the American scene on which they had turned their backs so scornfully in the preceding decade. The dynamic spirit of the Roosevelt administration during the president's first two terms of office also stimulated fresh interest in the American heritage and the country's cultural background—an interest encouraged by the government-sponsored guide books in which such subjects were explored in intimate detail. America, it appeared, had an unsuspected wealth of folklore, tradition, and local history that could profitably be re-examined.

The name of John Dos Passos is associated with the thirties (as Fitzgerald's is with the twenties), although his first novel, *One Man's Initiation—1917*, appeared as early as 1920 (the same year as *This Side of Paradise* and *Main Street*), and although only with his fourth novel, *Manhattan Transfer*, published just ten years later, did his special abilities become widely recognized. Dos Passos, too, was born in the Midwest. His background and experience were rich in variety, and are worth reciting. His grandfather was a Portuguese immigrant; his father became a successful New York lawyer; his mother came from Virginia; and his birthplace was Chicago. He lived his early life in such diverse places as New York, Mexico, Belgium, England, Washington, D.C., and Virginia. As a youth he went to Choate School in Connecticut and then to Harvard. (In 1916 he graduated from Harvard *cum laude*, but he thought his studies there had been useless.) After that he went to Spain to study architecture, just before going to war. Like Hemingway, he joined an ambulance corps in Europe before America's entry into World War I, an experience that provided material for his first novel.

But Dos Passos' talents were of a different order from those of either Fitzgerald or Hemingway, as the direction of his interests was different. In his work the nihilism of the lost generation gradually gave way to a concerned inquiry into social problems. A tragic society rather than the tragic individual became the protagonist of his stories. His criticism of society at large appeared as early as 1922 in a series of essays on the art and culture of Spain. But it was

John Dos Passos, author of more than thirty books, is best known for his trilogy U.S.A., an angry examination of industrial America during the period from 1898 to 1929. Social historian Matthew Josephson, who knew Dos Passos in New York and Paris in the 1920's, remembered him as being "a tall young man with a round, thinly covered head and a near sighted gaze. In manner he was uncommonly gracious, with an air both shy and eager to please."

in the 1930's, with a trilogy of related novels entitled *U.S.A.* (1938)—*The 42nd Parallel* (1930); *1919* (1932); *The Big Money* (1936)—that he most exhaustively stated his message of social crisis. With these three books he attempted to cover the entire social history of the United States in the twentieth century up to and through most of the Depression years. One critic suggested that if only because of its ambitious scope, *U.S.A.* might be considered as close to the "great American novel" as anything yet seen. Certainly, nothing quite as ambitious had ever been attempted in American fiction. But it is a tract of the times more than it is a timeless testament. It is a very sad epic that concludes in a massive indictment of American society. In his panoramic view Dos Passos saw American life only in terms of futility and frustration, corruption, and defeat for the individual, beyond hope of redemption by the most radical measures.

Of all this, however, he wrote in a startlingly original manner that has been likened to a cinematic technique, giving his message an unexpected sharp edge. He gave a running account of current events in a series of "Newsreels," using newspaper headlines to call attention to the fragmentary episodes in his story. Throughout the book he interspersed biographies of leading figures of the times—J. P. Morgan, Henry Ford, Eugene V. Debs, and others. The stories of swarms of ordinary people leading overlapping or parallel lives were woven together as "novels." From still another point of view, in "The Camera Eye" he provided personal impressions of all that was happening.

This exceedingly complex structure he put together with vivid and realistic effect in syncopated prose that resembles unrhymed poetry. No excerpt can suggest the total plan or quality of these novels, but a brief passage from one of his biographies gives some indication of the pattern of his incisive writing:

> Debs was a railroad man, born in a weatherboarded shack at Terre Haute.
> He was one of ten children.
> His father had come to America in a sailingship in '49,
> an Alsatian from Colmar; not much of a money-maker, fond of music and reading,
> he gave his children a chance to finish public school and that was all he could do. . . .

❀ ❀ ❀ ❀

> He was a tall shambledfooted man, had a sort of gutsy rhetoric
> that set on fire railroad workers in their pineboarded halls
> made them want the world he wanted,
> a world brothers might own
> where everybody would split even:
> *I am not a labor leader. I don't want you to follow me or anyone else. If you are looking for a Moses to lead you out of the capitalist wilderness you will stay right where you are. I would not lead you into this promised land if I could, because if I could lead you in, someone else would lead you out.*

In its entirety *U.S.A.* is a remarkable achievement, a technical accomplishment of rare virtuosity. It has been called a national epic, "the first great national epic of its kind in the modern American novel," and "a triumph of

thing in life." Paul nodded. Then she couldn't see his face anymore. The train had gone into a tunnel.

NEWSREEL XXXIV

WHOLE WORLD IS SHORT OF PLATINUM

Il serait Criminel de Negliger Les Intérêts Français dans les Balkans

KILLS SELF IN CELL

the quotation of United Cigar Stores made this month of $167 per share means $501 per share for the old stock upon which present stockholders are receiving 27% per share as formerly held. Through peace and war it has maintained and increased its dividends

6 TRAPPED ON UPPER FLOOR

How are you goin' to keep 'em down on the farm After they've seen Paree

If Wall street needed the treaty, which means if the business interests of the country properly desired to know to what extent we are being committed in affairs which do not concern us, why should it take the trouble to corrupt the tagrag and bobtail which forms Mr. Wilson's following in Paris?

ALLIES URGE MAGYAR PEOPLE TO UPSET BELA KUN REGIME

11 WOMEN MISSING IN BLUEBEARD MYSTERY

Enfin La France Achète les stocks Américains

How are you goin' to keep 'em away from Broadway Jazzin' around Paintin' the town

334

Dos Passos' U.S.A. comprises The 42nd Parallel *(1930),* 1919 *(1932), and* The Big Money *(1936). Interspersed throughout the trilogy are biographical sketches; impressionistic "Camera Eye" sections; and newspaper montages, or "Newsreels," in which Dos Passos attempted to report on current events and the temper of the times. The "headlines" reproduced above are from* 1919.

style." There are no happy people in it, but that stemmed in good part from the nature of the times. It did, once and for all, close the story of the lost generation and its private agonies. Later in his life Dos Passos' mood changed, and he rose to defend aspects of society that he had once so bitterly condemned; but he is best known for his earlier works.

William Faulkner, Dos Passos' junior by one year, wrote an American saga of an entirely different sort. In a cycle of novels and stories, many of the best of them written in the 1930's, he created a saga of the Deep South, which he found to be a world in itself—a stage large enough for the performance of human tragedy and human comedy in their most extravagant and elementary forms. Unlike Dos Passos, Faulkner wrote not in terms of recorded incidents and identifiable individuals but out of a wealth of imagination that was fed by long and intimate association with the region, its traditions, and its people. He wrote legends, not history.

Faulkner grew up in Oxford, Mississippi, and spent most of his life in that area. (For a short while he wrote scripts in Hollywood.) His great-grandfather, a Mississippi army officer, lawyer, railroad builder, and sometime author, was the prototype of one of the prominent characters in his fiction (Colonel Sartoris). With the outbreak of World War I, Faulkner joined the British Royal Air Force in Canada (at five feet five inches he was too small to qualify for the United States Army); but, like Fitzgerald, he never saw service beyond training. After several years of drifting in Europe and America, he settled back in Mississippi, and in 1929, with the publication of *Sartoris*, he produced the first novel in his long cycle.

For this series of more than sixteen novels (in addition to a number of shorter stories), written over a period of thirty-odd years, Faulkner created a long list of characters of every social stripe, from faded gentry and aggressive businessmen to humble Negroes and degenerate whites. He carried the story of their intermingling lives from early encounters with the Indians to his own day. As a background he invented a county in northern Mississippi, Yoknapatawpha County, which became, for his purposes, a sort of mythical land, but one that was complete in virtually every living detail. To clarify his made-up geography, for one of his books Faulkner supplied a fold-out map, here illustrated.

Six months after *Sartoris* appeared, Faulkner published *The Sound and the Fury*, a very angry book and one of the best in the series. *Sanctuary*, his most violent and most popular book came out in 1931; *Light in August*, another of his excellent works, in 1932; *Absalom, Absalom!* in 1936; *The Hamlet* in 1940; *Intruder in the Dust* in 1948; and so on. As his books multiplied, Faulkner's story of Yoknapatawpha came to seem like a legend of the entire Deep South. It is not a pretty legend. The good characters along with the bad all seem defeated by the circumstances of their lives, by the dead weight of a past that implacably dictates the present with its moral confusion and social decay —and all submit to their fate. That submissiveness, or passivity, is curiously combined with extremes of violence—rape, murder, and arson, along with incest, prostitution, and degeneracy. Faulkner was early criticized for the morbid and degenerate strains in his fiction. But it is more just to observe that, like Hawthorne, with whom he has often been compared, he probes the tragic

William Faulkner, "sole owner and proprietor" of the mythic Yoknapatawpha County, Miss., devoted a literary lifetime to exploring the Southern ethos. As he told his audience in 1950 at ceremonies awarding him the Nobel Prize for literature, he found in his microcosm "courage and honor and hope and pride and compassion and pity and sacrifice." The photograph above was taken that same year. The annotated map, reproduced opposite, was drawn by the author for inclusion in Absalom, Absalom! *(1936), but it applies broadly to the entire Yoknapatawpha cycle.*

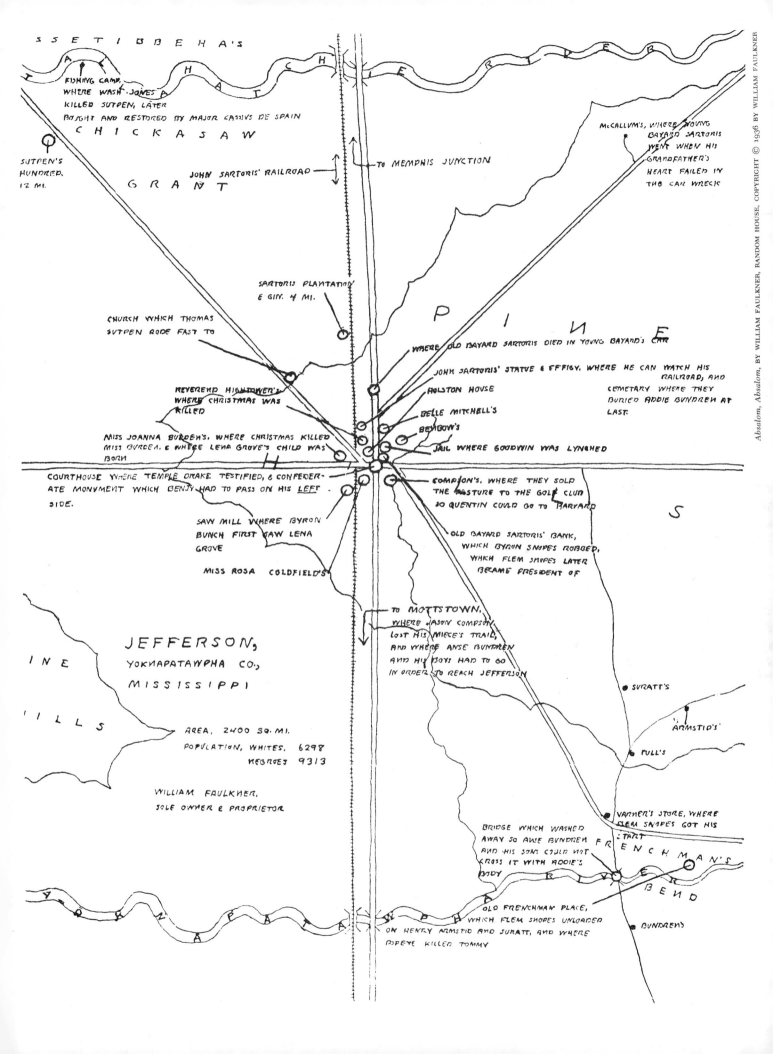

depths of human experience. He is outraged by the prospects his vision of life reveals, and that outrage takes the form of violent images.

The Yoknapatawpha series has been called the human comedy of the South, with flattering reference to Balzac's celebrated saga, *La Comédie Humaine*. It has also been described as "a modern epic of the fall and corruption of man." However, the early volumes had, on the whole, a lukewarm reception, which apparently made little difference to Faulkner. "I think I have written a lot and sent it off to print," he once said, "before I actually realized strangers might read it." In that same spirit, when the typesetter of his first book misspelled his name by adding a "u" to the family name Falkner, the author did not bother to change it. "Either way suits me," he remarked. Somewhat belatedly Faulkner earned due critical acclaim. In 1950 he received a Nobel Prize, and a quarter of a century after *The Sound and the Fury* was published, he finally won the Pulitzer Prize with *A Fable*. He continued writing until his death in 1962. By then he had produced a prodigy of imagination that had no equal in the American literature of its time.

Faulkner's fictional portrait of the Deep South was, obviously, not a smiling one. Observers and critics from other regions of the nation were quick enough to decry the "ignorant," "reactionary," and "uncivilized" aspect of things in the southern states—especially in Mississippi; and, unfortunately, there was some basis for their lament, if one applied the standard tests used by economists and sociologists to define "backwardness." Mississippi was, in truth, among the poorest states in the Union, with a relatively high degree of illiteracy among its people, along with other handicaps. Yet, as one Southerner pointed out, the year Faulkner received the Nobel Prize, "to find a novelist comparable to Faulkner in all the Northeast they [the literary intellectuals of Harvard University] have to go to more backward times and read Henry

Faulkner's landscape is filled with the imagery of decay—shattered ideals and crumbling walls that bespeak a culture at once grand and self-destructive. The old Shipp mansion, right, might be the model for the Sartoris family seat. Like so many houses that Faulkner knew first hand, only the memory of its elegance remains.

DAVID SCHERMAN

James." But Faulkner was not the only eloquent voice heard from the South during the twenties and thirties. The South was, in fact, enjoying a literary renaissance of its own during these decades. The regionalism apparent in this fresh flowering of Southern talent harks back to the earlier writings of George Washington Cable, Joel Chandler Harris, and others. But there was a difference. These new authors, and the critics who supported them, spoke with assurance of the "agrarian tradition" that they represented—a way of life they confidently pitted against the industrial tradition of the North, with its frantic, urbanized materialism. They were confident enough, especially the Southern poets, as Marcus Cunliffe has observed, to merge their regional pride in the general world of letters. They believed that their culture was a mature and valid continuation of the culture of the Western world at large. To insist on Americanism in letters, as so many of their northern contemporaries were doing, would be to restrict their viewpoint to chauvinistic manners. As the spokesman just quoted further tauntingly remarked of this apparent paradox:

> We must then conclude that the way to produce a John Ransom, an Allen Tate, a Robert Penn Warren, a Julia Peterkin, a Stark Young, a Eudora Welty, a Thomas Wolfe, a Jesse Stuart, an Elizabeth Roberts, is to have them be born and grow up in a backward Southern community that loves everything that Massachusetts condemns and lacks nearly everything that Massachusetts deems admirable and necessary.

He might have added the names of John Orley and Erskine Caldwell.

Several of those authors are still writing, their reputations still building, others have taken their place in history. Among the latter group, Thomas Wolfe, a Southerner by birth, belongs almost entirely to the 1930's. His first substantial book, *Look Homeward, Angel*, was published in 1929, and he died a young man just nine years later. In that short time he poured out such a torrent of words as threatened to overwhelm his editors. (Twelve publishing houses turned down *Look Homeward, Angel* before Scribner's undertook to edit and print the colossal manuscript Wolfe submitted.) As edited and printed, Wolfe's four huge novels (the three others are *Of Time and the River*, 1935; *The Web and the Rock*, 1939; and *You Can't Go Home Again*, 1940 —the last two issued posthumously) run to well over a million words. The last manuscript left with his publisher, shortly before Wolfe's untimely death, was in itself more than a million words long. One anecdote tells of Wolfe arriving at his publisher's bringing a manuscript in a truck; when the great editor Maxwell Perkins had cut and pruned it, only a taxi was required to take it away. As Wolfe once told Scott Fitzgerald, "a great writer is not only a leaver-outer but also a putter-inner."

Wolfe's four major works are, in a sense, one novel, and they are essentially autobiographical. His life was surcharged with formidable energy. Very briefly, he was born and raised in Asheville, North Carolina (the Altamont, Old Catawba, of his novels). After graduating from the University of North Carolina in 1920, he went on to Harvard to study play writing. After brief travels in Europe, he taught for a while at New York University, and then settled down to write for his few remaining years. He was a large man, with a

Son of a North Carolina stone-cutter, Thomas Wolfe looked no further than his own family and home town for the material of his first novel, Look Homeward, Angel. *The title, borrowed from Milton's* Lycidas, *held many meanings for the author, among them a reference to funeral statuary like this angel, which was produced in the elder Wolfe's workshop.*

341

Thomas Wolfe, shown above during a visit to Berlin, believed that "the artist has the only true critical intelligence." He imputed to America of the 1930's something of his personal unrest, declaring that "immense and cruel skies bend over us, and all of us are driven on forever and we have no home." Still, he loved his country and faced the future with hope. "I think," he wrote, "the true fulfillment of our spirit, of our people, of our mighty and immortal land, is yet to come."

consuming appetite for experience, which was never sated. Sinclair Lewis spoke of him as this "Gargantuan creature with great gusto of life." (Lewis praised *Look Homeward, Angel* in delivering his Noble Prize speech in 1930.) When he was still at Harvard Wolfe wrote his mother: ". . . [Life] is not all bad, but it is not all good; it is not all ugly, but it is not all beautiful; it is life, life, life—the only thing that matters. It is savage, cruel, kind, noble, passionate, generous, stupid, ugly, beautiful, painful, joyous—it is all these and more —and it's all these I want to know, and BY GOD, I shall, though they crucify me for it. I will go to the end of the earth to find it, to understand it. I will know this country when I am through as I know the palm of my hand, and I will put it on paper and make it true and beautiful."

That sounds a bit like an anxious young man, detached from his backland home, in quest of his soul in a larger world. However, all this he did try to do with desperate intensity, as a premonition of his early death formed within him. In all his writings Wolfe not only advances on his readers with a mighty barrage of words, he also engulfs them in feeling. In these two respects he is the exact antithesis of Hemingway, who was so sparing with his vocabulary and so chary of expressed emotions. Wolfe's great bursts of energy released lyrical qualities of poetic flavor with an explosive spontaneity that recalls the outbursts of Walt Whitman. With that spirit he strove to "set down America as far as it can belong to the experience of one man." In America, if he could encompass it completely, he would find the secret of his own identity. When he was abroad he nostalgically sought to recall in sharp detail the physical look of his native land. He discovered that land during his years overseas, he recalled, "out of his very need of her." In America—America as an idea as well as a land rivers and hills and cities—he would find the meaning of life, and the reassurance that he almost painfully wanted. He had to believe even in America of the Depression, which exactly spanned his own writing years. "Everywhere around me, during these years," he wrote, "I saw the evidence of an incalculable ruin and suffering. My own people, the members of my own family, had been ruined, had lost all the material wealth and accumulation of a lifetime in what was called 'the depression' . . . the staggering impact of this black picture of man's inhumanity to his fellow man, the unending repercussions of these scenes of suffering, violence, oppression, hunger, cold, and filth and poverty going on unheeded in a world in which the rich were still rotten with their wealth left a scar upon my life, a conviction in my soul which I shall never lose." Elsewhere he argued that such ruin and suffering was less an aspect of the times than the revelation of forces that were as old "as Time and evil and Hell"; a manifestation of the consequences of original sin. However, he could never renounce his need of an America he could comprehend. Later, he wrote in his last novel: "I believe we are lost here in America, but I believe we shall be found . . . I think that the true fulfillment of our spirit, of our people, of our mighty and immortal land, is yet to come." Those words appeared in print only after he had given up his quest and gone to his grave.

The most popular novel dealing with the Depression, and the most influential social novel of the period, was John Steinbeck's *The Grapes of Wrath*, with which he won a Pulitzer Prize in 1940. That work told of the epical migration of Oklahoma and Arkansas farmers, the "Okies," from their wasted lands in the Dust Bowl region to the promised land of California—a test of faith and endurance that recalled the pioneering western movement of earlier days. These people were also of old, God-fearing American stock, although they faced an economic frontier rather than a raw wilderness. But it was hard to recognize the spiritual heirs of Daniel Boone and Johnny Appleseed in such homeless and hungry migrants of the 1930's, looking for any work they could do to salvage a modicum of human dignity and fill their empty bellies. They took to the westward roads by the scores of thousands, in great caravans, traveling in jalopies that often ran on faith alone:

> The cars of the migrant people crawled out of the side roads onto the great cross-country highway, and they took the migrant way to the West. In the daylight they scuttled like bugs to the westward; and as the dark caught them, they clustered like bugs near to shelter and to water. And because they were lonely and perplexed, because they had all come from a place of sadness and worry and defeat, and because they were all going to a new mysterious place, they huddled together, they talked together; they shared their lives, their food, and the things they hoped for in the new country.

There were too many of them to meet with any welcome from settled towns-people and farmers, who also faced the troubles of the times and who found themselves threatened by these drifting hordes. Too often where they had hoped to find some new beginning, the Okies found only hatred and exploitation.

The Grapes of Wrath was read in many countries. (After Pearl Harbor the Nazis permitted its publication in translation, as anti-American propaganda. However, it proved to most German readers that, at the worst, Americans could still travel in automobiles and that, at a time when German literature was heavily consored, American writers could freely speak their minds.) The book was another of those tracts for the times in the vein of Harriet

Philip Reisman's ink drawing of "Okies" and "Arkies" en route to the promised land on the Pacific coast is one of a series inspired by John Steinbeck's The Grapes of Wrath.

Beecher Stowe's *Uncle Tom's Cabin*, Edward Bellamy's *Looking Backward*, and Upton Sinclair's *The Jungle*. Steinbeck's novel has frequently been reprinted, and it was made into a successful movie; and like those other tracts, it has had its consequences. The attention paid to improving conditions in the Dust Bowl of the Southwest in good part stemmed from the impact of this compassionate novel. Although it was an indictment of the American economy and of social callousness, it still struck a note of affirmation. At a point during a storm when one of the unfortunate young migrant women gives birth to a still-born child, as her family faces starvation, her mother cries, "We ain' gonna die out. People is goin' on—changin'a little, but goin' right on."

A number of Steinbeck's other familiar works were also written during the thirties, including *Tortilla Flat* (1935) and *Of Mice and Men* (1937). Many of his stories were laid in his native Salinas, California, about whose *paisanos* he has written with a mixture of good-humored laughter and serious social concern. *East of Eden*, published in 1952, his first major work after *The Grapes of Wrath*, was a family saga partly set in that valley. In 1962 he reported his tour of forty states of the Union with his poodle in a book under the title *Travels with Charley in Search of America*. That same year he became the seventh American author to win a Nobel Prize.

During the decades between the great wars more talented American poets were at work than at any other time in the nation's history. As earlier remarked, throughout these years Ezra Pound continued to serve as a major catalyst, not only by the example of his own verse but, more important, by his pervasive personal influence on poets of the rising generation. He tried to, and usually did, help everyone who came within his circle, among them T. S. Eliot, who was only three years his junior and who became largely responsible for the acceptance of modern verse in the post-World War I period.

Eliot was born in St. Louis into a family that jealously guarded its associations with New England. One of his ancestors had been president of Harvard, another a juror at the Salem witchcraft trials. His grandfather had gone West after graduation from the Harvard Divinity School and was a founder of Washington University in St. Louis. As he later recalled, Eliot had always been a New Englander in the Southwest and a Southwesterner in New England. "When I was sent to school in New England [he graduated from Harvard in 1910—in the same class with Walter Lippmann]," he wrote, "I lost my southern accent without ever acquiring the accent of the native Bostonian. . . . I remember a friend of my school-days, whose family had lived in the same New England seaport for two hundred and fifty years. In some ways his background was as different from mine as that of any European. My grandmother —one of my grandmothers—had shot her own wild turkeys for dinner; his had collected Chinese pottery [it was undoubtedly porcelain] brought home by the Salem clippers. It was perhaps easier for the grandson of pioneers to migrate eastward than it would have been for my friend to migrate in any direction."

He went on from Harvard for further study at the Sorbonne in Paris and at Oxford, and then remained in England to become a British subject. When his first book of poems, *Prufrock and Other Observations*, appeared in 1917, Eliot was an obscure clerk in Lloyds Bank, Ltd. A few years later he was already ac-

John Steinbeck, above, was well acquainted with the hardships and poverty of California's migratory workers. During the Depression he championed these humble and exploited "forgotten men" in such novels as The Grapes of Wrath. *His realism stirred the conscience of New Deal America, and his works were very well received.*

cepted, both in America and in England, as a leading poet and critic. The title piece of that initial volume, "The Love Song of J. Alfred Prufrock," was first published separately in Harriet Monroe's Chicago magazine *Poetry* in 1915. It had been rejected in England "with outspoken horror," but Pound persuaded Harriet Monroe to accept and print it. It tells the story of an aging young man ("with a bald spot in the middle of my hair") who faces the predicament of the modern world with mingled flippancy and despair, unable to commit himself either to love or life. (The First World War had just commenced.) The poem opens with the lines:

> Let us go then, you and I,
> When the evening is spread out against the sky
> Like a patient etherised upon a table;
> Let us go, through certain half-deserted streets,
> The muttering retreats
> Of restless nights in one-night cheap hotels
> And sawdust restaurants with oyster-shells:
> Streets that follow like a tedious argument
> Of insidious intent
> To lead you to an overwhelming question . . .
> Oh, do not ask, "What is it?"
> Let us go and make our visit.

T. S. Eliot, photographed in 1943 with Edith Sitwell, believed it "likely that poets in our civilization as it exists at present must be difficult. Our civilization comprehends great variety and complexity, and this variety and complexity, playing upon a refined sensibility, must produce various and complex results."

In 1922 Eliot published *The Waste Land*, which is considered his greatest achievement and has proved to be one of the most influential poems of our time. (Before the manuscript was released to the printer, it was heavily and expertly edited by Ezra Pound, to whom the poem was dedicated.) The "Waste Land" is the contemporary postwar world, a sterile and chaotic place —an "immense panorama of futility and anarchy" whose inhabitants are spiritually barren and desperate. Life is devoid of value. (This was the world, as Eliot wrote in another of his poems, that would end not with a bang but with a whimper.) That sordid scene is depicted with tremendous erudition. Eliot inserted passages in a half-dozen languages, including Sanskrit, as well as quotations from popular songs and allusions to some thirty-five different authors. One critic referred to Eliot's verse as "the most bookish of his time," and to Eliot himself as "a poet with dust and ashes for his theme." He did indeed demand a great deal of his readers with his use of myth, religious symbolism, and literary allusion, with his bold and sudden contrasts, sometimes ironic, between the grand style and colloquial usage, and with his variable moods developed through striking images, sometimes lovely, sometimes repulsive. (Eliot's position was that in a civilization so complex and so varied as that of the twentieth century a poet *had* to be difficult to express his message truly.) A brief quotation may serve to illustrate the nature of *The Waste Land*, although it cannot suggest the complexities of Eliot's construction or the skill with which he blended so many different elements into a coherent whole. The references in the following excerpt are from God's words to Ezekiel ("Son of Man, stand upon thy feet") and from Wagner's *Tristram and Isolde*.

> What are the roots that clutch, what branches grow
> Out of this stony rubbish? Son of man,

You cannot say, or guess, for you know only
A heap of broken images, where the sun beats,
And the dead tree gives no shelter, the cricket no relief,
And the dry stone no sound of water. Only
There is shadow under this red rock,
(Come in under the shadow of this red rock),
And I will show you something different from either
Your shadow at morning striding behind you
Or your shadow at evening rising to meet you;
I will show you fear in a handful of dust.
Frisch weht der Wind
Der Heimat zu
Mein Irisch Kind,
Wo weilest du?

After writing *The Waste Land* Eliot turned from skepticism to hope, from his sense of spiritual desolation to a vision of human salvation and of heavenly grace. In 1927 he renounced his American citizenship and became a British subject, and he joined the Anglican Church. Within that communion he found a sanctuary where his mind and his emotions could rest, a solution to man's dilemma; it was the faith he had called for at the end of *The Waste Land*—the faith he professed in his poem "Ash-Wednesday," published in 1930. He had become, as he said, "an Anglo-Catholic in religion, a classicist in literature, and a royalist in politics." With *Murder in the Cathedral* (1935), a versified tragedy on the death of Thomas à Becket, Archbishop of Canterbury, in A.D. 1170, Eliot sought to return poetic drama to the Church ritual in which it originated, to a form that would once more be viable on the stage. Eliot was an artist who never forgot to grow as he himself grew older. In 1943 he collected a cycle of his poems, *Four Quartets*, which was a meditative and lyrical counterpart of his plays. With the assurance of his faith, he concluded that "all will be well." He was awarded the Nobel Prize in literature in 1948, and six years later *Life* magazine solemnly announced to its mass audience that Eliot was "the world's most distinguished living poet."

William Carlos Williams felt that Pound and Eliot had injured the cause of American poetry by leaving their homeland and, in their expatriation, absorbing influences from alien (largely French) sources. However, although Williams, Sandburg, and certain other poets continued to emphasize the "Americanness" of the verse they wrote, much of the best American poetry of the postwar years had become international in character, generally independent of time and place for its impact. There were exceptions, of course, but on the whole the confrontation was now not so much between American and European kinds of verse and subjects as between traditional and innovative poetry.

E. E. Cummings stands out among the innovators of the postwar period. In 1922 he published a novel, *The Enormous Room*, recording his unique war experiences. He had been erroneously suspected of treasonable correspondence and was sent off to a prison in the south of France, where he spent several months. Modeled on *Pilgrim's Progress*, *The Enormous Room* demonstrated a new sensibility; it breaks "so completely with one tradition," Alfred Kazin observed, that it mechanically inaugurates another. Cummings' was an art transformed by the very experience of war; he established a language that powerfully conveyed the outrageousness and inherent meaninglessness of war. The enormous room became a metaphor for the imprisonment in chaos that is life without meaning. His was a hard language that sought, in Hemingway's words regarding his own purpose, to tell "the truth about his own feelings at the moment when they exist."

The passionate individualism of Cummings carried over into his poetry and makes it in tone and often in subject reminiscent of the Emersonian and New England tradition. He sought simplicity in an age of chaos; he wrought a new, grotesque poetic language, which allowed for the pride of self-knowledge within the integrity of art. Beyond that, his verse forms make a completely unconventional use of typography to express his message, as in the following poem, entitled "Buffalo Bill's":

BETTMANN ARCHIVES

> Buffalo Bill's
> defunct
>   who used to
>   ride a watersmooth-silver
>   stallion
> and break onetwothreefourfive pigeonsjustlikethat
>   Jesus
>
> he was a handsome man
>   and what i want to know is
> how do you like your blueeyed boy
> Mister Death

It has been said that through inadequate typesetting Cummings name appeared as e e cummings, without capitals or punctuation, on the title pages of some of his early poems, and since he liked it that way he continued using that curious form. (An imaginary interlocutor addressed him as "Mr. Lowercase Highbrow.") His odd syntax is another aspect of his revolt against standard conventions, a reflection of his distaste for the stereotyped slogans and the clichés used in the advertising world of the day and in mediums of mass communication generally (which he thoroughly castigated in some of his poems). A staunch individualist who asserted his views with a sort of highly personal romantic anarchism, he dismissed "mostpeople" (as he elided the two words) as snobs and bores, and abhorred the commercialism that so drably circumscribed their lives.

However fanciful and lighthearted his mannerisms make it seem, Cummings' verse is warm and lyrical (when it is not chillingly ironic). Love is imperative in his world, along with the other joys an individual can experience. One of his early poems, "since feeling is first," exemplifies the carefree charm that he could bring to his message:

> since feeling is first
> who pays any attention
> to the syntax of things
> will never wholly kiss you;
>
> wholly to be a fool
> while Spring is in the world

E. E. (Edward Estlin) Cummings, shown here in a self-portrait, juggled with syntax, punctuation, and typography, and coined and joined words to produce some of America's most amusing and ambitiously innovative poetry. His verse, writes one critic, like Alexander Calder's mobiles, is "a delightful merry-go-round, brightly rotating and rising and falling, in a Bank Holiday sunshine."

347

Marianne Moore, photographed at right, was once classified by T. S. Eliot as a "descriptive" poet. Her meticulously crafted poems, based on a structuring of facts, illustrate an avoidance of the "emotional slither" that Ezra Pound had condemned and, instead, sparkle like gems in their "hard, clear," cold exactitude. She believed that the poet's primary function was to be "a literalist of the imagination," a designer of "imaginary gardens with real toads in them."

my blood approves,
and kisses are a better fate
lady i swear by all flowers. Don't cry
—the best gesture of my brain is less than
your eyelids' flutter which says

we are for each other: then
laugh, leaning back in my arms
for life's not a paragraph

And death i think is no parenthesis

When Marianne Moore published a small book of verse called *Marriage* in 1923, T. S. Eliot wrote that she was one of the most exciting of living poets. She enjoyed such a reputation until her recent death at the age of eighty-four. W. H. Auden once remarked that her work was "a treasure which all future English poets will be able to plunder." Her poems are typically short, and she did not publish a large number; but her lines are fashioned with exquisite care and in a highly personal manner. Like so many other American poets, she had to devote herself to practical pursuits while creating her verse on the side. For a while, after graduation from Bryn Mawr in 1909, she taught stenography, typing, and bookkeeping at an Indian school in Pennsylvania, and later worked at the New York Public Library. From 1925 to 1929 she edited the magazine *Dial* and made it a great publication. For some years she lived in Brooklyn—until her favorite baseball team, the Dodgers, moved to Los Angeles, when (if not necessarily only for that reason) she returned to Manhattan.

Marianne Moore combined poetic wit with a rare sensibility and acute perception of the physical world, and with concern for the tonal variations of verbal sound and visual image. The results are creations of extreme originality. She had "a burning desire to be explicit" in whatever she wrote. As Marcus Cunliffe has observed, "her subjects are an anthology of rare and unexpected things, a poet's scrapbook of clocks and jewels and living creatures. . . . She can describe an ostrich or an elephant with equal felicity." Thus she wrote of "zebras, supreme in their abnormality," of "elephants with their fog-coloured skin and strictly practical appendages," or of a swan "with flamingo-coloured, maple-like feet."

It is difficult to excerpt passages from her poems, for the lines flow on throughout a work with inevitable continuity, as in "The Steeple-Jack":

> One by one in two's, in three's, the seagulls keep
>   flying back and forth over the town clock,
> or sailing around the lighthouse without moving the wings—rising
>   steadily with a slight
>   quiver of the body—or flock
> mewing where
>
> a sea the purple of the peacock's neck is
>   paled to greenish azure as Dürer changed
> the pine green of the Tyrol to peacock blue and guinea gray. You can see
>   a twenty-five-
>   pound lobster; and fishnets arranged
> to dry. The
>
> whirlwind fife-and-drum of the storm bends the salt
>   marsh grass, disturbs ·stars in the sky and the
> star on the steeple; it is a privilege to see so
> much confusion.

Marianne Moore's poems are not always easy to read. Once, after she had been reading from her works, a member of her audience asked what she had meant by the phrase "metaphysical newmown hay." The poet replied, "Oh, something like a sudden whiff of fragrance in contrast to the doggedly continuous opposition to spontaneous conversation that had gone before." To which her questioner replied, "Then why didn't you *say* so."

The life of Hart Crane, a somewhat younger contemporary of Marianne Moore's, was comparatively brief. He died at the age of thirty-three when, after a year's dissipated residence in Mexico, he leaped from the ship returning to the United States and was drowned at sea. Crane published only two books of verse during his life, but they were spotted with brilliant promise, and his major work, *The Bridge*, still stands as a literary landmark. That poem was intended as a "mystical synthesis of 'America'," an "organic panorama, showing the continuous and living evidence of the past in the . . . present."

LUKE "HOT POTATO" HAMLIN

The Brooklyn Dodgers were the favorite team of Marianne Moore, who followed their games avidly. A baseball card, above, shows Luke Hamlin, a popular Dodger pitcher of the early forties.

349

It was obviously influenced by *The Waste Land*, but its message was of a different order. Where Eliot's poem was written with despair, Crane's was conceived in a positive spirit of faith in the outcome of the American experience. In that spirit he used Columbus, Cortés, Pocahontas, Rip Van Winkle, Poe, Whitman, Melville, the subway, and, principally, the Brooklyn Bridge as symbols for man's creative power to unify the past and the present.

The lack of discipline that marked his tormented life, burdened as it was with sexual problems and excessive drinking, also robbed his epic of consistent quality. At his death he apparently did not believe he had achieved the "ecstatic goal" he had set for himself. Nevertheless, *The Bridge* contains passages of outstanding merit and power. One stanza in which the poet addresses the bridge, the great construction designed by John Roebling and still one of New York's most memorable monuments, Crane thought to be "almost the best thing I have ever written." It reads, in part, or rather in parts that suffer somewhat from the interrupted continuity, as follows:

> Down Wall, from girder into street noon leaks,
> A rip-tooth of the sky's acetylene;
> All afternoon the cloud-flown derricks turn . . .
> Thy cables breathe the North Atlantic still.
>
>   ❀   ❀   ❀   ❀
>
> O harp and altar, of the fury fused,
> (How could mere toil align thy choiring strings!)
> Terrific threshold of the prophet's pledge,
> Prayer of pariah, and the lover's cry,—
>
> Again the traffic lights that skim thy swift
> Unfractioned idiom, immaculate sigh of stars,
> Beading thy path—condense eternity:
> And we have seen night lifted in thine arms.
>
>   ❀   ❀   ❀   ❀
>
> O Sleepless as the river under thee,
> Vaulting the sea, the prairies' dreaming sod,
> Unto us lowliest sometime sweep, descend
> And of the curveship lend a myth to God.

There were other poets, more popular than Crane if of less enduring distinction, who looked to the American scene for inspiration. Stephen Vincent Benét begins his poem "American Names" as follows:

> I have fallen in love with American names,
> The sharp names that never get fat,
> The snakeskin-titles of mining claims,
> The plumed war-bonnet of Medicine Hat,
> Tucson and Deadwood and Lost Mule Flat.

The poem ends with the memorable line, "Bury my heart at Wounded Knee," a site that has recently had extensive publicity. Benét's reputation soared with the publication of his long poem *John Brown's Body* in 1928. Within a few months this epic of the Civil War was in the hands of a hundred thousand readers. Although one critic referred to Benét as only "an amiable and patriotic rhymster," another—as the result of an extensive poll of experts—ranked *John Brown's Body* as one of the best books of poetry of the decade

1926–35. In 1929 the author was awarded a Pulitzer Prize. Especially after the work was put to music, the refrain, "John Brown's body lies a mould'ring in the grave," became an enduring stock phrase for all America.

Archibald MacLeish had been an undergraduate at Yale with Benét. After serving in the artillery in France during the war, he went on to the Harvard Law School and to practice law in Boston. However, after three years he boldly gave up that profession in favor of a career as a poet. As his art matured, he, too, turned to the American scene and tradition for material for his verse. He found themes for his work in social issues of the day—the Depression, the peril of America in another world war, the need for peace, among other matters. He too won a Pulitzer Prize (1933). His commitment to his native land extended beyond his verse to a career as a public servant in the New Deal before he returned to Harvard as a professor of English.

Wallace Stevens was an older poet than any of the others that have been recently mentioned. However, he produced most of his work and his best work only after he was fifty years of age. Quite as extraordinary as that late, continued fertility of invention is the fact that throughout much of his writing career Stevens was employed full time as legal adviser to an insurance company in Hartford, Connecticut; he became vice president of the firm in 1934 and remained so employed until his death in 1955. He found his two lives as insurance executive and poet completely compatible—obviously, since he was one of the most accomplished American poets of our century. "It gives a man character as a poet," he remarked, "to have a daily contact with a job." He was such a man, he observed elsewhere, who "still dwells in an ivory tower, but who insists that life there would be intolerable except for the fact that one has, from the top, such an exceptional view of the public dump and

"The purpose of the expression of emotion in a poem," wrote Archibald MacLeish in one of his notebooks, "is not to recreate the poet's emotion in some one else.... The poem itself is a finality, an end, a creation." MacLeish, pictured at left, was a member of the foreign colony in Paris from 1923 until 1928, when he returned to the United States. In 1939 he was appointed Librarian of Congress, and during World War II he served as director of the Office of Facts and Figures, and later as Assistant Secretary of State.

Robinson Jeffers, above, settled in Carmel, Calif., in 1914, drawn there in part by the magnificent vista "through pines and sea-fog on Carmel Bay." Here on Point Sur the poet built with his own hands a stone house and tower— an aerie, where he lived secluded from a civilization he considered sick. Jeffers was a shy, introverted man; his poetry reflects his aversion to man and society and his preoccupation with the rugged Carmel setting. The pounding Pacific surf, the granite rocks, the soaring flight of the hawk, and the Monterey coastline with its graceful pines (as shown opposite) all figure in his verse.

the advertising signs. . . . He is the hermit who dwells alone with the sun and the moon, and insists on taking a rotten newspaper."

Imagination, Stevens maintained, must be based on realities. Actuality and art are inseparable, and his poems are filled with concrete imagery. Through the counterpoint of reality and imagination he arrived at a form of verbal music to which we must lend a ready ear as well as an attentive eye. His fondness for colors is everywhere apparent; he plays fastidiously with scintillating words; he seeks to delight, not to advise or deplore. And in all this he was witty and sophisticated and elegant. His poem "Disillusionment of Ten O'Clock" is a small but fair sample of his work.

> The houses are haunted
> By white night-gowns.
> None are green,
> Or purple with green rings,
> Or green with yellow rings,
> Or yellow with blue rings.
> None of them are strange,
> With socks of lace
> And beaded ceintures.
> People are not going
> To dream of baboons and periwinkles.
> Only, here and there, an old sailor,
> Drunk and asleep in his boots,
> Catches tigers
> In red weather.

The remarkable diversity of American poetry in the period between the two wars, and the difficulty of finding any common patterns in it, is clearly suggested by the fact that Robinson Jeffers was an almost exact contemporary of T. S. Eliot's. It would be hard to find two poets more different in their lives, their outlooks, and their expression. Eliot moved from the Midwest via Harvard to lead the life of an expatriate in London; Jeffers moved from Pittsburgh via Europe (as a youth) to live the life of a semirecluse on the Pacific coast, six thousand miles from London. Eliot found his way to a faith in mankind through religious orthodoxy; Jeffers renounced mankind as an ignoble breed ("the animals Christ was rumored to have died for"), wallowing in social degeneration. Eliot wrote of passion overweighed by thought (in a Puritan tradition); Jeffers wrote of passion as an uncontrollably destructive force— of violence, incest, murder, and elemental struggle, usually set against a realistic backdrop of the rugged, surf-beaten California coast near Carmel, its cypress-covered headlands and its nearby valleys.

Throughout his school and college days Jeffers was primarily interested in poetry, although he studied medicine at the University of Southern California and forestry at the University of Washington. However, he had little patience for the innovative poetry of his day with its "self-consciousness and naïve learnedness the undergraduate irony, unnatural metaphors, hiatuses and labored obscurity." When the war broke out he settled with his wife at Carmel, where he built with his own hands a stone house and a high tower for a study from which he could look down through the pines and fogs to the ocean below. From there, too, he could watch the soaring hawks and gliding peli-

cans and admire them, for he thought the "unsocial birds" were "a greater race" than human kind. His grim depreciation of his native land and its people was a far cry from the attitudes of Benét and MacLeish; and he isolated himself from the contamination of the city and the crowd. "Civilization," he once wrote, "is a transient sickness," but nature endures, everlastingly beautiful and completely indifferent to humanity. Thus, in "Gale in April," he wrote:

> Intense and terrible beauty, how has our race with the frail naked nerves,
> So little a craft swum down from its far launching?
> Why now, only because the northwest blows and the headed grass billows,
> Great seas jagging the west and on the granite
> Blanching, the vessel is brimmed, this dancing play of the world is too much passion.
> A gale in April so overfilling the spirit,
> Though his ribs were thick as the earth's, arches of mountain, how shall one dare to live,
> Though his blood were like the earth's rivers and his flesh iron,
> How shall one dare to live? One is born strong, how do the weak endure it?
> The strong lean upon death as on a rock,
> After eighty years there is shelter and the naked nerves shall be covered with deep quietness.
> O beauty of things go on, go on, O torture
> Of intense joy I have lasted out my time, I have thanked God and finished,
> Roots of millennial trees fold me in the darkness,
> Northwest wind shake their tops, not to the root, not to the root, I have passed
> From beauty to the other beauty, peace, the night splendor.

Jeffers did not go to war, but the disillusionment of the years between the two great conflicts found its extreme expression in his verse. He ended by feeling that no radical reforms could salvage the human race. "Blind war" was a better corrective of social ills than any planning could be. It cleansed civilization and led back to "the primal and the latter silences."

In all its diversity, during the years between wars American writing—fiction and poetry alike—rose to a dominating position in the wide world of letters. From a moribund Europe it appeared vigorous and new, bold and inventive. From the Fascist areas overseas it seemed as though American authors wrote with a dangerous freedom of expression that threatened authoritarianism everywhere. "In America," wistfully observed one German émigré to the United States, "the word still has real value; in Europe it is only make-believe." As eminent refugees from Europe's escaped to these shores—such men and women as Thomas Mann, Sigrid Undset, Bertolt Brecht, Jacques Maritain, among others—American literature was exposed to a new spirit of cosmopolitanism. Not very much more than a century earlier the witty Englishman Sydney Smith could ask his mocking question, "Who reads an American book?" Before the end of the 1930's it might better have been asked who could afford not to read American books.

LITERATURE
ON STAGE

The second decade of the present century witnessed a revitalization of the American theatre. To be sure, dramatic productions had been popular since colonial times, but native tastes ran mainly to such fare as tear-jerkers, side-splitters, and hair-raisers, and the commercial stage was dominated by great actors rather than talented playwrights. Arising in Europe in the 1880's, the little theatre movement reached America during World War I, and effected a clean break with the commercial stage and its thitherto inviolable conventions. Such experimental groups as the Provincetown Players and the Washington Square Players—later renamed the Theatre Guild—began to produce plays by unknown authors, to treat themes relevant to contemporary life, and to provide stimulus for a new drama.

RENAISSANCE OF THE

Eugene O'Neill, more than any other native playwright, was responsible for ushering in the modes and themes of the modern American drama. The son of a popular actor of romantic melodrama, he was nurtured in the traditions of the stage. Possessed of an insatiable wanderlust as a youth, O'Neill spent several years as a merchant seaman, drifting to various ports of call around the globe. In 1912, while confined with tuberculosis to a sanitorium, O'Neill turned his interests to drama. In 1913 he wrote his first one-act play—and embarked on a prolific period of experiment. The following year he attended George Pierce Baker's famous 47 Workshop at Harvard, and in 1916 was discovered by the Provincetown Players, who performed his *Bound East for Cardiff* that summer, and subsequently produced most of his pieces in New York until 1924. O'Neill achieved wide recognition as the nation's foremost playwright (and a modicum of financial success in the 1920's), and in 1936 he was awarded the Nobel Prize. Even O'Neill's early works illustrate such striking innovations as the use of realistic settings, simplified plots, and dialogue in the authentic idiom of a character's situation—"the gibberish of the vulgate" adapted to the theatre. He once explained: "I don't think, from the evidence of all that is being written today that great language is possible for anyone living in the discordant, broken, faithless rhythm of our time." His mature pieces, including *Desire Under the Elms, The Great God Brown, Strange Interlude,* and *Mourning Becomes Electra* reflect a mélange of Ibsenian realism and Brechtian expressionism, as well as a preoccupation with such social ideologies as those expressed by Marx and Freud. All these works, however, share the underlying theme of man's eternal struggle for understanding and "belonging" in an incomprehensible and often seemingly hostile universe. Rather than dealing with man's relation to man, O'Neill sought to explore man's relation to God, or to a force outside himself, and therein lies the greatness and tragic stature of his plays.

Eugene O'Neill, pictured at right, was assisted in his play-writing efforts by talented set and costume designers of the day. Their contributions are suggested, counterclockwise, by an art deco poster for Strange Interlude, *a nine-act stream-of-consciousness drama that had its premiere in 1928; an expressionistic jungle backdrop designed by Jo Mielziner for* The Emperor Jones; *and a Chinese bodyguard costume created for* Marco Millions *by Lee Simonson.*

Set designed by Oenslager for Steinbeck's Of Mice and Men

DESIGNS FOR PLAYWRIGHTS

During the nineteenth century American fiction frequently provided the stage with themes and plots for its productions. As early as 1822, James Fenimore Cooper's popular historical novel, *The Spy*, was dramatized by C. P. Clinch for a New York showing—an occasion recorded in a painting by William Dunlap (see page 64). Since then, a host of other fictional stories and tracts has been adapted for theatrical performances, including such an all time favorite as Harriet Beecher Stowe's *Uncle Tom's Cabin*. More recently, in 1957, Thomas Wolfe's autobiographical novel, *Look Homeward, Angel*, was dramatized by Ketti Frings and was awarded a Pulitzer Prize as a play. The scenes, laid largely inside or outside a grim late-nineteenth-century house, were designed by Jo Mielziner. However, as early as the 1920's and 1930's the growing trend in America was for playrights, not authors, to write plays. Even John Steinbeck's tragic novel *Of Mice and Men* (1937) was originally conceived in theatrical terms; when it was produced on Broadway as a play in 1938, with sets by Donald Oenslager, Steinbeck himself did the adaptation. Both Lillian Hellman and Arthur Miller have written almost exclusively for the stage. Hellman's *The Little Foxes* (1939), the story of a Southern family in decline, was one of her Broadway hits. Miller's *Death of a Salesman*, produced in 1949, with sets designed by Mielziner, was awarded a Pulitzer Prize.

Costume designs by Patricia Zipprodt for Lillian Hellman's The Little Foxes

Design by Mielziner for Arthur Miller's Death of a Salesman

A set, also by Mielziner, for Thomas Wolfe's Look Homeward, Angel

GREEK HERITAGE

A design by R. E. Jones for the stage setting of Eugene O'Neill's Mourning Becomes Electra *(1931), shows the play's American heroine, modeled on Aeschylus' Electra, a girl obsessed with her father's fate. She stands before her New England mansion, designed in the Greek Revival style. The Greeks not only originated the theatre but provided subsequent productions with inexhaustible source material.*

361

Costume designs by Patricia Zipprodt for Our Town

IN MODERN DRESS

Although modern American theatre, as it emerged in the twenties, exhibited a new naturalism, there were soon strong tendencies in the opposite direction. Even unsophisticated audiences readily accepted plays based on fantasy, symbolism, and poetry. Influenced by the regionalism of the Depression years, Thornton Wilder, in 1938, created the allegorical *Our Town*. The play ostensibly depicted New England life in the early 1900's, but it was intended to "present illustrations of harmony and of law . . . affirmations about mankind and his end." Rather than rely on such elaborate visual effects as Stuart Davis' cubistic costumes, right, for a 1922 play, Wilder staged *Our Town* without curtains or scenery, as indicated opposite. Similarly, Archibald MacLeish believed that "the imagination works better through the ear than through the eye," and in his *J.B.* of 1958 presented the story of Job in modern dress, as shown below, and in verse.

Above: Girl and Faun, Stuart Davis' designs for The Puritans, *1922; below: bride's main costume, by Norman-Bel Geddes for* The Miracle.

363

Lucinda Ballard's costume designs for Archibald MacLeish's J.B.

The Theatre Guild Presents
by arrangement with Sidney Harmon

BUT FOR THE GRACE of GOD

A Play by Leopold Atlas

GUILD THE...
52 nd ST. WEST OF

BIOGRAPHY

A PLAY BY
S.N. BEHRMAN

A THEATRE GUILD
PRODUCTION

AT THE
GUILD THEATRE
52ND ST. W. OF BROADWAY

A THEATRE GUILD production

DAYS WITHOUT END

A MODERN
MIRACLE PLAY
by
EUGENE O'NEILL

HENRY
MILLER
THEATRE
43RD ST. E. of Bway

THE THEATRE GUILD, Inc. Presents

GEORGE GERSHWIN'S AMERICAN FOLK OPERA

"PORGY and BESS"

(Based on the play "Porgy")

FORREST THEATRE
Two Weeks Commencing MON., JAN. 27th
Matinees Thursday and Saturday

THE THEATRE GUILD
PRESENTS

THE GOOD EARTH

DRAMATIZED BY OWEN AND DONALD DAVIS
FROM PEARL S. BUCK'S PULITZER PRIZE NOVEL
AT THE GUILD THEATRE 52 STREET W. OF BROADWAY

THEATRE GUILD

Of the estimated two thousand little theatres operating in this country by the mid-1920's, the Theatre Guild was the most successful. Organized in 1918, the Guild was an outgrowth of New York City's Washington Square Players, a semiamateur group that had begun performing one-act plays in 1915, and whose activities had been interrupted by World War I. Astute financial management, shrewd play selection, and skill in production enabled the Theatre Guild to go beyond the scope of the typical art theatre into commercial production. In 1925 the Guild erected its own million-dollar theatre, and in 1927 sent its first road company on tour. Increasingly elaborate plays by contemporary American and European authors were presented, as well as occasional revivals by the likes of Ben Jonson or Shakespeare. The Guild popularized George Bernard Shaw on the American stage, introduced dramas by Tolstoy and Dostoevsky, and performed such stridently experimental pieces as *The Adding Machine* (1923), by Elmer Rice. The variety of Theatre Guild offerings in the 1930's is illustrated by the posters, which range from Robert Sherwood's continental sex comedy, *Reunion in Vienna*, to an adaptation of Pearl Buck's novel, *The Good Earth*. By this time a group of insurgents felt that the Theatre Guild was becoming too conservative and founded their own Group Theatre. Nevertheless, the Guild had shown that new forms of drama could draw audiences, encouraged unknown playwrights to write avant-garde pieces, and bridged the gulf between what was possible in the rarefied atmosphere of the art theatre and what was possible on the commercial stage.

Donald Oenslager's set, a garish frontier hotel scene, for Ballad of Baby Doe, *1956*

Jo Mielziner's Broadway, designed for Guys and Dolls, *1950*

MUSIC
&
COMEDY

A blend of *opéra bouffe*, burlesque, minstrel show, Gilbert and Sullivan, and drama, the musical comedy is America's distinctive contribution to the stage. One of the first theatrical offerings to actually call itself a "musical comedy" was *Evangeline*, produced in 1874, and, like so many entertainments to follow, it borrowed freely from native history. Longfellow's sentimentalized Acadian heroine is further exaggerated by its stage adapter: she becomes "a creature of impulse pursued through love's impatient prompting by Gabriel, and with a view to audacious contingencies—by a whale." Despite the general literary trend toward realism in our century, "audacious contingencies"· and folk heroes remain rich narrative material. Three examples, represented here by their stage designers' sketches, are shown: Maxwell Anderson wrote the book and lyrics for *Knickerbocker Holiday* with a strong assist from Washington Irving; Abe Burrows' *Guys and Dolls* was inspired by Damon Runyon's "Idylls of Sarah Brown"; and John Latouche's libretto for *Ballad of Baby Doe* (a full-fledged opera set in Colorado) takes its flavor from Bret Harte's tales of the Old West.

Frank Bevon's costume for Peter Stuyvesant, lead character in Knickerbocker Holiday

367

Bradford Dillman, Jason Robards, Jr., Florence Eldridge, and Fredric March in O'Neill's Long Day's Journey into Night, *1956*

Ethel Waters, solo performance, 1953

Theatre by nature. is an art form that most people enjoy second hand, if at all. Performed principally in large cities, before small audiences, during limited engagements, most plays are known to the general public only through the eyes of syndicated newspaper critics—and the penmanship of a uniquely gifted artist, Al Hirschfeld. For more than fifty years now, Hirschfeld has been the American theatre's journalist-caricaturist, offering in the pages of the New York *Herald Tribune* and the *New York Times* his personal distillation of each season's most interesting productions. Working from preliminary drawings which he sketches in the dark during final rehearsals or out-of-town performances, he aims for characterizations that go deeper than physical appearances: "The playwright gives the measure of the man—villain or hero. All I'm trying to do is capture the playwright's dimensions." The task of finding that measure gets ever more difficult, the artist has complained, as bravura has gone out of acting and slice-of-life drama has gained literary favor. "They now try to imitate life rather than interpret it." Shown here are but a few of the thousands of studies Hirschfeld has contributed to contemporary theatre history.

Frank Fay in Harvey; *Laurette Taylor in Williams'*
The Glass Menagerie; *Judy Holliday in* Kiss Them
for Me; *and Frederic O'Neal in* Anna Lucasta, *1945*

June Havoc in the musical
Sadie   Thompson,   *1944*

A HIRSCHFELD ROUNDUP

Alfred Lunt and wife Lynn Fon-
tanne in O Mistress Mine, *1946*

Victor Moore in Nellie Bly, *1946*

Louis Calhern and Dorothy Gish
in The Magnificent Yankee, *1946*

I went to New York to meet Wittgenstein at the ship. When I first saw him I was surprised at his apparent physical vigour. He was striding down the ramp with a pack on his back, a heavy suitcase in one hand, cane in the other.

THE
PASSING SCENE

MUSEUM OF MODERN ART, JOSEPH G. MAYER FOUNDATION FUND

"But who can comprehend the meaning of the voice of the city?" queried O. Henry about New York, whose multifarious faces have been celebrated by many writers and artists, both native and foreign. British artist Eduardo Paolozzi's serigraph of 1965, Wittgenstein in New York *(opposite), juxtaposes robots, a portion of the Manhattan skyline, and a conglomerate of mechanism in such a way as to suggest the throbbing pulse of New York, an international cultural center and a city caught up in the agitations of the computer age.*

During the late 1930's, as the threat of full-scale war overseas steadily mounted, America's neutralism was stoutly reaffirmed from almost every quarter of the country. In 1935, 1936, and 1937 Congress passed a series of Neutrality Acts designed to prevent the sale of weapons and munitions to any warring power. When, in October, 1937, President Roosevelt declared in a speech that the aggressive nations that were violating the peace of the world must be "quarantined," his announcement was met by a storm of protest. As late as the autumn of 1940 both candidates for the presidency, Roosevelt and Wendell Willkie, insisted that they were opposed to leading the United States into the war. The neutralism of Americans at large died hard.

However, during that presidential campaign both candidates agreed upon the need to aid Europe's beleaguered nations. This had belatedly come to be seen by a majority of the voting public as a vital measure of self-defense. As Roosevelt had reminded his countrymen the year before when England declared war on Germany, "When peace has been broken anywhere, the peace of all countries everywhere is in danger." The truth of that observation was grimly emphasized when the German army, with lightning swiftness, invaded the Low Countries on May 10, 1940, and marched triumphantly into Paris just five weeks later. Nothing like this blitzkrieg had been known in the history of warfare. France was stunned. Such a demonstration of ruthless force was enough to sober the thoughts of most neutralists even in distant America. With his earlier conquests of Poland and Austria, of Denmark and Norway, Hitler now controlled virtually all western Europe. Britain's naval patrols on the high seas had often served in the past as a buffer against forces hostile to America; now Britain stood alone to confront with "blood, toil, tears, and sweat" Hitler's fanatical dream of conquest and empire. And German bombs were soon mercilessly raining on Britain, killing more than 14,000 civilians in London alone and blasting, among other targets, the cathedral city of Coventry.

Even in the face of these menacing developments and a rising fear that America was not so safe after all from the contagion of warfare, some advocates of isolationism held firm to their principles. Among them were such influential personages as Senators Gerald P. Nye and Burton K. Wheeler, the industrialist Henry Ford, the author Kathleen Norris, and one of America's most respected heroes, Charles Lindbergh. "Above all, let us stop this hysterical chatter of calamity and invasion," Lindbergh admonished while Hitler was forcing his way through to Paris. America also had its own home-grown Nazis, such as the German-American Bund, dedicated to Hitlerian principles and determined to keep the United States from joining the Allies in the war.

Nevertheless, with the fall of France, America greatly accelerated its defense output. During the Depression years, when many plants were shut down or working part time, the sharp spur of necessity had urged industry to more economical and more efficient methods. Now, with the brakes released, unheard-of levels of production were achieved, even though, starting in 1940, the military draft was siphoning off more and more manpower into the armed services. As one dramatic example, at the outbreak of the war the total output of American airplane factories was less than 6,000 units a year. In May, 1940, President Roosevelt asked the industry to gear-up to an annual production of 50,000 planes, a staggering increase at a time when designs were undergoing constant changes. Yet, in a few years, the planes of all types manufactured in the nation totaled nearly 100,000 a year.

All doubts about America's entry into the war came to an abrupt and indisputable end on December 7, 1941, when Japan made its devastating surprise attack on Pearl Harbor and, immediately afterward, Germany and Italy declared war on the United States. The nation sprang to arms with a unity of purpose it had not known in 1917—or ever before. This time young Americans went off to their battle tasks about the world with little of the crusading fervor that had launched those earlier expeditionary forces. There was not much flag-waving and there were few parades; the disillusionment following the First World War had left its scars, as had the Depression and the long, acrimonious debate that preceded our engagement in this conflict. What positive results would come from victory remained a large question, yet ultimate victory was all but a certainty in the minds of most Americans. Meanwhile, there was a job to be done; the future would have to take care of itself.

The victory that had been so confidently predicted came in 1945, but it brought only an uneasy peace. America emerged from the war the most powerful and the richest nation on earth. As well, she was burdened with all the unavoidable responsibilities that went with that position—world-wide responsibilities new to a country that had so long avoided entanglements with Europe's age-old problems, not to mention those of the Orient. After having been totally engaged in a global war and playing a crucial part in the peace settlements, the United States could not conceivably retreat toward its old isolationism. Probably no dominant nation in history ever assumed international leadership at once so reluctantly and so vigorously. As the cold war with Russia froze the world into separate camps, the United States assumed Britain's traditional role as defender of Western European civilization.

For some bigoted Americans the easiest explanation of the new problems that beset their country was simply that a Communist conspiracy had infiltrated every segment of society, from the federal government to Hollywood and even to the churches of the land. With the late Senator Joseph McCarthy as their most notorious spokesman, such zealots instituted witch hunts that, unbelievably shocking as it seems in retrospect, bred a mood of caution and nervousness, of fear and conservatism, new to American experience. While the mood lasted, it was not easy for writers to maintain their dignity.

Recalling the literary revival that had followed World War I, writers, critics, and the reading public had some reason to expect an equivalent revival in the years following the peace of 1945. However, the latter peace proved to be more than an uneasy one—it was hardly a peace at all. Where, in retrospect, the literary output of the twenties seemed to announce the dawn of a new era in writing, the novels and poems of the late 1940's and the 1950's were written in what seemed to be the shadows of an apocalyptic twilight. The violence of America's wartime experience around the world had apparently shattered the nation's sense of continuity with its own past. Americans tended to look back nostalgically to the heady informalities of the 1920's and to the dedicated efforts against adversity of the 1930's—and as well to the inspiring days of the nation's birth and the emotional drama of the Civil War (the latter crisis was the subject of innumerable books in the post-World War II years).

The renaissance of American letters, which, as earlier remarked, advanced by stages in the decades before Pearl Harbor, reached a zenith at some point between 1920 and 1940. American writing had by then truly come of age. The years between 1930 and 1936 alone saw the publication of Hart Crane's *The Bridge,* Wolfe's *Of Time and the River,* O'Neill's *Mourning Becomes Electra,* Dos Passos' *U.S.A.,* Eliot's *Murder in the Cathedral,* Fitzgerald's *Tender is the Night,* and Faulkner's *Absalom, Absalom!,* among still other great works. Looking back over the growth of an American tradition of letters, the English-born poet and critic W. H. Auden (who became an American citizen) remarked that the most interesting American writers, from Melville and James to Faulkner and Hemingway, gave an impression that no one had ever written before them.

"I should call ours an *age* of American literature," wrote Alfred Kazin in 1955. America had by that time, he observed, become its own tradition, with American writers learning from American novels and poems, finding a tradition in American examples, Emerson, Thoreau, Melville, Dickinson, and then Pound and Eliot, as instances, have had greater influence on American writing than all but a few English authors. Certainly the time was past when English commentators could fairly refer to American writing as "colonial," as they so often and so long had done. Even during the earlier period, when that time-worn notion had some justification, when much American writing patently deferred to English standards and conventions, there were already American books of a distinctively native character. In the century following the birth of this nation, Washington Irving in his comic *History of New York,* James Fenimore Cooper in his Leatherstocking tales, James Russell Lowell in his *Biglow Papers,* Mark Twain, and, emphatically, Walt Whitman all convinced even foreign critics that their work was not wholly to be accounted for by English tradition.

In the last generation that awareness of the separate and special strain in American writing has sharpened remarkably. As Kazin has also noted, what the French poet Charles Baudelaire had discovered in Poe, the Spanish author Federico García Lorca in Whitman, and Marcel Proust and Friedrich Wilhelm Nietzsche in Emerson, other, later Europeans were finding in Melville, Eliot, Hemingway, and Dos Passos. Jean-Paul Sartre, the French existentialist philosopher, at one time considered Dos Passos the greatest modern writer, a high distinction few American critics would claim for him. The debt of English authors to their American cousins is suggested by the praise D. H. Lawrence paid to Walt Whitman. "Whitman, the great poet," Lawrence wrote, "has meant so much to me. Whitman, the one man breaking a way ahead. Whitman, the one pioneer . . . Whitman like a strange, modern, American Moses . . . the great leader. . . . He was a great changer of the blood in the veins of men." How much England—and all Europe—owes to the creative use of tradition by such poets as Pound and Eliot can hardly be measured.

One aspect of American writing that particularly appealed to European audiences was the tough, hardened violence that coursed through some of the best of it; not only human violence but the violence of Nature as a force in the shaping of human affairs and a symbol of fundamental verities, as in the works of Cooper, Melville, Stephen Crane, Faulkner, and Hemingway for example. There is reason enough for America's concern with such factors of life. In one of his brief essays the critic W. H. Auden pointed out that Englishmen live in a mild climate of "weather, whereas Americans live in a climate of violent extremes"; in England, he observed, "there is no primitive wilderness left and no uninhabitable area, but within fifty miles of New York City you can get fatally lost in the woods, and a breakdown of its irrigation system would turn most of Southern California into a desert within a few days." Such books as *Walden, Moby Dick, Leaves of Grass,* and *Huckleberry Finn* contain for us a racial memory of the wilderness that was for so long omnipresent in American life. Yet, Auden remarked, "if America is a land of heat waves, cold waves, tornadoes, droughts, floods, it is also, as a land only half-full and half domesticated, still a land of the Open Road, where the openness of the future does not seem wholly dependent upon technological advance and political wisdom. It is true that Huckleberry Finn can no longer light out for a Wild West, but he still feels that if to-day he fails, he can make a wholly new start somewhere else to-morrow; he can remember the past if he likes but he doesn't have to, and its only meaning to him is its relevance to the present."

A number of the leading writers of the twenties and thirties—Faulkner, Hemingway, Dos Passos, and O'Neill, along with such poets as Marianne Moore and Robert Frost, T. S. Eliot and Ezra Pound—continued to write for some years after the war. Robert Penn Warren, James Gould Cozzens, and others still continue. Meanwhile, a new generation of authors came to maturity in the postwar years: novelists, poets, and essayists whose work more directly reflects the temper of later times. These times have been turbulent, full of unexpected crises, new anxieties, international disorders, and rapid changes of perspective. Twice the United States has engaged in "hot" wars, in far-off Korea and Vietnam. At home leading Americans—President John F. Kennedy, Martin Luther King, Robert Kennedy, and Malcolm X—have been brutally assassinated. The country has been torn by debates over civil rights, particularly the pathetically long-deferred rights of the black minority. Meanwhile, too, Americans have walked and driven over the surface of the moon and returned safely to earth—adventures that, except for science-fiction writers and far-seeing scientists, were all but inconceivable in prewar years. How to define a society in such constant and sometimes violent flux and how to find in it a coherent role for the individual posed unprecedented problems for the writer (as for the artist) if he were to give expression to the age he lived in. It also suggested limitless answers and opened fresh paths to new talents.

Time will undoubtedly winnow out the most deserving of those talents more effectively than any short-range judgment of the moment can do. Since 1945 a fair number of literary reputations have already risen and fallen in critical, and popular, estimation; literary trends have come and gone. Such fluctuations in taste and values have always been the case, of course, but in recent decades the rhythm has become more rapid, as the pace of history itself has accelerated—and more books in more different forms by more authors are being published than ever before. To name all the writers who have won favorable notice over the years since the war would call for a list that would fill more pages than remain in this book. However, amid this wealth and variety of evidence there are some works that can be suggested as truly representative.

As might be expected, a number of capable young writers found themes for their work in their wartime experiences. One of the first important examples, still widely considered the best, was Norman Mailer's *The Naked and*

Novelists who wrote of the experiences, adventures, and tragedies of World War II; clockwise, starting at the near right, James G. Cozzens, James A. Michener, James Jones, Norman Mailer (at a party), John Hersey, and Herman Wouk

the Dead, published in 1948, when the author was twenty-five years old. This book, like others on the same general subject, owed some of its popularity to the fact that so many readers shared experiences of the kind Mailer wrote about. Sinclair Lewis thought of Mailer as "the greatest writer to come out of his generation." Ernest Hemingway, on the other hand—somewhat jealously, perhaps—referred to *The Naked and the Dead* as "poor cheese, pretentiously wrapped." In any case, the book immediately launched Mailer on a conspicuous and a somewhat flamboyant career that has hardly been free of controversy. Recalling the remark earlier quoted from W. H. Auden, one critic has written that Mailer "thinks as if no one in the history of the world has ever thought before him[;] . . . the only ideas he can feel and understand and use are those he himself has put forward."

As a commentary on the quality of a number of novels about the war, four of them won Pulitzer prizes: John Hersey's *A Bell for Adano* (1945), James A. Michener's *Tales of the South Pacific* (1948), James Gould Cozzens' *Guard of Honor* (1949), Herman Wouk's *The Caine Mutiny* (1952). James Jones' *The Thin Red Line,* published in 1963, did not win this particular distinction (nor did *The Naked and the Dead*), although it approached Mailer's book in the intensity of horror that it conveys. Jones had won wide attention twelve years earlier with *From Here to Eternity,* a naturalistic novel about army life at a Hawaiian base just before the Japanese attack on Pearl Harbor. Hersey wrote his book while the war was still in progress; Jones wrote *The Thin Red Line* eighteen years after the war was over. The continued popularity of the general theme is suggested by the fact that Rodgers and Hammerstein converted Michener's book into the enormously successful musical comedy *South Pacific,* and that Wouk's book was adapted both to the stage and the movies.

All these authors wrote other books on different subjects, of course, some of them more distinguished than their war novels, but the fact remains that the war and its consequences were shaping factors in their lives, as they were on American life in general. In a thoughtful essay entitled "The White Negro" Mailer refers to the psychic havoc caused by the ghastly horrors of the concentration camps and the atomic bomb:

> For the first time in civilized history, perhaps for the first time in all of history, we have been forced to live with the suppressed knowledge that . . . we might still be doomed to die as a cipher in some vast statistical operation in which our teeth would be counted, and our hair would be saved, but our death itself would be unknown, unhonored, and unremarked, a death which could not follow with dignity as a possible consequence to serious actions we had chosen, but rather a death by *deus ex machina* in a gas chamber or a radioactive city. . . .
>
> The Second World War presented a mirror to the human condition which blinded anyone who looked into it. For if tens of millions were killed in concentration camps out of the inexorable agonies and contractions of super-states founded upon the always insoluble contradictions of injustice, one was then obliged also to see that no matter how crippled and perverted an image of man was the society he had created, it was nonetheless his creation, his collective creation (at least his collective creation from the past) and if society was so murderous, then who

Phillis Wheatley was an African-born slave of the 18th-century Boston tailor John Wheatley, who educated her and encouraged her talent for writing verse. Thomas Jefferson was among those who vouched for the originality of her poetry when it was questioned.

could ignore the most hideous of questions about his own nature?

Worse. One could hardly maintain the courage to be individual, to speak with one's own voice, for the years in which one could complacently accept oneself as part of an elite by being a radical were forever gone. A man knew that when he dissented, he gave a note upon his life which could be called in any year of overt crisis. No wonder then that these have been the years of conformity and depression. A stench of fear has come out of every pore of American life, and we suffer from a collective failure of nerve. The only courage, with rare exceptions, that we have been witness to, has been the isolated courage of isolated people.

The war altered the patterns of life in this country in countless ways. Hitler's mad insistence on Aryan superiority, his depraved and murderous persecution of millions of Jews, made many Americans re-examine their own ethnic prejudices, and, all too often, to find senseless and malignant, not only their feeling about Jews, but about Negroes and other ethnic groups. In American literature, as in common parlance, both Jews and Negroes had all too frequently been reduced to comic stereotypes—"kikes" and "niggers"— as in earlier years had been the Germans and the Irish who came to this country to find a better life. A remarkable indication of changing attitudes could be read in the election returns of 1960 when a Roman Catholic of recent Irish descent was elected to the presidency of the United States.

No other group benefited more from the war than the Negroes. Their valuable service in the armed forces and in defense projects and other civilian activities during a time of crisis was an insistent reminder that no citizens of

A group of prominent black writers; clockwise, starting at the near left, James Baldwin, Imamu Amiri Baraka (assumed name of Leroi Jones), Richard Wright, W. E. B. Dubois, Ralph Ellison

377

this nation could be considered second rate. Racial discrimination did not disappear with that realization or with the enactment of laws designed to reduce or eliminate it from American life, but the process already under way was accelerated. A distinctive Negro culture had enriched American life for centuries past through its peculiar and colorful dialect, its folklore, celebrating such heroes as John Henry and his rivals, which gave rise in white America to the popular Uncle Remus stories; the rhythms of the blues and the spirituals; and the skills of individual musicians and practitioners of the other arts.

For all their richness of expression, such contributions did not flow directly into the mainstream of American culture, although they are inseparable components. As far back as the eighteenth century there were black poets like the Senegalese-born slave Phillis Wheatley and another slave, Jupiter Hammon, whose verse, indifferent in quality as it was, astonished the white world simply by having been created under the circumstances. The Lady Huntingdon, who entertained Miss Wheatley, must have considered her a benighted savage who, by the grace of God and the good will of a tailor (her master) from Boston, had learned to turn an ode as well as any of the school of Alexander Pope. (Miss Wheatley did not complain of her bondage in America; rather, she rejoiced that "young in life, by seeming cruel fate [she] was snatched from Africa's fancy'd happy state.") Even in recent years black writers, like black artists, have too often been thought of as Negroes first and as writers and artists second.

There were black writers of merit at work in the nineteenth century, such as Charles W. Chesnutt, whose short stories were published in the *Atlantic Monthly* and whose novels continued to appear into the present century. Chesnutt was a better novelist than many who followed him, and a better writer than the times could afford with competition from the popular romances of the day. He did not feel obliged to use the novel to air the very real grievances of the Negro, but rather to find with it a means for dramatizing basic human conflicts, hopes, and fears. While Chesnutt was producing his stories, around the turn of the century, Paul Laurence Dunbar was writing lyrical poems in which he used to good effect Negro refrains blended with typical humor and pathos.

However, it was in the early decades of this century that the Negro found a new and audible voice, a voice of affirmation and of protest—affirmation of his right to take an equal place beside white Americans, protest against the difficulties of securing that right. That voice grew in volume and in eloquence in the 1920's, the heyday of what became known as the Harlem Renaissance, when such writers as Langston Hughes, Claude McKay, W. E. B. Dubois, Countee Cullen, Jean Toomer, and James Weldon Johnson, to name but a few, were creating novels and poems that commanded the attention of a wide reading public. In passing, this was an active period in the lives of such notable Negro performers as Paul Robeson, Roland Hayes, Louis Armstrong, Duke Ellington, and Josephine Baker. (The Harlem scene of that decade was vividly and sympathetically described by Carl VanVechten, a white writer, in his novel *Nigger Heaven*.)

In the decades that followed, talented black writers were winning even wider and more enthusiastic audiences. Langston Hughes, one of the most prolific of all and a highly developed, self-conscious artist, produced poems, librettos, short stories, and autobiographies, as well as novels. Like a number of other Negro authors of the time, and like Chesnutt more than a generation before him, Hughes could write with more interest in life itself than in propaganda for his race, as in his outstanding novel *Not Without Laughter*. As did a growing number of other writers, he gave us the actual manners and speech of the Negro without undue deference to white conventions of deportment and cultivation. He is best remembered for his poems, often sardonic and untraditional in form, in which he caught the inimitable tang of Negro expressions and the pulsing rhythms of jazz. "We younger Negro artists," he once remarked, "now intend to express our individual dark-skinned selves without fear or shame."

When Richard Wright's novel *Native Son* appeared in 1940, the author was widely hailed as the leading American Negro writer of the time. It is a passionately honest and passionately angry book, written with an intention to represent the sufferings of members of his race through a story of grotesque and violent crime. It is also a deliberately sensational book that yet asks for the reader's pity and compassion. (It was successfully dramatized and made into a film—in Argentina—with Wright himself in the leading role.) Some critics have blamed Wright for writing a mechanically contrived, if slick, "protest" novel, and, in doing so, having robbed his major character of human credibility. But Wright's own indignation is true, and he wrote *Native Son* at a time during the late years of the Depression when the airing of social grievances found a sympathetic reception. Born in Mississippi, Wright had had to go on relief during the 1930's, and for a while he was a member of the Communist party. (In those days he also received a prize for the best book by anyone associated with the Federal Writers' Project.) After the war he expatriated himself to Paris, where he continued to write.

James Baldwin, born in Harlem, sixteen years later than Wright, also spent years as an expatriate in Paris. (He finished one recent book in Istanbul.) When his first novel, *Go Tell It on the Mountain*, was published in 1953, it was acclaimed as a major story of Negro life in America; Baldwin himself was hailed as a rising leader among Negro writers. Virtually by popular acclamation he was nominated a spokesman of his people. (His portrait appeared on the cover of *Time* magazine, and action pictures of him were run in *Life* magazine, as tokens of his popular image.) Baldwin has had a proclivity for turning the emotional complications of his own life into symbols of the crisis of black experience in America. In spite of his acknowledged literary talent, his self-appointed role as a very "angry Black" is confused by the fact that he is a homosexual and that accordingly his personal problems, his particular concern for sexual matters, represent to some extent those of a minority of his own minority race.

When Ralph Ellison's novel *The Invisible Man* was published in 1952, it won a National Book Award. Thirteen years later a panel of two hundred authors and critics nominated it as the work of American fiction most likely to endure of all those issued since 1945. *The Invisible Man* tells the story of a young black searching for his identity as an individual, for his place in

A sampling of Jewish authors; Bernard Malamud (left), Arthur Miller and Saul Bellow (below left to right) conversing with John Steinbeck, J. D. Salinger (far right)

relation both to his race and to American society. It was written before the more violent explosions of Negro protest, and has the more power for not assuming the nature of a tract, as so many later novels of protest did. Yet, it remains, as Marcus Cunliffe termed it, "a furious fantasy, as savage in its concluding account of a Harlem riot as the apocalyptic novels of . . . Jack London, or as Richard Wright's . . . *Native Son.*" In that one novel of his, Ellison looks beyond the plight of the Negro to a vision of the universal condition of man as such white authors as Melville and Faulkner had projected it. When it is finally defined, Ellison has pointed out, the "image of the American" must be an amalgam of black and white. Like other forms of Negro expression, Negro literature is in the end an inseparable part of American culture. That is a thought to consider as the number of books by and about Negroes mounts with each passing season, books by such young writers as William Melvin Kelly, John Williams, and others too numerous to mention.

Although the annals of American history, since the days before the Revolution, are studded with the names of illustrious Jews, the position of the Jew in American society, like that of the Negro, has been somewhat ambiguous and apart as a member of a separate minority that has managed to retain a particular identity in the overwhelming majority of Christians. The greater number of Jews in the country descend from immigrants who came here after 1880, mainly from Russia, Austria-Hungary, Poland, and Rumania. Like other newcomers to America from such "outlandish" places, they were considered an alien strain that would be difficult, if not impossible, to assimilate into traditional American culture. On the lighter side, Jewish jokes and vaudeville acts provided stock entertainment on the street and stage. Potash and Perlmutter were classic comics in the early years of this century; as Leslie A. Fiedler has observed, the Jew entered American culture "on the stage, laughing." (Interesting sidelights on this sort of caricature appear in the solemn message inscribed on the base of the Statue of Liberty welcoming "the wretched refuse, the homeless, tempest-tost" peoples of the world, written by the Jewess Emma Lazarus; and in the fact that the Pulitzer prizes were founded with an endowment established by the Hungarian-born son of a Jewish immigrant, journalist Joseph Pulitzer, who died in 1911.)

Today, relatively so few years later, the Jew is no longer seen as an alien in a traditionally white Protestant culture. Jewish authors, indeed, have been among the outstanding interpreters of American life for Gentile and Jew alike. Having been less brutally excluded than the Negroes from conventional American society, Jewish writers have felt less reason to be militant about the place they so rightfully won in public acceptance of their talents. One recent British reviewer has remarked that Jewish authors have added ambition to the already ambitious American ego. In their writings, he adds, "the Id seems to have shot up into the head. Sex is certainly in the head. And this has led to either a comic or ugly disparagement of women, which leads one to think adolescence hangs on as a rage not outgrown." Such words almost automatically bring to mind the work of Philip Roth, whose first popular success, *Portnoy's Complaint*, was published in 1969. Like others of his generation of writers, Roth is explicit in his references to sex—to a degree that would have had his book banned a mere decade earlier. He is also fascinated by the details of his own Jewish childhood. There is in his work, Kazin writes, "the calculated profanation of mother, father, the most intimate offices of the body. . . ." He traces his own experience back to the infantile rejections he recalls in detail and to the resentments that came of them. And in his obsession with the Jewish family, as Kazin also observes about Roth, he managed to remove all the mystery from the Jewish experience.

The Jewish writers Herman Wouk and Norman Mailer have been mentioned. A third, Saul Bellow, has been called "America's finest living novel-

Beat authors and poets of recent years; clockwise, starting at the top, Lawrence Ferlinghetti, Jack Kerouac, Gregory Corso, and Allen Ginsberg. The work of the beats (so called largely by their own choice) began to be noticed in the cafés and cabarets of San Francisco in the early 1950's and then succeeded to recognition.

381

ist" by more than one critic. Bellow was born in Canada of parents come there from Russia, and he was brought up in Chicago. Two of his major novels, *The Adventures of Augie March* (1953) and *Herzog* (1961), serve to represent his special accomplishments. In both these, typically, his main characters are Jewish; the non-Jewish others are obsessed with Jews. Life in America is presented through the experience of Jews whose background is in the ghettos of eastern Europe, whose immigrant parents had been nothing but Jews to the tyrants of their homelands—Jews whose offspring graduated from the slums of Montreal or Chicago to emancipation in a wider world. "Look at me going everywhere!" cries Augie March, a young Chicago Jew, amazed at the liberation and enlightenment he found in picaresque adventures that took him far from his childhood environment into situations where he lives sensitively and with new awareness of a life in which his Jewishness remains important. *Herzog* is the odyssey of a scholarly American Jew, who in Bellow's story becomes one of the most credible and articulate intellectuals in all of modern fiction—a man with an indomitable belief in commanding his own experience by thinking it through. Here, as elsewhere in Bellow's works, the Jewish experience represents in sharp focus a life and a world any American of discernment could recognize as his own.

"All men are Jews," remarked Bernard Malamud, a Jewish author who was born in Brooklyn of immigrant Russian parents. Malamud writes with equal care and facility about Jew and Gentile alike. For instance, his first novel, *The Natural*, published in 1952, is a story of the game of baseball in terms of the skilled player who becomes an American folk hero, told with comic overtones. In such later works as *The Assistant* (1957) and *The Magic Barrel* (1958), he is concerned with the daily life of Jews in America, with the travail and indignity which they may happen to face. His characters speak with a vigorous Yiddish accent common to the streets of New York. He writes with piercing insight into such situations, tempered by Jewish sense of self-irony that reveals a fundamental faith in man.

J. D. Salinger is a writer of a different stripe. For some years his novel *The Catcher in the Rye*, published in 1951, was considered "the testament of the postwar generation." In it Salinger views the American scene through the eyes of an unhappy, quixotic teen-age boy, disturbed by the "phoniness" of his moral environment and at odds with the adult establishment. The book has been described as a latter-day version of *Huckleberry Finn*. For a generation of readers it served as a sensitive commentary on an adolescent adrift in an unlovable world—a theme much in the mood of the times—and it enjoyed immense popularity, especially among those who were eager to identify themselves with its principal character. In his few but brilliant shorter stories, such as *Franny and Zooey* and *Raise High the Roofbeam, Carpenters*, most of which first appeared in *The New Yorker*, Salinger uses his unique prose to describe young urban Americans of middle-class parentage, all faced with the corruption that goes with growing up, which, at least until recently, has remained a postwar problem of our youth.

Such a spirit of youthful revolt against the established formalities of life and literature characterizes the so-called Beat Movement that we associate in American writing with the 1950's and with San Francisco. Beat writers—Jack

Kerouac, Allen Ginsberg, Gregory Corso, and Lawrence Ferlinghetti, to name a few, and some not quite youthful—looked for illumination and fulfillment in completely disassociating their style of life and letters from that of the conventional world into which they were born. Aided by drink and drugs, they expressed themselves in their own "hip" language, using inspirational phrases from the Zen philosophy that influenced them. They are one of the latest in an old and honored American tradition of protest that would include among its exponents Thoreau and Whitman. But it is doubtful whether the contribution of the beats to that tradition has added much that will be valued by later generations, except as a historical phenomenon. Their undisciplined, intemperate, and spontaneous celebration of the individual personality as a matter of commanding importance lacks both the craftsmanlike qualities and the sense of shared experience that for long ages have been the essential stuff of enduring literature. Nevertheless, something of the spirit that dominates beat writing, its improvisations and chance irregularities, is present not only in the writing of Salinger, but in the later work of Mailer and Saul Bellow, and in the work of such older writers as the poet Kenneth Rexroth and the novelist Henry Miller. Miller's best-known book, *Tropic of Cancer*, was banned in the United States for twenty-seven years after it was first published in Paris in 1934. The custodians of American morals considered it obscene. Miller wrote that book, and *Tropic of Capricorn* (1939), as an expatriate in Paris during the Depression, and he was writing about more than sex. He was expressing his intense individualism, his quest of intellectual and aesthetic adventure, as well as his love of personal freedom. His work remains of major interest today.

That American society of the postwar period was re-forming in new patterns was obvious enough, although what those patterns would eventually come to be was all but impossible to judge; what they *should* be was another question, one open to wide argument. More objective witnesses than the beats put their minds to the matter. One basic problem was to try to determine, amid the rapid changes that were taking place, what was actually happening in American life, and to this end a number of analytical books were addressed that had

Southern writers; from left to right, Flannery O'Connor, Eudora Welty, and Truman Capote, with pet. Miss O'Connor died in 1964 at the age of thirty-nine. Miss Welty and Capote are producing new works, the former in Mississippi, the latter in New York City.

considerable influence. In *The Lonely Crowd*, published in 1950, David Riesman saw the emergence of "other-directed" patterns of social behavior, as different from the "inner-directed" patterns of earlier years. The venerable traditions of the "Protestant work ethic" and of "rugged individualism," for so long basic premises in the definition of American culture, were being reconsidered. *The Organization Man,* by William H. Whyte, Jr., reenforced the conclusion that representative Americans, in spite of the voices raised in dissent, were becoming mass-organized conformists whose standards were not fixed or fundamental, but were shaped by shifting circumstance to those of their neighbors and business associates. American men eager for success, for instance, wore gray flannel suits (or uniforms), as in Sloan Wilson's popular book *The Man in the Gray Flannel Suit* (1955), and complied with regulations prescribed by the large, paternalistic business corporations that controlled their futures. It was in the same dispassionate spirit that Dr. Alfred Kinsey compiled his controversial statistical reports on American sexual behavior. Such books were sociological studies rather than creative literature, but they tended to take over one of literature's most characteristic functions, the investigation and criticism of manners and morals.

Nevertheless, the continued diversity of American culture and the vitality of creative American literature was undeniable. One of the most productive sources of fiction was the South, where such distinguished writers as Carson McCullers, Eudora Welty, Truman Capote, and Flannery O'Connor produced novels and stories that still seem among the best of the period. Although before her death in 1967 McCullers had long lived in New York, she was a Georgian who set the scene of most of her work in her native state. Her first novel, *The Heart is a Lonely Hunter*, was published when she was twenty-three, on the eve of the war, but it strikes a note that was repeated with variations in her subsequent postwar work—a note of "spiritual isolation," as she called it, which provided the pivot for her plots. Love, she held, was the answer to life's dilemma; but in her stories love relationships appear as solitary and obsessed attachments that perform no magical transformations in her characters.

The humorist S. J. Perelman, left, enjoying a good laugh. In his cartoon "House and Woman" James Thurber plays on one of his most popular themes; with formidable spirit a predatory, all-embracing female confronts a properly apprehensive male, reduced in scale by the overwhelming odds he faces. Until his death in 1961 Thurber was a frequent contributor to The New Yorker, *for which magazine Perelman continues to write his sophisticated and witty nonsense.*

Flannery O'Connor, another woman author from Georgia, wrote some of her best fiction in the shadow of what she knew would be her early death. In her two gothic novels, *Wise Blood* (1952) and *The Violent Bear It Away* (1960), and her book of short stories, the fiction is frequently grotesque and understated. Her characters inhabit a world of "Guilt and sorrow"; they are souls in the wrong world who resent that fact of their lives and who are presented with clear and terrible vision and with relentless pity.

Although he was born in New Orleans, Truman Capote prefers not to consider himself a Southerner. *In Cold Blood*, a meticulously documented examination of a notorious multiple murder in Kansas (the author worked from six thousand pages of notes), tells a true, tragic story that if presented as fiction would seem scarcely credible enough for publication. (Capote called it a "nonfiction novel.") That book, extravagantly promoted and publicized before it was issued, won more attention than any of Capote's other works; it made a celebrity of him and made him a fortune.

In Cold Blood, a very highly stylized performance, was serialized in *The New Yorker* before it appeared in book form. Over the years this magazine has welcomed to its pages a variety of literary stylists whose use of the American language in short stories and in the books that have often resulted from them set standards of excellence. One of the most brilliant and witty of *The New Yorker*'s contributors was E. B. White, an original writer in the classic tradition of Thoreau whose regard for the written word is unsurpassed in American letters and whose influence has been important but unobtrusive. White also wrote a long series of essays for *Harper's Magazine*, published as *One Man's Meat*, which he produced from a salt-water farm in Maine while "engaged in trivial, peaceable pursuits, knowing all the time that the world hadn't arranged any true peace or granted anyone the privilege of indulging himself in such trivialities." (Those words were written during the war years.) Clifton Fadiman praised White's "ability to write of the small and large at the same time, even in the same sentence. Thus the subject may be a raccoon hunt or a lambing or a park for caravans; but it is also freedom and democracy and the American notion of individuality." He is a humane, civilized, and sensitive craftsman who, as Fadiman wrote, "sees through things to the truths that lie behind appearances." "His modulated sentences," Fadiman remarked, "have in them both the whir of the wings of poetry and the plain honest accent of twentieth-century American speech."

Another truly inimitable humorist very closely associated with *The New Yorker* was James Thurber, whose essays, fables, stories, and drawings repre-

The fame of John Cheever (upper left) continues to grow with each new work. He, like John Updike (above), has been a frequent contributor to The New Yorker. *Over the past thirty years, the poems, novels, and essays of Robert Penn Warren (below) have won a notable place in American letters.*

sented a heightened form of fantasy that was never disassociated from reality and the commonplace. His contributions to the magazine began in 1927 and continued until his death in 1961. Of his humorous tales and drawings he once said, "the little wheels of their invention are set in motion by the damp hand of melancholy." "Humor," he remarked, "is a kind of emotional chaos told about calmly and quietly in retrospect." He wrote and illustrated large truths in the simplest and most polished style. As Russell Lynes observed in 1957, Thurber was one of the few humorists of the twentieth century whose reputation will remain increasingly secure. The fantasies of his subdued, puzzled little men, surrounded by predatory women and resigned dogs, cut through all the transient crises of modern society to lead us, as they did Thurber's appealing "hero" Walter Mitty, toward dreams of ultimate glory.

One other contributor to *The New Yorker* whose style has defied any successful imitation is the humorist S. J. Perelman. From the late 1920's to the present day his lightly handled satirical pieces have lampooned the vacuities so carelessly repeated by advertising agents, in motion picture dialogues, in popular fiction, and in the daily press. Perelman has done for literature what the Marx brothers did for the motion pictures. By his skillful manipulation of words and clichés he creates from commonplace incidents a surrealistic world that is endlessly entertaining and almost believable. He was, in his own words, "rapier sharp, button cute." After reading Perelman's always unexpected play with words one reads everything else more carefully.

John Cheever and John Updike are still two other writers associated with *The New Yorker,* authors with distinctive styles and individual approaches to those aspects of the world about them that they chose to define and describe. Cheever's world is New England suburbia, whose generally affluent and domesticated dwellers, disenchanted with the quality of their lives, and in a heartbreakingly comic manner act out their inner conflicts through eccentric adventures. Like their distant Puritan forebears, they find life in America as they know it merely a way station on the long road to some Promised Land. Cheever's first long work of fiction, *The Wapshot Chronicle,* published in 1957, won a National Book Award.

Updike, a stylist of great gifts, has provided brightly lighted pictures of American society since the mid-1950's—in particular, the American society observable near his small home town in southeastern Pennsylvania. In such books as *Rabbit, Run* (1960), *The Centaur* (1963), and *Rabbit Redux* (1970), one critic has observed, he writes "as if from an inexhaustible intelligence" and "with a poet's sensibility." His ultimate reputation is still in the making, for like that of Cheever and others among his talented contemporaries, his work is by no means finished.

It is possible to view the work of Robert Penn Warren in deeper perspective because he has been writing fiction, verse, and critical essays since the 1920's In 1947 he was awarded a Pulitzer Prize for his novel *All the King's Men* and in 1958 another prize for *Promises: Poems 1954–1956*. Born in Kentucky, Warren has close associations with the traditions and issues of the South. *All the King's Men,* for example, is a complex account of provincial political tyranny in that region; it is a richly colored story that has no equal in American fiction in the treatment of that subject. One verse from *Original Sin: A Short*

Story (1942) will serve as a sample of Warren's closely structured poetry:

> Nodding, its great head rattling like a gourd,
> And locks like seaweed strung on the stinking stone,
> The nightmare stumbles past, and you have heard
> It fumble your door before it whimpers and is gone:
> It acts like the old hound that used to snuffle your door and moan.

In late years Warren's poetry has become increasingly sensuous and personal. Writing about modern poetry in 1966, Warren observed: "The collected editions are now settled comfortably on the shelves, some, even, gathering a little dust. The authors of some of those books are dead. We are witnessing, in other words, the end of a poetic era, the end of "modernism," that school of which the founding fathers were Eliot, Pound, and Yeats. It is true that in the quarter of a century since the end of World War II a new poetry expressive of a new sensibility has emerged. To select names from the list of varied talents that have won popular recognition and critical applause in recent years must appear invidious. Yet any selection of representative poets would at the very least have to include Theodore Roethke, Karl Shapiro, Robert Lowell, Richard Wilbur, and John Berryman all of whom received Pulitzer prizes.

Roethke was the oldest of this group, a great hulk of a man, a nimble tennis player, and a precocious artist. His favorite theme deals with the cycle of birth, growth, decay, and death—as indeed he had ample occasion to witness it in the greenhouses of his family's large floral establishment in Saginaw, Michigan. Thus he wrote about a child in such a greenhouse:

> The roses kept breathing in the dark
> They had many mouths to breathe with.
> My knees made little winds underneath
> Where the weeds slept.
>
> There was always a single light
> Swinging by the fire-pit,
> Where the fireman pulled out roses,
> The big roses, the big bloody cinders.

A quartet of Pulitzer Prize-winning modern poets; clockwise, starting at the top, Karl Shapiro (1945), Theodore Roethke (1954), Robert Lowell (1947), and Richard P. Wilbur (1957). Like Robert Frost, Archibald MacLeish, Robert Penn Warren, John Berryman, and other American poets (and Pulitzer Prize winners), all four have been influential through their teaching at various colleges and universities as well as through their writings.

Until his sudden death in 1963, Roethke passed through several distinct stages of development, his verse ranging from nonsense rhymes to poems of surrealistic darkness. The rich imagery he sustained in his best work is suggested by the first and last verses of "Elegy for Jane: My student, thrown by a horse":

> I remember the neckcurls, limp and damp as tendrils;
> And her quick look, a sidelong pickerel smile;
> And how, once startled into talk, the light syllables leaped for her,
> And she balanced in the delight of her thought,
> A wren, happy, tail into the wind,
> Her song trembling the twigs and small branches.
> The shade sang with her;
> The leaves, their whispers turned to kissing;
> And the mould sang in the bleached valleys under the rose.
>
> ❋   ❋   ❋   ❋
>
> If only I could nudge you from this sleep,
> My maimed darling, my skittery pigeon.
> Over this damp grave I speak the words of my love:
> I, with no rights in this matter,
> Neither father nor lover.

The influential author, teacher, poet, and critic Allen Tate has written that not since the advent of T. S. Eliot had poetry seen "that final honesty which is rare, unpleasant, and indispensable in a poet of our time" that could be found in the work of Karl Shapiro. He won his Pulitzer Prize with a book of verse written while he was a soldier in the South Pacific. The first and last verses of "Nostalgia" offer a tantalizing sampling of his rare talent:

> My soul stands at the window of my room,
>   And I ten thousand miles away;
> My days are filled with Ocean's sound of doom,
>   Salt and cloud and the bitter spray.
> Let the wind blow, for many a man shall die.
>
> ❋   ❋   ❋   ❋
>
> Laughter and grief join hands. Always the heart
>   Clumps in the breast with heavy stride;
> The face grows lined and wrinkled like a chart.
>   The eyes bloodshot with tears and tide.
> Let the wind blow, for many a man shall die.

Lowell, a great grandson of James Russell Lowell and a namesake of his brother, Robert Traill Spence Lowell, has been hailed as the most accomplished of postwar poets—indeed, as "America's best living poet." He has been a nonconformist who, despite his family heritage, shied away from Harvard, became a convert to Catholicism, and was jailed as a conscientious objector during the war. He has written with disenchantment, but with quiet authority and deep personal concern, about aspects of the American scene he cannot with good conscience tolerate. In "Mr. Edwards and the Spider" he recalls the observations recorded by Jonathan Edwards as a child in the eighteenth century. The first two verses read (Edwards is speaking):

> I saw the spiders marching through the air,
> Swimming from tree to tree that mildewed day

> In latter August when the hay
> Came creaking to the barn. But where
>   The wind is westerly,
> Where gnarled November makes the spiders fly
> Into the apparitions of the sky,
>   They purpose nothing but their ease and die
> Urgently beating east to sunrise and the sea;
>
> What are we in the hands of the great God?
> It was in vain you set up thorn and briar
>   In battle array against the fire
>   And treason crackling in your blood;
>   For the wild thorns grow tame
> And will do nothing to oppose the flame;
> Your lacerations tell the losing game
> You play against a sickness past your cure.
> How will the hands be strong? How will the heart endure?

John Berryman was another poet who found a theme in Puritan New England, with *Homage to Mistress Bradstreet*, published in 1956, one of the most highly regarded long poems recently written in America. In this richly allusive biographical ode he inquires into the personal and spiritual life of Anne Bradstreet to relate its significance to the present day. With another long work, *77 Dream Songs*, Berryman won the Pulitzer Prize for poetry in 1965. One critic has written that this work "is about a poet writing a poem that is the poem one is reading." He had started this long sequence ten years earlier, and he continued to compose other "Dream songs" in following years. Berryman, in a fresh and often surprising idiom, wrote of an imaginary character, Henry, who talks about himself sometimes in the first person, sometimes in the third, or, again, in the second. In "Dream song 14" he wrote:

> Life, friends, is boring. We must not say so.
> After all, the sky flashes, the great sea yearns,
> we ourselves flash and yearn,
> and moreover my mother told me as a boy
> (repeatedly) 'Ever to confess you're bored
> means you have no
>
> Inner Resources.' I conclude now I have no
> inner resources, because I am heavy bored.
> Peoples bore me,
> literature bores me, especially great literature,
> Henry bores me, with his plights & gripes
> as bad as achilles,
>
> who loves people and valiant art, which bores me.
> And the tranquil hills, & gin, look like a drag
> and somehow a dog
> has taken itself & its tail considerably away
> into mountains or sea or sky, leaving
> behind: me, wag.

Berryman died a suicide in 1972.

Richard Wilbur, another war veteran, writes with technical virtuosity and with a wide learning that he wears lightly in his precisely composed, graceful, and catholic poetry. As in the case of the other creative talents briefly mentioned here, the full savour of Wilbur's work can only be had with much wider acquaintance than can be introduced in these pages. The temptation to quote one of his poems, "Beasts," is, however, irresistible and this may serve to remind us of how much delight awaits us in the further reading of the authors here mentioned:

> Beasts in their major freedom
> Slumber in peace tonight. The gull on his ledge
> Dreams in the guts of himself the moon-plucked waves below,
> And the sunfish leans on a stone, slept
> By the lyric water,
>
> In which the spotless feet
> Of deer make dulcet splashes, and to which
> The ripped mouse, safe in the owl's talon, cries
> Concordance. Here there is no such harm
> And no such darkness
>
> As the selfsame moon observes
> Where, warped in window-glass, it sponsors now
> The werewolf's painful change. Turning his head away
> On the sweaty bolster, he tries to remember
> The mood of manhood,
>
> But lies at last, as always,
> Letting it happen, the fierce fur soft to his face,
> Hearing with sharper ears the wind's exciting minors,
> The leaves' panic, and the degradation
> Of the heavy streams.
>
> Meantime, at high windows
> Far from thicket and pad-fall, suitors of excellence
> Sigh and turn from their work to construe again the painful
> Beauty of heaven, the lucid moon
> And the risen hunter,
>
> Making such dreams for men
> As told will break their hearts as always, bringing
> Monsters into the city, crows on the public statues,
> Navies fed to the fish in the dark
> Unbridled waters.

Six years ago the English poet and critic Stephen Spender observed that the center of poetic activity in the English language had shifted for the predicable future from London to the United States, and there is good reason to accept that judgment. Somewhat earlier, Robert Frost pointed out that a poem "begins in delight and ends in wisdom," as does so much of his own verse. American poetry of our time is rich in such delights. American literature in all its forms has long since taken deep root in native soil and, like American painting and architecture, has spread out to make its fresh and ample contribution to the culture of the world at large.

THE ART OF LITERATURE

American writers and artists have often shared their interests. As earlier told, some writers have drawn or painted with variable results, and some artists have written commendable verse and prose. As has also been remarked, a number of prominent painters have used their talents to illustrate literary works—traditionally with more or less straightforward pictorial representations of scenes and persons described in such texts. Grant Wood's Midnight Ride of Paul Revere, *below, painted in 1931, is a fanciful rather than a literal interpretation of Longfellow's poem. It is much more an evocative pattern than a realistic depiction. In late years, during the vogue for abstractions, artists have occasionally used literature merely as a point of departure for their inspirations, eschewing all traces of representational art in their efforts to approximate the mood of a poem or prose passage in visual terms. A selection of these is reproduced on the following pages.*

METROPOLITAN MUSEUM OF ART

391

A CARAFE, THAT IS A BLIND GLASS
A kind in glass and a cousin, a spectacle and nothing strange a single hurt color and an arrangement in a system to pointing. All this and not ordinary, not unordered in not resembling. The difference is spreading."

"A PETTICOAT
A light white, a disgrace, an ink spot, a rosy charm."

"A TIME TO EAT
A pleasant simple habitual and tyrannical and authorised and educated and resumed and articulate separation. This is not tardy."

"A FIRE
What was the use of a whole time to send and not send if there was to be the kind of thing that made that come in. A letter was nicely sent."

"A BROWN
A brown which is not liquid not more so is relaxed and yet there is a change, a news is pressing."

"A SOUND
Elephant beaten with candy and little pops and chews all bolts and reckless reckless rats, this is this."

Gertrude Stein, from "Objects," in *Tender Buttons*

Like most artists, the painter Bradley Walker Tomlin experimented with a variety of styles, including a rather decorative cubism and a mode close to expressionism and action painting. It was only toward the end of his life that he found a very personal expression in works such as Number 9: In Memory of Gertrude Stein (1950), reproduced above. It is fitting that Tomlin, who has been so much a part of the artistic revolutions of the 20th century, should pay homage to Gertrude Stein, one of the chief advocates of modernism in all the arts. In her poetry and prose she sought to create a literary equivalent of post-impressionism and cubism, and through experiments in syntax "to get to the very core of the communication of the intuition."

Poem

I will always love you
though I never loved you

a boy smelling faintly of heather
looking up at your window

the passion that enlightens
and stills and cultivates, gone

while I sought your face
to be familiar in the likeness

or to follow your sharp whistle
around a corner into my light

that was love growing fainter
each time you failed to appear

I spent my whole life searching
love which I thought was you

it was mine so very briefly
and I never knew it, or you went

I thought it was outside disappearing
but it is disappearing in my heart

like snow blown in a window
to be gone from the world

I will always love you

Frank O'Hara

*One of the finest instances of American collaboration between artists and authors was
21 Etchings and Poems, published in New York in 1960 by the Morris Gallery (the imprint of
poet Morris Weisenthal). The portfolio includes twenty-one etchings in black and white,
each of which appears with the poem that either inspired it or complements it. Franz Kline's
bold abstraction, above, provides a counterpoint to Poem, written by Frank O'Hara.*

"Among the rain
and lights
I saw the figure 5
in gold
on a red
firetruck
moving
tense
unheeded
to gong clangs
siren howls
and wheels rumbling
through the dark city."

William Carlos Williams, "The Great Figure"

METROPOLITAN MUSEUM OF ART, ALFRED STEIGLITZ COLLECTION, 1949

Charles Demuth's painting I Saw the Figure 5 in Gold *(1928), which remains one of his most important works, was dedicated to his close friend, the imagist poet William Carlos Williams, and was based on his poem, opposite. Williams greatly admired the painting and called it a "literary" picture.*

*"It was the whiteness of the whale that above all things appalled
me. But how can I hope to explain myself here; and yet, in some dim,
random way, explain myself I must, else all these chapters
might be naught.*

*Though in many natural objects, whiteness refiningly enhances
beauty, as if imparting some special virtue of its own,
as in marbles, japonicas, and pearls . . . yet for all these
accumulated associations, with whatever is sweet, and honorable,
and sublime, there yet lurks an elusive something in the innermost
idea of this hue, which strikes more of panic to the soul than
that redness which affrights in blood.*

*This elusive quality it is, which causes the thought of
whiteness, when divorced from more kindly associations, and coupled
with any object terrible in itself, to heighten that terror
to the furthest bounds. . . . That ghastly whiteness it is which imparts
such an abhorrent mildness, even more loathsome than terrific,
to the dumb gloating of their aspect. . . .*

*Is it that by its indefiniteness it shadows forth the heartless
voids and immensities of the universe, and thus stabs us
from behind with the thought of annihilation,
when beholding the white depths of the milky way? Or is it, that
as in essence whiteness is not so much a color as the
visible absence of color, and at the same time the concrete of
all colors; is it for these reasons that there is such
a dumb blankness, full of meaning, in a wide landscape of snows—
a colorless, all-color of atheism from which we shrink? . . .*

*And of all these things the Albino Whale was the symbol.
Wonder ye then at the fiery hunt?"*

Herman Melville, from "The Whiteness of the Whale," in *Moby Dick*

*Abstract painter Sam Francis worked primarily in blacks,
grays, and tinted whites until the early 1950's, when he began
introducing patches of luminous colors in his canvases. His
painting* The Whiteness of the Whale *(1957–58) is a study in
the tension between white and opposing forces of color. The
title is the same as that of the chapter in* Moby Dick *devoted
to a disquisition of the terrifying nature of the color white.*

"I would sing in my copious song your census returns of the
    States,
The tables of population and products, I would sing of your
    ships and their cargoes,
The proud black ships of Manhattan arriving, some fill'd with
    immigrants, some from the isthmus with cargoes of gold,
Songs thereof would I sing, to all that hitherward comes would I
    welcome give,
And you would I sing, fair stripling! welcome to you from me,
    young prince of England!
(Remember you surging Manhattan's crowds as you pass'd with
    your cortege of nobles?
There in the crowds stood I, and singled you out with attach-
    ment;)
Nor forget I to sing of the wonder, the ship as she swam up my
    bay,
Well-shaped and stately the Great Eastern swam up my bay, she
    was 600 feet long,
Her moving swiftly surrounded by myriads of small craft I
    forget not to sing;
Nor the comet that came unannounced out of the north flaring
    in heaven,
Nor the strange huge meteor-procession dazzling and clear
    shooting over our heads,
(A moment, a moment long it sail'd its balls of unearthly light
    over our heads,
Then departed, dropt in the night, and was gone;). . . ."

Walt Whitman, from "Year of Meteors," in *Leaves of Grass*

*Robert Indiana, master of hard-edge painting, became inter-
ested in the artistic possibilities of the circle in the 1950's
when he was living near Coenties Slip on the tip of Manhattan.
His painting, Year of Meteors (1961), is named after a Walt
Whitman poem. Indiana's love of American literature and the
probability that the Great Eastern sailed into New York via
Coenties Slip contributed to the inspiration for the painting.*

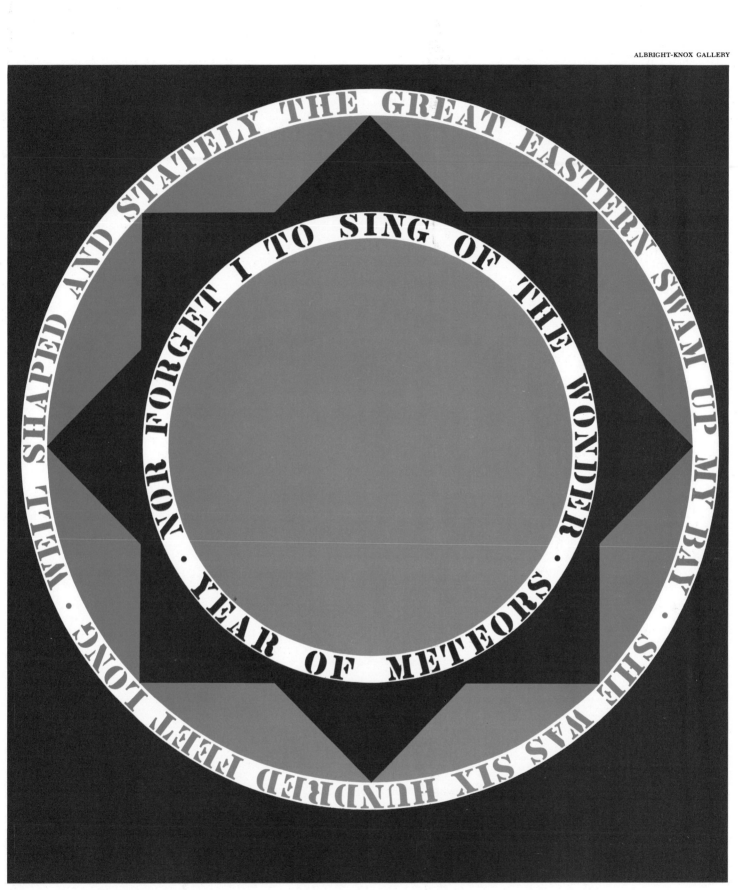

ACKNOWLEDGMENTS

The numerous quotations used in this book have largely been taken from the publications here listed. We gratefully acknowledge our debt to the editors and publishers of these works.

Adams, Henry, *The Education of Henry Adams, An Autobiography*, Houghton Mifflin Company, Boston.

Adams, Henry, *The Letters of Henry Adams (1858–1891)*, Worthington Chauncey Ford, ed., Houghton Mifflin Company, Boston.

Anderson, Sherwood, *Winesburg, Ohio*, Copyright © 1919 by B. W. Huebsch, Inc., 1947 by Eleanor Copenhaver Anderson. Reprinted by permission of The Viking Press, Inc., New York.

Benét, Stephen Vincent, "American Names," from *Ballads and Poems*. Copyright © 1931 by Stephen Vincent Benét. Copyright © 1959 by Rosemary Carr Benét. Reprinted by permission of Holt, Rinehart and Winston, Inc., New York and Brandt & Brandt, New York.

Berryman, John, "Dream Song 14," from *77 Dream Songs*, Farrar, Straus & Giroux, Inc., New York. Copyright © 1959, 1962, 1963, 1964 by John Berryman. Reprinted by permission of Farrar, Straus & Giroux, Inc., New York and Faber and Faber, Ltd., London.

Brooks, Van Wyck, *The Flowering of New England*, E. P. Dutton & Co., Inc., New York.

Cather, Willa, *A Lost Lady*, Alfred A. Knopf, Inc., New York. Copyright © 1923 by Willa Cather; renewed 1951 by Executrix of the Estate of Willa Cather. Reprinted by permission of Alfred A. Knopf, Inc., New York.

Crane, Hart, "The Bridge," from *The Collected Poems and Selected Letters and Prose of Hart Crane*. Copyright © 1933, 1958, 1966 by Liveright Publishing Corporation, New York. Reprinted by permission of Liveright Publishing Corporation, New York.

Cummings, E.E., "Buffalo Bill's," copyright © 1923, 1951 by E.E. Cummings; "since feeling is first," copyright © 1954 by E.E. Cummings; both from *Complete Poems 1913–1962*. Reprinted by permission of Harcourt Brace Jovanovich, Inc., New York and MacGibbon and Kee, Ltd., London.

Dickinson, Emily, "Wild Nights—Wild Nights!" in *The Literature of America: Nineteenth Century*, Irving Howe, ed., McGraw-Hill, Inc., New York. Reprinted by permission of the Trustees of Amherst College.

Dos Passos, John, "Lover of Mankind," from *U.S.A.*, Houghton Mifflin Company, Boston. Reprinted by permission of Elizabeth H. Dos Passos.

Edwards, Jonathan, *Images or Shadows of Divine Things*, Perry Miller, ed., Yale University Press, New Haven.

Eliot, T. S., "The Love Song of J. Alfred Prufrock" and *The Waste Land*, from *Collected Poems 1909–1962*. Copyright © 1936 by Harcourt Brace Jovanovich, Inc., New York. Copyright © 1963, 1964 by T.S. Eliot. Reprinted by permission of Harcourt Brace Jovanovich, Inc., New York and Faber and Faber, Ltd., London.

The Founding Fathers, Benjamin Franklin: A Biography in His Own Words, Thomas Fleming, ed. Letter to Mme Brillon, translated by Sandra Gary, Newsweek Books, Inc., New York. Reprinted by permission of the American Philosophical Society.

Frost, Robert, *The Poetry of Robert Frost*, Edward Connery Latham, ed. Copyright © 1916, 1923, 1969 by Holt, Rinehart and Winston, Inc., New York. Copyright © 1936, 1942, 1944, 1951 by Robert Frost. Copyright © 1964, 1970 by Leslie Frost Ballantine. Reprinted by permission of Holt, Rinehart and Winston, Inc., New York.

James, Henry, "Crapy Cornelia," from *The Finer Grain*, Charles Scribner's Sons, New York.

Jeffers, Robinson, "Gale in April." Copyright © 1924 and renewed 1952 by Robinson Jeffers. Reprinted by permission of Jeffers Literary Properties.

Literary History of the United States, Robert E. Spiller, Willard Thorp, Thomas H. Johnson, Henry Seidel Canby, Richard M. Ludwig, eds., The Macmillan Company, New York.

Lewis, Sinclair, *Main Street*. Copyright © 1920 by Harcourt Brace Jovanovich, Inc., New York, Reprinted by permission of Harcourt Brace Jovanovich, Inc., New York and Jonathan Cape, Ltd., London.

Lindsay, Vachel, "The Congo," from *Collected Poems of Vachel Lindsay*. Copyright © 1914 by The Macmillan Company, New York. Renewed by Elizabeth C. Lindsay. Reprinted by permission of The Macmillan Company, New York.

Longfellow, Henry Wadsworth, *The Complete Poetical Works of Longfellow*, Houghton Mifflin Company, Boston.

Lowell, Amy, "Patterns," from *The Complete Poetical Works of Amy Lowell*. Copyright © 1944 by Ada D. Russell. Reprinted by permission of Houghton Mifflin Company, Boston.

Lowell, Robert, "Mr. Edwards and the Spider," from *Lord Weary's Castle*.

Copyright © 1946 by Robert Lowell. Reprinted by permission of Harcourt Brace Jovanovich, Inc., New York and Faber and Faber, Ltd., London.

Mailer, Norman, "The White Negro." Copyright © 1959 by Norman Mailer. Reprinted by permission of G. P. Putnam's Sons, New York.

Moore, Marianne, "The Steeple-Jack," from *Collected Poems of Marianne Moore*. Copyright © 1951 by Marianne Moore. Reprinted by permission of The Macmillan Company, New York and Faber and Faber, Ltd., London.

Morison, Samuel Eliot, *Builders of the Bay Colony*, Houghton Mifflin Company, Boston.

The Oxford Anthology of American Literature, William Rose Benét and Norman Holmes Pearson, eds., Oxford University Press, New York.

Pound, Ezra, "In a Station of the Metro," "The Game of Chess," and "Hugh Selwyn Mauberley, V," from *Personae*. Copyright © 1926 by Ezra Pound. Reprinted by permission of New Directions Publishing Corporation, New York and Faber and Faber, Ltd., London.

Pound, Ezra, "Canto LXXVII" and "Canto CXVI," from *The Cantos*. Copyright © 1966, 1972 by Ezra Pound. Reprinted by permission of New Directions Publishing Corporation, New York and Faber and Faber, Ltd., London.

The Puritans, Perry Miller and Thomas H. Johnson, eds., Harper & Row, Publishers, New York.

Robinson, Edwin Arlington, "Tristram," from *Collected Poems*. Copyright © 1937. Renewed 1955 by Ruth Nivison and Barbara R. Holt. Reprinted by permission of The Macmillan Company, New York.

Robinson, Edwin Arlington, *Collected Poems*, Charles Scribner's Sons, New York.

Robinson, Edwin Arlington, "Miniver Cheevy," from *The Town Down the River*. Copyright © 1907 by Charles Scribner's Sons; renewed © 1935. Reprinted by permission of Charles Scribner's Sons, New York.

Roethke, Theodore, "Elegy for Jane." Copyright © 1950 by Theodore Roethke. "The Return." Copyright © 1946 by The Modern Poetry Association, Inc. Both from *Collected Poems of Theodore Roethke*. Reprinted by permission of Doubleday & Co., New York.

Sandburg, Carl, *Chicago Poems*, Harcourt Brace Jovanovich, Inc., New York.

Sandburg, Carl, "The People Will Live On," from *The People, Yes*. Copyright © 1936 by Harcourt Brace Jovanovich, Inc., New York; renewed 1964 by Carl Sandburg. Reprinted by permission of Harcourt Brace Jovanovich, Inc., New York.

Shapiro, Karl, "Nostalgia," from *Selected Poems*. Copyright © 1942 and renewed 1970 by Karl Shapiro. Reprinted by permission of Random House, Inc., New York.

Steinbeck, John, *The Grapes of Wrath.* Copyright © 1939, 1967 by John Steinbeck. Reprinted by permission of the Viking Press, Inc., New York.

Stevens, Wallace, "Disillusionment of Ten O'Clock," from *The Collected Poems of Wallace Stevens.* Copyright © 1923 and renewed 1951 by Wallace Stevens. Reprinted by permission of Alfred A. Knopf, Inc., New York and Faber and Faber, Ltd., London.

Taylor, Edward, *The Poems of Edward Taylor,* Donald E. Stanford, Yale University Press, New Haven

Warren, Robert Penn, "Original Sin: A Short Story," from *Selected Poems: New and Old, 1923–1966.* Copyright © 1942 by Robert Penn Warren. Reprinted by permission of Random House, Inc., New York.

Wells, H. G., "Stephen Crane from an English Standpoint," in *The Shock of Recognition,* Edmund Wilson, ed. Copyright © 1943 by Doubleday, Doran & Company, New York. Copyright © 1955 by Edmund Wilson. Reprinted by permission of Farrar, Straus & Giroux, Inc., New York.

Wigglesworth, Michael, "The Day of Doom," in *The Literature of America: Colonial Period,* Larzer Ziff, ed. Copyright © 1970 by McGraw-Hill, Inc., New York. Reprinted by permission of McGraw-Hill, Inc., New York.

Wilbur, Richard, "Beasts," from *Things of This World.* Copyright © 1956 by Richard Wilbur. Reprinted by permission of Harcourt Brace Jovanovich, Inc., New York and Faber and Faber, Ltd., London.

Williams, William Carlos, "The Red Wheelbarrow" and "At the Ball Game," from *Collected Earlier Poems.* Copyright © 1938 by New Directions Publishing Corporation, New York. Reprinted by permission of New Directions Publishing Corporation, New York and Laurence P. Pollinger, Ltd., London

The editors also appreciate the generous assistance provided by many individuals and institutions during the preparation of this book. They especially wish to thank the following:

Joseph Blumenthal

The Brooklyn Museum
  Linda S. Ferber, Assistant Curator of Paintings and Sculpture

Mark Twain Memorial, Hartford, Conn.
  Wilson H. Faude, Curator

Jo Mielziner

New York Public Library
  Maude D. Cole, Rare Books Division
  Elizabeth Roth, Prints Division

Charles P. Noyse, III

Donald Oenslager

David Scherman

S. Morton Vose, Vose Galleries of Boston

Mrs. Thomas R. Wilcox

INDEX

A